Comm

A Foundation Course 2nd Edition

Communication

A Foundation Course 2nd Edition

Shirley Tyler

Chris Kossen

Charmaine Ryan

PEARSON
Prentice Hall

Copyright © 2005 Pearson Education Australia Pty Ltd

First published 1999
Second edition 2005

Pearson Education Australia
Unit 4, Level 2
14 Aquatic Drive
Frenchs Forest NSW 2086

www.pearsoned.com.au

All rights reserved. Except under the conditions described in the Copyright Act 1968 of Australia and subsequent amendments, no part of this publication may be reproduced, stored in a retrieval system or transmitted in any form or by any means, electronic, mechanical, photocopying, recording or otherwise, without the prior written permission of the copyright owner.

Acquisitions Editor: Michelle Aarons
Project Editor: Rebecca Pomponio
Copy editor: Jennifer Coombs
Proofreader: Margaret Rose
Cover and internal design: Liz Nicholson, designBITE Pty Ltd
Cover illustration by Getty Images
Typeset by Laserwords Private Limited, Chennai, India

Printed in Malaysia (CTP-VVP)

7 8 9 10   13 12 11 10

Tyler, Shirley, 1942– .
    Communication: a foundation course.

    2nd ed.
    Includes index.
    For tertiary students.
    ISBN 0 7339 7137 7.

    1. Communication. 2. Written communication. 3. Oral communication. 4. Problem solving. I. Kossen, Christopher, 1963– . II. Ryan, Charmaine, 1947– . III. Title.

    302.2

Every effort has been made to trace and acknowledge copyright. However, should any infringement have occurred, the publishers tender their apologies and invite copyright owners to contact them.

An imprint of Pearson Education Australia
(a division of Pearson Australia Group Pty Ltd)

Contents

Preface ... x

Part One Communication overview ... 1

Chapter 1 Why study communication? ... 3
Academic life ... 4
Professional life ... 4
Interpersonal skills ... 5
Ethics and communication ... 6
Summary ... 6
Key points ... 7
Review question ... 7
Exercises ... 7
Bibliography ... 7

Chapter 2 What is communication theory? ... 8
Defining communication ... 9
The nature of communication theory ... 10
Working with communication theory ... 14
Theories of communication ... 16
Perception in communication ... 26
Task analysis: A strategic approach
  to communication ... 34
Summary ... 36
Key points ... 36
Review questions ... 37
Exercises ... 38
Bibliography ... 38

Part Two Written and electronic communication ... 41

Chapter 3 Electronic communication ... 43
Defining electronic communication ... 44
Computer-mediated communications ... 45
Newsgroups ... 53
Discussion groups ... 53
Electronic bulletin board (EBB) ... 54
Knowledge acquisition and management ... 54
Summary ... 56
Key points ... 56
Review questions ... 57

	Exercises	*57*
	Bibliography	*57*
Chapter 4	Effective writing skills	58
	Task and audience analysis	59
	Criteria for effective writing	60
	Vocabulary	61
	Sentence structure	63
	Active and passive voice	64
	Paragraph structure	65
	Unity and transitions	66
	Logical sequence	67
	Style and tone	67
	Summary	*68*
	Key points	*68*
	Review questions	*69*
	Exercises	*69*
	Bibliography	*70*
Chapter 5	Letters, memos and email	71
	Letters	72
	Memos	80
	Email	82
	Tone and style	82
	Summary	*83*
	Key points	*83*
	Review questions	*83*
	Exercises	*84*
	Bibliography	*84*
Chapter 6	Extended writing—essays and reports	85
	Essays	86
	Reports	96
	Editing and proofreading	104
	Tone and style	105
	Summary	*105*
	Key points	*105*
	Review questions	*106*
	Exercises	*106*
	Bibliography	*107*

Part Three Oral communication 109

Chapter 7	Oral presentations/speeches	111
	Oral presentations	114
	Types of speeches	114

Preparation and practice	121
Delivering the speech	122
The speech itself	123
Seminar presentations	124
Discussion	125
After the speech	126
Summary	*128*
Key points	*128*
Review questions	*128*
Exercises	*129*
Bibliography	*129*

Chapter 8 *Interviews* 130

Questioning	131
Interview structure	135
Summary	*138*
Key points	*139*
Review questions	*139*
Exercises	*139*
Bibliography	*139*

Part Four Problem solving, decision making and persuasion 141

Chapter 9 *Decision-making strategies* 143

Logical and creative thinking	144
Creative problem solving	144
Problem-solving and decision-making sequence	146
Case studies	149
Summary	*153*
Key points	*153*
Review questions	*153*
Exercises	*154*
Bibliography	*154*

Chapter 10 *Persuasion* 155

Source credibility	157
Appeals to emotion	157
Rational appeals	158
Persuasive strategies	159
Summary	*162*
Key points	*162*
Review questions	*162*
Exercises	*162*
Bibliography	*163*

Chapter 11 Clear thinking, logic and argumentation — 164

- What is logic and argumentation? — 165
- Arguments — 165
- Truth and validity — 168
- Deductive and inductive reasoning — 168
- Fallacies — 169
- *Summary* — *175*
- *Key points* — *175*
- *Review questions* — *175*
- *Exercises* — *176*
- *Bibliography* — *177*

Part Five — Interpersonal and professional communication — 179

Chapter 12 Nonverbal communication — 181

- Important aspects — 182
- Interrelationships between verbal and nonverbal communication — 186
- Types of nonverbal communication — 188
- *Summary* — *194*
- *Key points* — *195*
- *Review questions* — *195*
- *Exercises* — *195*
- *Bibliography* — *196*

Chapter 13 Interpersonal communication — 197

- Intrapersonal communication — 199
- Interpersonal communication — 204
- Role theory: As a tool for skill development — 205
- Styles of relating: In interpersonal communication — 206
- Conflict — 210
- *Summary* — *215*
- *Key points* — *215*
- *Review questions* — *215*
- *Exercises* — *216*
- *Bibliography* — *217*

Chapter 14 Group communication — 218

- Group dynamics — 221
- Conflict in groups — 227
- Leadership — 229
- *Summary* — *232*
- *Key points* — *232*
- *Review questions* — *233*
- *Exercises* — *233*
- *Bibliography* — *234*

Chapter 15 Organisational communication 235

    The communicative climate 240
    Organisational culture 245
    Summary *248*
    Key points *248*
    Review questions *248*
    Exercises *249*
    Bibliography *249*

Part Six — Communication problems and solutions — 251

Chapter 16 Barriers 253

    Physical barriers (or external barriers) 254
    Intrapersonal barriers 255
    Interpersonal barriers 265
    Intercultural barriers 267
    Semantic barriers 271
    Additional barrier management approaches 272
    Summary *274*
    Key points *275*
    Review questions *275*
    Exercises *276*
    Bibliography *276*

    Glossary 277
    Index 285

Preface

We can think of communication as the oil that greases social, educational, professional, indeed all human interaction. Effective communication facilitates the smooth transfer of messages and ideas; it provides the means for us to express our feelings and needs; it allows us to build friendships and maintain relationships; it enables managers to manage effectively and subordinates to know what should be done, by whom, when and how. Communication does indeed permeate all aspects of our lives. It is, therefore, important that we become as expert in communication as possible.

This text is broad based, covering most aspects of communication from theories of how communication functions to how to write effective essays and reports; from how to solve problems and make effective decisions to how to communicate in groups and organisations. For this reason, a balance has had to be found between the demands of theory and application. We have also had to be selective in terms of what we consider to be the most important aspects of the areas being covered. A central thread of the text, because it is of such vital importance in effective communication, is task and audience analysis.

The text is divided into six parts. Part 1 outlines the advantages of effective communication in everyday life and provides an overview of communication as a process. Shirley Tyler wrote Chapter 1 and Chris Kossen wrote Chapter 2. Part 2 deals with communication technology and written communication. Charmaine Ryan wrote Chapter 3 while Shirley Tyler wrote the remaining three chapters in this part. Part 3, concerned with oral communication, and Part 4, about problem solving, decision making and persuasive communication, were written by Shirley Tyler. Part 5 relates to communication between people, both one to one and in larger organisational groups. Shirley Tyler wrote Chapter 12 while Chris Kossen wrote the remainder of this part and Part 6 dealing with problems that can arise in communication and ways in which such problems can be overcome or avoided.

Revising the text for this edition has given us the opportunity to bring the text up to date, to fill in some gaps and to expand on some areas. In addition to review questions, exercises are now provided for each chapter. Chapter 2 has extended discussion of communication theory to application of theory for maximum effect. Other major additions include material on Web services and SMS messaging in Chapter 3, material on seminar presentations in Chapter 7, haptics in Chapter 12 and emotional intelligence in Chapter 13. New material has been added on topic analysis, evaluative reading and essay writing in Chapter 6 while dysfunctional communication is given greater prominence in Chapters 14 and 15. The authors and Pearson Education would like to thank the following reviewers for their invaluable contributions to this edition they are: Eleanor Kiernan, University of Southern Queensland; Geoff Danaher, Central Queensland University; Alison O'Day, Australian Catholic University; Jane Madden, Victoria University; Lesley Roberts, University of Southern Queensland; Peter Pierce, James Cook University; Nina Weekarody, Deakin University; and Teresa O'Connor, James Cook University.

Shirley Tyler
Chris Kossen
Charmaine Ryan

Part One

Communication Overview

Why study communication?

CHAPTER 1

Upon completing this chapter you should be able to:
- appreciate the importance of, and need for, studying communication;
- understand the benefits of studying communication, including its relevance to both academic and professional life;
- demonstrate a knowledge of the major areas incorporated within communication; and
- be aware of the importance of communicating ethically.

Communication permeates our lives at all levels, academic, professional and personal. If we think of communication as involving any transaction, verbal or nonverbal, conscious or unconscious, intentional or unintentional, by which messages are sent or received, then we can see that we are communicating all the time, all day, from the moment we first wake up to when we finally go to sleep—and if there is anyone else in the room with us we can be communicating even when we are asleep.

This centrality of communication within our day-to-day lives is double edged. It means that communication is vitally important in every facet of our lives but it also leads to an assumption that because we are communicating all the time we already know how to do it and do not need to spend time learning anything about it. We take communication for granted as part of the background of our lives.

Unfortunately, few of us reach our communication potential and probably all of us have encountered communication problems from time to time. We have all had the experience of saying or doing something and being surprised to find that someone else interprets our words or actions in a way that we never intended, indeed never even considered. Communication is a complex, dynamic process with many opportunities for mistakes and misunderstandings to occur. We will examine how miscommunication can occur in more detail throughout the text, but miscommunication does occur—frequently. Studying communication, however, can help minimise miscommunication.

Let us look at the importance of communication in terms of our academic, professional and personal lives.

Academic life

The most obvious areas of communication at university are written and oral communication, both of which are of considerable importance in professional life as well. Extended writing, such as essays, forms a primary assessment mechanism at university. Writing effective essays requires communication skills and abilities. It requires the ability to research effectively; to think critically; to apply content knowledge to the completion of particular tasks; to develop a thesis and construct a logical and coherent argument to support that thesis; and, most obviously, it requires the ability to communicate in a clear, understandable and correct written form. Do your essays come back with good marks and comments such as 'A clear and lucidly expressed exposition of the problem', or are the comments along the lines of 'There is evidence of research and indications of some good ideas but the essay lacks structure and cohesion and the development of a sustained argument'?

At university, and in professional life, we will be required to present our ideas orally, in the form of speeches or seminar presentations. Presenting our ideas orally involves the same skills of critical thinking, analysis and logical development of argument that are needed for essays or reports, but it also requires the ability to adapt often complex material to the constraints and demands of an oral presentation format. Of course, it also requires the ability to communicate effectively through spoken language. Success at university and in professional life depends on how well we can solve problems; on how self-motivated and self-directed we are; on how effective we are at thinking and learning independently; and on whether we have the mental flexibility and adaptability to cope with the career changes that will probably occur in our working lives.

Professional life

There is sometimes a perception that, yes, communication is important in those 'people-oriented' professions like human resources, public relations and so on but not really vital if you are, say, an information technology person. This is not, however, the case and good communication skills—being able to express ourselves fluently in writing and speaking, being able to work well and co-operatively with colleagues and clients, being skilled at interviewing, being able to work effectively through other people—are increasingly demanded across all industries and professions.

Good communication skills help us get the job in the first place and you can test this out for yourself by looking through job advertisements in any newspaper. How many employers specify the need to have good communication skills—written, oral or interpersonal? How many of the advertisements place those communication skills among the essential criteria? You will notice that in Positions Vacant advertisements employers identify two levels of skills and abilities: essential and desirable. Essential means that there is no point in applying for the job unless you have those particular skills or abilities. The employer considers them so important that applicants without them will not be considered. Desirable means that the employer considers the skills and abilities important but is prepared to forgo them if an applicant has strengths in other areas. So placing good communication skills among the essential criteria signals the importance of these skills in professional life.

As well as helping in obtaining the job, good communication skills can help us succeed in the job and, importantly, move up the career ladder. In the information technology supplement 'Next' in *The Sydney Morning Herald* of 27 July 2004, Paul Edwards interviews CIOs, or chief information officers (people who have risen to the top in the information technology professions), and the people who recruit these top executives. Both the executives and the recruiters, the 'headhunters', stress the importance of good communication skills, especially good written and oral communication (including oral presentation skills) and strong interpersonal communication skills.

Can you persuade others to your viewpoint, or are you often tongue-tied and embarrassed when presenting your ideas orally? In an interview situation do you know how to phrase your questions appropriately to elicit the information you require? Do you know how to interpret what an interviewer is really looking for and frame your answers accordingly? How good are you at solving problems and making decisions? How skilled are you at reading nonverbal cues? If you plan to work in sales, marketing, export or the diplomatic service, how adept are you at reading nonverbal cues from different cultural backgrounds? These are vital professional skills that can make the difference between success and failure in your career but, unfortunately, they are often poorly developed.

Interpersonal skills

Do you find it difficult to say 'no' to any request and end up fuming about being forced to do something you do not want to do because you could not refuse? How do you cope with conflict? By pretending it does not exist, by going in 'boots and all' or by trying to find a compromise that allows both parties to 'save face'?

Increasingly, groups or teams are part of the decision-making process in industry and the professions. What are your responsibilities as a group member or leader? How effectively can you operate within groups or teams?

No matter which profession you follow, it is likely that you will be working within an organisation of some kind. How can you ensure that your communication within the organisation is efficient and effective?

These are only some of the multitude of questions that could be asked about our communication abilities. This is because communication is not only what we write or say; it is how we write or say a message; it is how we stand; how we use time; how we interact with others; even how we feel about ourselves.

So, why study communication? Good communication is essential in both personal and professional life, at university or college, at work and play. To be a good communicator means learning the principles and techniques, what makes up the communication process and how to improve communication performance. That is the basis of this text—to assist readers to develop fundamental skills on which they can build their own communication expertise.

Ethics and communication

We have seen how central communication is to all aspects of our lives, providing the mechanism for our interactions with individuals and groups. How we communicate, and how effectively we communicate, is influenced by who we are, by the type of person each of us is and by the way we view others. In Chapter 13 on interpersonal communication, in the section dealing with different communication styles, for example, we can see the problems that can result from an aggressive or non-assertive communication style. These problems arise from a failure to respect the rights of all participating parties.

So what do we mean when we speak of 'ethics'? Ethics form an entire branch of philosophy and philosophical definitions of ethics can be quite detailed, but ethics is always linked to morality. When we speak of ethics we speak, not of what is legal or permissible, but of what is morally right—what is 'good'.

If we think, then, of the styles of communication mentioned earlier, we can see that failure to respect the rights of all communicating parties, whether by taking all rights to ourselves as the aggressive communicator does, or by denying all rights to ourselves as the non-assertive communicator does, is not communicating ethically. Persuasive communication and the use of logic and argumentation are also areas where unethical communication can often be found.

There are many variations on what constitutes ethical communication, but perhaps we can think of ethical communication as involving:

* honesty;

* respect for individual rights;

* concern for others;

* open-mindedness in terms of differing views, cultures, religious beliefs, gender,— being tolerant of diversity;

* clarity—tailoring the message to the audience and task so the meaning is as unambiguous as possible; and

* lack of manipulation and coercion.

However, and this is at the heart of ethics, as ethics is often concerned with what we could call 'grey' areas, there may be times when we will deliberately breach one of the guidelines in order to meet other guidelines. For example, where does the 'little white lie' fit in? As Ruben and Stewart (1998) note, if a friend who is ill and really looks ill asks how he looks, should we be honest or try to cheer our friend up by being less than honest? Should our concern for our friend's psychological welfare override our concern for honesty?

SUMMARY

This chapter has outlined the importance of communication in all areas of our lives, introducing the main areas of communication that will be covered in this text and linking communication ability to academic, professional and personal life. Unfortunately, because communication is an everyday activity we often assume that we communicate adequately, that there is no need to study communication. This is not the case. Few of us have achieved our communication potential and the remaining chapters of this book deal with ways in which we can improve our ability to communicate effectively in writing, speech, interpersonally, in groups and within organisations.

KEY POINTS

- Communication permeates our lives at all levels: academic, professional and personal.
- Communication problems can, and do, occur. The more we know about communication, the greater chance we have of avoiding or overcoming communication problems.
- Success in academic life requires the ability to communicate effectively in writing and orally, to think critically, to research effectively and to construct a logical argument.
- Employers are placing increased importance on good communication skills when recruiting employees.
- Important to our communication effectiveness is our ability to interact interpersonally and to function within groups and organisations.

REVIEW QUESTION

1. Why is good communication important?

EXERCISES

1. Think of an example from your own experience when a communication problem occurred. What caused the problem? What do you think could have been done to avoid or overcome the problem?
2. Look through the Positions Vacant section of any major newspaper on any Saturday. What percentage of the advertisements specify that communication skills are required? What percentage of those advertisements say that communication skills are essential?
3. In the chapter on extended writing, mention is made of plagiarism, of stealing someone else's intellectual property or ideas and passing them off as our own. What are the ethical implications of plagiarism?
4. Can you think of examples from your personal or professional life that involved unethical communication or where you had to make the type of decision mentioned earlier in relation to the sick friend?

BIBLIOGRAPHY

Edwards, P. 2004, 'Take me to the top', *The Sydney Morning Herald,* 27 July.
Ruben, B. & Stewart, L. 1998, *Communication and Human Behaviour,* 4th ed. Allyn & Bacon, Boston.

What is communication theory?

CHAPTER 2

Upon completing this chapter you should be able to:

- understand and appreciate the complexity involved in defining and understanding the term 'communication';
- understand and explain the nature and importance of strategic communication.
- explain each of the 'process theory-models' of communication, critically evaluate each model, and understand the practical issues involved in applying communication theory effectively;
- describe the processes involved in perception;
- understand how task and audience analysis processes can be used to make communicative tasks manageable and communication more effective.

Communication pervades every aspect of our lives. It is infinitely complex and as alluded to earlier we cannot choose not to communicate, for example no matter what you wear people will still make interpretations about the way you look including your clothing, your posture, facial expressions and so on. When life seems to be going well for us we may not give a great deal of thought to communication. However, good communication skills can provide us with a means by which to best manage the difficult times and the challenges life presents personally, professionally and academically.

While good communication techniques and practices can be critical to future success and happiness it is also important to acknowledge that communication in itself is not a 'cure all' i.e. not the answer or complete solution to all problems. Nonetheless, developing our ability to communicate more effectively is very important in relation to success in our pursuits and our quality of life.

The aim of this book is to help build upon your existing understanding of communication (with an emphasis on professional and academic contexts) and to provide you with 'tools' for making communication effective.

In this chapter we examine the foundations of communication theory. Communication theory helps us to better understand communication and the better our understanding of how communication work, the better placed we are to make decisions about how to communicate effectively. Indeed, the communication theory as presented provides the very basis upon which the communication strategies and techniques that make up the bulk of this book are based.

Defining communication

Communication is a very broad concept and therefore difficult to define in a clear and precise way. Barker acknowledges the problematic nature of defining communication, saying that:

> defining communication is similar to trying to define love. Intuitively, you feel you understand it, but it's difficult to put into words.
>
> [and that] communication theorists have never completely agreed on a single definition of communication.

(Barker 1984, p. 5)

When thinking about what makes a good communicator we often think of people who are outgoing and appear to speak clearly. In other words, good communicators seem to be 'well spoken' and have 'the gift of the gab', a cliché for people who are talkative and find speaking to others quite easy. This stereotype can be misleading as it tends to convey the impression that good communicators are very outgoing people who talk a lot and that communication is primarily about speaking.

However, good communicators are not necessarily talkative or extroverted. In fact, 'good' or effective communication requires a broad range of skills. This is reflected in the number of chapters in this book.

While communication is very broad in nature, at this point we will begin with a simple definition of communication as: *the process of information exchange by and among people.*

The purpose of this book is to examine ways in which we can make our communication as effective as possible. Hence, a great deal of emphasis is placed on developing skills that will help us to enhance our abilities to exchange information with people effectively. In essence, we are concerned with developing abilities in the following domains:

✱ comprehension: abilities to listen, learn, read, research and understand, critique and evaluate ideas and information accurately.

✱ expression: abilities to formulate and present ideas and information to others—in ways that inform, convince and persuade, in both oral and written forms.

In keeping with the aim to communicate as effectively as possible, it is important that we approach communication strategically. Indeed we already use communication strategically in our lives but we may not always realise it. Communicating strategically involves communicating in an effort to have your needs and desires met (your desires would include your goals), and as such it means communicating with a goal in mind. However, in the context of this textbook **strategic communication** means deliberately taking a well-planned approach to a communicative task or activity in an effort to achieve a specific goal or goals. Communication provides the primary means by which we seek to have our needs and desires met. Taking a well-planned approach to communication is the central focus of this textbook.

The nature of communication theory

Before progressing with the main content of this book (the theories and concepts that can be used to enhance effectiveness in communication) we will try to build an understanding of how theories and concepts operate. Indeed, if we wish to apply theory well, then it is wise first to give consideration to the nature of such theoretical knowledge. Interestingly, this pursuit of thinking about the nature of theory is in itself a field of inquiry, known as *meta-theoretical inquiry*. The prefix 'meta' means 'about', so the term meta-theory means 'about theory', but it is also worth mentioning that this field of inquiry is philosophical and becomes very complex. Given the scope of this text, we will limit discussion to the level appropriate to foundation communication.

What is 'theory'?

In simple terms a theory is an explanation. However, the word 'theory' often conveys the idea that it refers to something that is not totally correct or complete, and indeed this is true of theory. However, it is also reasonable to assume that being 'human' brings with it limitations, as human beings cannot gain a 'perfect' understanding of their world or the phenomena in it. Despite this, our 'humanly' constructed theories can prove very useful. 'Knowledge is not a perfect map of the thing known but without it one has to move through the environment with no map at all' (McGuire 1981, p. 42). Accordingly, a good theory is one that provides us with the most adequate and effective explanation on a given area at a given time. In doing this, theories can provide us with a greater understanding of our environment and ultimately assist us in gaining a greater degree of control over it.

Functions and features of theories

Theories have the following functions and features. They:

* provide tentative explanations (on a given area);
* help organise ideas and therefore make information and ideas more manageable;
* provide a repository for knowledge. In this way, a theory functions as a framework upon which knowledge can be structured. The communication theory-models in this chapter provide a base from which we then develop principles and strategies and also more specific theories, for example, on interpersonal communication;
* explain relationships between the *specialised* concepts (or variables) they incorporate;

* provide us with a greater understanding and therefore allow us a greater degree of control;

* have prescriptive value, that is, provide principles to follow in order to maximise the likelihood of a desired outcome;

* are predictive, that is, can be used to try to predict outcomes, for example *If I do A, then it is more likely that B will follow;*

* provide us with a certain kind of perspective on an area, and therefore function like a lens to shape our perception, and therefore the way we view or come to see phenomena; and

* are progressively superseded, as tentative explanations, by more adequate/accepted theories over time.

Theories take the form of descriptive statements and can also incorporate diagrammatic models, for example the communication models presented later in this book. Many researchers view models as a type of theory that lends itself to modelling, for example a visual representation. Theories are based on building blocks called concepts, or variables, and theories provide explanations about the relationships that exist between these concepts. In this way, they can be thought of as extensions to concepts (as they are explanations about concepts). We now turn our attention to the topic of concepts.

THE FUNCTIONING OF CONCEPTS

Human beings devise concepts in order to comprehend the world. This process of conceptualisation involves attaching labels (or names) to the phenomena we perceive so that we can think and communicate about them. In English, for example, the letters *d-o-g* put together allow us to communicate the concept (or notion) of *dog,* because we all understand and agree that it refers to the same kind of animal/thing. We can then go on to make finer distinctions which enable us to communicate about various breeds of dogs, such as *boxers* and *terriers.* Concepts range from basic tangible or 'concrete' concepts, like that of 'dog', to more advanced and abstract notions such as *love, loyalty, social justice* and *economic rationalism.*

American theorist George Lakoff makes the following points about the process of categorisation:

> Every time we see something as a kind of thing, for example, a tree, we are categorizing. Whenever we reason about kinds of things—chairs, nations, illnesses, emotions, any kind of thing . . . [w]ithout our ability to categorize, we could not function at all . . . understanding how we categorize is central to an understanding of what makes us human.

(Lakoff 1987, pp. 5–6)

Figure 2.1 represents theoretical knowledge (explanations of the world *per se*) as being a result of the extensions we make from the phenomena we encounter in life, to conceptual naming through to our explanations about relationships between such concepts.

Costs associated with conceptualisation

While we need to conceptualise the world in order to communicate and think about it, in doing this we impose our own human/cultural order upon it. Many theorists believe that our perception of the world is shaped by the concepts we devise and use to understand it. The theory of linguistic relativity goes so far to posit that '. . . different languages give rise to different views of the world' (O'Sullivan *et al.* 1994, p. 168).

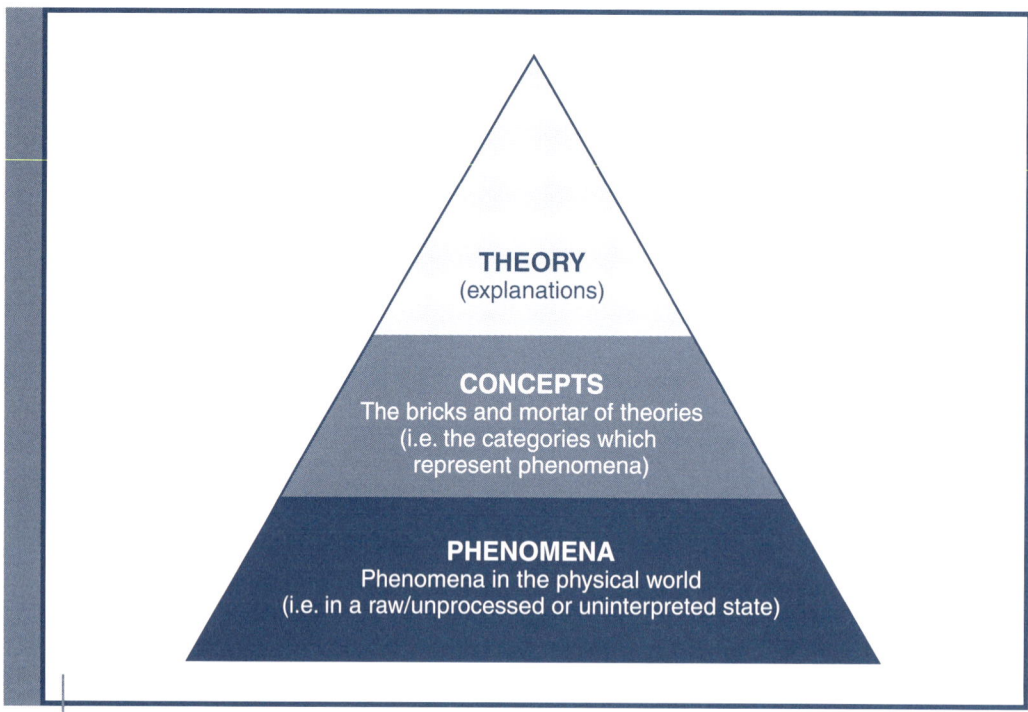

FIGURE 2.1 | The Construction of Theoretical Knowledge

While it draws quite a bit of criticism, the theory of linguistic relativity does appear to be evident in particular kinds of language, for example technical language. Mackay (1994) explains that an accountant may be inclined to view life in terms of the concepts and language used by accountants. In other words they may have a tendency to see things in terms of cost, profit and loss and return on investment. Alternatively, an architect may be inclined to view their surrounds in terms of form and function. 'Professional deformity', as Mackay calls it, contends that our occupational experience and exposure to specialist concepts and terminology can not only influence but bias our perception.

> [an economist] may become so preoccupied with the economic consequences of a particular policy that the human consequences may be entirely overlooked.
>
> *(Mackay 1994, p. 81)*

So theories come at a cost or with a price attached. However, theories (and their associated concepts) gain their power because they highlight particular aspects of reality for special consideration (Walker 1975). Medical theories, for example, are used to focus and explain phenomena pertaining to health and disease. Consequently, the discipline of medicine uses concepts such as 'virus' or 'germ' to develop theories to explain and subsequently treat a range of illness. In this instance, the value of theory is evident in the progress made in the area of medicine over the past century. In spite of this, however, in the process of highlighting certain aspects, theories also operate to de-emphasise other aspects.

The emphasising and de-emphasising function of theories can be compared to another kind of theory making we know as stereotyping. Stereotypes, if used cautiously, can at times provide us with a convenient device for making some useful generalisations. For example, they may give some clues as to what to expect and how to behave when visiting an overseas country. In spite of this, stereotypes function to deny people and situations their true individuality and complexity. For example, by viewing all individuals in a grouping, as all being alike, we begin to disregard people's individuality. For instance, Australians are known 'stereotypically' for their friendliness, but in reality not all Australians are the same and nor is every Australian citizen a friendly person.

Theories also tend to function in this way, hence we need to adjust them rationally in order to apply them successfully to specific 'real-life' cases, that is, we need to apply this kind of knowledge in case-specific or case-sensitive ways. In other words, we should try to assess each situation on its own particularities or merits as opposed to seeking standard 'one fits-all type' theoretically based solutions. Communication theories can become problematic because of our human tendency to inadvertently over-extend them. So keeping this in mind can help us to apply them with maximum success.

THE STRUCTURE OF THEORY: FORMAL AND FOLK THEORIES

In essence, the process of 'theorising' is not all that mysterious; indeed it can be seen as an everyday activity. We theorise whenever we try to understand or explain things in a systematic or ordered fashion. The process of theory making (the way in which theories are 'put together') is comparable not only to stereotyping but also to kinds of generalisations we call myths or clichés. Theories of this kind are sometimes referred to as **folk theories** and these are the kinds of theories that provide us with our commonsense and informal knowledge about the world.

Myths, including clichés, become popular because they seem to impart an important element of truth; for example, 'Don't count your chickens before they hatch' and 'Don't put all your eggs in one basket'. These kinds of generalisations are often challenged as not being quite true for every situation. This is also a problem when applying principles derived from communication theory. In other words, a principle or approach may have a good deal of merit, but not an applicability rate of 100 per cent. The main difference between informal and formal theories is that formal theories are more rigorously tested by the scientific and academic community and as such they carry greater authority and credibility, and are normally more accurate and reliable.

The gap between theory and practice

It is important to remain alert to the fact that theories and concepts are abstractions from reality. They provide representations of the 'real' world and hence differ from reality. In other words, they are not direct objective copies of what they represent, and necessarily provide an incomplete view.

Furthermore, concepts (as labels) and theories (as explanations) as humanly constructed representations of reality do not reflect 'reality' in holistic, accurate or unbiased ways (or with a *God's eye* view). It is on this basis that some people, particularly those who view theory negatively, argue that all theories are fundamentally flawed. While this is not entirely untrue, remaining alert to the nature and potential limitations of theoretical information can help us to approach this information in a more informed and practical manner. But simply discarding theory-based knowledge on the grounds of incompleteness or imperfection is essentially a naïve argument, and one that is misguided and poorly informed.

The abstract concepts we use in theories are not always precise or mutually exclusive. In other words, the world does not always fit neatly into the conceptual boxes we devise to comprehend it. However, we still have a tendency unwittingly to assume that these abstract concepts do, and should, match reality precisely (refer to Figure 2.2). In contrast, abstract concepts come with ambiguity and contain overlaps (i.e. are not mutually exclusive), and as such should be thought of as fluid concepts as opposed to being 'black and white'.

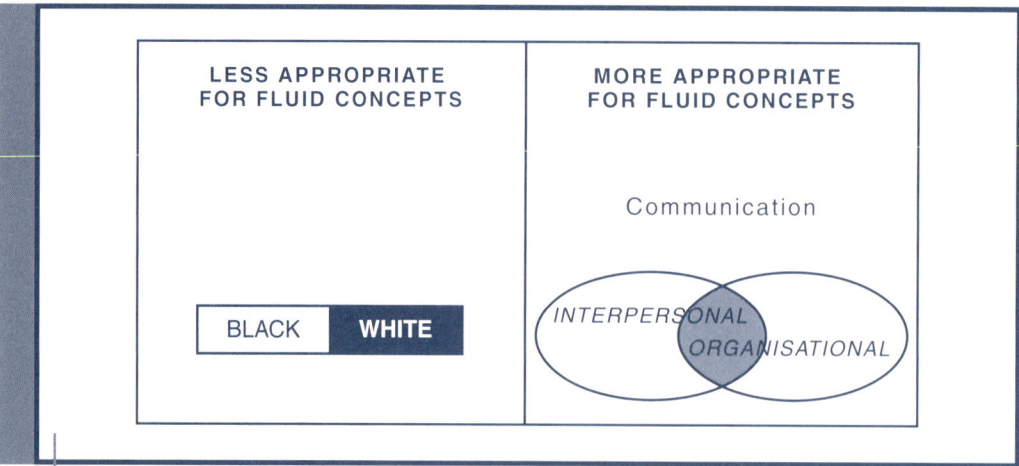

FIGURE 2.2 | Rigid Versus Fluid Thinking on Categorisation

We create conceptual categories to distinguish between things which then tend to appear as 'clear-cut', when in fact these kinds of distinctions are intertwined in highly complex ways. Accordingly, our perceptions of phenomena are most accurate at the point where we can see and understand the distinctions being made (and how this is useful) while also seeing and understanding the fluid and intertwined nature of the area being examined. Figure 2.2 provides a communications-based example whereby an instance of communication in an organisation can be categorised as being interpersonal communication (face-to-face communication between people) and organisational communication (communication within an organisation) at the same time. Accordingly, the distinctions we select and emphasise depend on the purpose at hand, for example whether we wish to view communication from an organisational or interpersonal perspective or possibly both.

As previously discussed, some people try to discredit theory as a form of knowledge by looking for cases where it does not match reality, subsequently attacking it on the grounds of lack of applicability. Approaching theory in this way is an unproductive strategy, especially at tertiary level. However, if we are aware of, and sensitive to, the nature of theory we are able to approach it in a prudent manner and apply it in ways that are responsive to the situation or reality at hand. We can use theory in these kinds of ways to capitalise on the benefits theory can offer.

The gap between theory and practice means that one needs to make decisions about which principles and strategies, and ways of applying them, may provide the most beneficial way of dealing with the particular situation at hand. It is thus evident that communication theories do not provide simple 'one size fits all' solutions. Furthermore, theoretical knowledge should be approached critically, as opposed to being accepted as completely true or accurate. You can do this by thinking about their applicability to the problem or task at hand, and remaining alert of potential pitfalls.

Working with communication theory

This text has conceptualised communication into categories, by the way of chapters. This allows us to focus our attention on specific features of communication so that we can develop a greater understanding of how certain aspects of communication function. Ultimately we use this knowledge to help improve our communicative abilities.

Communication is a complex process with many variables operating simultaneously, so when we are studying particular aspects of communication we need to be aware that the specific theories and concepts are only parts of a much bigger picture. While it is often necessary to look very closely at certain features of a communication task or problem, it is also important to stand back periodically and consider how these features relate to the overall context (the bigger picture) because we can lose sight of this by getting lost in the detail. The danger of losing sight of the bigger picture is shown in the classic fable about the three blind men describing an elephant. The first man likens it to a rope after examining its tail; the second man describes it as large rubber hose after feeling its trunk; and, after examining its leg, the third man describes it as being like a large tree stump.

This fable helps to demonstrate that failing to keep the overall picture in mind can lead to problems. In this case, the three men each failed to produce an adequate account of what an elephant is like. Keeping perspective is an important skill in achieving effective communication. With this in mind it is also important to be aware of a common pitfall in producing assignments, which is spending too much time and effort on less important aspects of the work to the detriment of more important aspects of it, for example the physical presentation or use of eye-catching graphics as opposed to the quality of writing and argument. Heightening our levels of awareness (or internal radar) is important so that we can monitor our progress by asking ourselves questions relating to such matters.

Applying theory: Striving for optimum balance

Applying theory well requires a flexible and balanced approach but it is virtually impossible to achieve a perfect equilibrium (i.e. 100 per cent effective communication). The best balance becomes the means by which we can communicate and learn with the greatest success. To illustrate this point further, imagine a 100 per cent efficient engine. This is, of course, a theoretical ideal but a practical impossibility. However, this theoretical ideal gives engineers a goal to strive for, that is, to continue to develop engines that become progressively closer to that ideal. While the meticulous application of all our communication theory to a situation will not result in 100 per cent efficient communication in practice, striving for the theoretical ideal of 100 per cent efficient communication helps us to develop and improve our abilities in this area.

In approaching many problems or situations, professionals and scholars alike need first to decide what they wish to achieve and then consider which approaches would assist them to realise their goals. Aiming for success in communication whether at a tertiary or professional level involves striving for the most effective balance in the use and selection of communication strategies. This also entails an effort to not *overdo* or *underdo* things when applying strategies and principles. In sum, a good or effective balance helps to maximise one's chances of attaining desired goals at a very high level. In fact, success in tertiary study is assessed against one's ability to apply the theoretical ideas covered in a course in assignment work. Accordingly, you can think of assignments as hypothetical realities or simulated practical-type problems that lecturers produce to assess your understanding and ability to apply theoretical content.

When applying theoretically based principles to assignments it is worth keeping in mind that these kinds of principles, not unlike the 'ten commandments' (or the tenets of other religious tradition), are typically much harder to apply consistently and apply well than as they first appear. Principles tend to appear more uncomplicated when you see them in written form than is the case when you need to apply them. However, taking on this kind of challenge with a 'healthy' learning attitude should also help make it a stimulating and rewarding way to advance your ability to think, problem solve and communicate effectively.

Theories of communication

This section outlines some of the main ways in which communication has been theorised and modelled. While these theoretical models are by their very nature incomplete simplifications, they nonetheless enable up to make very complex processes comprehensible and thereby advance our understanding.

Theory 1: The linear process model

The *linear view*, also known as the *transmission model* (shown in Figure 2.3), was modelled in 1949 by Shannon and Weaver. This *transmission theory* was based on an earlier *information theory* that was extended beyond its traditional engineering base to help explain the process of human communication. This model emphasises the notion of a **sender** sending information to a **receiver**. This model views communication in terms of information transfer and divides it into a number of stages. These stages are seen as components in the communication process and are also known as *communication variables*. These components are:

Sender:	the source
Receiver:	the destination
Message:	the information
Code:	the form the message takes
Channel:	the means or medium used
Noise:	physical interference, for example sound, light and so on

These components help us to understand and study communication. The first component, the sender, is responsible for formulating and sending a message to a receiver in such a way that the sender's message or meaning is effectively transferred to the intended receiver. As the originator of the message and selector of the code and channel through which the message is to be conveyed, the

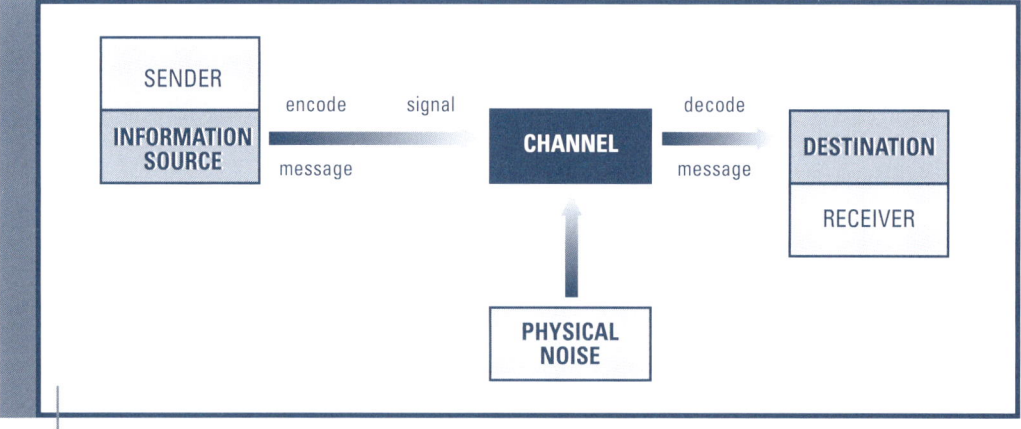

FIGURE 2.3 | The Linear Process Model

Source: Based on Shannon and Weaver (1949).

sender carries a great deal of the responsibility for the effectiveness of the communication. However, receivers also carry a degree of responsibility for effective communication because the amount of attention they pay to messages directed at them will influence the outcome. As a strategic communicator, the sender should formulate the message code in a manner that is aimed at persuading the receiver. Note that the practice of targeting messages for receivers is discussed later on in the chapter under the heading 'Audience analysis: Tailoring communication to address others' perceptions'.

CODE AND CHANNEL

Before thought can be transferred from the mind of a sender to a receiver, it must be put into a form in which it can be sent, so it is understandable to the receiver. This requires the use of a system of representation that will enable communication to occur. Hence it must be understood by both the sender and the receiver. These systems of representation in communication are known as **codes**; a verbal language is an example of a code. Verbal language codes, for example English, can also be subdivided into the codes of written and spoken language.

A concept closely related to code is **channel**. The term channel refers to the medium through which the message is sent. If the sender has chosen to use the code of written English they will choose a medium appropriate to that code, for example a letter or an email. Note that channels also include technologies such as facsimile machines, television, video, telephone and so on. Our five (5) senses are also embedded into the concept of channel, as we can receive messages visually, for example an email in written form, or through hearing, for example, spoken words over telephone and also via multiple sensory channels, for example vision and hearing from television.

The notion of codes also includes other means by which to signify meaning, including nonverbal forms such as gestures. It is often the case that nonverbal codes or forms of communication are more open, that is, less structured and precise, but nonetheless important. The area of nonverbal communication is considered in more detail in Chapter 12. However, at this point, the distinctions in Figure 2.4 are useful.

The use of codes entails the notions of encoding and decoding messages. A sender must **encode** the original idea or message before it can be transferred to the receiver. Subsequently, the receiver of such a message must then **decode** the contents in order to interpret the message and make sense of it.

NOISE

Noise can be defined quite simply as anything that interferes with the effective transmission of a message. However, this model is concerned with physical noise. Physical noise includes any environmental or physical factors that impede the interpretation of messages, for example anything that interferes with audibility, such as the sounds created by a lawn mower or a jack hammer, or even poor amplification in a public communication situation. The distraction of a mobile telephone phone ringing is yet another contemporary example of noise. However, physical noise also includes eye-catching distractions occurring nearby, such as a mouse running across the floor of a classroom. In addition to this, noise also includes environmental factors such as poor lighting, a cold room or a hot location and even equipment failure, for example a malfunctioning projector or computer during a presentation.

CRITICAL COMMENTS ON LINEAR PROCESS MODEL

As an early theory/model of communication, the linear view model provides us with a number of key concepts useful to understanding the process of communication. While it can be argued that this model provides an adequate account of communication forms like some mass media forms

FIGURE 2.4 Communication Codes

Source: Based on Saville-Troike, 1994

(e.g. radio, television) and older technologies such as the telegraph, it falls short as an adequate explanation of other common kinds of communication, particularly those in which feedback is quite evident, for example in interpersonal communication such as a conversation. But even so many still argue that it also falls short of adequately accounting for communication through radio and television technologies because feedback does occur via audience ratings, for example though ratings feedback, which is not all that obvious to us because most of us are not directly involved in the ratings process and therefore tend to overlook it. The linear model frames communication as a one-way process of communication from a source or sender to a destination or receiver. Hence it has been criticised heavily for describing communication as a mechanical process rather than one that is inherently human, thereby reducing human complexity to a view that sees people as being essentially machine-like. Developments evident in the following model also work to reveal shortcomings in this first model.

Theory 2: The interactive process model

The interactive view is an advancement on the linear-transmission model and addresses some of its inadequacies (refer to Figure 2.5 for an overview of the interactive model). First, the assumption that all communication is intentional is problematic, because people will interpret aspects of our behaviour—including our appearance—irrespective of whether we are intentionally trying to communicate information (e.g. make a certain impression) or not. So whether you are dressed to impress or have not put much thought into what you are wearing, people will nonetheless make interpretations about you on the basis of your appearance. Accordingly, this interactive model makes use of the broader term—behaviour—to incorporate the intentional and unintentional information that occurs in communication.

The linear model views communication as a one-way process from sender to receiver, and as such does not adequately account for the interactive nature of communication as a two-way

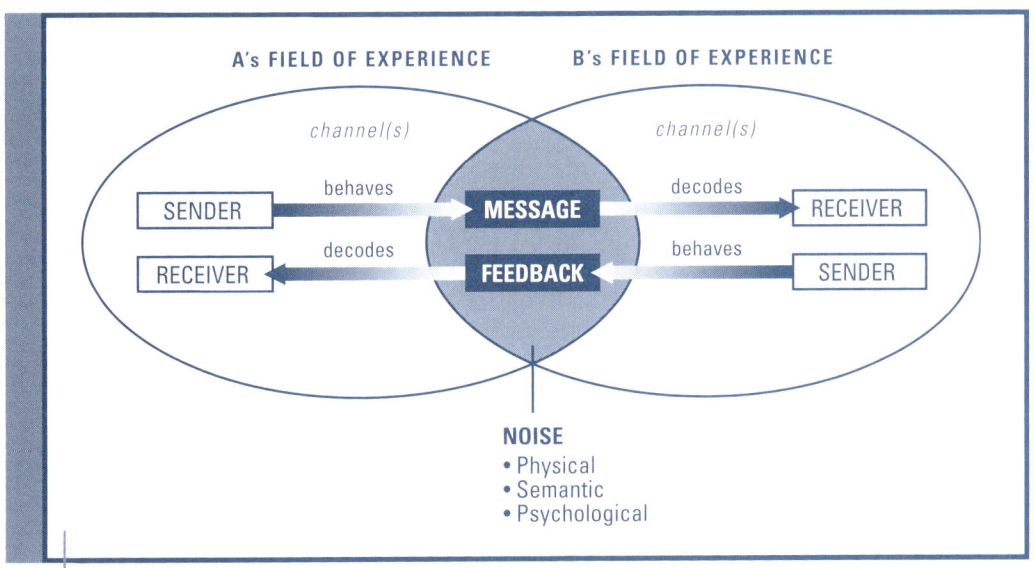

FIGURE 2.5 | The Interactive Model

Source: Based on Looking Out/Looking In: Interpersonal Communication, *Eighth Edition by Ronald B. Adler and Neil Towne, copyright © 1996 by Holt, Rinehart and Winston, reprinted by permission of the publisher.*

process involving information exchange between sender and receiver. Hence the interactive model incorporates the concept of *feedback*.

Feedback refers to a receiver's response to a message. This model views the receiver as a more active participant in the process. Examples of verbal feedback include responses such as, 'Could you explain that again?', 'I don't think I can help you,' and 'I don't agree with you on that point.' However, much of the feedback we send and receive is in nonverbal form, for example nodding in agreement or frowning in disagreement. Nonverbal feedback also occurs in the form of vocal sounds such as 'um' and 'ah'.

However, feedback is not always of the immediate kind, which typically occurs in spoken face-to-face communication. Delayed feedback is a function of written communication, for example the marker's written comments on a returned university assignment. Feedback provides an important means by which senders can evaluate and enhance the effectiveness of their communication. Successful communicators use feedback to tailor and adjust the messages they send to meet the needs of their receivers to help enhance the effectiveness of their messages.

Senders and receivers possess their own respective and overlapping **fields of experience**. The overlap shows that the sender and receiver must have a degree of shared understanding, or knowledge, for communication to occur. For example, they will typically share a common understanding and knowledge of the language (i.e. code) being used. Field of experience refers to the past experiences of an individual and this ultimately influences the way one perceives the world. The past experiences include gender, age, culture and education and so on.

We all know that in communication the receiver never interprets the message in exactly the same way the sender intended or understood it. The interactive model shows the sender and receiver as occupying their own individual space, or field of experience, and as such accounts for the fact that senders and receivers have their own unique views and ways of interpreting information.

Hence this model replaces the older linear view of meaning as being something that resides within the actual code (e.g. the actual words being used), and instead views meaning as something that resides within the minds of senders and receivers. Indeed, there is wide agreement among communication theorists today that meaning exists within people's minds and not in the words or code being used. This model starts to address this by expanding the concept of noise, beyond physical noise, to include anything that interferes with the original intended meaning of a message (the meaning that resides in the mind of the sender) being received into the mind of the receiver. In addition to physical noise, noise can take the form of:

* **Psychological noise**—individual factors such as mood/emotion, expectations, biases and so on in cases where they impact negatively on communication.

* **Semantic noise**—differences in people's understanding of the meaning of certain words (which is influenced by their field of experience including their culture).

Psychological noise refers to the influences of individual factors including psychological make-up, mood and emotion. The area of psychological noise is highly complex and can be very difficult to manage. In spite of this, it is an area of great importance and hence this text pays a good deal of attention to the factors that relate to psychological noise, such as perception and audience analysis (as discussed in later chapters and sections).

As a receiver, a person's psychological make-up is influenced by factors such as personality traits, upbringing, education and so on that make up someone's field of experience. A person's mood is also an influencing factor. If you were fined for speeding on your way to a university lecture, you may well be less receptive to the information being presented in the lecture than you would have normally been. The influences of illness and fatigue also fall into this category.

While a great deal of attention is devoted to the importance of the psychological factors influencing the receiver in the study of communication, the influence of our own psychological make-up as the senders in the process is often neglected. The influence of our psychological make-up is discussed later in the section 'The impacts of our own perceptions'.

Semantic noise refers to distortion due to differences in people's understanding of the signals being used in a message. The term *semantics* refers to the study of meaning and, particularly, the study of meaning of words in language. **Semantic noise** occurs because individuals attach different meanings to words. In some cases a receiver may not even be familiar with a word being used. For example, if I were to use the word 'semantics' in a message to a young child it is quite likely that the child will not understand what it means. One way to overcome this meaning problem would be to introduce the term with an explanation.

While semantic noise can occur at the level of denotation, the literal or dictionary meaning of a word, problems can also arise at another level called *the connotative level*. Connotative meaning refers to the emotional overtones conveyed by a word; for example, the word *dog* may connotatively convey impressions of *companionship* and *friendliness* for one individual but *fear* and *loathing* for another.

As senders of messages we need to choose words carefully so that the connotative meaning received does not interfere with the intended meaning. For example, if a male approached a group of mature women and asked, *What are you girls up to?*, the word *girls* could be interpreted as derogatory and thereby swamp the meaning as originally intended by the sender as one of endearment.

So far we have seen that the interactive model addresses many of the shortcomings of the first model, and the third model goes even further to address more of the complexities involved in communication.

Theory 3: The transactional process model

The transactional view provides us with yet another advance on the modelling of communication and presents communication as a far more dynamic process (refer to Figure 2.6 for an overview of the transactional process model). First, it accounts for the way in which we receive and send information simultaneously when communicating. In this way, the human mind can be likened to a computer processor when it is involved in what is called *multitasking*. In other words we not only are capable of but are typically involved in the sending and receiving of information at the same time. This model incorporates the use of double feedback arrows and refers to both the sender and receiver as 'communicator' in an effort to show how each communicator is both sending and receiving messages at the same time.

COMMUNICATION AS ONGOING AND RELATIONSHIP BASED

The transactional model also views communication as an *ongoing process* or continually unfolding process, as opposed to a static process consisting of discrete instances of communication.

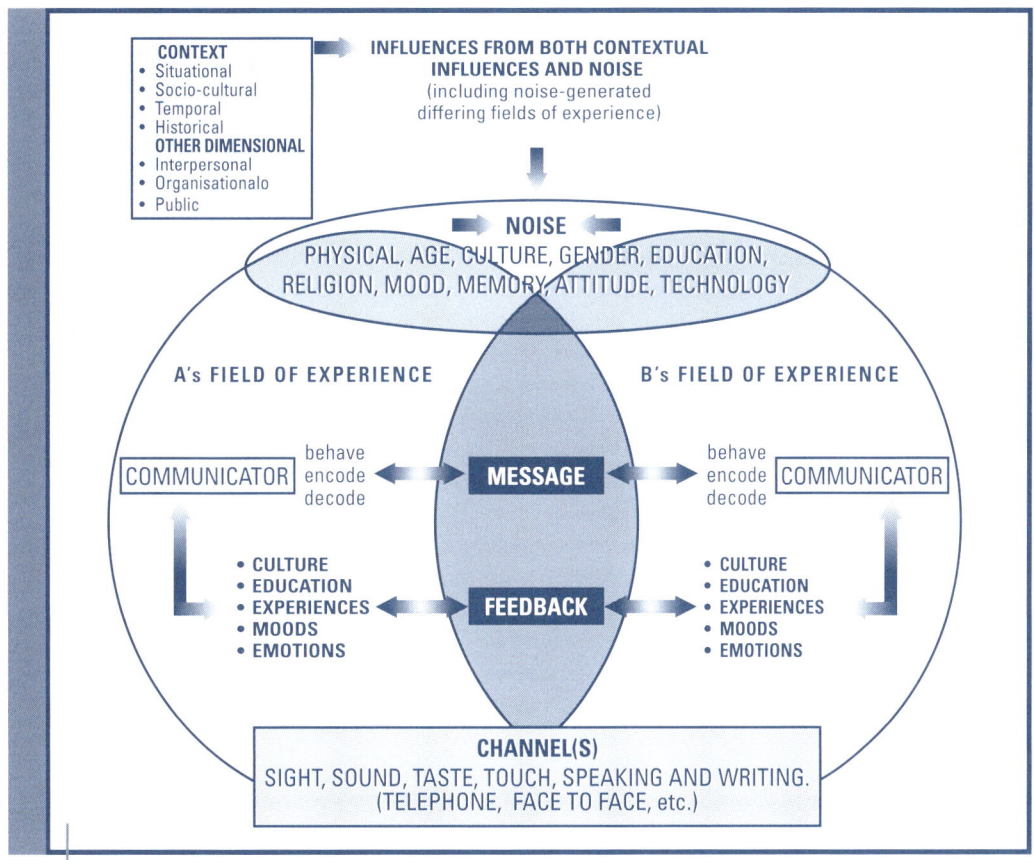

FIGURE 2.6 | The Transactional Process Model

Source: Based on Looking Out/Looking In: Interpersonal Communication, *Eighth Edition by Ronald B. Adler and Neil Towne, copyright © 1996 by Holt, Rinehart and Winston, reprinted by permission of the publisher.*
Note: The model has been simplified in this representation.

Rather than seeing communicative situations as being separate isolated events, communication is viewed in terms of an ongoing and continually unfolding phenomenon. In this way, the model can be used to help us understand the continuing drama of our lives (much like a soap opera) where our communicative interaction with someone we know takes place within the context of previous communicative exchanges. In other words, we do not start communication anew or by *going back to the 'drawing board'* each time we communicate with a colleague, but rather in the context of our previous communicative interactions (or shared history).

While viewing communication as discrete instances may help account for certain kinds of communicative situations, such as a one-way letter or an invoice, it does not adequately account for the interpersonal and ongoing communicative exchanges that characterise much of the communication in our lives. Hence the transactional model incorporates a *relationship dimension* into the process of communication. That is to say, when we communicate, we are also involved in relationship with the person involved. The kinds of relations vary from intimate relationships to working relationships and through to more impersonal kinds of relationships, such as a relationship between a customer and salesperson. So from a transactional viewpoint, when communicating with people we are also relating to people. (The relationship dimension is explored in more detail in Chapter 13, 'Interpersonal communication'.)

COMMUNICATION AS TRANSACTION AND NEGOTIATION

The idea that communication involves processes of transacting and negotiating is central to the perspective the transactional model takes. From a transactional model perspective, a conversation can be viewed in terms of two people exchanging their individual feelings and points of view. From a transactional view, this also involves transactions in which each individual negotiates and arrives at their own personal understanding of what the other party has expressed. In other words, each individual brings their own perspective and background to the negotiating 'table' where the currency being exchanged consists of people's respective ideas, feelings and points of view.

The idea that meaning is something that is negotiated between people also accounts for the innate differences in meaning between the message received and the message as intended by the sender. This again highlights the importance of audience analysis—discussed later in the chapter.

In terms of communication strategy then, we need to speculate about the other party before sending messages, with probing questions like: 'In what way may this person interpret my message?' For example, a request to 'Wash up your cup after you've finished' may be taken as an insult in some situations—even if the sender of the message did not intend it to be. So the meaning of a message is not a *given,* rather it is constructed through negotiation based on interactions with others.

The meaning of words are also negotiated between people with differing views about a concept, for example 'What is meant by professionalism?' It can mean different things to different people as can *professional standards* and *ethical behaviour.*

The relationship dimension of the transactional model is also helpful to us here by showing that communication involves the negotiation of the 'status' of each individual within a relationship dynamic. For example, the way in which you communicate with your boss will influence their perception of you and as such your status in the relationship at a given point. So each time you communicate a process of renegotiation comes into play (often subtly) on a variety of very important levels including those of power, status, credibility and trust.

We will also explore meaning negotiation at another level, specifically the social level, further on under the heading 'The structuralist perspective', in particular how the 'discourse' of environmentalism has had its position renegotiated from marginal (a less well-accepted idea or cause) to one that is central (legitimate and widely accepted as worthwhile). Environmentalism today is a cause that has moved from marginal status to one with a great deal of political power and credibility.

CONTEXT

The transactional version of the model also incorporates a range of other factors that influence communication, namely the **context** of a situation. Communication never takes place in total isolation because it must occur within a context. Dwyer defines context in the following terms:

> Context is the situation or setting within which communication takes place or the circumstances that surround a particular piece of communication.
>
> *(Dwyer 1990, p. 11)*

The context, at this level, is quite specific and is used to describe the specific situation or setting in which communication is taking place and is therefore best referred to as the **situational context** (*or dimension*). The situational context has a major determining influence over the kinds of communicative behaviours and messages that will be produced. For example, the kind of communication that is likely to occur in a setting such as a football grand final will differ greatly from that which people would expect to see in a setting such as a church service. The context of a situation also enables us to interpret what is occurring in an accurate and appropriately informed manner. For example, in the context of having to produce an academic essay or paper, one needs to become familiar with the conventions that 'contextualise' that task in order to be able to produce work which is appropriate to that situation (e.g. the use of formal language as required and avoidance of informal language such as slang).

The **temporal context** relates to time factors. This can refer to the time of day and also the timing of an event (e.g. choosing good timing to request a pay rise). Timing can be crucial in communication, for instance being late for an important meeting or a date can have a negative impact on your ability to communicate at that meeting. The importance of time and timing in communication is discussed in the section on chronemics (i.e. time as a factor in communication) in Chapter 12 on nonverbal communication.

The **historical context** refers to our historical placing in time, for us the beginning of the twenty-first century, often referred to as the new millennium. This is a time when certain values, norms, technology and knowledge exist; for example, it is common for people today to conceptualise human thinking in relation to how a computer processes input. Conceptualising life in this way was not even conceivable until after computers were invented and became a feature of our time. Arguably, we also live in a time where there is less tolerance of discriminatory behaviour and language; for instance, the use of sexist or gender-biased language is tolerated less in our society today than it was 30 years ago and this is evident in this textbook, for example. More recent historical influences may also accompany and influence communicative acts, for example the history behind a particular relationship or the history behind an ongoing criminal trial.

The *historical context* is also closely related to and intertwined with the **sociocultural context** and includes the kind of culture and society where communicative interactions occur. Sociocultural factors also include the kinds of governmental systems in place (e.g. democratic) along with the key political issues of the time, for example debate over whether paid maternity and/or paternity leave should be available to those with newborn babies. Sociocultural factors also include prevailing attitudes and values in a culture, for example commonly held views about fairness and equality. Equality in Australia (also known as *Australian egalitarianism*) has traditionally been associated with the social-cultural notion that home ownership should be within the reach of all Australians.

The transactional model incorporates a range of characteristics that are particularly prominent in direct face-to-face/interpersonal communication. This model presents a more adequate explanation of communication than either the linear or interactive model. It also provides us with the most detailed account of communication as a process in line with the aims of this textbook.

While providing any one definition of communication remains problematic due to its broad nature from the transactional model perspective, communication could be described as: an ongoing process involving a relationship between communicators who occupy individual but overlapping fields of experience, who are involved in the simultaneous sending and receiving of messages where meaning is interactively negotiated but also subject to distortion from various forms of noise.

Comments on the process models

Preference is given to the transactional view as it provides a comprehensive theory-model that allows us to focus on communication in a way that facilitates our key aim, which is to maximise our effectiveness as communicators. Nonetheless, it is acknowledged that it emerged from the earlier model of linear transmission. The original linear-transmission model and the later interactive model are based on the notion of receiving and sending information effectively. These models have made significant contributions by providing a strategic basis upon which to formulate written and scripted forms of communication. The two later models also provide the basis for one of the most important concepts in communication, that of audience analysis, which helps us to tailor our messages to suit the needs of a receiver(s) and enhance the effectiveness of our communication. The third, 'transactional' model of communication provides a yet deeper and more comprehensive understanding so that we can develop strategies and techniques to enhance further our effectiveness as communicators. However, it is important to note that there are numerous other theoretical approaches to the study of what is classified as communication from the arts to mass media forms of entertainment, as is the case with the structuralist approach discussed below.

The structuralist perspective (an alternative theoretical perspective)

While this book is primarily concerned with process models of communication, we briefly divert to introduce another theoretical perspective called *structuralism*, also known as *semiotics*. Semiotics is often referred to as the science of signs and sign systems and it concerns itself with the levels at which signs generate meaning. As a substantial area of study beyond the scope of this book, it provides a very different perspective on communication from the process models. Nonetheless, it is introduced in this section to show that there are other kinds of theories and perspectives on communication besides the process models approach which underpins this particular textbook.

Semiotics is concerned with how we produce meaning using signs and sign systems and places its emphasis on viewing signs and meaning production in terms of structured systems. In its broad sweep, it also views meaning as being produced by and within the structures of our political and cultural systems.

COMMUNICATION AS 'STRUCTURED'

The English language provides an example of a sign system. A particular word such as 'Wednesday' is an example of a sign within that sign system. As the word 'structuralism' suggests, this perspective views communication as something that is based on structures (e.g. the English language provides a structured system that enables communication to occur). To illustrate further, a structuralist would argue that a sign can only generate meaning via its relationship to other signs within a system. For example, the sign 'Wednesday' can only communicate meaning because of its relationship to the other signs in a system known as the *days of the week*. Take the following examples:

Wednesday means:	*cool* means:
• not Monday;	• not cold;
• not Tuesday;	• not hot;
• not Thursday, etc.	• not warm.

Wednesday derives its meaning by virtue of the *social world* fact that it fits into a structure known as the days of the week. If you have had musical training, or are familiar with the dynamics of music, you will notice the same kind of principle—with the role that notes play in putting together a melody or tune. That is, that melodies are more the result of contrasting relationships between certain notes than the direct result of notes in themselves. A practical example of this principle is that a song can be played and sung in a different key (i.e. in a range which uses lower notes, or a range that uses higher notes).

Semiotics identifies further structural elements in relation to communication and some of the key elements include: discourse, ideology, myth and metaphor. Semiotics provides a means by which the communication outputs and products—such as television programs, newspaper and magazine articles, advertisements, art, cinema, music and so on—can be interpreted in ways that help reveal how the signs being used (for example in a news article) function to generate meaning at the structural levels of discourse, ideology and myth. Semiotics can be used to analyse the signifiers (or content) of a classic or popular movie (as a social artefact), guided by questions such as 'What is the moral of the story?'; 'What values are being promoted?'; 'Are myths being utilised to sustain commonly held views?'; or 'Does the movie content challenge and call into question mainstream views?'

DISCOURSE: ADVANCED COMMUNICATION THEORY

Semiotics views the concept of **discourse** as a key structural element in communication. It is a complex concept which eludes a stable and precise definition, but the following information is helpful in developing an understanding of the concept. In contemporary semiotics the term discourse refers to the systematic ways in which people, or groups, within a society produce and communicate information and it also functions to construct the various domains of knowledge in a society. O'Sullivan *et al.* discuss discourse in terms of:

> The social process of making and reproducing sense(s). Discourses are the product of social, historical and institutional formation, and meanings are produced by these institutionalized discourses.
>
> *(O'Sullivan et al. 1994, pp. 93–94)*

In terms of mainstream institutionalised domains of knowledge within a society, we can identify and analyse discourses such as:

* medical discourse;
* scientific discourse;
* economic rationalist discourse;
* environmental discourse;
* communication discourse, and so on.

Accordingly, it is evident that communication and society incorporate a very wide range of discourses. Discourses carry with them their own particular perspectives on life; for example, the discourse of medicine focuses on the notions of healthiness, disease and managing and curing illnesses. In semiotic theory, discourses are seen as being composed of other structural elements, such as ideology and myth.

Ideology is another complex concept, and for our purposes can be viewed in terms of the values, or value system, that underpin a discourse. For example, the discourse of environmentalism is one that places a great deal of value on protecting the environment and managing it in sustainable ways.

The term **myth** refers to the common beliefs or belief systems of a society which reside within its discourses. In this sense myths are not thought about in terms of being necessarily untrue or misnomers, as per the traditional sense of the word, but simply refer to widely held beliefs within a society. For example, within the discourse of *traditional Australian identity* there exists a range of myths that Australians believe that everyone is entitled to *a fair go*, that is, to be treated fairly and equally (other cultures have variations on these kinds of beliefs and values). The cultural tenet of *a fair go* is evident in a related myth called *the great Australian dream*, that is, that all Australians should be entitled to own their own home. This myth then is supported by an ideology that places a high value on the idea of equality (or equal-ness) among people rather than a society based on social classes. You may be aware that in recent times many people argue that Australia is becoming a less egalitarian society.

Semiotics is itself an example of a discourse or sub-discourse of knowledge that resides within the discourse of *communication studies* and as such it carries its own particular perspective, or *frame of reference*, for understanding communication as something which functions to structure power relations. So discourses, as constructed perspectives and associated bodies of knowledge (which include theory), are viewed as being in competition with each other for power and legitimacy. A semiotic analysis of the discourse of environmentalism over the past 30–40 years reveals that this discourse evolved from being a marginalised discourse with very little legitimacy or mainstream acceptance. For example, newspaper headlines and stories from the past used terms such as *ratbag-greenies* when reporting on the environmentalists movement as a means to marginalise it. However, the situation today is quite different. The 'Green' movement, as a discourse, is associated with a great degree of political power and social legitimacy. For example, corporations today wish to be associated with 'Green' values, while we also have government ministers for the environment and even a political 'Greens' party dedicated to promoting environmental values of environmental sustainability.

From a discourse perspective, the act of communicating is never neutral, as it involves the constructing of a particular world view or perspective that exists within a culture or society. So when we communicate we are also imparting particular views and values within our society and in most cases without being consciously aware of this. (This theoretical perspective is compatible with that of *social constructivism*, discussed further on—a view which posits that knowledge and understandings are actively constructed though our communicative interactions.) On a final note the structuralist/semiotic approach has also been criticised quite heavily in recent times from other perspectives, notably *post-structuralism* and also *postmodernism*. Post-structuralists contend that communication and society are considerably less structured than structuralism suggests.

Perception in communication

Perception lies at the very heart of the communication process. It is the process by which we make sense of and understand ourselves and others. It is important to remember that perceptions of reality can, to varying degrees, overtake reality, so there is some truth in the cliché that 'when perception takes over, reality no longer matters.' Therefore, it is worth remembering that when dealing with others we are also dealing with their perception.

The process of perception can be broken down into two major domains: selection and organisation or interpretation. However, these two domains are not clearly separate from each other (nor do they work in isolation of each other) but are intertwined with points at which they overlap and also influence each other.

Selection

Through the course of our daily lives we are constantly subjected to a large number of stimuli. If you happen to be studying at a library, for example, you are surrounded by stimuli such as the colour scheme, décor and the sound of quiet conversations and other activity. Because we are surrounded by more stimuli than we can manage, we have to be selective about what to focus on simply so that we can cope with life. Accordingly, people tend to pay attention to what seems to be important and significant to them and to varying degrees they discard the rest. Selection (paying more attention to some things) is far from an objective process and depends on what one has learned from past experiences including one's likes and dislikes. For example, someone interested in football may pay a great deal of attention to a conversation about the game while others with little interest in it 'tune out'.

We all have the capacity to select and focus on certain things, for example the courses you choose to study and the time you devote to these. We make these choices based on what we feel is in our own best interest. However, it is important that we realise that we are not always good at judging which options are really in our best interests. An awareness and appreciation of this is important to effective communication (including learning and self-management) because it draws attention to the fact that we need to think carefully about the decisions and courses of action we take.

It is also important to be mindful that a lack of interest in a given topic lessens the likelihood that a person will further their understanding in that area. This has ramifications for learning, for instance when you are required to do an assignment on a topic that you do not find interesting. The best advice in such cases is to try to muster an interest in the topic from within, for example 'Can you look at it differently or search for an interesting aspect to it?' You need to search for a means by which to motivate oneself and thereby boost the chances of performing the task well.

It is important to realise how attitudes and beliefs play a role in determining a person's performance and achievements. In the study of communication, this determining influence is known as the phenomenon of *self-fulfilling prophecy*. **Self-fulfilling prophecy** explains how 'existing attitudes and beliefs tend to influence a person's behaviour in ways that increase the likelihood of outcomes that support those attitudes and belief' (Adler *et al.* 1998). Take the following negative scenario: a belief that—*I'll never be good at playing sport* increases the likelihood that I will continue to avoid playing sport and subsequently fail to develop skills or learn to enjoy sport. This outcome can then work to reinforce that belief and 'sport-avoidance' behaviours. (Issues relating to this are explored in greater detail in Chapter 13 on interpersonal communication and Chapter 16 on communication barriers.)

Finally, getting back to the main topic of selection in perception, the nature of life is such that it constrains possibilities. In other words, as an individual you cannot choose to pursue a large range of endeavours; for example, it would be very difficult to become a surgeon and a pilot and a rock star as well as an athlete. Hence making *life choices* is often difficult and as such they need to be carefully thought through. The flip side of this is that we can become too restrictive in our views about what we can achieve and enjoy—which is not the case with a group of surgeons in the United States who also enjoy playing in a rock band. So it is also worth remembering that 'choices' become choices only after we perceive them as being real and available to us as options.

Organisation/interpretation

Once again, all perception involves some degree of distortion because we do not have direct access to 'reality'. Our interpretations are subject to a range of factors including our physical senses and cognitive tendencies. So it is important to remain aware that our view of the world is our reconstruction of it rather than a direct copy of it. Indeed, there are times when the discrepancies between the two stand out. For example, the bent appearance we see when a stick is partially submerged in water reminds us that there are differences between what we perceive or see and the (physical) reality. Earlier discussions also revealed that the conceptual and linguistic resources (e.g. concepts) we use also influence perception.

Lakoff (1987) explains that we process stimuli through organising structures or mental models, also called **idealised cognitive models (ICMs)**, which evolve from past experiences and learning. Interpretation involves the weaving of selected stimuli through these preconceived sense-making models (or preconceptions). A person's individual cognitive tendencies shape a person's view of the world, and this is some times referred to as an individual's **personal world view**.

While our personal *world view* allows us to make sense of the world, it does so at the price of distorting it. So it is important to understand that we are predisposed to interpreting the world in ways that accord with the perceptual biases that reside within the sense-making models that constitute our world view. For example, if an employer has a tendency to view older workers as generally slower and more lethargic than younger workers, then contact with a very energetic older worker may be interpreted as a one-off instance where this worker stands out as being an exception to the rule (Kossen 2003). Once established, these mental models are resistant to change because they are flexible enough to accommodate contradictory information. In other words, our attitudes, assumptions and established ways of thinking and understanding have a strong tendency to resist change, but in spite of this cognitive tendencies do change slowly over time to accommodate new learning and a changing world.

However, self-development and learning is hindered in those who are more closed-minded. In essence, our experience of life shapes the interpretive models through which we see the world. In other words, through life we learn to see or perceive things in certain ways. The visual gestalt (see Figure 2.7) can be used to help show how stimuli can be perceptually organised in two different ways—as a duck or a rabbit: 'Which of these do you see?'; 'Try looking at it both ways so that you can see the two images'. How we approach the diagram determines the view we construct; for example, viewing the protrusions on the left as a beak gives the impression of a duck, while viewing them as long ears gives the impression of a rabbit.

The point being made here (using a simple concrete-based example) is that once you become accustom to seeing something one way it can be very difficult to see it in another (not so difficult with the duck–rabbit image though). Keeping in mind that we rely on a perceptual frame of reference to interpret phenomena, shifting an established frame of reference in order to view phenomena from another point of view can be difficult. A perceptual frame of reference, for example a theoretical point of view, also can function to hinder and block our perception because once we get used to seeing or understanding something in a certain way it becomes harder to see it differently, and hence it can restrict our capacities to perceive and comprehend.

FIGURE 2.7 | Duck/Rabbit Visual Gestalt

However, being aware of this and keeping an open mind (being open to and interested in alternative points of view) helps to loosen these restrictions, allowing us to be more flexible in our thinking. It is important that we try and understand alternative points of view; however, it does not mean that we have to abandon our views or necessarily agree with alternative views.

Attitude is another major shaping or organising force in the way we perceive information, ourselves and others and it refers to a predisposition to respond to stimuli in a particular way (Taylor *et al.* 1983). Attitudes are interlinked with and also shape our preferences, biases, values and so forth (psychographics found under the heading 'Factors of influence in perception'). These are the factors within an individual that structure the way they perceive the world. They provide the basis upon which we organise and make sense of experience.

COMMON TENDENCIES THAT DISTORT PERCEPTION

* The tendency to view the world in ways that best suit our established attitudes, beliefs and conditioned ways of thinking. This is especially problematic if our views are unrealistic or we are closed minded (less open to new and alternative ideas).

* Selective perception, that is, overlooking information that contradicts one's views as in the prejudice towards older workers in the scenario outlined above. In other words, only seeing the things we wish to see and which confirm our established attitudes and beliefs.

* The tendency to believe that most people think and feel much the same way as we do; for example, if you prefer hot weather to cold and then assume other people feel the same way, as well as being critical of people whose views, tastes or preferences differ from your own.

* The tendency to judge ourselves more generously than we do others, particularly in the way we account for the situations and hardships we and others face in life. For example, if I fail an examination I may attribute blame to external causes, but if someone else fails I am much more likely to attribute the blame towards the character of the person involved, for example 'It is because she is lazy and does not study'.

* The halo effect, a tendency to perceive someone we like ('it may be because they are handsome and well mannered or excel at sport') in ways that exaggerate positive qualities and overlook

or play down negative qualities. The flip side of this effect works in reverse for people we dislike such as discounting a valid point from someone we dislike because we discount their ability to make a good point.

* The tendency to view things in overly simplistic ways rather than developing more detailed and comprehensive understandings. A theoretical explanation for this would be that we interpret reality through ICMs that simplify and distort perception. A genuine commitment to open-mindedness and lifelong learning provides us with a means by which we can manage and lessen the distortive influences associated with ICMs.

The differences in people's perceptions

The interactive and transactional models of communication acknowledge the idea that the message one receives is never exactly the same as the one intended by the sender. The types of stimuli we focus on and the ways in which we organise them vary from person to person. And the way an individual perceives depends on a large number of complex factors including: their interests, attitude, personality, upbringing and past experience. For example, eyewitness accounts to police after a robbery often vary greatly because different people select from and make sense of the same situation differently. Someone interested in clothes and fashion may be more likely to notice and give a more detailed description of the clothing worn by a robber than someone less interested in fashion. The variability that exists between people's perceptions of the world is signified in both the interactive and transactional model via the separate, but overlapping, fields of experience. A potential dilemma in perception is simply that *everyone has a different one*. We are all unique and occupy a different subjective place in the world. This strikes right at the heart of what communication is about—relating to and exchanging ideas with others who occupy their own unique subjective position. This then provides a strong support for the importance of audience analysis for effective communication (audience analysis is explored below).

Factors of influence in perception

The list of variables that influence perception is virtually endless. Some significant influences follow.

DEMOGRAPHIC FACTORS

Reasonably accessible variables:

* physical location;
* culture;
* language (including conceptual categories);
* gender;
* age;
* past experiences (note: age influences this variable);
* education;
* religion;
* socio-economic position; and
* occupational status, etc.

PSYCHOGRAPHIC FACTORS

Less accessible psychological or mental variables which can be known with less certainty:

- assumptions;
- preconceived ideas;
- biases and prejudices;
- attitudes;
- values and beliefs;
- interests;
- likes and dislikes;
- perspectives (points of view);
- professional bias or disposition;
- personality;
- expectations;
- tastes and preferences (e.g. fashion, music); and
- mood, motivation, etc.
- world view (personal and cultural)

'Cultural' world view (commonsense knowledge)

While every individual is unique and perceptions vary from person to person, people nonetheless share a great deal of common culture-based knowledge. Theorist Alfred Schutz noted that 'the unique biographical situation in which I find myself within the world . . . is only to a very small extent of my own making' (Schutz 1973, p. 163) and hence he developed an interest in the everyday world of *commonsense* knowledge within a society which is that knowledge which is 'taken for granted'. This theoretical view, **social constructivism**, posits that commonsense knowledge is socially constructed through people's interactions with one another and with wider society and its institutions such as educational and mass media (Berger and Luckmann 1991 [1966]). This theory is compatible with the *ICM* discussed earlier, because it also involves the use of 'sense-making' structures but on a wider sociocultural scale. Commonsense knowledge stems from cultural frames of reference that shape our expectations and views. For example, the behaviour many of us would expect from a school teacher is that which is in keeping with community standards for someone in that role. These established and prevailing views cohere into what can be referred to as the **world view** of a culture, or a **cultural world view**, as a culturally shared sense-making framework that also shapes the ways in which an individual will come to see and understand the world. In spite of this, social constructivism also posits that people actively construct meaning and understanding, as opposed to a view that perception is merely a passive process. Hence it also accounts for changes in culture—as people interactively construct our social realities, for example community expectations along with outcomes that stem from these.

A distinction often made about a Western society world view, in contrast to some other Eastern societies' world views, is that of 'individualism' (emphasising freedom and autonomy of individuals) as a Western world view in contrast to that of 'collectivism'. In terms of audience analysis, it is important that we gain an understanding of the nature of the collective world view of such cultures—particularly in cases where you are required to communicate and interact in a cultural context different from your own. Intercultural communication is covered in more depth in Chapter 13, 'Interpersonal Communication', and then further in Chapter 16, 'Barriers'.

Culture-based world views are made up of the ideas, values and beliefs that are dominant in a culture at a given period and, while world views are quite stable, they nonetheless change over longer time frames. For instance, the traditional Western view of 'history' was that it was objective and singular, whereas today it is widely accepted that history is not singular and objective but that there are multiple subjective histories, for example histories from the point of view of Aboriginals, histories from a feminist point of view, and so on. Major changes in the structures of understanding (as in history above) that mark a major shift or move away from the orthodox thinking of a world view are called *paradigm* shifts, that is, major shifts or changes in a world view. The term **paradigm** can be traced to Thomas Kuhn, who used it to explain how theories are developed out of frameworks that are based on a set of world view assumptions, which in essence function as pillars upon which a given mode of knowledge rest.

Since then, Kuhn and others have also shown that what emerges as a 'fact' in science depends upon the frame of reference used by an observer (Selden and Widdowson 1993). Accordingly, the assumptions that frame a world view affect the way the world is viewed. Ideally, this should serve as a powerful reminder that our world view is only one of many, and of the need to appreciate and respect cultural world views that differ from your own. Finally, earlier discussion regarding the visual gestalt shown in Figure 2.7 also supports the (meta-theoretical) principle, that how we come to view phenomena is dependent upon the framework through which we view them.

Audience analysis: Tailoring communication to address others' perceptions

The difficulties that arise because of differences in the way people come to perceive things make audience analysis a communication imperative. The rationale for audience analysis is that it provides us with information that can help us tailor messages in ways that cater for the needs and wants of our intended receivers. Consideration of the demographic and psychographic factors listed above help us to generate useful information. The better our understanding of the assumptions, attitudes and knowledge level of our audience (or receiver or other party), the better placed we are to communicate effectively.

Demographic information is by nature the more accessible and concrete, so if we have access to a person's age then we can be certain about that person's age. Furthermore, a person's age will affect the nature of their life experiences.

Demographic information can also assist in speculations about a psychographic profile. For instance, communication and English lecturers may be more pedantic about grammar and spelling in assignments than a mathematics lecturer. However, if this assumption is arrived at solely on these demographics then there would be no guarantee that this assumption would be correct. Nonetheless demographics can provide valuable information when trying to gain a better understanding of our receiver or audience. For example, information about the teachings of a given religion may provide some reasonably reliable insights into the values and beliefs common among members of that religion.

While we do need to approach psychographic information with care, psychographic information can be obtained using a number of methods including direct contact with the party of interest especially over an extended time frame (getting to know people); contact with reliable sources, for example interviews with knowledgeable informants; and even through questionnaires directed at obtaining information regarding values, beliefs, preferences and so on when appropriate to do so. In sum, audience analysis can be understood using the cliché of 'doing your homework' or more precisely making sure you are appropriately prepared in terms of knowing your audience's/or receiver's points of view, expectations, desires and pertinent issues they face.

In writing assignments, it is important that you meet the lecturer's expectations. An audience analysis strategy could entail the testing of your interpretation of a task by seeking clarification with your lecturer.

The impacts of our own perceptions on ourselves

While audience analysis plays an extremely important role in maximising the effectiveness of our communication, the influence of our own perceptions as both senders and receiver-learners is often overlooked, although not by Hugh Mackay, who points out that:

> It is easy to accept that we are the products of our own experience, but not so easy to acknowledge that we are also prisoners of our experience.
>
> *(Mackay 1994, p. 61)*

Our past experiences, including all our learning to date, enable us to make sense of the world and to function in it. For example, we even rely on this knowledge to execute everyday tasks such as crossing a road safely. However, this knowledge, incorporating our perspective on life, which includes prejudices, biases, assumptions and so on, can also work to impede our ability to learn new ways of thinking and to accommodate new ideas that conflict with our existing point of view. As Verderber (1990, p. 33) notes:

> Some people have very accurate perceptions of their world; others may distort what comes to them through their senses to such an extent that their perceptions of the world, themselves and others have little to do with reality. Thus, their communication loses its potential effectiveness.

An awareness that the experiences (or baggage) we bring to situations also functions to hinder effective communication is important if we are to begin managing their obstructive effects. You may have heard the cliché that 'he [or she] is his own worst enemy', and while it does sound harsh it applies to all of us from time to time. In other words, we have all on occasion acted in ways that run counter to our best interests and wellbeing. As noted earlier, our perceptions of the world can deceive us in ways that can make it hard to truly recognise 'What is in our own best interest?', that is, 'What kinds of things will bring us happiness and allow us to develop and enjoy a rewarding career?' So in pondering these questions it is important to be mindful of the differences that can, and often do, exist between:

1. what we see as being in our best interests; and
2. what may actually be in our own best interests.

Accordingly, it is (often) in our own best interests to think carefully about the choices we make because after all it is our interests that are at stake. Unfortunately, it is all too easy to get it wrong; however, being aware of this provides us with a start for helping to 'get it right' more often. Self-monitoring, such as regular self-evaluation and readjusting goals and behaviours, also provides us with strategies that help keep us 'on the right track'.

The ways in which we think and interpret information become our 'thinking habits' and some of our unproductive thinking habits can, and do, at times impede our ability to learn and develop. For example, thinking critically at tertiary level requires us at times to question and confront our existing views on life. This can be discomforting, but being aware of this dynamic can assist us in negotiating a way through the proverbial 'learning curve'.

Hence a genuine effort to try to periodically identify and evaluate factors that may inhibit our learning and development is a worthwhile self-management strategy, in other words, to try to manage one's perspective and accompanying biases in order to remain open minded and receptive so that one can continue to learn and develop and stay in touch with reality.

These 'self-management' type of strategies involve processes of *self-monitoring* in an effort to detect potential biases and *critical self-reflection*, for example giving due consideration to potential biases identified and reviewing one's outlook as deemed necessary. These concepts are discussed in more detail in Chapters 13 and 16, which deal with *interpersonal communication* and *barriers to communication* respectively. In addition, keeping an open mind in relation to alternative views and receptiveness to feedback are important skills that we must continually develop in order to maximise our effectiveness and success as communicators, learners and professionals.

Task analysis: A strategic approach to communication

Along with audience analysis, task analysis is one of the most important and fundamental principles for maximising communicative effectiveness and efficiency. Task analysis is often taken for granted and seen as something that is straightforward and plain commonsense. However, these are the kinds of underestimations that can lead to poor communicative performance.

Task analysis is the process of working out the purpose and defining what kinds of things need to be achieved—including the division of a task into more manageable subtasks—and the development of aims, objectives and scope (refer to Figure 2.8). From this point, we can begin to consider strategies and techniques by which these aims and objectives can be best achieved.

A generic approach to task analysis

The following chapters of this book provide specific information on planning communication including task analysis for approaching particular communicative tasks, for example essays and interviews. At this point, however, we introduce an overview of a general approach to analysing communicative tasks.

AIM

In order to maximise the likelihood of successful outcomes, it is most important to be very clear about what needs to be done. Task analysis, along with the rest of the principles and strategies presented in the text, is a kind of skill (or series of related skills) and practice (or doing) provides

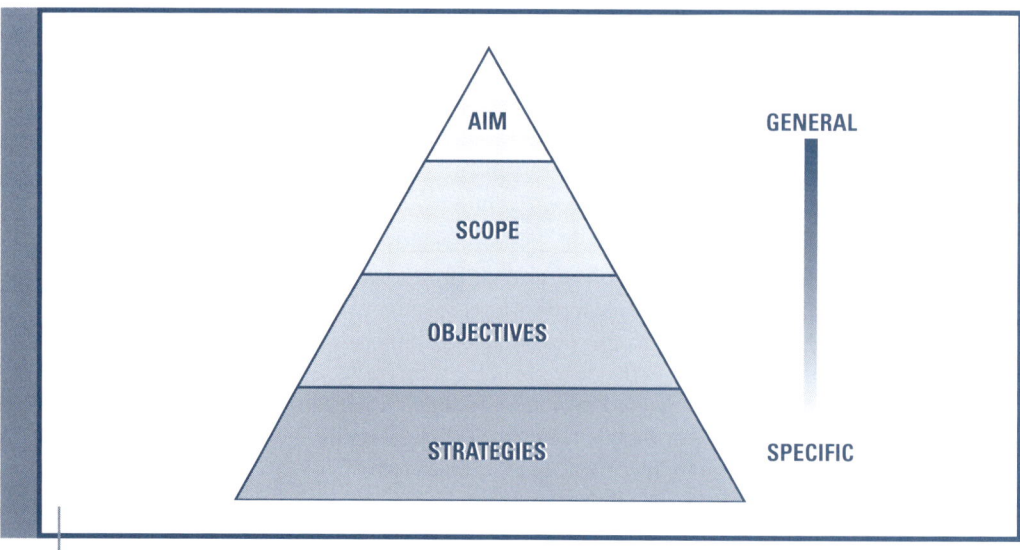

FIGURE 2.8 | The Task Analysis Process

the means by which we develop our proficiency. In developing the aim one needs to formulate a statement of intent at a very general level. In business terms we could equate a stated aim with the mission statement of an organisation.

The specific ways in which a task analysis is performed depend on the nature of the task being undertaken. In the context of university studies, students often have to address assignment questions. In this case analysing the question becomes quite important. This is discussed in detail in later chapters, for example Chapters 4 and 6, 'Effective writing' and 'Extended writing' respectively.

STATING THE AIM

To develop the aim one needs to formulate a clear statement that outlines what is to be achieved. In brief, a thesis statement represents the stated aim for an essay (refer to the relevant chapters mentioned above for more detail on developing thesis statements).

SCOPE

In the scope, you develop the parameters of the task. You will need to identify what areas are to be covered in the project and also the limitations. For example, specify what areas are to be analysed while also making reference to the limitations (what is not going to be analysed) in an essay or report.

OBJECTIVES

The objectives stem from the aim and the scope and detail what needs to be achieved in order to fulfil what is required to reach the aim successfully. Identifying and gaining an understanding of the objectives is a critical process and requires a great deal of effort in the way of depth of analysis. The task here is to determine at a specific level the kinds of criteria that need to be satisfied in order to achieve the aim. The assessment criteria (on an assessment criteria sheet) provide you with important information here. The objectives break the task down into more manageable tasks or subtasks. Once determined, the stated objectives can be used to help formulate strategies to fulfil them.

STRATEGIES AND TECHNIQUES

At the level of strategies things become very specific. Hence strategies are not discussed in detail here and are instead presented in the remainder of the text. For the purpose of providing an example, however, one will typically use library research strategies in an effort to identify and evaluate relevant information for an essay or report.

Generic 'task management' model

TASK ANALYSIS

* Analyse the task, question or problem and develop an aim statement.
* Identify, analyse and state objectives required to reach the stated aim.
* Plan by dividing the task into more manageable subtasks.
* Proceed with (initial) subtasks (e.g. research the literature).

AUDIENCE ANALYSIS

* Analyse the audience/receiver (e.g. expectations, dislikes).
* Select strategies appropriate to the audience and incorporate these into the task plan (e.g. the use of formal English and technical terms required for an essay or report).

EXECUTING TASK (ALL SUBTASKS)

* Structure information (introduction, main arguments and conclusion).
* Periodically review strategies while in progress (e.g. Will my argument be convincing and clear for the receiver? Am I on task, that is, am I addressing the question well?).
* Develop drafts and continue to develop and refine; proof final draft and present the work (e.g. essay).

EVALUATION

* Use the feedback to evaluate the strategies and techniques used (e.g. What weaknesses may need to be addressed in future work?).

The *generic task management model* as presented appears to be linear in process, in that it shows task analysis as a process where tasks can be broken into discrete step-by-step stages, or subtasks, which are easy to follow. In reality, however, these stages are dynamic (not as linear as they appear) and as such task analysis requires us to do quite a lot of 'backwarding' and 'forwarding' between stages. Being aware of this may be just enough to keep you from becoming too overwhelmed and help you to preserve your stamina and confidence when the models, theories and ideas you are using do not unfold easily or the way you originally planned. It is important to note that presenting models in a linear form (as per the model above) can be very useful, as it allows us to represent complex processes in a way that makes them easier to comprehend. But in applying such a model we need to realise that the process is by its very nature one that is non-linear.

SUMMARY

This chapter provides a foundation for studying the main content of the book, which chapter by chapter will deal with specific principles and strategies for maximising effectiveness in communication. In laying this foundation, we have considered the importance of approaching theoretical ideas in a flexible and open-minded manner and thinking about them critically by weighing up possible benefits and costs. Remember that the theoretical ideas presented in this book are fundamentally the ideas, concepts and principles we can use to understand communication better. Ultimately we can use this knowledge to enhance the effectiveness of our communication. Equipped with this core knowledge, we now proceed to the main content in the following chapters, which contain the more specific principles and strategies for communication on areas such as written communication, interpersonal communication, group communication and teamwork and so on.

KEY POINTS

- Communication is a very broad and complex concept and therefore difficult to define in a precise way. But, in essence, it pertains to the exchange of information among people. This requires skills in comprehending and expressing information. Our capacity to communicate derives largely from our ability to conceptualise (assign categories, names and explanations).

- Explanations which are formalised are called *theories*. Reflecting on the ways in which theories function and how they are constructed is referred to as consideration at the meta-theoretical level.

- Theories provide us with a greater degree of understanding and control, but remain inherently incomplete. Theories and concepts also shape our perceptions and have the potential to distort them. Hence they need to be applied carefully in order to maximise benefits and minimise potential costs.

- The first theory-model of communication, the linear model, emphasises the notion of a sender sending information to a receiver.

- The interactive model is an advance on the linear model and incorporates the concepts of feedback, unintentional aspects of communication, people's fields of experience and a notion of noise that goes beyond physical impediments.

- The more advanced transactional model views communication as an ongoing process involving relationships between participants who occupy individual but overlapping fields of experience, and who are involved in the simultaneous sending and receiving of messages which are subject to various forms of noise.

- According to the transactional model, communication is also a process whereby the meanings in messages are negotiated by the communicators.

- Structuralism (or semiotics) provides yet another perspective on communication and concerns the levels at which signs generate meaning systematically through the social formations of discourse, myth and ideology.

- Perception is central to communication and involves the selection and organisation (or interpretation) of stimuli and is influenced by demographic and psychographic factors.

- Our own perception impacts upon our ability to learn and communicate, so it is important that we reflect upon the implications of this and work on keeping an open mind to new and alternative ideas.

- Task analysis is the process of determining what needs to be achieved, dividing it into more manageable subtasks, including the development of aims, objectives and scope. This then allows us to develop the kinds of strategies by which these aims and objectives can best be achieved.

- Audience analysis involves researching the expectations and desires of those with whom we wish to communicate in an effort to help effectively tailor our communication accordingly.

- Communication theory, as presented in this chapter, provides a framework for strategies and techniques used to maximise effective communication in specific contexts including written, interpersonal and group communication. The remainder of this text examines strategies and techniques for a range of specific situations and context types as signalled in the respective titles of each chapter.

REVIEW QUESTIONS

1. What does the notion of effective or successful communication mean to you? To start you thinking, some people may see it in terms of satisfying relationships, productive alliances or successfully attaining goals. So how do you see it?

2. What, in your view, are the key elements to effective communication?

3. What kinds of benefits and costs are associated with theories and what are the implications of these?

4. What are the differences between formal and folk theory?

5. Are there any forms of communication that the linear or interactive models account for more adequately than the transactional model?

6. What kinds of noise can occur in communication and how can their effects be minimised?

7. Describe, using examples, the way in which contextual aspects of a situation can influence communicative behaviour.

8. Provide your own examples of situations that help illustrate how meaning is negotiated in communication as explained in the transaction model.

9. How could the message 'Wash up your cup after you've finished with it' be taken as an insult, even though the sender did not intend it to be insulting?

10. Summarise the key elements of the semiotic or structuralist approach to communication. How do they help advance and deepen our understanding of communication?

11. Describe the processes involved in perception. How do they function to influence it?

12. In what ways do think your perceptions hinder your effectiveness as a communicator (in certain situations)?

13. Describe the key aspects of task and audience analysis. What are the major benefits of the task/audience analysis approach to communication?

EXERCISES

Note: After formulating your responses it is important wherever possible to discuss them with a peer or group of peers. If you are not in a classroom setting, then an appropriate electronic discussion board would be ideal.

1. In a group or with a peer or friend discuss for what reasons the statement that 'all theories are flawed' is correct.
   Given that this is the case, what measures can you use so that you can productively apply theoretically based knowledge to real situations or problems?

2. In a group or with a peer or friend identify one or more situations (real or hypothetical) in which the differences between someone's perceived best interests (i.e. as perceived by that person) and their actual best interests has led that person to act in a way that ran counter to their interests, for example their benefit or wellbeing.

   – Provide a theoretical analysis of this scenario. In other words, what theoretical principles can you use to explain it?

   – Put forward strategies and/or techniques you can use to counter these kinds of pitfalls.

3. In what ways can an accurate perception of yourself help you to communicate more effectively? Discuss in a group.

4. Identify one or more situations (real or hypothetical) in which attempts to communicate have actually become counter-productive, that is, actually made a situation worse? Use theory to explain the unfolding of this scenario. Can you draw any conclusions about the nature of communication based on this scenario?

BIBLIOGRAPHY

Adler, R., Rosenfeld, L., Towne, N. and Proctor, R. 1998, *Interplay: The Process of Interpersonal Communication,* 7th ed., Harcourt Brace & Company, Florida.

Adler, R. and Towne, N. 1996, *Looking Out/Looking In: Interpersonal Communication,* 8th ed., Harcourt, Brace Jovanovich, Orlando, Florida.

Barker, L.L. 1984, *Communication,* Prentice Hall, Englewood Cliffs.

Berger, P.L. and Luckmann, T. 1991 [1966], *The Social Construction of Reality: A Treatise in the Sociology of Knowledge,* Penguin, Victoria.

Dwyer, J. 1990, *The Business Communication Handbook,* 2nd ed., Prentice Hall, Sydney.

Fiske, J. 1982, *Introduction to Communication Studies,* Methuen, London.

Gottdiener, M. 1995, *Postmodern Semiotics: Material Culture and the Forms of Postmodern Life,* Blackwell Publishers, Cambridge.

Hodge, R. and Kress, G. 1988, *Social Semiotics,* Polity Press, Cambridge.

Kossen, C. 2003, 'Underemployment among older workers: A barrier to financial security', *Age, Work and Employment: Thinking about the Future,* Stirling Management Centre, University of Stirling, Scotland, June, pp.139–66.

Lakoff, G. 1987, *Women, Fire, and Dangerous Things: What Categories Reveal About the Mind,* University of Chicago Press, Chicago.

Lakoff, G. and Johnson, M. 1980, *Metaphors We Live By,* University of Chicago Press, Chicago.

Lewis, P.V. 1987, *Organisational Communication: The Essence of Effective Management,* 3rd ed., John Wiley & Sons, New York.

McGuire, W.J. 1981, 'Theoretical foundations of campaigns', in *Public Communication Campaigns,* eds R. Rice and W. Paisley, Sage Publications, Newbury Park.

Mackay, H. 1994, *Why Don't People Listen: Solving the Communication Problem,* Pan Macmillan, Sydney.

Mohan, T., McGregor, H. and Strano, Z. 1992, *Communicating!: Theory and Practice,* 3rd ed., Harcourt, Brace Jovanovich, Sydney.

O'Sullivan, T., Hartley, J., Saunders, D., Montgomery, M. and Fiske, J. 1994, *Key Concepts in Communication and Cultural Studies,* 2nd ed., Routledge, London.

Richmond, V. and McCroskey, J. 1985, *Communication: Apprehension, Avoidance and Effectiveness,* Gorsuch Scarisbrick, Scottsdale.

Saville-Trokie, M. 1994, *The Ethnography of Communication: An Introduction,* 3rd ed., Basil Blackwell, Oxford.

Schutz, A. 1973, in *Collected Papers I: The Problem of Social Reality,* ed., M. Natanson, Martinus Nijhoff, The Hague.

Selden, R. and Widdowson, P. 1993, *A Reader's Guide to Contemporary Literary Theory,* Harvester Wheatsheaf, Hertfordshire.

Shannon, C. and Weaver, W. 1949, *The Mathematical Theory of Communication,* University of Illinois Press, Champaign.

Taylor, A., Rosegrant, T., Meyer, A. and Samples, B. 1983, *Communicating,* Prentice Hall, Englewood Cliffs.

Verderber, R. 1990, *Communicate!,* 6th ed., Wadsworth Publishing Company, Belmont.

Walker, D. 1975, 'Curriculum development in an art project', in *Case Studies in Curriculum Change,* eds W.A. Reid and D. Walker, Routledge and Kegan Paul, London.

Part Two

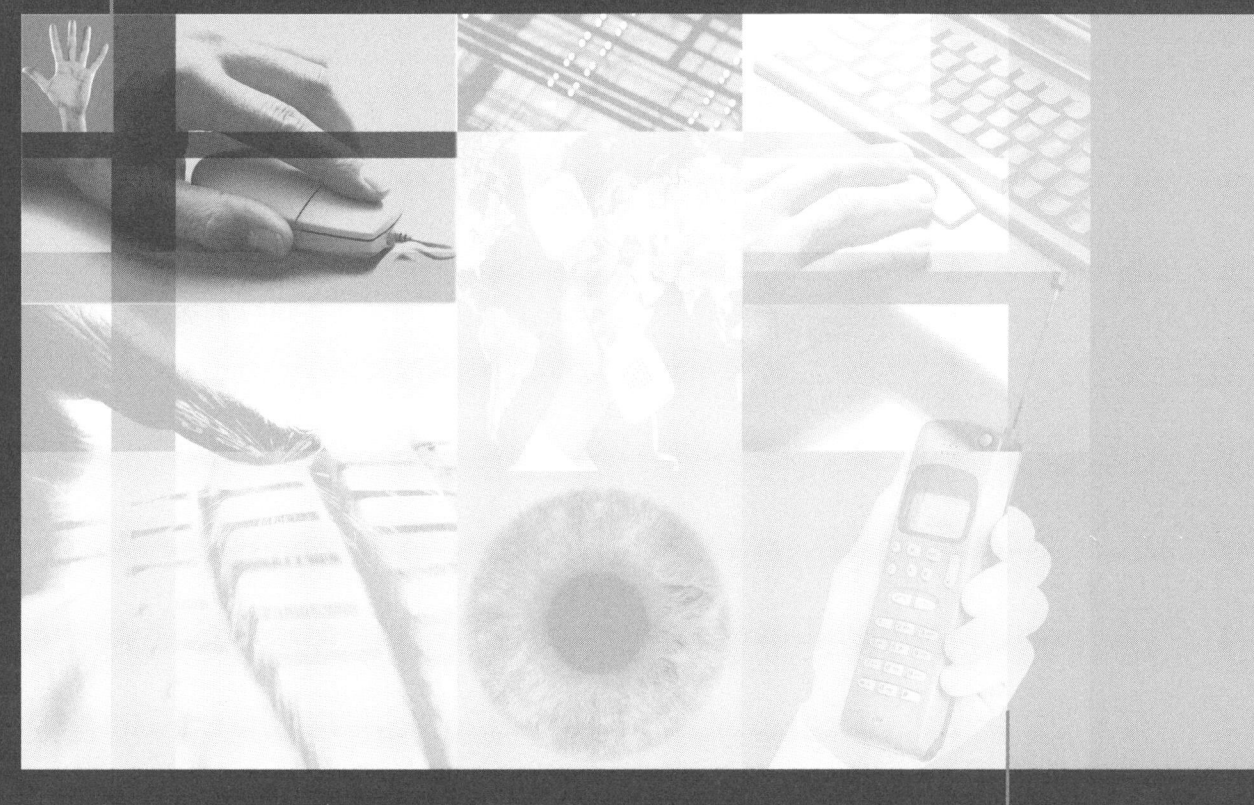

Written and Electronic Communication

Electronic communication

CHAPTER 3

Upon completing this chapter you should be able to:
- understand the distinguishing characteristics of electronic modes of communication;
- demonstrate an awareness of the various electronic media and their functionality;
- appreciate the importance of adjusting tone and style to suit the chosen electronic medium;
- demonstrate the capacity to choose the appropriate electronic medium for the task and audience; and
- understand the opportunities and limitations of the various electronic communication media.

This chapter introduces you to the dynamic world of electronic media. This media can support rapid communication between two or more persons situated at different localities: across the desk, down the hall, down the street or around the world. In this chapter we address the use of text, audio and/or video forms in electronic communications in both synchronous (at the same time) and asynchronous (at a different time) modes. You will learn some of the features that are available to support these various communication forms.

In particular, attention will be focused on when and how to use the various forms, and how to take advantage of the computer's speed of delivery, its capacity to capture and store the communication contents for reuse and its support for distributed work groups. You will be asked to consider issues of electronic media choice, effectiveness of use, limitations and avoidance of common pitfalls.

Defining electronic communication

What is electronic communication? Broadly speaking, this term refers to any information that is exchanged between two or more computers via a computer network. A computer network is the physical connection between two or more computers that allows the computers to exchange electronic data or to 'talk to each other'. A worldwide collection of open computer networks has been developed and this forms the Internet (see Figure 3.1). The Internet enables the transfer of data between any two computers connected to the worldwide network.

In this book we use the term electronic communication in a more specific way. We use it to refer to any person-to-person(s) interaction that occurs via or with the support of a computer network and the appropriate communication software. An organisation may have an internal computer network that may or may not be connected to an external computer network such as the Internet.

FIGURE 3.1 The Internet

The popularity of the Internet has far exceeded expectations. Indeed, from its original goal as a research and communication tool for the defence department and academics in the United States, the growth and popularity of the Internet has been nothing short of extraordinary. Its growth continues to be dynamic and, currently, it is in the process of revolutionising some aspects of our communications and commerce. To suggest that in 10 years' time it will be as common a communication tool as the telephone would be a conservative forecast. Indeed, it is predicted that telephone communication will soon be conducted via the Internet rather than via dedicated lines as it is today.

The Internet was developed initially as a text-based communication tool but can now also transmit voice and video data. Many computer systems can capture one or more of these forms, convert them to an electronic format, transmit them, then, at the receiving location, convert them back to the original form for use by the receiver. In many ways, the Internet does not create new methods of communication but is an additional medium by which to transport or exchange information. Indeed, many of the rules and guidelines that have been developed for traditional communication may apply equally to electronic communication. It does not merely mimic the various forms of traditional communication media but also offers some unique and useful features. These include:

* speed of delivery of text;
* convenience;
* ease of distribution to large groups of people;
* capacity to capture and store the communication contents and decision outcomes for later use; and
* support for distributed work groups.

To enable us to examine the functionality of features and decide how best to use them, we require some familiarity with the computer systems that offer these functions. I say 'some', because there are a number of categories, many of which overlap in their functionality. So don't be disheartened if initially you find it confusing trying to differentiate between categories. The major advantage of electronic communication is its ability to reduce considerably the relevance of the geographical distance between the communicating persons and its functionality that allows businesses (or individuals) to receive personal communication from its customers or potential customers. Thus, I believe an effective approach is to consider the support functionality offered by these computer systems from a time and place combination, similar to Johansen *et al.*'s (1991).

Communication, electronic or traditional, occurs between two or more persons at the same location or at different locations. Such communication may take place synchronously or asynchronously. Table 3.1 compares electronic communication forms and traditional forms along these two dimensions. It also includes the medium's ability to capture automatically the exchanged data for later reference or use. Returning often to this table as you study the different types of electronic media will assist you in identifying the functionality of the various categories.

Computer-mediated communications

Electronic communication is often categorised under the label of computer-mediated communications (CMC). CMC is any use of computers to initiate communications, store the communication contents, deliver to one or more participants and process the communications. Chat programs, discussion groups, electronic mail, Short Message Service (SMS), web services, webcam and voice

TABLE 3.1 Comparison of traditional and electronic communication functionality

	Traditional communications	Automatic storage for reuse	Electronic communications	Automatic storage for reuse
Same time/ Same place	Face-to-face communications	✗	Group decision Support systems	✓
Same time/ Different place	Telephone conversations	✗	Video conferences Audio conferences Chat systems	✓
Different time/ Same place	Memos Reports Noticeboard	✓	Electronic mail Voice mail Discussion list	✓
Different time/ Different place	Letters Reports	✓	Electronic mail Voice mail Computer-mediated conference Newsgroup Mailing list	✓

mail are some common examples of CMC. As electronic mail, or email as it is commonly called, is the form of electronic medium that is most frequently used in business, we shall examine it first.

Electronic mail

Electronic mail is a text-based messaging system similar to a memorandum or a letter. Organisations may use email as an internal-only or as both an internal and external communication medium. Electronic mail systems that are internal-only systems allow employees to communicate with other employees only within that organisation via a local area network (LAN). External access allows the employees to communicate with anyone who has an email address anywhere in the world via the Internet.

Email differs from a letter or memorandum with regard to its emerging communication protocol and its mode of delivery. First, email has developed a communication protocol that is more informal and more conversational in style than that of its physical counterpart. Second, it is delivered electronically, from one computer to another, rather than physically from one place to another. Email may be sent from any computer that has a mailing software package and is connected to a computer network to any other computer similarly connected.

CREATING EMAIL

To create an email open the mailing program on your computer and then choose the new mail option. Typically, you are presented with a form that has a fill-in section at the top and a section below where you write your message. The layout is similar to that of a memorandum, except that there is no section in which to insert the date or the sender's name. Each of these is added automatically by the computer. The date includes the current local day, date and time that the message left the sender's electronic mailbox. Interestingly, if the sender is in a different time zone to the receiver, the time shown will reflect that time difference, sometimes making it appear that the

J.

Will do. Have a great time tomorrow. See you Monday.

C.

────── Original Message ──────

From: Julie Townsend
Sent: Friday, February 20, 200X 6:23 PM
To: Christine Robertson
Subject: RE: Training workshop

Hi C,

I'm just finishing off my handouts for the xxxxx Service Club workshop tomorrow, on how to develop an 'Informative Club Newsletter'.

Why don't you give me a call at work when you're ready on Monday — around 11am or later. We can cut the handouts, then have lunch as a reward. Can you bring your photos along? We can decide then where we want to eat! I think I'd prefer somewhere off campus — xxxxxxx? But who knows by then?

Jaded Julie

────── Original Message ──────

From: Christine Robertson
Sent: Friday, February 20, 200X 6:16 pm
To: Julie Townsend
Subject: RE: Training workshop

J.

I am printing the handouts at the moment and am hoping to get them finished tonight, so on Monday any time after 11am suits me. What would you like to do for lunch, go to a restaurant or bring lunch to eat while we are working?

C.

────── Original Message ──────

From: Julie Townsend
Sent: Friday, February 20, 200X 9:05 AM
To: Christine Robertson
Subject: RE: Training workshop

C:

Any idea what time?

J.

────── Original Message ──────

From: Christine Robertson
Sent: Friday, 20 February 200X 9:04 AM
To: Julie Townsend
Subject: RE: Training workshop

Yes, suits me for guillotining and lunch. I'll give you a ring when I'm ready to come over.

Ta Christine

FIGURE 3.2 Internal Email *continued*

> ——— Original Message ———
>
> **From:** Julie Townsend
> **Sent:** Friday, February 20, 200X 8:41 AM
> **To:** Christine Robertson
> **Subject:** RE: Training workshop
>
> Yes. I'll be available on Monday and we could cut them on one of two guillotines here. How about lunch as well?
>
> Does that suit?
>
> Julie
>
> ——— Original Message ———
>
> **From:** Christine Robertson
> **Sent:** Friday, 20 February 200X 8:21 AM
> **To:** Julie Townsend
> **Subject:** Training workshop
>
> Julie
>
> I hope to print the handouts for the workshop next week but I will have a problem cutting them. The blade on our guillotine needs replacing as it currently leaves a rough edge. Do you have access to one in better condition that I (we) could use?
>
> Christine

FIGURE 3.2 Internal Email

email has been received before it was sent. The form received by the addressee will include the information as shown in Figure 3.2.

Most initial email messages begin with a salutation. The salutation may be simply the name of the receiver or it may be preceded by a 'hello', a 'hi' and occasionally a more formal 'Dear <name>'. If the message is being sent to a group or a number of individuals, the salutation often includes the word 'all', that is, 'hello all' or 'hi all'. There may be a complimentary close, but it may be just the name of the sender or that may be preceded by a 'thanks', 'regards', 'bye' or 'cheers'. These salutations and complimentary closes reflect the conversational style that is emerging as part of the electronic communication style.

The conversational style becomes more apparent as emails focusing on or discussing the one topic are sent backwards and forwards. Examine the series of emails in Figure 3.2. Contrary to the traditional method of adding to a message, note how a new message is added to the top of the page rather than to the bottom. Reading the messages from the bottom of the box to the top, you will notice that the primary purpose of the communication is to arrange a suitable meeting venue and time to produce some handouts for a training workshop. Notice also that a salutation was used in the initial email but as the conversation continued the salutation was either shortened or omitted. Similarly, as the conversation proceeded, both contributors shortened their signature. Such informality is common in email use even between work colleagues and is closer to the communication style used in conversation than either that of a traditional letter or memorandum.

It is interesting to note also that, similar to a conversation and unlike either a memorandum or business letter, secondary goals were interspersed in the conversation about the primary goal as the communication proceeded. This email conversation took place between two employees of the same organisation who work on the same site. Why didn't one or the other pick up the telephone and arrange the meeting? Experience had demonstrated that usually it was quicker to send an email than to telephone. That experience included knowledge about the other's work responsibilities and habits. Work responsibilities meant that each was not always at her desk and work habits were such that each checked and replied to her email regularly throughout the day. So sending an email could achieve the desired outcome in an acceptable time frame and probably would be more efficient as time would not be wasted ringing and re-ringing if the other were away from her desk. Another benefit to choosing an email over the telephone in this instance might have been that Julie may have needed some time to check her diary as well as the availability and condition of the guillotines before she could reply.

Some regular email users are embedding their replies into the original email overriding the sequential memo style. In this instance, the original email is typically structured as a series of questions which the respondent answers immediately following the original text. Colour or font can be used to differentiate each person's contribution to the ongoing discussion. This style not only allows a more cohesive conversation to develop but makes categorisation easier and storage and retrieval of the contents more convenient.

An important factor to note here is that, regardless of the style used, the success of email, and any communication tool, is the level of use of both (all) parties. If the sender knows that the receiver checks her email only rarely, then that knowledge alone would be a strong indicator not to use this medium for any message that required an answer within a short time frame.

REPLY TIMES

A characteristic of the email culture is the implicit pressure for an immediate reply. Unlike traditional postal delivered documents, where a turnaround of a day or two or even up to a week is quite acceptable, email users have an expectation that the message will be responded to immediately. The typically rapid turnaround of an email conversation can be both a benefit and a drawback. It can reduce substantially the time taken by a distributed group to discuss a problem and decide upon a solution. In the process, the group distribution facility can allow everyone concerned the opportunity to peruse all contributions and to add to the discussion. On the negative side, the rapid turnaround decreases the opportunity for in-depth consideration of the issues while at the same time increasing the amount of information to be processed.

EMAIL RECEIPTS

The sender of an email may request a receipt generated automatically and returned to them when the email arrives at the receiver's mailbox and/or when the email is opened.

ORGANISING INCOMING EMAIL

Modern email packages, sometimes referred to as enhanced email, allow users to set up folders in which to filter their incoming email. The filters will check the incoming mail and deliver the mail to a particular folder according to a predefined set of rules. Filters are particularly useful in separating regular and low-priority mail from high-priority mail. Low-priority mail, such as messages from distribution lists, can be redirected into a separate folder for attention at a later and more convenient time, leaving higher-priority mail in the main folder, making it easier to attend to this mail first.

Regular mail sent between the members of a group can use this feature to advantage by agreeing upon a common identifier to include in the subject field of the email. The email filter can be set to redirect all mail that includes that identifier in the subject field to a particular folder. An additional advantage to the separation of mail by subject is that it allows for easier search and retrieval of information at a later date.

STORAGE AND SEARCH

One common function of many email packages is the automatic recording of each interaction. The complete text of the conversation is recorded and automatically stored. Unless it is deliberately deleted, it is kept in a format that can be searched.

DISSEMINATION OF INFORMATION

Email has the capacity to transmit data to a large number of people simultaneously and individually. This is achieved by including multiple email addresses in the 'To' field. This task, if it is a regular occurrence, is made easier by creating a distribution list. A distribution list contains the email addresses of each member on the list. When an email is to be sent to the list, the user inserts the list name into the 'To' field. Once given the command to send, the email is automatically sent to each member on the list.

ATTACHMENTS

In modern PC-based email systems, another file or files may be attached to the email and sent with it. Any type of file may be sent, for example a word processing file, a spreadsheet file or a clip art file. Attachments are very useful for distributed groups with joint responsibility for completing a particular task that requires the use of computer files. For instance, a group may be writing a joint report or submission. Each member may be responsible for a different section of the report. They may choose to allow one member to complete their section and then pass it onto the next member. Alternatively, they may each complete their section individually and then email it to the group leader to merge the documents and complete the report. Careful consideration should be given before attaching files to an email. The first consideration is whether the receiver has compatible software in which to import the sent file. Ideally, the software should be saved in a format that is known to be readable by the receiver's software. While many software packages have the functionality to import data from other software packages, portability of data is by no means universal. Indeed, earlier versions of the same software packages frequently cannot successfully import data saved in later versions of the same software package. However, later versions of a software package usually allow the file to be saved in an earlier version's format. The transfer of graphical data, for example tables and figures, from one word processor brand to another remains problematic. For word processing files, if the sender is unsure of the receiver's software, saving the file as a rich text format should ensure compatibility.

Another consideration is the size of the attachment file. Many people are allocated a quota for the quantity of data they are allowed to receive over the computer network lines. Once their quota is exceeded, many are required to pay for the excess. Courtesy demands that the sender should ensure that the receiver is aware of the size of the attachment and wishes to receive it before it is sent.

DISTRIBUTION LISTS

A distribution list comprises a collection of email users who have a defined focus of interest. Postings to the list are restricted to issues discussing or imparting information about that focus. An individual list member may send an email to the list and it is then forwarded to all members or a nominated subgroup of the list. The email is sent from the distribution list's email address and the identity of individual list members is not revealed on the sent email. Some lists do allow their members access to the full membership list upon request.

Many distribution lists moderate the incoming messages to ensure that they are addressing the list's focus while others rely upon the list members to ensure that they restrict themselves to posting appropriate material. My experience of distribution lists is that they begin by being self-monitoring and only move to a moderated list when the volume of inappropriate messages becomes a problem to the list's membership. Members who send inappropriate messages to the list may have their membership of the list terminated.

Distribution lists with a large membership and ongoing active discussions on a number of different appropriate issues may create subgroups within their lists. Individual members are asked to nominate the focus of their submission and it is forwarded only to those members who have chosen to belong to those particular subgroups.

Distribution lists can be a valuable tool for professionals to exchange information and discuss difficult issues with their peers. On the other hand, an active list can be one of the major contributors to information overload, which will be discussed in the next subsection.

INFORMATION OVERLOAD

While electronic mail has many advantages, its very ease of use has encouraged its overuse. It is just as easy to send an email to multiple people as it is to send it to one person. Similarly, it is easy to forward any email or document to multiple people. Indeed, it would seem that some email users feel that they must pass on any information that may be of some interest to others, regardless of how minor that interest may be. Consequently, the time taken to read and process email can be considerable.

The most common complaints I hear about email is the volume of junk mail that individual users receive. Junk mail is any mail that the receiver considers is not essential information for them to receive and which they would prefer not to have received. Users adopt many strategies to rid themselves of the burden of excess mail. One is deleting, without reading, any email that does not appear from the nominated subject to be of interest to them. Another is to prioritise the incoming mail and process high-priority mail immediately, leaving the rest to be processed during less busy periods. Of course, there is a risk that important mail may be ignored, deleted or placed with the low-priority mail. Thus, if users are not to be overwhelmed by the volume of information that comes via their emails, organisational guidelines need to be developed and respected.

Many organisations do draw up guidelines to assist their employees to be more discriminating in the email they generate. Guidelines can include restricting email to organisation business and minimising the posting of emails to groups. It is also possible to restrict the posting of group emails to low-volume time, for instance emails to all employees to be sent at the end of the day. Another strategy is for the organisation to set up discussion groups for specific topics. These can work well for topics that have broad interest within the organisation but where employees who may wish to take part in the discussion may not be easily identified.

COMMUNICATION CUES IN EMAIL

Electronic mail has developed a culture that has some characteristics of traditional text documents such as the letter and memorandum and some characteristics of a conversation. However, while it can be used to simulate a traditional letter or memorandum, it is not as easy to simulate a traditional conversation. The traditional conversation always includes auditory cues and, often, visual cues. Both types of cues are absent in the email conversation and the conversation is dependent upon the written word and/or symbols. Consequently, care needs to be taken in the construction of the email message to ensure that the text does not convey an ambiguous message or one that may be misunderstood.

Short Message Service (SMS)

Short Message Service (SMS) is a service that allows alphanumeric messages to be sent from mobile phones, fax machines and/or a computer connected to the Internet. The messages have either a maximum of 160 or 244 characters depending on the bit mode available. If the mobile phone is not active or out of range when the SMS is sent, it will be stored for a period until the phone becomes active and within range. SMS messages can also be used to notify the receipt of a voice mail or email.

The most interesting aspects of SMS is that its popularity, particularly with the young, has resulted in the evolution of a shorthand language. This language makes use of symbols, digits and characters in word construction and considerable word economy in its message construction. The message construction is similar in some respects to that used earlier in telegraphic messages but is much more highly developed. Some commonly used 'words' are BTW for 'by the way', C for 'see', 2DAY for today. The language is not restricted to English words. In Arabic some sounds can not be represented by roman letters so numbers are used as a substitute, 'Fa6oom' and '5waly' (Danet and Herring 2003). In additions, the set of emotion symbols that started to evolve in the early text days of computers continues to expand because of their popular use in this medium. Examples are the well-known ☺ for happy and X = for fingers crossed (see <http://www.askoxford.com/betterwriting/emoticons/>).

The challenge with SMS messages is to develop our message using language that the receiver can read and understand. As with all languages, regular users will have a greater vocabulary than casual or novice users. Communication with someone from the latter groups requires the use of simpler SMS words (or symbols) than with the former group.

To learn more about SMS and its evolution, you might like to explore the following websites to get you started:

<http://www.askoxford.com/betterwriting/emoticons/>

<http://esl.about.com/cs/reference/a/bl_sms2.htm>

<http://www.mob1le.com/sms.html>.

Web services

Today many businesses offer their customers the opportunity to contact the company via the company's website. This communication is facilitated by the presence of an interaction point on the company's website. The interaction point may contain a 'Frequently Asked Questions' (FAQ) section where the customer can access information about commonly requested questions and an email link to the company's service division for questions that are not covered or fully covered in the FAQ. When interaction points were first developed any email request was handled manually, but as the service grew in popularity businesses became overwhelmed with the quantity of email contacts and were unable to attend to the queries in a timely manner. To meet this demand, linguistics tools were developed to be used in conjunction with the company's knowledge bases. The linguistics tools assess the text of the query to identify its primary content. The content is used to search the knowledge bases for the appropriate information to provide an answer to the customer. If this search is successful, the answer is automatically emailed to the customer. Only if the search cannot identify a suitable answer are emails forwarded to customer service personnel for attention. For many companies the use of these tools has proved to be a satisfactory solution for clearly defined and known problems.

As a user, we can make the most effective use of these services by first checking the FAQ to see whether our question can be answered there and, if not, try to articulate our question in a clear and concise manner using similar terminology to that used on the company's website, particularly that found in the FAQ.

The advantage of the automated email is that we should receive the automatic reply very quickly. Queries that are passed on to the service personnel typically take longer. Often the reply includes an invitation to rate the appropriateness of the answer together with an invitation for a further clarification if our needs are not fully met. These ratings are used to develop further and improve the information stored in the company's knowledge bases as well as refining the efficiency of the linguistic search tools. In this way, the company's knowledge base is continually being updated in response to customers' queries and their successful solutions.

The company's knowledge bases are used by telephonic call centres as well. In these circumstances, service personnel ask customers a set series of questions designed to identify the source of the problem quickly, entering the replies into the knowledge base search facility progressively. The 'best' solution or series of potential solutions are displayed on the computer screen. On the basis of this information, the service personnel discuss the most likely solution or solutions with the customer. Again if the solution cannot be identified immediately the details are sent to an expert for investigation and the caller is advised that they will be contacted at a later time with a reply.

Some of these telephonic call centres are automated so that the call connects to a computer and the caller is asked to press a particular number or say a particular word to access a particular service. If the request is a common request, the caller may be given an automatic answer rather than being put through to the service personnel. In most instances there is the opportunity to speak to one of the staff if the customer prefers it.

Newsgroups

Newsgroups are similar to a noticeboard, only in this instance they are a worldwide noticeboard with enhanced features. Any user of the Internet may read or post a message to a newsgroup. A newsgroup typically has a specific focus, and discussion and information sharing on issues relating to that focus is encouraged.

Individuals post relevant items to the noticeboard for the interest and comment of others. In return, other individuals may continue the discussion by posting their comments. Newsgroups allow group discussion via the Internet and are a public facility. There are many thousands of newsgroups on the Internet focusing on a wide variety of interest and research areas.

The messages are not delivered to the user's electronic mailbox. To read or contribute messages to the discussion, users have to access the newsgroup's site. Using newsgroups for group discussion is a very effective way of contributing to the control of information overload. However, newsgroups can be very active and the volume of messages can be large, so many groups use software that filters the messages into related groups. In newsgroups this process is known as 'threading'. Threading encourages continued participation, particularly on busy newsgroups, by streamlining participants' searches for messages in their interest areas. Users may choose to read only the messages that address the threads that are of interest to them.

Discussion groups

Newsgroups within an organisation with access restricted to members of the organisation are often referred to as 'discussion groups'. These discussion groups may be available for all members of the organisation or they may be limited to a defined group within the organisation. These groups have a clearly identified focus for discussion and seem to be more productive when they have one or more facilitators. The facilitator has two important roles. One is to monitor the messages to ensure the discussion is not drifting away from the defined focus. The second is to summarise the messages if the volume of postings is likely to cause interested employees to withdraw from the discussion. This prevents information overload.

By way of example, I will describe the very effective use of discussion groups by unit leaders within our university. Discussion groups are created at the beginning of each semester to facilitate communication between students within a particular unit. Ground rules are set by the unit leader and are monitored by them according to these rules. Some unit leaders take an active role in the group's conversation while others regard it as the 'students' space' and only intervene if the conversation wanders away from the goals of the group. In addition, most unit leaders use the group as a noticeboard where they can post updates of materials or interesting references.

Such groups are particularly useful where there are off-campus students as well as on-campus students. Students who use the group commonly report that they feel less isolated than they might otherwise and find the contact with other students helpful to their studies. There is no doubt that students benefit greatly from discussing the unit content between themselves. It does much to help them identify and clarify concepts they may be having some difficulties understanding. Of course, students may contact the lecturer for clarification but, in my experience, many feel reluctant to do so until they have established that 'they are not the only one who is having the difficulty'. On-campus students have the opportunity to enter into such discussions with their fellow students before and after lectures and tutorials. The discussion groups extend this opportunity to the off-campus students.

As previously mentioned, discussion groups have a noticeboard capability. As well as posting a text message to the group, other files including graphic files (e.g. Powerpoint lecture slides) may be posted to the group. Then these files are available to the group members and may be downloaded.

Interestingly, I have found that the number of postings does not necessarily give a true indication of the level of use by students. Many students who use the group to receive information never post an item. The groups are just as popular with on-campus students as with off-campus students and the off-campus students enjoy the interaction with the on-campus students. To assess the true level of usage, one should take into account both the number of students who have accessed the list and how many times each has done so. To assess the usefulness of the groups, one would need to survey the student group.

To summarise, a discussion group can be a very useful communication tool for a group of people with a common interest, but its success depends on the setting of appropriate guidelines and on the quality of the contributions of the group members themselves.

Electronic bulletin board (EBB)

An electronic bulletin board (EBB) is like a traditional noticeboard. Authorised persons can post electronic messages for all to read. These messages may result in a user directly contacting the person who posted the notice but rarely result in a group discussion. It is similar to walking down the hall to view the notices on a public noticeboard.

Knowledge acquisition and management

In the years since the first edition of this book both the number of available sites connected to the Internet and the use of the Internet has increased dramatically. Currently, the Internet has millions of sites that contain information on all manner of interests. The availability of this information from our desktops can be an excellent source of information on a particular topic. However, the nature of the Internet should be considered when using it as a resource. The Internet gives each one of us a relatively easy way of publishing our work to a very large readership. One just needs to obtain Internet access, develop a web page, place the desired information on the website and make the website available to the Internet community. From there, anyone with access to the Internet can access the site and use the information contained within it. Many of these sites contain information that is very specific and excellent in content; others are clearly presented as personal or group opinion or belief; while still others have content that is personal opinion presented as proven facts. Just as when using traditional sources of information, we need to be discriminating in our use of information from individual websites. The sheer volume of the information available makes extracting specific information a challenging task. So how do you minimise your search efforts and maximise your desired 'hits' (targeted sites)?

Let's address the latter first. When searching for information we want to be able to identify sites that have an acceptable level of rigour for our particular purpose. The level of rigour required may range from low to high. Low rigour may be acceptable if we wanted to identify web users' opinions on a particular subject. A moderate level of rigour may be acceptable if we were writing a creative essay and wanted to broaden our knowledge of the topic before we commenced. A high level of rigour would be required if we wanted to write a literature review of an academic area. We should take the same steps to identifying the level of rigour of information on the Web as we do with printed materials. This is particularly necessary when searching for information with a high level of rigour. One should ensure that the website is maintained by a highly regarded person or organisation within that area of knowledge. Many academic journals are published on the Web now and you will be able to ask your discipline leaders what their level of standing is within your discipline area. Journal that accept academic papers using a blind peer review process are the most highly regarded. EBSCO Information Services <http://www.epnet.com/> host many such journals.

Information gathered from the Web must be treated in the same way as information gathered from any other sources. If another's thoughts are included in your work, their contribution and its source must be acknowledged. Most referencing systems give guidelines for referencing websites but there are some that have not yet defined their requirements. In such instances keep in mind that the primary purpose for including details of the source is to allow the reader of a document to return to the original source. The details of the reference must give the reader sufficient information to be able to access the original source. If your discipline's referencing system does not have guidelines for websites then you might consider adjusting the format for a printed source and replacing the publisher's name and place with the web page address and the date the information was obtained from that address. As a web page is a volatile source, I find the inclusion of the date of sighting is very helpful as I have had a number of occasions when I returned to a web page only to find that the site no longer exists. Sometimes this is a consequence of an expansion and updating of the website—the page remains on the Web but the site address has changed.

Finding information

A most efficient and effective method of finding information on the Internet can be to obtain website addresses from informed sources, such as textbooks, journals, magazines and so on. However, there are many occasions when we want to initiate an investigation and do not have immediate access to those sources. A search of the Internet using a search engine can identify many sites (sometimes thousands) for you to investigate. The Internet has many excellent search engines freely available for use. Your home site may have a default search engine. However, you are at liberty to use any of the other search engines freely available on the Web. Different search engines may be more efficient in some topic areas than others as many have been developed to search for a particular type of information. If you search regularly for information in a particular discipline area, your search may be considerably improved by finding the search engine that consistently produces a higher number of quality sites focusing on that topic. A search for search engines will give you a choice of many sites to investigate. For an introduction to and a review of well-regarded engines, the site <http://www.searchengineguide.com/searchengines.html> (accessed July 2004) is recommended. Other sites that are worth a visit include:

* <http://www.windweaver.com/searcherguide.htm>
* <http://www.searchability.com/definitions.htm>
* <http://www.google.com>
* <http://search.msn.com>

A search may be further refined using the advanced features of an engine. A search can be conducted for websites that contain a particular word or series of words, are written in any language or in a particular language, within a specific domain, have been modified on a given date or within a defined period and/or contain various types of graphic files. You can opt to have summaries of the sites shown, restrict the number of pages shown within a particular domain or website to one and/or sort the results. Search engines have many options that can be used with finesse to maximise the appropriateness of the search results.

Storing information

Once you have found a site that is useful you may wish to save the address for later use. Depending upon the software you use, you can store the address in your 'favourites' or 'bookmarks'. In software that stores 'favourites', you can access the 'Favourites' menu option to add web addresses, organise those addresses into separate folders or subdirectories that you create and/or retrieve them when you wish to revisit the site. Similar options are available in other Internet software.

SUMMARY

In this chapter you have been introduced to electronic communication media. You should have developed an understanding about when and how to use the various forms of electronic media and how they complement the traditional forms of media. Although electronic media is similar in many aspects to traditional communication media, each form has a unique combination of functions that complement traditional forms rather than being a direct alternative for any particular medium. They allow us a greater range of choice when deciding which communication method is the most appropriate by which to convey our message.

KEY POINTS

- Electronic communication media complements the traditional forms of communication media.
- Speed of delivery is not affected by geographical distance.

- Email has developed a format that is more similar to a conversation than a letter or memorandum.
- The email culture exerts implicit pressure for an immediate reply.
- Electronic messages are stored automatically and are able to be searched electronically.
- The ease of sending and forwarding email messages can result in information overload.
- Newsgroups, discussion groups and electronic bulletin boards have evolved in an attempt to reduce information overload.

REVIEW QUESTIONS

1. What is electronic communication media?
2. Explain how the Internet works.
3. What factors would you take into consideration when choosing whether or not to use email?
4. What steps can you take to prioritise the emails you receive?
5. How could you help reduce information overload?

EXERCISES

1. Form a group with two other email users. Have one member search the Internet for sites about email, another for newsgroups and the third for discussion groups. Communicate your results to the other group members electronically. Discuss your experiences with one another electronically.
2. Identify a newsgroup or discussion group about communications. Post a message to the group and report on any replies you receive.
3. Conduct a search on the Internet for a topic of interest. Note how many websites are identified. Refine the search using at least one of your search engine's advanced options.
4. Conduct an Internet search for articles about the evolution and use of the SMS language and write a critique on its influence on traditional writing styles in young people.
5. Find a company with web services as part of their website and evaluate the service with regard to usability, response time, appropriateness of response.

BIBLIOGRAPHY

Danet, B & Herring S (2003), "Introduction: The Multilingual Internet", *Journal of computer mediated communications,* 9, no. 1. <http://www.ascusc.org/jcmc/vol9/issue1>

DeTienne, K.B. 2002, *Guide to Electronic Communication,* Prentice Hall, Upper Saddle River.

Johansen, R. *et al.* 1991, *Leading Business Teams,* Addison-Wesley, Reading.

Kolsky, E. 2004, *Marketscope: Email Response Management Systems, Gartner,* 1H04, Research Note, M-22-0610.

Kolsky, E. 2004, *Marketscope: Web Self-Service, Gartner,* 1H104, Research Note, M-22-0475.

Morris, M. and Ogan, C. 1996, 'The Internet as mass medium', *Journal of Communication,* 46, no. 1, 39–50.

Palme, J. 1995, *Electronic Mail,* Artech House, Norwood.

Effective writing skills

Upon completing this chapter you should be able to:
- demonstrate an awareness of the role of task and audience analysis in effective writing;
- understand the basic principles of effective writing; and
- demonstrate an awareness of the relationship between writing style and tone.

The ability to communicate effectively in writing is integral to success, both academically and professionally, regardless of whether the profession is in health care or business, the arts or sciences. Everyone who is literate can write a letter, memo or report but that, unfortunately, does not mean that the letter, memo or report will be effective. Effective writing is writing that achieves its purpose, whether that is to influence or persuade, to motivate, to get or give information or to get action. How effective messages will be in achieving the desired results depends on how well each message is tailored to the task and the audience, and on how easily accessible it is to the reader.

The tools available for writing are words, sentences and paragraphs. Within the constraints of correct usage, word choice or the vocabulary used will be determined by both the objective and the audience. Chapter 2, on communication theory, introduced the concepts of task and audience analysis. However, the ability to analyse both task and audience is so central to effective communication that we will revisit the concepts again, applying them to effective writing.

Task and audience analysis

Task analysis

The first requirement for analysing a task is to be very clear about the purpose—both the general purpose and the specific purpose. The general purpose will determine whether the communication is designed to persuade or influence, to get or give information or to get action. The specific purpose will be precisely what you want the message to achieve. For example, if you want action the specific purpose will be exactly what action you want to stimulate. Imagine that you want an extension on an assignment. The general purpose is to persuade. The specific purpose is to get an extension of so many days on the assignment. However, task analysis does not end here. The scope of the communication also has to be determined—in other words, just what needs to be covered in terms of the content in order to achieve the objective, an extension on the assignment. Because it is at this point that task and audience analysis overlap, it is appropriate now to consider analysing the audience.

Audience analysis

Our audience is the person to whom our communication is directed, whether that is the reader of the letter, the person on the other end of the telephone or a colleague on the other side of the desk. **Empathy** is important in analysing an audience. Empathy is not sympathy. We can empathise even if we do not like the other person. Empathy means sitting in the other person's chair. It means imaginatively putting ourselves in the place of the receiver or audience so that the message can be tailored most effectively and the receiver can be targeted with the greatest accuracy.

Some of the questions we need to ask are:

* What sort of person is the audience or receiver?
* Does the receiver have any interests, views or beliefs that need to be taken into account in writing the message?
* What does the audience already know about the subject?

Let us return to the example of the letter requesting an extension on the assignment. What do we know about the task and the audience? Does the request fall within existing guidelines; in other words, do we have a legitimate reason for requesting an extension? If not, is the lecturer or tutor likely to be favourable or otherwise to the request? Most importantly, what information should be included in the letter and how should the message be structured to maximise the chances of success?

In analysing the task, we are concerned with what we want to achieve. In analysing the audience, we are concerned with the person(s) we want to influence. Both task and audience analysis will determine how the task is completed, that is, how the letter, memo or report is written.

Criteria for effective writing

Analysing the task and the audience effectively enables the writer to decide the most appropriate way to convey the message. No matter who the audience is, effective writing will always be: appropriate; correct in terms of spelling, grammar and punctuation; and easily accessible by the reader.

Appropriate

Appropriate writing is writing that is suitable both to the task and to the audience. This involves both task and audience analysis, and style and tone. (Style and tone are dealt with later in this and subsequent chapters.) Imagine that you are sending an invitation to an office function to three different people. One is an old friend whom you know well; one is your superior; and one is a valued client. You could, of course, send exactly the same message to all three recipients but you would probably use a more informal, relaxed style with your friend than you would with your superior or with your client.

Correct

Effective writing is correct in terms of spelling, grammar and punctuation. Incorrect spelling, grammar or punctuation is noise, adversely affecting the message. Let us suppose you have applied for a job for which there were some 50 applicants. The first screening is done on the written applications. No matter how well you fit the job description, no matter how well qualified you may be in the field, if the letter of application and résumé contain spelling, grammatical or punctuation errors it is unlikely you will be shortlisted for interview.

Nowadays, most people write using a computer, which will normally have a spelling and grammar checker. However, it is a mistake to rely exclusively on the computer. The spell checker will alert you to errors in spelling but it will not tell you if you should have written 'their' rather than 'there', or 'affect' rather than 'effect'. It simply scans the words to match them to those in its memory. The grammar checker will scan the writing for grammatical errors. However, software packages vary and they are not infallible. So while the software on the computer can be a help in final editing, the responsibility for the correctness of the finished writing rests with the writer. In other words, the writer still needs to know the basics of spelling, punctuation and grammar. By all means, use the checking facilities of the computer but merely as a double-check that you have not missed any errors.

Accessible

All professional people, whether they are arts administrators or sales managers, educators or psychologists, are busy people; their time is limited. Your letter, memo or report will have a greater chance of success if it is readable. What is meant by readability is a text that is easy for the reader to access and understand.

Ease of access depends on vocabulary and sentence and paragraph structure. At a simplistic level, we can adapt the KISS acronym: Keep It Simple and Straightforward. We can say that text is readable if it uses a vocabulary of simple, commonly used words in short, simple sentences. However, this is too simplistic, because producing effective text involves more than simple words and short sentences. A letter written in short, simple words and sentences only can seem jerky and lacking in cohesion; it can also seem patronising. There should be a balance between short, simple words and sentences and longer words and more complex sentences. However, do not try to write in a style with which you are not comfortable. Sometimes students think they should write in what they consider to be an 'academic' style and their writing is often awkward or unclear as a result. Do not use words unless you really know what they mean. Do not use long, involved sentences unless you know that the sentences are complete, clear and easy to understand.

Vocabulary

Considerations in choice of vocabulary should be: familiarity, simplicity and straightforwardness, freshness and vitality, level of abstraction, jargon and acronyms and—always we come back to this—task and audience analysis. The basic rule in our choice of vocabulary should be what will enable us to get our message across most effectively, what will most accurately express our ideas and what will be most easily understood by our reader.

Before discussing vocabulary choice we should be aware of the fact that words have both a denotative and a connotative meaning. The **denotative meaning** of a word is what we could call the dictionary definition, or the generally agreed meaning. The **connotative meaning** of a word involves the emotions or feelings aroused by the word. For example, the denotative meaning of 'chair' could be 'a piece of furniture with four legs, a seat and a back on which people sit'. However, the connotative meaning of 'chair' would be the particular chair (recliner, office chair, deck chair, rocking chair, plastic chair, dentist's chair, etc.) of which *you* were thinking. All those aspects of differential perception dealt with in Chapter 2 influence how we each interpret words and the meanings we ascribe to them.

Familiarity

Although there may be occasions when an extensive, even esoteric vocabulary is appropriate (writing for professional or academic journals, for example) in most written communication it is words in common use, words with which most readers can be expected to be familiar, that are most effective. The following list of synonyms will illustrate what we mean.

Unfamiliar	Familiar
heterogeneous	mixed
combust	burn
predilection	bias/prejudice
suffrage	right to vote
undulating	wavy
prior to	before
subsequent to	after

Simplicity and straightforwardness

Remember the KISS formula. Keep the writing simple, straightforward and direct. This means not repeating yourself or using unnecessary words or phrases.

Avoid	Better
totally honest	honest (either people are honest or dishonest so 'totally' is unnecessary)
bigger in size	bigger (bigger relates to size so adding 'in size' is unnecessary)
as for example	as for example ('as' and 'for example' both mean the same thing so you are really saying 'for example for example', or 'as as')

There are many more examples. Indeed, it can be a game to read the newspaper and spot all the redundancies.

Freshness and vitality

Clichés make writing seem flat, tired and boring. Interestingly, clichés are also often wordy, using several words where only one is necessary.

Cliché	Better
first and foremost	first
over and above	over
few and far between	few/rare
at this moment in time	now
here and now	now
enclosed please find	enclosed is

Level of abstraction

What is meant by 'levels of abstraction' in relation to words, or what is meant by **concrete words** and **abstract words**? At the lower levels of abstraction are words that we could call 'concrete'. These can be words that refer to concrete objects—things we can see, hear, touch or smell—but they are also words that contain sufficient detail to present a precise and specific idea. For instance, if we refer to *Home and Away*, many people will have a clear and precise idea of the television show to which we are referring. However, as language becomes more abstract, detail is lost and words become more general, less specific. If we refer to a television soap opera our audience will not know whether we are referring to *Home and Away, Neighbours, Days of Our Lives* or any of the other soap operas on television. If we refer simply to a television show, our audience will not know whether we are referring to a current affairs or news program, a sporting program, a film, a soap opera, a situation comedy or any of the other programs shown on television. As Severin and Tankard (1992) note, abstraction involves selection and omission of details with a corresponding weakening of contact with reality. Indeed, abstract words can be so lacking in detail that it can be difficult to find a common meaning for them. There are also words such as 'love', 'loyalty' and 'happiness', which deal with abstract concepts, with matters that we cannot touch, feel or smell. Such words are difficult to define and there are as many definitions as there are individuals. Just think of the word 'happiness', for example. Not only is your idea of happiness probably different from that of your friend or neighbour, but your own idea of happiness will change according to the situation or how you are feeling.

To be effective, writing should contain both concrete and abstract words. Writing that contains only concrete words will be boring and simplistic and the subject matter will be severely limited. However, when we use abstract words or generalisations we need to bring them down to concrete detail by placing them within particular contexts. If we are talking about 'happiness', for example, we would need to place it within a context that gives a clear indication of what we mean by 'happiness'.

Jargon and acronyms

Jargon has had a bad press in recent years, but using jargon can be an effective way of getting our message across. **Jargon** is a type of professional shorthand that enables people from the same profession or discipline to convey complex information with the minimum of words. However, jargon is only effective if all members of the audience are familiar with the terms. If not, jargon will make our writing inaccessible to our readers. If you were among a group of computer experts, how easy would it be to understand their talk of kilobytes and gigabytes? If you were also a computer expert, it would be easy but it would probably be very difficult if you were not. So remember that jargon is not necessarily bad; it all depends on the audience.

Acronyms are in a similar category to jargon. **Acronyms** are initials that are used instead of spelling the name out in full: ABC for Australian Broadcasting Corporation or CHOGM for Commonwealth Heads of Government Meeting, for example. They provide a short cut, but only if the audience knows what the acronym means. The easiest way to ensure this is to use both the acronym and the full name the first time the acronym is used.

Sentence structure

Words are the building blocks for sentences. Each sentence should contain only one central idea and no sentence should contain unrelated ideas. If we have unrelated ideas we need to write two sentences not one. Sentences can be simple, compound or complex. However, whether simple, compound or complex, sentences must be complete.

Simple sentences

Simple sentences are sentences containing one independent clause. A clause consists of a subject and a verb. Clauses can be independent—that is, capable of standing alone; or dependent—that is, incapable of standing alone. 'The teacher called the roll' is a simple sentence.

Compound sentences

Compound sentences contain two or more independent clauses joined by a conjunction such as 'and', 'or', 'nor' and 'but'. The two clauses should be closely related in terms of the ideas being put forward. 'The tutor called the roll and noted any absentees' is a compound sentence consisting of one clause, 'the tutor called the roll', and the second clause, '[the tutor] noted any absentees'. Since both clauses deal with the same matter—checking student attendances—they can be joined to form one compound sentence.

Complex sentences

Complex sentences contain one main clause (usually an independent clause) and at least one subordinate clause (usually a dependent clause). Let us look at our compound sentence 'The tutor called the roll and noted any absentees'. If we write 'When calling the roll, the tutor noted any absentees' we have written a complex sentence. The main clause is 'the tutor noted any absentees'. This is an independent clause. It makes sense on its own. 'When calling the roll' is the subordinate clause. It is a dependent clause. It does not make sense on its own but it adds to the main clause, in this case placing the tutor noting any absentees within a time context.

Referring to the KISS formula, our writing will generally be more accessible if our sentences are mainly simple and straightforward. However, as noted earlier, using only short, simple sentences will make our writing seem choppy and simplistic, even patronising, so we need to use a combination of sentence structures.

In *Studying and Writing Effectively* Mahony (2004) suggests making key sentences (and topic sentences are key sentences) brief, while sentences that support or explain the topic sentence can be longer. This is a useful suggestion as topic sentences are the primary sentences for conveying your message. Keeping topic sentences simple and straightforward helps to ensure that they are clearly focused and easily accessible to readers, while using longer, more complex sentences to explain, illustrate or support the topic sentences produces a more varied and interesting writing style. It is, however, better to avoid sentences that are so long and involved that the reader has trouble following what is being written.

Let us look at an example of a long, involved sentence.

> It is important that clerical staff take care when using office equipment because we have had far too many breakdowns of equipment which considerably reduce office efficiency and leave people standing around waiting for equipment to be fixed instead of doing their jobs as well as far too many service calls which, because they have been urgent, have had to be paid for at penalty rates.

Is there just one idea in that sentence or are there several? Let us break the sentence up into several shorter sentences.

> It is important that clerical staff take care when using office equipment. We have had far too many breakdowns of equipment. Such breakdowns considerably reduce office efficiency by leaving people standing around waiting for equipment to be fixed instead of doing their jobs. There have also been far too many urgent service calls which have to be paid for at penalty rates.

Which of the two examples can you understand more quickly and easily?

Active and passive voice

This section could have been included in the tone and style section, because active and passive voice are integral to the tone of any piece of writing. What do we mean when we talk about active and passive voice? **Active voice** is shorter, more direct, stronger and usually more positive—more active, in fact. In active voice, the subject does the action. For example, 'I shut the door' is active voice. **Passive voice** is longer, more indirect, weaker. 'The door was shut by me' is passive. In passive voice the subject receives the action rather than performs it. This changes the emphasis. In active voice the emphasis is on the subject; in passive voice it is on the object.

Usually, it is appropriate for the emphasis to be on the doer of the action. Therefore, most of the time active voice will be preferable. However, there are occasions when passive voice is more appropriate.

Passive voice gives prominence to the object rather than the subject and thus provides a way to de-emphasise a point, for example, non payment of an account. This can result in a more tactful or diplomatic message.

> **Active:** You have not paid your account.
>
> **Passive:** Payment for your account has not been received.

Active voice here imparts an accusatory tone. Passive voice conveys the same information—namely that the account has not been paid—but it does so in a less accusatory, more tactful manner.

Passive voice distances the writer from the action. This is useful if you are conveying bad news, such as refusing a request or conveying criticism.

> **Active:** We have to refuse your request for a refund.
>
> **Passive:** Your request for a refund has to be refused.
>
> **Active:** You will have to restructure your essay.
>
> **Passive:** Your essay will have to be restructured.

Paragraph structure

As words are the building blocks of sentences so sentences are the building blocks of paragraphs. Paragraphs should have unity and internal coherence and consistency. So, although a paragraph often consists of several sentences, each paragraph should deal with only one major idea because a new paragraph signals to the reader that we are moving on to a new idea or a further development of the idea of the previous paragraph. The basic rules for paragraphs are much the same as for sentences. Keep your paragraphs predominantly short and simple but use some longer, more complex paragraphs to provide variety and to prevent your writing becoming stilted.

Read the following paragraph.

> I want to call a meeting for tomorrow. We need to discuss the new K7 blender. It will have to be carefully marketed to recoup the research and development costs. The monthly store figures are in and we should go over them. We need to look for possible trends in relation to the last six to seven monthly figures to help us with forward planning. *Product Magazine* has increased its advertising costs. Our advertising in this magazine has been successful in the past but the increased costs mean that we should decide if our advertising dollar can be better spent. Perhaps we should look at another magazine, or maybe even think of radio advertising or direct mail.

A paragraph should have only one central idea. How many ideas are contained in this paragraph? There are actually three separate ideas. First, there is the marketing of the K7 blender. Second, there is the issue of the monthly figures. Finally there is the problem of the increased advertising costs for *Product Magazine*. This paragraph would work much better if it was broken up into three smaller paragraphs.

> I want to call a meeting for tomorrow to discuss three matters:
>
> 1. Marketing the new K7 blender
> Research costs in the development of this blender were high.
> We need to discuss how best to market the blender to recoup the research and development costs.
>
> 2. Monthly store figures
> The monthly store figures have now come in. We need to examine them in light of the previous six or seven monthly figures to see if any trends are developing that can help us in forward planning.
>
> 3. Increased advertising costs
> *Product Magazine* has substantially increased its advertising costs. While our advertising in this magazine has been successful in the past, the increased costs mean that we should decide if our advertising dollar can be better spent. Possible options are to advertise in other magazines or even on radio. We could also look at direct mail advertising.

Notice that not only has the material been divided into three paragraphs, each dealing with a central idea, but that it has been set out in the form of numbered points with headings. This may not be appropriate in all situations but it can be an efficient method to make the writing more easily accessible to readers.

A paragraph can be thought of as a micro essay in that it will often have a **topic sentence** that contains the central idea of the paragraph, sentences supporting the topic sentence and some sort of concluding sentence. A topic sentence gives readers an overview of the paragraph, and consequently of the writing as a whole. The rest of the paragraph will consist of supporting material such as data or statistics, anecdotes, examples, explanations or additional detail. Often the topic sentence is the first sentence in the paragraph but it may appear anywhere in the paragraph. However, not all paragraphs have a topic sentence so it is probably better to think of the main idea of the paragraph rather than of just a topic sentence.

What is the main idea in the following paragraph? In other words, what is the paragraph about?

> The best university students usually have the ability to read critically or evaluatively. **That is,** they do not uncritically accept what they read but analyse and evaluate any piece of writing. **Since** most academic writing is concerned with arguing for a viewpoint, identification of the main idea is one of the more important aspects of evaluative reading. **However,** the main idea needs to be adequately supported by subordinate ideas and credible evidence so identification of supporting ideas and evaluation of evidence are also important aspects of critical reading.

We could consider the first sentence to be the topic sentence but, in this paragraph, we need to think of the main idea rather than a topic sentence and the main idea concerns critical and evaluative reading. Notice how the linking words or transitionals (in bold print) link sentences and indicate the progress of the exposition in the paragraph.

Unity and transitions

The paragraph about critical reading demonstrates the importance of smooth transitions between sentences. A frequent problem in essays is lack of cohesion. Instead of being unified segments, paragraphs are a collection of sentences that seem to be rather unrelated to each other. So, how do we achieve unity in both paragraphs and in the essay as a whole, and how do we move smoothly from sentence to sentence and idea to idea? Our writing can be unified by repetition of words or phrases, by picking up ideas or concepts, even by common imagery. Let's look at the following passage:

> The focus of an **essay** is the **thesis statement** which functions as the conclusion of the extended argument that constitutes the **essay** itself. Since the **thesis statement** is the point toward which the **essay** moves, and the factor which determines both the content and structure of the body of the **essay,** it is crucial that it is clear, relevant and focused on the **topic.**
>
> The **thesis statement** must develop from a close **analysis** of the **topic.** Initially this **analysis** involves identification of task or determining words and **key or defining words,** but this surface analysis needs to be deepened to an identification of the **central issue,** problem or idea behind the **topic.** While all **key words** are important, there may be a **hierarchy of importance** within the **key words** in terms of identifying the **central issue.** It is, therefore, necessary to determine if there is a **hierarchy of importance** among **key words.**
>
> Determining which **key words** lead to the **central issue** . . .

As we can see, the paragraphs above are unified by repetition of key words or phrases and these key words or phrases also provide a smooth transition between paragraphs. For example, the last paragraph begins where the second last paragraph ends, that is with the idea of the importance of key words in relation to the central issue.

Logical sequence

Every piece of writing should have an introduction, a body and a conclusion.

The introduction will set out the issue or problem to be dealt with, will indicate our approach and our stance in relation to the topic, will set out any limitations and will give readers an overview of how our argument will develop.

The body contains the message and it is here that how we organise our material is important. Logical organisation of material is one of the most difficult aspects of writing and because it is so closely related to the task and the audience it will be dealt with in more depth in the following chapters. As a general rule, however, we need to bear in mind both our task analysis and audience analysis. What are we trying to achieve? To whom are we writing? Both questions will help us to organise our material in the most effective way.

The conclusion draws the writing together. It enables us to restate our main points, provide a summary and restate our position. Importantly, it allows a final interpretation of the analysis and data contained in the body of the essay.

Style and tone

Style and tone are dealt with together because they are integrally related. **Style** results from the vocabulary used and the way the words are structured in sentences and paragraphs. **Tone** is the feeling or atmosphere engendered by style. Style comes from the writer and from that style the reader gets the tone of the writing. Consider the following examples from the point of view of tone and style.

> It is expected that all students will adhere to the Faculty's guidelines in relation to assignment deadlines. Failure to do so without prior approval will result in mark penalties.

> Get your assignments in on time—otherwise you'll lose marks.

If we look at both examples we can see that, although they both say the same thing, the tone is quite different. What gives the examples their particular tone?

In the first passage the sentence structure is formal and grammatical. There are no contractions such as the 'you'll' that we find in the second example. The vocabulary in the first example is formal. Words such as 'expected', 'adhere', 'guidelines', 'failure', 'result', 'penalties' and phrases such as 'in relation to' and 'prior approval' impart a formal, official tone to the passage. In the second example we have a less formal sentence structure with the sentence broken by the dash after 'time'. The vocabulary is more informal. Words such as 'get' and 'you'll' and the phrase 'lose marks' are almost colloquial. Notice also that the first passage is impersonal. The student is not addressed directly in the first passage while the second passage is more personal, speaking directly to the student: 'your assignments' and 'you'll'. The styles of the two passages are what give them their particular tone. In the first passage the tone is formal and official; in the second passage it is more informal and, interestingly, more direct.

SUMMARY

This chapter has provided an overview of the major principles of effective writing. It is beyond the scope of just a chapter to cover effective writing fully but there are many books devoted to the subject and you will find some of them listed in the Bibliography.

A vital element in effective writing is task and audience analysis. Without a clear purpose and an awareness of the audience even the most stylish writing will not be effective. Effective writing also demands a knowledge of the basics of grammar and spelling. It involves choosing the most appropriate vocabulary, sentence and paragraph structure and producing the most appropriate tone and style to suit both the task and the audience.

The following chapters on letters, memos and extended writing will put the principles of effective writing dealt with in this chapter into more direct application.

KEY POINTS

- Task analysis involves determining the purpose and scope of the communication. It is concerned with what we want to achieve.

- Audience analysis enables the writing to be tailored to the reader's level of interest and knowledge. It is concerned with who we want to influence.

- Effective writing is appropriate, correct and accessible to the reader.

- Words, sentences and paragraphs are the building blocks of writing.

- Choice of vocabulary should be determined by level of familiarity, simplicity and straightforwardness and freshness and vitality.

- Language can be concrete or abstract. Concrete words are less likely to be misinterpreted than abstract words, so if abstract words are used it is wise to place them within a concrete framework that minimises the possibility of misinterpretation.

- Jargon and acronyms are not necessarily bad or to be avoided. It all depends on the level of knowledge of the audience.

- Sentences can be simple, compound or complex. Effective writing should have a mixture of different sentence structures.

- Most writing will be in active voice but there are situations in which the de-emphasising quality of passive voice is preferred.

- Paragraphs should contain one central idea that is supported by sentences containing detail, evidence, examples and so on. There may be a concluding sentence recapitulating the main point.
- Style results from the choice of vocabulary, sentence and paragraph structure. Tone is the feeling the reader gets as a result of the style.

REVIEW QUESTIONS

1. What is effective writing?
2. What is involved in task analysis?
3. Why is audience analysis important?
4. How can writing be made accessible?
5. What principles should guide you in using jargon and acronyms?
6. What is the effect of using passive voice? When is it appropriate to use passive voice?

EXERCISES

1. Turn the following sentences in passive voice into active voice.
   - The assignment was marked by the lecturer.
   - The English examination was taken by all students last week.
   - Lecture theatres are locked by security personnel by 7 pm every day.

2. Simplify the following passage.
   It is not too much to hope that the trouble caused by your predilection for being totally honest in the most inconvenient circumstances might finally, at long last, make you realise that, sometimes, honesty is not the best policy. First and foremost, we need to get on with each other. After all, we are a heterogeneous bunch of people and, at this moment in time, it is important that we all work together.

3. Take two passages of writing, one from an academic journal and one from a student newspaper, and analyse the differences in tone and style. How are the different tones achieved? Provide examples from the two passages to illustrate how the differences are achieved.

4. Take a passage from a newspaper and find all the redundancies.

5. You are writing an essay on the advantages of a university education. Note the points you would make to support the advantages of a university education and indicate how you would organise and link the points to provide a logical sequence and a sense of unity and coherence.

6. The following sentence in bold type ends a paragraph.

   The initial research phase of essay writing often results in a rather chaotic collection of random facts and ideas.
   Which of the sentences below would best start the paragraph?
   - We probably find that we have too much material so we need to select and organise it for it to be effective.
   - These random facts and ideas can be thought of as the bricks of our writing, but they need to be organised before they can become an effective wall, or an effective essay.
   - Equally important is the ability to organise our material into a coherent and logical argument.

BIBLIOGRAPHY

Anderson, J. and Poole, M. 2001. *Assignment and Thesis Writing,* 4th ed., John Wiley & Sons, Milton.

Bate, D. and Sharpe, P. 1996, *Writer's Handbook for University Students,* Harcourt, Brace & Company, Sydney.

Burdess, N. 1998. *Handbook of Student Skills,* 2nd ed., Prentice Hall, Sydney.

Hay, I., Bochner, D. and Dungey, C. 1997, *Making the Grade: A Guide to Successful Communication and Study,* Oxford University Press, Melbourne.

Mahony, D. 1996, *The Student Guide for the Preparation, Writing and Presentation of Assignments,* QUT, Brisbane.

Mahony, D. 2004, *Studying and Writing Effectively,* QUT, Brisbane.

Palmer, R. 1992, *Write in Style: Guide to Good English,* Spon, London.

Petelin, R. and Durham, M. 1996, *The Professional Writing Guide: Writing Well and Knowing Why,* Pitman, Melbourne.

Severin, W.J. and Tankard, J.W. 1992. *Communication Theories: Origins, Methods, and Uses in the Mass Media,* 3rd ed., Longman, New York

Letters, memos and email

CHAPTER 5

Upon completing this chapter you should be able to:
- show a knowledge of the formal elements of letters and memos;
- demonstrate an awareness of the different types of letters and memos;
- understand the relationship between structure and purpose in letters and memos; and
- appreciate the relationship between purpose, audience and tone and style.

Chapter 4, on effective writing skills, dealt with the building blocks of written communication: vocabulary and sentence and paragraph structure. It also discussed the importance of analysing both the task and the audience. In this chapter we will apply the principles of effective writing to letters, memos and email messages.

Letters, memos and email messages provide a written communication network that encompasses both people working within the same organisation and people outside the organisation. Letters are normally written to people outside the organisation—to customers or clients, to suppliers, to government bodies, to competitors, to any one of the host of people any organisation communicates with in order to pursue its goals. However, if the subject matter is important, letters can also be written to people within organisations. Such letters usually deal with matters affecting an employee's working conditions or career, for example promotion, salary increase or redundancy.

Memos—or inter-office memorandums or just memoranda—are always written to people within the organisation. This can be someone in another state, or even in another country in the case of multinational companies, but memos are never written to people outside the organisation.

Email messages can be written to people both within and outside the organisation. We will begin our discussion of the forms of professional written communication with letters and memos, and we will deal first with the conventions that govern their layout. By conventions, we mean the formal elements that writers are expected to include in letters and memos.

Letters

Although the use of emails is increasing, letters are still written and there are certain formal elements that need to be included. The formal elements of letters can be divided into those that are regarded as essential and those that are optional. The essential parts of letters are:

* the letterhead or return address;
* the date;
* the inside address; and
* the signer's identification.

Some of the optional elements are:

* notations such as 'Personal and Confidential';
* attention lines;
* the salutation;
* the complimentary close;
* *reference initials;
* *PS notation; and
* *enclosure or c.c. notation.

While the above elements are labelled 'optional', those marked with an asterisk may be a required part of a letter. For example, reference initials are normally required if the writer did not type the letter. The enclosure or c.c. notation is essential if the letter contains an enclosure or is being copied to someone else. Similarly, if something has been added after the end of the letter, a PS notation would be necessary.

Essential elements

These elements are essential because they fulfil vital functions within letters.

THE LETTERHEAD/RETURN ADDRESS

Every letter should have some means of telling the reader where the letter is from. In business and professional letters this information is found in the letterhead, which contains all the information that the reader needs in order to respond to the letter. Information included in the letterhead is the name, address, email address and telephone and fax numbers of the organisation. The letterhead will often also contain a description of the business of the organisation, such as 'Solicitors' or 'Chartered Accountants'.

The return address takes the place of the letterhead in letters written by private individuals. It gives the address of the person writing the letter. It does not, however, give the name as this is included in the signer's identification section.

DATE

Letters must be dated. This is particularly important where legal matters are concerned.

THE INSIDE ADDRESS

The inside address gives the name, position if appropriate and address of the person to whom the letter is being written. This identifies the receiver, providing a permanent record of what was written and to whom.

SIGNER'S IDENTIFICATION

This identifies the person who wrote the letter both by name and, if appropriate, position.

REFERENCE INITIALS

These identify the writer and typist of the letter. Note that reference initials are not used if the writer types the letter him/herself.

Optional elements

'PERSONAL AND CONFIDENTIAL'

This appears on both the letter and the envelope. It indicates that the letter contains confidential material and should only be opened by the person to whom it is addressed.

ATTENTION LINE

An attention line is normally used if the letter is addressed to a company rather than to a specific individual. The attention line is then used to direct the letter to a particular person in the organisation. If an attention line is used, the salutation will be 'Dear Sir' or 'Dear Madam'.

SALUTATION

The salutation is the equivalent of 'hello' in a conversation and helps to establish the tone of the letter. For example, if the salutation is 'Dear Mr Wilcox', the tone that is established is immediately more formal than a salutation such as 'Dear Jim'.

COMPLIMENTARY CLOSE

This allows the writer to 'sign off'. If a salutation has been used, then a complimentary close must be used. If there is no salutation, a complimentary close is not used. The complimentary close may be 'Yours sincerely', 'Yours truly', 'Sincerely yours' or whatever the writer considers most appropriate. However, if the salutation is 'Dear Sir' or 'Dear Madam', the complimentary close must be 'Yours faithfully'.

PS NOTATION

PS stands for 'postscript', which means something added after the letter has been written. Originally it enabled the writer to add something that had been forgotten, but in today's professional letters it is used to give prominence to a particular point by separating it from the body of the letter.

ENCLOSURE OR C.C. NOTATION

Often material will be included with a letter. This may be a cheque, a brochure or price list, a copy of correspondence or any other material the writer thinks the reader needs. When material is enclosed with the letter, the notation 'enc.', or 'encs' if there is more than one enclosure, alerts the reader to the fact that there is more than just the letter in the envelope. This is important if the enclosure is small and valuable like a cheque, in which case the enclosure notation will often include 'cheque', for example 'Enc.: cheque'.

Copies of letters are indicated by c.c. notations, short for carbon copy from the days when copies of letters were made by placing pieces of carbon paper between the sheets of typing paper. These notations let the reader know that someone else has a copy of the letter. For example, in responding to a letter of complaint, it can be useful to signal to the reader that the complaint has been passed on to the appropriate person and the c.c. notation enables the writer to do that.

The sample letter in Figure 5.1 shows all the elements mentioned above. Note that if the letter had not had an attention line the inside address would have been:

Ms J Perlane
Personnel Officer
Buckleigh Engineering
PO Box 95
FORTITUDE VALLEY QLD 4006

Types of letters

Letters are written to get or give information, to get action or to persuade. Depending on the subject matter letters can be divided into a number of different categories but they will all fall within three broad divisions: neutral/good news letters, refusal letters and persuasive letters.

NEUTRAL/GOOD NEWS LETTERS

These are the most common letters written, both professionally and privately. They include letters giving and requesting information (requests for product information, enrolment procedures); letters requesting action (sending travel information, ordering goods); collection letters; and letters giving or requesting credit.

BRITERITE ENGINEERING [Letterhead/return address]

37 Tregear Street
BRISBANE QLD 4000

GPO Box 345
BRISBANE QLD 4001

Telephone: (07)3947.8898
Fax: (07)3947.8899
e-mail: briteriteng@com.au

2 May 200X

Buckleigh Engineering
PO Box 95 ← [Inside address]
FORTITUDE VALLEY QLD 4006

ATTENTION MS J PERLANE, PERSONNEL OFFICER ← [Attention line]

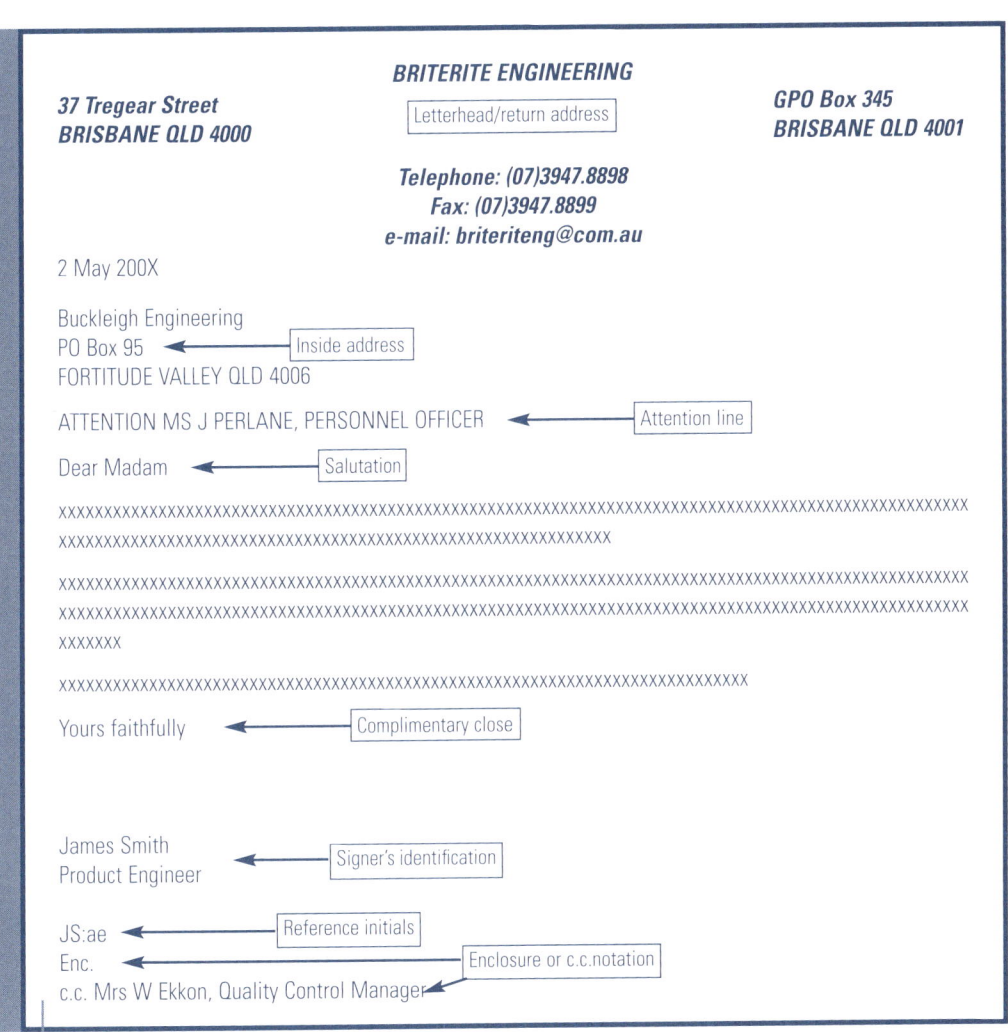

Dear Madam ← [Salutation]

xxxxxxxxxxxxxxxxxxxxxxxxxxxxxxxxxxxxxxxxxxxxxxxxxxxxxxxxxxxxxxxxxxxxxxxxxxxxxxxx
xxxxxxxxxxxxxxxxxxxxxxxxxxxxxxxxxxxxxxxxxxxxxxxxxxxx

xxxxxxxxxxxxxxxxxxxxxxxxxxxxxxxxxxxxxxxxxxxxxxxxxxxxxxxxxxxxxxxxxxxxxxxxxxxxxxxx
xxxxxxxxxxxxxxxxxxxxxxxxxxxxxxxxxxxxxxxxxxxxxxxxxxxxxxxxxxxxxxxxxxxxxxxxxxxxxxxx
xxxxxxx

xxxxxxxxxxxxxxxxxxxxxxxxxxxxxxxxxxxxxxxxxxxxxxxxxxxxxxxxxxxxxxxxx

Yours faithfully ← [Complimentary close]

James Smith
Product Engineer ← [Signer's identification]

JS:ae ← [Reference initials]
Enc. ← [Enclosure or c.c. notation]
c.c. Mrs W Ekkon, Quality Control Manager

FIGURE 5.1 Sample Letter Showing the Essential Elements of a Business Letter

REFUSAL LETTERS

Refusal letters also convey information but because the information is likely to be unwelcome to the reader, involving refusal of a request, these letters need to be written in a particular way. This will be dealt with in detail later in this chapter.

PERSUASIVE LETTERS

Every communicative act has elements of persuasion and every letter should have an underlying goodwill purpose as well as the specific purpose. Here, however, we are talking about letters such as sales letters that have persuasion as a primary purpose.

Letter purpose and structure

LETTER PURPOSE

If you recall the work in the previous chapters on task analysis, you will remember that it involves having a clear focus on what you want to achieve and that this precisely defined objective will influence how the message is structured. This applies just as much to letter writing as it does to any other communicative act, so the purpose of the letter will affect how it is structured and how the material is presented.

LETTER STRUCTURE

A letter, like a memo, an essay or a report, has an introduction, a body and a conclusion. However, within the constraints of an introduction, a body and a conclusion there are three basic methods of presenting material: the direct method, the indirect method and the AIDA formula for persuasive letters.

Direct method

This method is used for neutral/good news letters. We write to achieve a particular goal, and we are more likely to achieve our goal if we have analysed both our task and our audience. In the direct method we come to the point—the object of the letter—immediately. This is where the subject line can be helpful, for it enables our reader to know immediately what we are writing about.

The first paragraph of the letter functions as an introduction. It places the letter within a context and tells the reader what we are writing about. It introduces us and our subject matter.

Introduction

The following are three examples of letter openings for good news or neutral letters.

1. We have received your letter of 9 May asking for increased credit.
2. I am writing in response to your telephone call requesting enrolment information.
3. I wish to apply for the position of administrator of Eurabeen Retirement Hostel, which you advertised in *The Australian* on 29 June.

Each of the above opening sentences places the letter within a context and tells the reader why we are writing. Each opening sentence gives all the necessary information, such as relevant dates or references to previous communication, that the reader needs to identify the communication.

Body

Subsequent paragraphs comprise the body of the letter and these expand on the first paragraph, providing additional information and supporting detail. Below are ways we could expand on the opening sentences in the examples above.

1. You have been a customer of this firm for many years. Your credit rating has always been good, and the increase you request is within company guidelines. We are, therefore, pleased to grant your request for increased credit.
2. I enclose a copy of our general booklet 'What You Need to Know About Enrolment'. This will give you general information on the enrolment procedure.
    You will not be able to enrol until the official enrolment period, which begins on 30 January, but all the information you need will be included on the enrolment forms, which should reach you within the next week.

3. I am interested in this position, not only because it is a logical career progression for me, but also because my family are all now living in Perth, and working at Eurabeen will enable me to relocate to Western Australia.

   You will see from my résumé that for the last three years I have been Director of Nursing at Collowood Nursing Home. As a fully qualified nurse, I have the medical qualifications and experience, which will be of great use at Eurabeen where the residents, although still relatively independent, are, I understand, often frail. I also have considerable administrative experience through my role at Collowood, where I was directly responsible for a staff of 30 full- and part-time nurses and nursing aides, as well as having delegated responsibility for an ancillary staff of five kitchen staff and three clerical staff.

Conclusion

The final paragraph provides the conclusion and tells the reader what we expect to happen next; in other words what we will do or what we want the reader to do. Remember that letters should finish on a positive, friendly note.

1. Please complete the enclosed credit form and return it to us. Your increased credit will begin as soon as we have acknowledged receipt of the completed form.

2. If you have not received your enrolment forms within ten days or if you need any more information, please ring or write to us.

3. Providing that I have sufficient warning to arrange for someone to take over my duties, I can be available for interview at any time. I can be contacted during office hours on (xx) cccc cccc or on (xx) cccc cccc outside office hours. I look forward to hearing from you in due course.

Indirect method

No one likes to have requests refused, so if we use the direct method and give the bad news or refusal straight away, it is likely that our audience will read no further. It is important for maintaining goodwill that our reader knows why we have had to refuse a request. So, with refusal letters, we delay the actual refusal until our audience has read the reasons for refusal. We use the indirect method of structuring our letter.

Introduction

Even though we are using the indirect method, the reader still needs to know immediately what the letter is about so the opening sentence will fulfil the functions of the introduction for the good news or neutral letter. It will tell the reader why we are writing and will provide the reader with all the information necessary to put the letter into context. It is, however, important to do this without giving any indication of whether the request will be granted or not.

   We have received your letter requesting a refund on tickets to the 'Stars Under the Stars' concert next week.

Body

The next section of the letter, the body, gives the reasons for the refusal. Providing a rationale for the refusal serves two purposes. First, it helps to maintain goodwill by demonstrating that there were valid reasons why it was not possible to agree to the request. Second, it prepares the reader for the refusal. By the time the reader has read through the reasons, it is obvious that the answer is going to be 'no'. It is better to avoid using vague generalities such as 'company policy' or 'financial constraints' as the reason for the refusal. The more specific we can keep our reasons, the more credibility those reasons will have.

> This has been a very expensive concert to mount. Using an outdoor venue has meant considerable set-up costs in terms of preparation of the stage and the sound systems. It is, indeed, because the concert will take place in an outdoor venue that we have had to make our tickets non-refundable. As you will see from the concert brochure and from the information on the back of the ticket, no refunds can be given.

Notice that the actual refusal is written in the passive voice. This distances the writer from the action, implying a sense of events outside the writer's control. Note, too, that the refusal is written as a subsidiary part of a sentence. It is not given the prominence of a sentence to itself. It is also preferable not to start a sentence or paragraph with the refusal as this gives it prominence and we want to downplay the refusal rather than make it stand out in any way.

Conclusion

Finally, conclude the letter with some sort of positive alternative and goodwill close.

> The concert is on for two nights, and we may be able to arrange an exchange of nights. Alternatively, you may find someone to purchase the tickets from you.
>
> We do hope you can come to the concert as it promises to be a wonderful experience.

Persuasive letters

As mentioned before, all letters have elements of persuasion, but in this section we are looking at letters that are written primarily to persuade, whether what is being sold is a product or an idea. A common method of structuring persuasive letters according to Galvin, Prescott and Huseman (1992), Andrews and Andrews (1992) and Eunson (1996), among others, is the AIDA formula where A stands for attention, I for interest, D for desire and the final A for action.

Attention

With unsolicited sales letters we have only one sentence in which to catch the attention of the reader. If we do not get the reader's attention in the first sentence, the letter will most probably end up unread and in the bin. So, how do we get a reader's attention in the first sentence? In all communication, it is important to make a direct connection with the audience. The question to be asked is: 'What is in it for the audience?'. This is particularly important with persuasive letters. The more closely we can link our message to the needs and desires of our reader, the more successful our persuasive appeal will be. The letter therefore needs to begin with something significant about what we are selling that will make a direct connection with the reader. In other words we should start the letter with what the reader will consider the primary benefit of what we are selling.

We can begin the letter with a rhetorical question, some startling statistics, a reference to current affairs—anything that provides an attention-getting opening that is relevant to what is being sold. The last point is important because as well as getting the attention of the reader the opening of the letter has to lead naturally into the body of the letter detailing what we are selling.

Following are three possible opening sentences. The first example is from a letter selling a dishwasher, the second is from a letter asking for support for an environmental organisation and the third is from a letter selling washable crayons.

1. If you have prepared just two meals a day for a family of three, you have washed 21 900 pieces of crockery, cutlery and pots and pans last year.
2. Do you want your children's children to see trees only in picture books?
3. We challenge you to write your name on the wall with the enclosed crayon.

Notice that all the suggested openings emphasise the reader. They are written in a 'you-oriented' style and they are directly relevant to what the writer is selling.

Interest

The interest and desire sections form the body of the letter. We will deal with interest and desire as two separate sections here but often they will merge into each other and be difficult to separate.

After we have gained the reader's attention we need to develop that attention into interest in the product. Emphasise the benefits of the product or idea, making close links between what the product or idea offers and how it will benefit the reader. Appeals can be made to the head or the heart, to logic and reason or to the emotions. We deal with emotional and logical appeals in more detail in Chapter 10 on persuasion. Most appeals will involve a mixture of appeal to reason and to the emotions, but it is important to stress 'what's in it for the reader'.

Let us develop the dishwasher opening into the interest section of the AIDA formula.

> Imagine having a Dishace to do all those dishes and pots and pans for you. Just think of all the interesting things you can do with the time you save—play golf, play bridge, sit in the sun, shop 'til you drop.

Desire

The desire section gives more product information. In this section the writer needs to develop reader interest, moving the reader from a feeling of 'I am interested in this' to 'I really want this'.

An important element in any persuasive message is credibility. A message will only be persuasive if it is also credible, so avoid exclamation marks and 'over the top' language. There is so much hyperbolic language used nowadays that people have become suspicious of exaggerated claims.

In the following paragraphs notice that the language is simple and everyday. It is not highly emotional but there are still strong emotional appeals present. There is the appeal of saving time and having increased leisure, which links with the opening sentence of the letter. There is the appeal of the fact that the Dishace is quiet and will not take up much space and there is an appeal (partly emotional and partly rational) to saving money. Notice how the product price is downplayed, preceded by the word 'only' and embedded in a paragraph emphasising how economical the product is and how little it will cost to have the washing up done by the Dishace.

> The Dishace is easy to stack. You can put in a full load in only three minutes. Think of the time you will save on the 20 minutes a normal wash up takes.

> The Dishace is quiet and compact. Although capable of doing a full family washing up in only half an hour, it is so quiet you won't even know it is operating.

> The Dishace is economical. It uses no more water than conventional washing up, and it runs for only $1.00 an hour. So for a cost of only $1100 you can have your washing up done for 50 cents every day, all year for years and years.

Action

This is the real purpose of the persuasive letter. This is where we tell the reader what we want to happen next.

> Getting your new Dishace is as easy as picking up your phone. Phone free call xxxxx xxxxx for an obligation-free trial of the Dishace in your own home. What can you lose?

In the action section, it is important to make the action we require as easy and inexpensive as possible. Here the request is not to write a letter or fill in a form but just to make a simple—and free—phone call.

Memos

Email has largely taken over as the primary means of in-house written communication. However, memos are still written so we need to deal with them.

There are many similarities between letters and memos. The major layout differences stem from the fact that memos are in-house documents, distributed only to people within the same organisation. This eliminates the need for an inside or return address. There is also no salutation or complimentary close.

Elements of memos

Even though memos are written only for internal distribution it is still necessary for the receiver to know who wrote the memo, and there is a necessity for a permanent record of who the receiver was. These requirements are met by the 'To' and 'From' sections of the memo.

To

The 'To' section takes the place of the inside address in the letter. It gives the name and, sometimes, position of the person to whom the memo is sent.

From

The 'From' section corresponds to the letterhead/return address and signer's identification sections of the letter, giving the name and, sometimes, the position of the writer of the memo.

Date

All written correspondence should be dated, so memos also have a section giving the date.

Subject

Memos also have a 'Subject' section. This takes the place of the subject line in letters but is not optional as the subject line is in letters. The 'Subject' section tells the reader what the memo is going to be about.

Enclosure and c.c. notations

Memos can also have enclosures and c.c. notations.

Sometimes organisations will have preprinted memo forms, but nowadays the writer usually generates the form at the time of writing. Below are samples of the ways in which the parts of memos mentioned above can be set out.

```
MEMORANDUM
TO:                           FROM:
DATE:                         SUBJECT:
```

```
MEMORANDUM
TO:
FROM:
DATE:
SUBJECT:
```

> **MEMORANDUM**
>
> TO: John Dixon, Director   FROM: Sarah Jones, Account Executive
>
> DATE: 7 October 200X   SUBJECT: SCOTTLEY ACCOUNT
>
> I have had discussions with David Pryor at Scottley about the possibility of mounting a campaign to launch their new hair care product. David seems interested and will be here tomorrow at 11.
>
> I think it would be a good idea for him to meet you and some of the creative team as well. Can you let me know whether you will be available and whether you would like to join us at lunch later?
>
> SJ

FIGURE 5.2 Sample Memo Using Direct Method

Memos are usually brief and direct. They can, like letters, be used to get and give information and to initiate action. They often form part of the regular reporting mechanisms within organisations such as weekly sales figures, monthly financial analyses and so on. They can be used to confirm or reinforce oral communication such as a telephone call or a face-to-face meeting. They are useful for passing on complex information and provide an efficient method of reaching a large number of people simultaneously.

Like letters, memos may be written according to the direct or indirect method, depending on whether they are conveying neutral material or good news, or refusing a request. Most memos, however, deal with routine matters and will be written using the direct method.

Figure 5.2 is a sample memo written using the direct method. You will see that the first sentence fulfils the same function as the opening of a letter. It serves as an introduction, putting the communication within a context. The following sentences form the body of the memo, giving more information and detail. The final sentence concludes the memo by pointing to what happens next, to what action the writer wants or expects.

Note that the signer's identification is reduced to just the initials.

Indirect method

The indirect method is used for refusals. In the sample memo Figure 5.3 you can see the similarities with the letter of refusal. The memo begins with a sentence putting the memo into context but giving no indication as to whether the request will be granted or refused. The body of the memo gives the reasons for refusal. When the refusal does appear, the writer is distanced from the action. Compare 'You do not qualify' with 'I have to refuse your request' to see how the writer is absent from the first phrase but centrally involved in the second. The memo concludes with a positive alternative and a friendly invitation.

> MEMORANDUM
> TO: Tom Winton DATE: 3 May 200X
> FROM: Maria Tilling SUBJECT: ANNUAL LEAVE
>
> I note that you have asked to take your annual leave in December/January.
>
> As you know, because that is the period of the school holidays it is the most popular vacation time and this year 80% of staff have requested leave at this time. Because we are a service industry we have to maintain our services to our customers so, although we can function on a reduced staff, we still need at least 50% of our staff available during this period. We have, therefore, had to limit annual leave at this time to staff with school-age children. Unfortunately this means that you do not qualify for leave during December/January.
>
> There would be no problem with your taking leave at another time and I am available to discuss the matter at any time.
>
> ST

FIGURE 5.3 Sample Memo Using Indirect Method

Email

Email has been dealt with in Chapter 3, Electronic Communication, so this section will merely provide a brief overview of email as part of the written communication network of organisations. Email can be sent to people both within and outside an organisation. In terms of format, email is closer to the memo than to the letter, although most email messages do begin with some sort of salutation. Sometimes this will just be the name of the receiver. Sometimes the name may be preceded by 'hello' or even 'hi there'. There is usually no complimentary close, just the name and, sometimes, the email address of the sender.

Material can be attached to email messages in rather the same way that material is enclosed with letters and this allows entire, even lengthy, documents to be sent by email. Basically, if the material is on computer disk it can go by email.

One disadvantage of email is that it is usually less secure than letters and memos, so confidentiality can be a problem. If you are writing anything confidential it is better to use a conventional letter or memo.

Tone and style

Chapter 4, on effective writing skills, included a discussion on how choice of vocabulary and sentence and paragraph structure contributed to the writer's style upon which the tone of the communication depended. In terms of formality, letters are normally more formal than memos and memos are normally more formal than emails. However, the degree of formality will depend on the relationship between the writer and the reader and on the subject matter.

Letters, even professional letters, can be quite informal if the writer and the receiver are friends and if the subject matter is routine and unimportant. However, even between friends matters of importance will usually be conveyed formally, even though the salutation may remain 'Dear Bill'.

The level of formality of memos depends on the relationship between writer and reader, especially in terms of status. Memos written to peers will often be more informal than memos written to superiors or even to subordinates. Again, the subject matter will affect how formal or informal a memo is. If we are writing to a friend about a routine matter, our memo will probably be less formal than a memo to the same person about a serious matter.

Emails are often almost conversational in tone, although the relationship between sender and receiver and the subject matter will still influence the level of formality. The tone in emails can often create misinterpretation. Writers sometimes appear brusque and unfriendly because they take shortcuts with language. This can lead to misunderstanding.

SUMMARY

In this chapter we have looked at letters, memos and email messages. You should now be aware of the formal elements of letters and memos, which serve important functions in terms of identifying the writer and the receiver, noting any enclosures and so on. Letters, memos and emails fall into three broad categories: neutral or good news letters, refusal letters and persuasive letters. In most correspondence the writer should come to the point immediately; however, there are occasions (when refusing a request) when a more indirect method is preferable. Although email messages are usually more informal than letters and memos, the tone and style of any correspondence will be influenced by both the task and the audience.

In the next chapter we will deal with more extended writing—that is, essays and formal reports.

KEY POINTS

- Letters and emails can be written to people within or outside an organisation. Memos are written to people within an organisation.
- There are certain formal elements necessary in correspondence. These elements identify both the writer and the receiver and include information such as the date of the correspondence, whether enclosures or attachments are included, whether anyone else has received a copy of the correspondence and anything else important relating to the correspondence.
- Letters, memos and emails fall into three broad categories, which influence the way the material is presented. Correspondence containing neutral or good news information is written in the direct method. Correspondence refusing requests is written in the indirect method, while persuasive messages follow the AIDA formula.
- Although letters are normally more formal than memos, and email messages are the most informal, the degree of formality and the tone and style of any message will be influenced by the relationship between the writer and the reader, as well as by the content of the message.

REVIEW QUESTIONS

1. What are the essential formal elements of letters and memos, and why are they important?
2. What purpose does the opening of a letter or memo using the direct method serve?
3. What is the indirect method, and why would you choose to use it?
4. What is the AIDA formula? Select any advertisement in print or on television and analyse it in terms of the AIDA formula. What is the attention section? How is interest and desire generated? What is the action section?
5. What are the advantages and disadvantages of email?

EXERCISES

1. You are a member of the Student Union and you are organising a student barbecue for an anticipated 500 people. You need to hire cooking equipment. Write to Betta Bar-B-Qs of Sunnybank Road, Holthurst 3560, to inquire about price, and terms and conditions of hiring equipment to cook for the function.

2. You are the Credit Manager of QPC Brakes. Lindways Garage is two months overdue in paying for their last order and owes $1200. Write to Lindways Garage of Burnage Road, Smithville 4698, to request payment of the overdue account.

3. You are setting up a part-time business doing mowing and gardening. Write a flyer that you can put through local letterboxes selling your services.

4. Write a letter to your lecturer appealing against a failing grade for your last assignment.

5. You work part-time in a local coffee shop. For personal reasons you will not be able to work next Saturday. Write a memo to your supervisor asking if you can have next Saturday off.

BIBLIOGRAPHY

Andrews, D.C. and Andrews, W.D. 1992, *Business Communications,* 2nd ed., Macmillan, New York.
Barker, A. 1993, *Letters At Work,* The Industrial Society, London.
Cormier, R.A. 1995, *Error-Free Writing: A Lifetime Guide to Flawless Business Writing,* Prentice Hall, Englewood Cliffs.
DeVries, M.A. 1994, *The Elements of Correspondence,* Macmillan, New York.
Eunson, B. 1996, *Writing in Plain English,* Jacaranda Wiley Ltd, Brisbane.
Freeman, J. 1996, 8 June. 'Write & Wrong', *The Sydney Morning Herald,* Employment Section, p. 1.
Galvin, M., Prescott, D. and Huseman, R. 1992, *Business Communication: Strategies and Skills,* Holt, Rinehart and Winston, Sydney.
Keithley, E.M., Flatley, M.E. and Schreiner, P.J. 1988, *Manual of Style for Business Letters, Memos and Reports,* 4th ed., South-Western Publishing Company, Cincinnati.
Kogen, M. 1989, *Writing in the Business Professions,* National Council of Teachers of English and the Association for Business Communication, Urbana.
Lindsell-Roberts, S. 1995, *Business Letter Writing,* Macmillan, New York.
Lowell, T. 1989, *The Australian Handbook of Business Letters,* Information Australia, Melbourne.
Mahony, D. 2004, *Studying and Writing Effectively,* QUT, Brisbane.
Morenberg, M. 1991, *Doing Grammar,* Oxford University Press, Oxford.
Petelin, R. and Durham, M. 1996, *The Professional Writing Guide: Writing Well and Knowing Why,* Pitman, Melbourne.
Snodgrass, G. and Murphy, E. M. 1986, *Letter Writing Simplified,* rev. ed., Pitman, Melbourne.
Tarling, L. 1989, *The Australian Handbook of Business Letters: The Essential Writing Reference,* Information Australia, Melbourne.

Extended writing—essays and reports

CHAPTER 6

Upon completing this chapter you should be able to:
- understand the distinguishing characteristics of an essay and a report;
- demonstrate an awareness of the importance of task analysis;
- demonstrate a knowledge of the skills necessary to undertake task analysis;
- show the capacity to find and evaluate research sources;
- appreciate the importance of tailoring tone and style to the task and audience; and
- realise the importance of accuracy and presentation in the finished product.

This chapter applies task and audience analysis and good writing skills to the production of effective pieces of extended writing, namely, essays and reports. It should be noted at the outset that essays do not normally form part of professional writing. In business and the professions it is usually reports rather than essays which are required. However, the skills needed to write a good essay are precisely those that are necessary to write a good report, so we will start by looking at what is needed for a good essay.

Essays

We will look at essay writing in a fairly simple, almost formulaic way, but when you are more experienced in writing essays, you can be more sophisticated, even innovative. Essays, like seminar or tutorial papers, dissertations and theses, form part of academic writing or written communications required as part of academic study. First, what is an essay? An **essay** is a sustained piece of writing that tests a student's ability to write clear and correct English and to conduct effective research. More importantly, however, essays enable an assessment of a student's grasp of the higher-level skills of analysis, synthesis, selection and organisation of ideas and material, and the ability to construct sustained, logical and coherent arguments. An essay, in fact, is an extended argument in which we try to persuade our readers to accept our viewpoint, our thesis, on the basis of the reasons we put forward to prove that thesis and the evidence we provide to support those reasons. Because essays can be used to judge so many important academic skills and abilities, they are, possibly, the most common form of assessment at tertiary institutions. The ability to write effective essays is, therefore, critical to eventual university success.

Note the importance given to the development of an argument. What is meant when we talk of an essay having a well-developed, coherent argument is an essay that provides a clearly structured series of points supported by research that is designed to prove a particular viewpoint or thesis in relation to the essay topic. We will deal with this in more detail later in the chapter, but almost every university essay will require the development of an argument.

So, let us begin by looking at what constitutes a good essay or good academic writing.

Effective academic writing

Good academic writing has certain characteristics:

* It addresses the question that has been set and does not deviate into irrelevancies. It is clearly focused on the topic and particularly on the central issue or problem at the core of the topic.

* It shows evidence of intelligent and relevant research that has been correctly referenced.

* It has a central thesis or idea, which is supported or proved by a clear, logical and reasoned argument.

* It displays an understanding of vocabulary and concepts relevant to the discipline.

* It is correct in terms of spelling, grammar and punctuation.

* It is appropriately presented, preferably typed, with appropriate use of white space such as margins and double line spacing.

Analysing the topic/question

If any communication is to be effective, whether it is a letter or a speech, an essay or a report, it needs to be focused. In allocating time to a task, at least 80 per cent should be spent preparing to write and a maximum of 20 per cent on the actual writing. Analysing the task and audience, thinking about the topic, research, collection, selection and organisation of material should take at least 80 per cent of the time allocated to any assignment.

The first characteristic of a good essay involves focusing on the topic, in other words answering the question. Before we even begin our research we need to have a very clear idea of the task. Much thought should be expended on the essay topic before any writing takes place. We need to analyse the essay topic. This means more than a quick read through. It means really thinking about the question, and finding out *exactly* what we are being asked to do. Unfortunately, students often do poorly in essays and reports because they fail to answer the question or address the topic. A common fault is to write on the subject but not on the topic. Let us put that into context by looking at a question that was set in a recent examination.

> Nonverbal communication is more important than verbal communication. Do you agree? From your knowledge of nonverbal communication, substantiate whatever view you take with regard to the first statement.

Some of the answers dealt with kinesics, proxemics, paralinguistics, chronemics and semiotics but did not address the topic, did not 'answer the question' and, consequently, were awarded very low marks. The topic was not 'write all you know about nonverbal communication'. The question required knowledge about nonverbal communication to be applied to a specific aspect of the subject. Writing all you know about a subject is, first, descriptive not analytical and, second, it does not test real understanding. We can write an essay on something we do not really understand if all we are being asked to do is to write all we know about a topic. It takes an understanding of content to apply that knowledge in particular ways required by different topics.

For these reasons university essays will normally require application of knowledge in terms of a particular problem to be solved or a specific topic to be addressed. Therefore, it is vitally important for success at university to be skilful in analysing what you are being asked to do. It is also a skill equally important in professional life. If you cannot analyse a problem there is very little chance that you will be able to solve it, and solving problems is a major component of professional life. The skills required to analyse an essay topic are also the skills required to analyse a problem in professional or business life. (We will deal with problem solving in more detail in the chapter on decision-making strategies, Chapter 9.)

So how do we analyse a topic? How do we decide what we are being asked to do? Basically, what we do in analysing the question or topic is task analysis. We need to break the topic down into its component parts, thinking critically about exactly what is required. We should first realise that essay topics contain task words and key words. **Task words** tell us what we should be doing and how we should treat the areas to be considered. Almost every tertiary essay will require you to analyse, even if the topic also has aspects of description or summary.

Task words that call for description rather than analysis are:

describe	define	comment	give an account of
state	list	narrate	
enumerate	outline	classify	
review	summarise	relate	

Task words that ask for analysis rather than description are:

analyse	assess
compare	contrast
discuss	criticise
evaluate	find causes (why)
examine	

Sometimes a question may require both description and analysis, but the analysis section will usually be of more importance. Analysis is a higher-level skill than description for it requires not only knowledge of the topic but, more importantly, real understanding of the subject matter. Analysis goes beyond content and moves into the realms of intellectual activity, into the formulation and exposition of a thesis, that is, our own position in relation to the topic.

If we look at our examination question, the task words are 'do you agree'. We could substitute 'discuss' for 'do you agree' because it means almost the same in terms of what we are required to do. So we are asked to analyse nonverbal and verbal communication in terms of their relative importance.

However, the question goes on to specify that we should substantiate whatever view we take from our knowledge of nonverbal communication, so we are clearly meant to view the question from the perspective of nonverbal communication. In other words, while we need to deal with both verbal and nonverbal communication, we are meant to write from the perspective of nonverbal rather than verbal communication.

Key words define the areas we need to consider. They define the areas we are asked to investigate and add to our understanding of what we are being asked to do. The first thing to realise is that, while every word in the assignment topic is important, not all the words in a topic are of equal importance. There will always be a hierarchy of importance in the words in assignment topics. Let us look at the examination question again. What are the key words? Certainly words such as 'nonverbal communication' and 'verbal communication' are important. But what about 'more important'? We are being asked to decide whether we do, or do not, consider nonverbal communication to be more important than verbal communication. So the words 'more important' define the way in which we are being asked to evaluate nonverbal and verbal communication.

The previous examination question was straightforward. Essay topics, however, are often more complex. Let us look at another topic.

> What role does gender play in communication? Do gender influences in communication have an effect on power and status and, if so, what effect do they have?

Let us italicise the task words and bold the important key words.

> *What* role does **gender** play in **communication**? *Do* gender influences in communication *have an effect* on **power and status** and, if so, *what* **effect** do they have?

You may think there are more key words, but we do need to be selective in deciding on the most important key words because we will use those key words to work our way to the central issue or problem in the topic. If we have included almost all the words in the topic in our important key words, the resulting lack of focus will make it difficult to uncover that central problem. Most essay topics are concerned with a conflict or issue arising from a problem, and it is this problem that we must uncover before we can develop our thesis. It is the key words that lead us to this deeper level of analysis. If we decide for this topic that the key words are gender, communication, power and status, we can decide that the issue is the relationship between gendered communication and power and status. It can be useful to think of the central issue as a question. So here our question could be: 'Does gender influence communication in ways that impact on, or reflect, power and status?' Once the central problem or issue has been identified, preferably in one simple question, we can develop our thesis, that is, our viewpoint in relation to that issue.

Thesis development

When we have a very clear idea of the central problem or issue in the question it is time to develop our thesis. A thesis is simply a theory we hope to prove; it is our viewpoint or stance in relation to the topic. We need to express our thesis in the form of a thesis statement. This should be a clear, *precise* expression of our viewpoint on the topic, which we hope our essay will prove. I have put 'precise' in italics because our thesis *must* be precise. It should be one relatively short sentence. If we take several sentences to state our thesis we need to go back to our analysis of the central problem and focus our thesis much more clearly. Because our thesis is the point that our whole essay is written to prove, it is essential to the development of a logical argument that our thesis statement is clear, concise and focused. If our thesis statement is vague or ill defined, we have no focus for our argument and no clear point towards which our essay is leading. Some topics virtually write our thesis for us. Let us assume our topic is:

> The interactive model of communication is the most appropriate model for all communicative acts. Do you agree?

This topic is straightforward, and our thesis would be either to agree, disagree or agree/disagree with qualifications. If we agree, our thesis would be 'The interactive model of communication is the most appropriate model for all communicative acts'. Of course, this thesis would be difficult to prove because the interactive model of communication is not the most appropriate model for *all* communicative acts. In fact, it is the most appropriate for only a small proportion of communicative acts, mainly those concerned with written communication or communication where there is a time lag between sending and receiving feedback. It is certainly not the most appropriate model for face-to-face communication. So, our thesis could be 'While the interactive model of communication is appropriate for some forms of communication, it is not the most appropriate model for all communicative acts'.

However, topics are often more open. The topic on gender and communication is an example of a more open topic where our thesis is not written for us in the topic itself, but where we have to develop our own thesis. With a more complex topic, identification of the central problem or issue is necessary because it is from our analysis of the central problem or issue that we can develop our thesis.

Research

It is important to keep the topic in mind throughout our research because it is easy to become sidetracked. We need to refer constantly to the topic when researching to ensure that our research is still 'on track'.

With a straightforward topic our research can be focused from the beginning. Once we have analysed our topic and decided on a tentative thesis (I use the word 'tentative' advisedly as research may well lead us to alter, perhaps even completely change, our viewpoint) we can begin the research. With a more complex, open topic, however, initial research will take the form of wide reading (all the time, of course, keeping the topic in mind), which will help us to refine our ideas, to come to a better appreciation of the complexities of the central problem and to develop our own thesis. At this point our research can become more closely focused.

Research can be based on primary or secondary sources. **Primary sources** will normally be unpublished material, usually our own research. Primary sources include surveys, questionnaires, structured interviews, observation and experimentation. **Secondary sources** are published material such as books, journals, newspapers, government publications and, increasingly, electronic sources such as discussion lists and the internet. However, in some disciplines such as literature, primary sources consist of material by the writer we are researching and secondary material is other published material such as works by other writers, background history, cultural studies material, philosophy, critical theory and so on that is related to the author and topic.

SELECTION OF SOURCE MATERIAL

How do we select the best references for our purpose?

* It is preferable to use a recent text although the importance of using recent texts varies from discipline to discipline. In areas such as taxation or computing, for example, it is important that references are as recent as possible. This is why journals are important sources. In some disciplines, in the time it takes for a book to be published material can already be outdated. In other disciplines, such as literature, material is superseded less rapidly.

* Evaluate the author's claims to scholarship. What are the author's qualifications and experience in the subject matter? How well regarded is the author in the area of the research?

* Is the publisher a reputable one, especially in the discipline area? If the publication is a journal, is it a **peer-reviewed/refereed** journal?

TEXT EVALUATION

Even texts that meet all of the above criteria still have to be assessed in terms of relevance and usefulness for the particular task. To evaluate the usefulness of a text, we need to be able quickly to get an overview of its content and perspective. The introduction will give an overview of the text with some idea of the author's perspective; however, the index at the back of the book is also useful because it lists the contents of the book alphabetically by subject. The index functions in the same way as the subject catalogue in the library so, for example, if we were researching the examination topic we would look up 'nonverbal communication' in the index. Sometimes, we might not find what we want under a particular word and may need to look up synonyms or associated terms involved in the task. For example, if we were working in the area of written communication, we might need to look up 'written communication', 'letters', 'memos', 'reports' and so on. We would probably find several references, some to only one page and some to two or more pages. The longer references are likely to be more useful, so we would probably start with them. We could also find some cross-references that could usefully be followed up.

The contents page at the front of the book, which lists the contents of each chapter, is also useful in providing an overview of the contents of the book as a whole.

Time constraints often mean that it is not possible to read every word in each text, but reading the opening and closing paragraphs, any headings and subheadings and the topic sentences of paragraphs (usually the first sentence in the paragraph) will provide enough material for us to judge whether a text is likely to be useful or not. If a text seems particularly relevant and useful, it can then be read in more detail. Initially, this will mean reading for meaning, reading sufficiently carefully to obtain the sense of the material.

Ultimately, the text will need to be read critically. A common weakness among students, especially in the early part of their courses, is uncritical acceptance of what is read, a failure to assess and evaluate sources. Critical or evaluative reading is a vital academic skill. It means evaluating what we read in terms of the following:

* How credible is the source, both in terms of the author and the publication in which the information appears?
* How reliable is the information? Is it substantiated by other sources? What evidence is provided to support the argument and how credible is that evidence?
* What is our evaluation of the argument? Is there a focused and logical progression? Do all the points made help support or prove the thesis?
* How comprehensive is the coverage? Is there anything important omitted? Is there sufficient breadth and depth?
* Is the information free from errors?
* What value assumptions are inherent in the writing?
* What bias is present and how is it evident?

At this point, it is important to note that every piece of writing will contain bias of some kind. This may be conscious or unconscious. It may exist in what is said, but equally it may exist in what is not said, in arguments or viewpoints that are not advanced. No matter how bias is evident, we need to be aware constantly that once knowledge is processed, that is, put into a form that enables it to be transmitted, bias is present.

Referencing

It is important in any research to take full notes of the sources of any material so that the material can be correctly referenced. **Referencing** means acknowledging the source of the quotation or idea we are using. This is done for three reasons. Firstly, it is unethical to use someone else's words or ideas—their intellectual property—without acknowledging the fact. It is theft; it is called **plagiarism** and is heavily penalised. Secondly, quoting the opinions of experts in the field will validate the points we are making. It will provide support for our argument. Thirdly, acknowledging sources enables our reader to follow up any points that may be of interest.

Because there are many different referencing systems (and during your university career you will probably be required to use more than one system depending on the discipline or subject you are studying at the time), we will not go into particular referencing systems here. However, whatever system is used the information required would be the name of the author, the title of the book, the publisher and place and date of publication, as well as the numbers of the pages where the material was found. How this information is arranged and punctuated will depend on the particular referencing system being used. You will need to refer to a style manual to make sure the referencing is correct. The referencing system in this text is the Author/Date or Amended Harvard System. When making notes it is helpful to make source notes in the referencing format to be used in the finished essay. This makes it easier when the essay is written and ensures that nothing important is omitted.

Essay structure

Every essay should have an introduction, a body and a conclusion.

INTRODUCTION

The introduction is one of the most important parts of our essay because it orients our reader to both our thesis and our argument. Although the introduction is the first paragraph (sometimes paragraphs) of our essay, it is probably, like the conclusion, written after we have drafted the body of our essay; in fact the introduction will possibly be written even after the conclusion.

The introduction is a crucial section of the essay. As Mahony (2004) notes, the introduction should fulfil certain important functions. It should provide:

* an explanation of the central issue or problem set by the topic;

* any necessary definitions of key terms;

* an orientation to our perspective and approach to the topic; and

* a statement of our thesis.

The introduction gives an overview of the essay as a whole and foreshadows what is to follow in the body of the essay. However, it is important that we remember that, while the introduction does orient our readers to our thesis and argument, it should not be a mini essay. If our introduction lists all the points we intend to make in our essay and we then repeat those points (with amplification, evidence, examples and so on) in the body of the essay and then reiterate the points in the conclusion, we have an essay that will probably be boringly repetitive and give the reader a sense of stagnation, rather than a sense of an argument moving forward. The bulk of our introduction should be taken up with the explanation of the central issue or problem, defining any terms (including explaining any limitations we have had to place on our material) and, of course, our thesis statement. Probably only about one-third of our introduction will normally be concerned with indicating our approach to the topic, that is, how we intend to support or prove our thesis.

Let us look at a sample introduction:

Topic: Interviews have been called structured conversations. This implies a certain equality of power and responsibilities. To what extent are interviews exchanges of views between equals in terms of power and responsibilities?

Introduction: To describe interviews as structured conversations is an acknowledgement of the central purpose of all interviews, which is an exchange of ideas, but an exchange of ideas within certain well-defined parameters that exist to ensure the objective of the interview. While there could be interviews in which power and responsibility are shared equally by both interviewer and interviewee, it can be argued that the very structure of the interview process militates against equality of power and responsibility. Through a study of a number of types of interviews, it is possible to analyse the power relations and dynamics between participants and to determine if there is equality of power and responsibilities within the normal interview process.

How well do you think the above paragraph functions as an introduction in relation to the topic? How well does it fulfil the functions of the introduction? Is there a thesis statement and, if so, what is it? How well does the writer orient the reader towards both content and perspective?

Thesis statement

How introductions are organised can vary but the introduction *must* contain our thesis statement. The thesis statement is the conclusion that the essay is designed to prove. 'Conclusion' in this context is not 'conclusion' in terms of essay structure, that is, the final section of our essay that draws together the main points of our argument. We are talking of 'conclusion' here in terms of logical argument, that is, the viewpoint that our essay sets out to prove. (We will deal with logical arguments in more detail in the chapter on clear thinking, logic and argumentation, Chapter 11.) If we have not formulated a clear thesis statement we have nothing to use as the basis for an argument in our essay. Essays without a clear thesis statement are usually descriptive rather than analytical and have no, logically developed argument. Sometimes, essays contain an implied thesis but, in almost every case, such essays lack a clear focus and development of an argument. They tend to be diffuse and often just miss achieving success. So, our thesis must be stated clearly somewhere in our introduction. Where it appears in the introduction is a matter for individual judgement. Basically, there are three primary structures that we can follow for our introduction. There is the pyramidal structure:

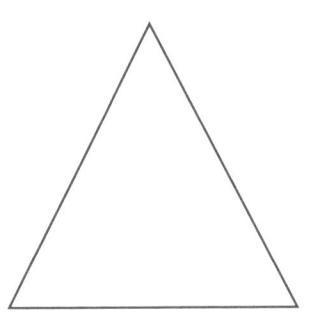

Here we begin with our thesis statement and then proceed to outline how our argument to support that thesis will develop. This form of introduction works quite well with the straightforward topic where the thesis is virtually worded for us.

There is the reversed pyramid:

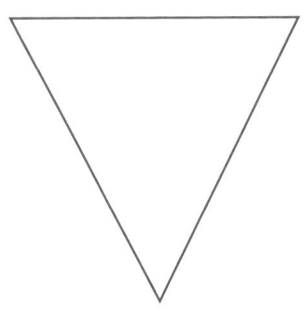

Here we begin by overviewing our topic and argument, perhaps providing background information and definitions, and finish with our thesis statement.

Finally, there is the hourglass:

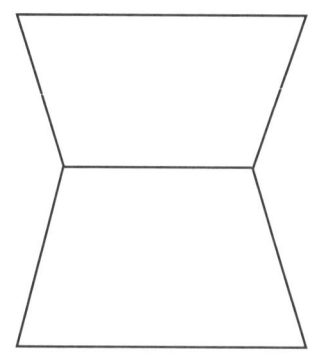

Here we begin with, perhaps, some background information, maybe some definitions, then move to the thesis and complete the introduction by overviewing how our argument will develop. The inverted pyramid and the hourglass work well with more complex topics that require us to develop our own thesis.

BODY

The body of the essay is where we provide the research data and detailed analysis foreshadowed in the introduction. This is where we make the points that support or prove our thesis. Let us return to the topic involving the relative importance of nonverbal and verbal communication. If we had decided that both nonverbal and verbal communication were equally important and that their relative importance in relation to each other depended upon the type and context of the communication, the body of the essay is where we would make the points that support that thesis. In broad terms (and we would probably divide these broad points into more detailed subpoints), we may write about the relationship between verbal and nonverbal communication, noting that verbal communication primarily conveys ideas, while nonverbal communication is the primary means of conveying feelings or emotions. We may also make the point that nonverbal cues can complement, reinforce or undermine words. We may also put these differences into specific contexts or examples.

The custom has been for essays to be written in sustained prose without subheadings. However, increasingly writers are using subheadings as signposts for readers. If you use subheadings, you would certainly not use a heading 'introduction' or 'conclusion' as these sections should be self-evident. Whether you use subheadings or not should be determined by your audience, that is, what your reader wants or expects and by the demands of your content and argument.

Important considerations

Maintain focus

It is important in the body section not to deviate from our thesis statement. One way to stay focused on the topic is to prepare an essay outline containing the main points. Sometimes this outline can consist of topic sentences from the paragraphs but even short notes are often enough. References and research data can be indicated in the essay outline.

Write an outline

An outline serves a number of purposes. By providing the skeleton, which will be fleshed out with sentences and paragraphs, an outline:

* can help keep the essay on the topic;

* enables us to ensure that our argument is clear and logical and that the points we are making are relevant and, importantly (and often badly done), linked to the topic and thesis. Always remember that nothing in an essay is neutral. If the points made do not support our thesis they will detract from our argument by making it less clear;

* can help ensure that the points we are making are sufficiently supported by relevant evidence.

Develop an argument

It is important that readers can easily see the relationship between the research, the topic and the thesis. Also, since every essay is concerned with the formulation of an argument, it is necessary that readers can clearly follow the logic of our argument.

Linking words, sometimes called connecting words, are useful in helping readers to follow an argument. Linking words can be as simple as 'and', 'but' or 'yet', but they are useful in two ways. They provide smooth transitions between sections of an essay, and they signal developments in the argument. Linking words provide signposts that help our readers follow our argument. 'And' indicates that we are not developing our argument at this point, just adding to it, whereas 'but' and 'yet' indicate a qualification or change in direction within the argument. 'Also' or 'as well' move the argument forward, while 'however' or 'although' signal a change in the direction of our argument. We can see this in operation in the second sentence of this paragraph, which started with the idea that linking words can be simple *but that* (slight change of direction) they are useful.

Linking words can be used to:

* introduce examples or illustrations ('for example', 'that is', 'in other words', 'for instance');

* indicate comparison ('similarly', 'likewise'), contrast ('on the other hand', 'in contrast') or the adoption of an alternative view to the argument being put forward ('however', 'but', 'yet', 'though');

* show relationships such as causal relationships and indicate that a conclusion is being reached ('therefore', 'as a result', 'hence', 'consequently'); and

* alert the reader to the fact that we are summarising ('as mentioned/noted before', 'to summarise').

It is important that our writing has a logical flow both within and between paragraphs. Look at the following paragraphs. Note how repetition of words, phrases or information can provide unity and smooth transitions. The bold words and phrases provide unity within the paragraph, while the italicised phrases provide a smooth link between paragraphs.

> The social changes wrought by the Industrial Revolution gave rise to **bourgeois domestic ideology.** An important element in this **domestic ideology** was the **concept of separate spheres** which characterised the **public domain of work,** economic usefulness, politics, public culture and all areas of society where power and influence were wielded as masculine, while women were confined to the purely private and **domestic sphere of home and family.** This **separation of public and private, work and home** reinforced both masculine supremacy and female dependence. **The family** reflected the gender power imbalances extant in the **wider society** and **the public dominance of men** gave the family its **patriarchal structure. Family and society, private and public spheres** were mutually affective and reinforcing.
>
> *The association of men with the* cultural, rational, organising, economically productive, *public areas of society* while **women** were progressively **confined to the circumscribed, private,** enclosed world of the home both extended and reinforced **patriarchal hegemony.**

Female exclusion from the masculine domain effectively defined home, wife and children as other and powerless. Industrialism, then, **empowered men** who could rise from working class to wealth, and commensurately **disempowered women** who were economically marginalised and for whom the gender role was increasingly restrictive.

CONCLUSION

The conclusion should follow logically from the body of the essay. It should recapitulate the main points made in the essay and function to summarise, to draw the essay back to a central point and to provide the conclusion to the evaluation or analysis with which the essay has been concerned. The conclusion also provides the opportunity for a final interpretation of the data and points found in the body of the essay.

Reports

In terms of task analysis and the importance of ensuring a logical sequence and a coherent argument, reports are similar to essays. However, in essays we are being asked to put forward an argument and to prove our thesis, while in reports we are usually being asked to solve a problem.

Types of reports

Reports form an important part of professional written communication, providing one of the primary means of problem analysis and management advice within organisations. Reports fall into two main categories: informational and analytical.

INFORMATIONAL REPORTS

Informational reports are usually short reports, often written in the form of a memo or letter. Short informational reports include routine reports such as regular departmental reports, sales reports, production reports, progress summaries, status reports and so on, as well as irregular reports such as accident reports. Sometimes, informational reports are simply forms to be filled in, for example accident reports for insurance companies.

ANALYTICAL REPORTS

Analytical reports are written to investigate or analyse problems or situations with the aim of providing recommendations designed to solve the problems. Although written in a style that conveys a factual, objective, unbiased tone, these reports are persuasive documents, for the report is successful if management adopts and implements the solutions set out in the recommendations. Analytical reports can be informal reports, short reports set out in a memo or letter format. However, they are often long documents that are sometimes called **formal reports** because of the formal requirements that need to be met in terms of required sections and format.

Report format

FORMAL REPORTS

We will begin our discussion of report format with the long or formal report. The conventions governing report format vary slightly from organisation to organisation and you will, of course, follow the format favoured by whatever organisation employs you. However, there are certain elements common to almost all formal or analytical reports. These are:

* transmittal document;
* title page;
* table of contents;
* summary, synopsis or abstract;
* introduction;
* body;
* conclusion(s);
* recommendations;
* bibliography or list of references; and
* appendix or appendices (not always required).

Transmittal document

The purpose of the transmittal document (see Figure 6.1) is to introduce the report to the reader. If the report is going to someone outside the organisation the transmittal document will be a letter. Usually, reports written for someone within the organisation will be written for someone senior in the organisation, in which case the transmittal document may still be a letter. However, if the report is going to someone within the organisation who is not very senior, the transmittal document could be a memo.

Whatever form the transmittal document takes, there is certain information that should be included. This is:

* the transmittal;
* the report overview; and
* a courteous close.

LETTERHEAD

Date

Inside Address

Salutation

Attached is the report you commissioned on 28 September investigating the best computing system for Berryman Enterprises.

The report examines three computing systems, Unissa, Bettacomp and Zweixa, concentrating on suitability for your needs, price and warranty, reliability and service. Although each system had certain positive and negative features it was possible to recommend one of the systems as being best for your needs.

I will be available if you have any queries or wish to discuss any part of the report in more detail.

Complimentary close

Signer's identification

FIGURE 6.1 Example of a Transmittal Document

If you have had help with the report you can acknowledge such help, and this would normally appear before the final courteous closing paragraph.

Title page

The title page (See Figure 6.2) will contain the title of the report; the name, title and organisation of the person who authorised the report (the receiver or audience); the name, title and organisation of the person who wrote the report (the sender or source); and the date (unless it is included in the report title, in which case it is not always necessary to repeat it).

```
TITLE PAGE

An Investigation of Networked Computer Systems for
Berryman Enterprises, Investment Advisers


Prepared for
Mr Alan Bryce, Senior Partner
Berryman Enterprises, Investment Advisers


by
Virginia Metcalfe
Senior Consultant
Computican Pty Ltd


25 August 20--
```

FIGURE 6.2 Example of a Report Title Page

Table of contents

The table of contents (see Figure 6.3) lists the divisions and major subdivisions of the report with the numbers of the pages on which the divisions and subdivisions will be found. If the report contains a number of tables or illustrations, a list of tables or a list of illustrations will also be necessary. If only one or two tables or illustrations have been included, a contents page for these may not be necessary, although if the tables or illustrations are important and are referred to constantly throughout the report, it could be worthwhile using a contents page for them.

The table of contents serves two major functions. Most importantly, it enables the reader to find any particular part of the report quickly; however, it also provides an overview or outline of the report as a whole, rather in the way that the contents page in reference books gives a picture of the complete text.

The summary, executive summary synopsis or abstract

The important thing to remember about the summary is that it is just that—a summary. For a 2000-word report, it should be no more than one-third of a page and, regardless of report length, it should never be more than one page. Although the report itself will be typed in double spacing, the summary is typed in single spacing. The purpose of the summary is to provide a concise overview of the report for people with too little time to read the whole report (see Figure 6.4).

The summary should include the problem, research methodology, principal arguments and important issues, findings and recommendations.

Table of Contents

Summary			iii
1.0	Introduction		
	1.1	Background	1
	1.2	Authorisation	1
	1.3	Aim of the Report	1
	1.4	Scope and Limitations	1
	1.5	Sources of Data	2
2.0	The Unissa System		
	2.1	Capabilities and Special Features	3
	2.2	Reliability and Warranty	5
	2.3	Service	6
	2.4	Price	7
3.0	The Bettacomp System		
	3.1	Capabilities and Special Features	8
	3.2	Reliability and Warranty	10
	3.3	Service	11
	3.4	Price	12
4.0	The Zweixa System		
	4.1	Capabilities and Special Features	13
	4.2	Reliability and Warranty	15
	4.3	Service	16
	4.4	Price	17
5.0	Conclusions		18
6.0	Recommendations		19
Bibliography			20

FIGURE 6.3 Example of a Table of Contents

SUMMARY

Owing to a substantial increase in its client base, Berryman Enterprises are finding that its existing stand-alone computers are inadequate. A networked system capable of using flexible database software is needed. Confidentiality of client records is important so computer security is a primary consideration.

Three systems were investigated. These were the Unissa, Bettacomp and Zweixa. The systems were compared in terms of capacity to meet the special requirements of Berryman Enterprises, reliability and warranty, service and purchase price.

All systems were capable of meeting the needs of Berryman Enterprises. The Unissa was fractionally the fastest but the Zweixa had greater memory capacity. In the area of computer security the Bettacomp was the best, although the Zweixa also had adequate security systems installed. In terms of initial purchase price the Unissa is the cheapest system but the cost of upgrading the security system would make it the dearest of the three systems. The Zweixa is the next cheapest but the warranty period is only three months and there have been some problems with service in the past.

The Bettacomp system is recommended. Although the initial purchase price is higher than the other two systems, this is offset by the extended warranty, excellent after-sales service and reputation for reliability.

FIGURE 6.4 Example of a Report Summary

Introduction

The introduction in the report fulfils the same functions as the introduction in an essay. It puts the report in context by giving the background (the problem, why the report was commissioned); the authorisation; the purpose of the report; the scope of the report; the research methodology; sources of data; any limitations affecting the report if they are relevant; and definition of terms if appropriate.

Body

The body of the report contains the research findings. The material in the body of a report can be organised in different ways, and the method selected will be determined by the purpose and the audience. Report material can be organised using similar methods of organisation to those used in oral presentations; that is, it can be organised chronologically; geographically or spatially; in terms of topics and subtopics; in a parallel order such as problem/solution, advantages/disadvantages, cause/effect; inductively (from the particular to the general); deductively (from the general to the particular); or in order of familiarity (usually starting with the most familiar and moving to the least familiar).

Whatever method is selected, it is important that a clear argument is developed and that readers can easily follow the logic. If this seems similar to the material in the section on essay writing, it is. Development of a logical argument is as important in a report as it is in an essay. The primary difference is that in an essay we need to formulate our own thesis statement, our viewpoint on the topic. In a report we need to formulate a short, simple and straightforward statement of report aim.

Analytical reports are commissioned if there is a problem, and their purpose is to present recommendations designed to solve the problem. In the case of Berryman Enterprises, for example, the problem is that the existing computer system is inadequate. The task facing the report writer, therefore, is to evaluate appropriate computer systems in terms of what Berryman Enterprises requires, particularly in terms of what are considered to be key needs. For example, how important is speed of response? Is ability to use particular software a major concern? The report writer needs to gather data, to analyse that data and, ultimately, to recommend the best replacement computer system.

The body of the report is where the data and analysis are set out. Headings and subheadings help the reader by:

* providing an overview of the structure of the argument and the logic;

* highlighting central ideas; and

* indicating a hierarchy of importance in terms of data and ideas.

Let us look at how material can be organised in a report in terms of Berryman Enterprises. The sample contents page shown in Figure 6.5 indicates that the material in the body of the report is organised in topics and subtopics, in this case the various computer systems being investigated.

This seems to be a satisfactory method of organising the material in the report. We have our main sections (the Unissa system, the Bettacomp system, etc.), which are divided into the subsections of capabilities and so on. However, let us think back to why the report was commissioned. Let us remember that this is a persuasive document. We need to persuade our reader to accept our recommendations, so we need to make it easy for our reader to see why our recommendations will solve the problem. What does Berryman Enterprises want from the report? Berryman Enterprises needs to know which computer system will be best for its purposes, so the report needs to make it as easy as possible for the reader to make the comparisons and to see why we are recommending one particular system over the others. Does the arrangement above do that, or could the material be organised in a way that would make it clearer to the reader why Bettacomp is the recommended system? Suppose we reorganise the material (see Figure 6.6). Does the reorganisation make it easier for our readers to understand how we arrived at our conclusions and, therefore, to accept those recommendations?

```
2.0    The Unissa System
       2.1    Capabilities and Special Features
       2.2    Reliability and Warranty
       2.3    Service
       2.4    Price

3.0    The Bettacomp System
       3.1    Capabilities and Special Features
       3.2    Reliability and Warranty
       3.3    Service
       3.4    Price

4.0    The Zweixa System
       4.1    Capabilities and Special Features
       4.2    Reliability and Warranty
       4.3    Service
       4.4    Price
```

FIGURE 6.5 Example of Contents Page Showing Organisation in Terms of Topics

```
2.0    Capabilities and Special Features
       2.1    Unissa
       2.2    Bettacomp
       2.3    Zweixa

3.0    Reliability and Warranty
       3.1    Unissa
       3.2    Bettacomp
       3.3    Zweixa

4.0    Service
       4.1    Unissa
       4.2    Bettacomp
       4.3    Zweixa

5.0    Price
       5.1    Unissa
       5.2    Bettacomp
       5.3    Zweixa
```

FIGURE 6.6 An Alternative Presentation of Topics

Conclusion(s)

There may be one or more conclusions that should follow logically from the body of the report and point to the recommendations. The conclusions summarise the report, restating the main points and drawing them together. However, the conclusion section does more than this for it is where interpretation of the data set out in the body of the report takes place. The conclusion should provide the analysis of what the facts mean, what their significance is and what their importance is in relation to the report purpose.

Recommendations

The conclusions follow logically from the analysis in the body of the report. The recommendations follow logically from the conclusions.

In many ways reports are similar to case studies. In each, a problem is presented that needs to be solved. The introduction, body and conclusion(s) form the problem-solving part of the report. The recommendations are the decision-making section.

Recommendations, which are usually numbered, are short, direct, action statements, which provide detail on what should be done, by whom, when, where and how. In the case of the Berryman Enterprises report, for example, there would probably be only one recommendation and that would be that Berryman Enterprises purchases and installs the Bettacomp system as soon as possible. However, sometimes a report can result in several recommendations. Make sure that each recommendation incorporates only one action or response. If, for example, we incorporate more than one action in a recommendation and our readers disagree with one of those actions, the entire recommendation may be rejected. Similarly, if some recommendations are likely to be more acceptable than others, it can be helpful to put the more acceptable recommendations first to establish a climate of acceptance before the less attractive recommendations are reached.

Bibliography

If we have used secondary sources as part of our research for the report, we need to identify these in a bibliography.

Appendices and glossary of terms

These sections are optional. Appendices contain information that is not essential to the report but that could be helpful for our readers. If our research was centred on a survey or questionnaire, for example, we could provide a copy of the questionnaire in an appendix for any reader who was interested.

INFORMAL REPORTS

Short or informal reports range from form reports such as accident reports and regular information reports such as progress reports and monthly sales figures to shorter versions of the analytical or problem-solving formal reports. In this chapter we deal only with the informal report as an analytical or problem-solving document. Analytical or problem-solving informal reports will normally either deal with a relatively simple and straightforward problem or may be an investigatory report written as a preliminary to a more detailed formal report.

Informal reports can be written in memo or letter form, depending on whether the report is going to someone within or outside the organisation. Even if the report is going to someone within the organisation, however, a short report can be, and indeed often is, a letter, especially if it deals with a matter of importance or is going to someone much higher in the organisation. The difference between memo and letter reports is found in the layout. The memo report is set out as a memo with the 'To', 'From', 'Date' and 'Subject' headings common to memos. The letter report is set out as a letter with the letterhead or return address, the date, inside address, salutation, complimentary close and signer's identification elements common to letters.

Introduction

Although we are dealing with an informal report many of the elements of the formal report are retained, albeit in a less formal way. The short report still needs an introduction, which will give the subject of the report, the authorisation, purpose and scope, as well as sources of information, but these are not identified by subheadings as is the case with a long report (see Figure 6.7). If the Berryman Enterprises report had been written as an informal report, for example, the introduction would still contain all the information set out in the Table of Contents in Figure 6.3 but this would be contained in the first few sentences or paragraphs of the letter or memo. Figure 6.7 shows a simple sample introduction.

While the sample introduction could provide more detail, you will see that it does contain the background (why the report was commissioned, in this case a computer system in need of replacement); the authorisation (from Mr Bryce); the aim (to recommend a replacement system); scope and limitations (Australian companies) and sources of data (technical literature and discussions with experts). Notice that there is no heading 'Introduction'. Informal reports can have headings but they will be headings that relate, except for the conclusions and recommendations, to content rather than to format. For example, in the Berryman Enterprises report there would be no heading 'Introduction' or 'Body'. There could be headings for 'Capabilities and Special Features' and subheadings for each system in line with the sample contents page in Figure 6.5. There would also be a heading for 'Conclusion(s) and for 'Recommendations'.

The letter report would end with the complimentary close and the signer's identification, as well as any enclosure notations and so on, if appropriate.

Computican Pty Ltd
GPO Box 769
SYDNEY NSW 2001

25 August 2001

Mr Alan Bryce
Senior Partner
Berryman Enterprises
GPO Box 301
SYDNEY NSW 2001

Dear Mr Bryce

We submit our report written in response to your request that we locate a computer system to replace your present system which is proving inadequate to deal with your rapidly expanding needs. For the purposes of ease of servicing, we restricted our investigation to Australian companies. Analysis of technical material and discussions with information technology experts in the accounting field led us to narrow our investigation to the three major companies who specialise in systems of the type you require.

FIGURE 6.7 Example of an Introduction to an Informal Report

Body, conclusion(s) and recommendations

The body of the report contains the data and analysis and, like the long report, can be organised chronologically, in terms of spatial relationships, parallel order, topic order, inductively or deductively. The conclusion follows logically from the body of the report. It provides the opportunity for a final interpretation of the data and analysis contained in the body of the report, as well as providing a summary and leading into the recommendations, which, as in the long report, are short, direct action statements detailing how the problem will be solved.

Report organisation

It may seem logical that any report should begin with the introduction, move through the body and finish with the conclusion(s) and recommendations. This is a useful method if it is possible that the receivers may disagree with the findings or if the conclusions can only be understood if the readers have worked their way through your analysis. However, the people for whom reports are written are usually busy people. This is why they often read the summary only and why they often prefer to have the conclusions and recommendations first in the report. The method selected will depend upon an analysis of the task and the receiver.

Graphics

Illustrations and graphics can add value to a report. Although not every report will need graphics (usually called 'figures'), graphics (line charts, bar charts, pie charts) as well as tables and graphs do allow us to display quantitative information in a way that enables the reader to access the information easily and directly. For example, graphs and tables are useful for illustrating quantitative relationships (comparison, contrast), while diagrams and maps are an effective means of showing spatial relationships. However, use graphics only if they will help you get your message across clearly. If you do use graphics they need to be integrated into the text, and we do this by referring to them in the report ('as you will see in Figure 1, below', for instance).

Editing and proofreading

This is a vital part of any report or essay writing. Poor editing, leaving spelling, punctuation and grammatical errors uncorrected, will undermine the credibility of your document and diminish the persuasiveness of your writing. Certainly use the spell and grammar checks on your computer but remember, as we noted in Chapter 4, on effective writing skills, that computer software is not all encompassing, nor is it infallible. The spell check, for example, will not read 'affect' as an error even if the correct word should be 'effect'. Also check that you are using Australian, not American spelling. As the writer of the report, it is your responsibility to ensure that no errors slip past, so proofreading is important. Every word should be checked, especially to ensure that there are no errors in the name, position or company of the person to whom the report is going. It is also necessary to check the mechanics. This is particularly important because it is so easy to add and delete text with computers. We, therefore, need to make sure that the page numbers in the contents page have not changed and that references to figures are accurate. For example, the figure that might have been below when the report was first typed could, by the time we have a finished product, be on the next page.

Editing means going through the report with the reader's eyes. Does the introduction fulfil all the functions required of it? In the body of the report is the logic clear; can your analysis be followed easily? Does the conclusion follow logically from the analysis in the body of the report?

Are the recommendations the logical outcome of the conclusions? Is the style appropriate? Do you need to change some of the words to make them less subjective, more impartial? Is there only one idea per sentence and paragraph? Does the text flow? Is there anything that could irritate the reader (repetitions, lack of flow between paragraphs, jargon)? Are the figures (your graphics) integrated into the text?

It is a good idea to leave your report or essay for a few days, or even a week, before re-reading it. This helps you pick up any errors in spelling, grammar or style, or any areas where you have not made your point as clearly as you had earlier thought.

Tone and style

Tone in both essays and reports should be formal. Slang, colloquial expressions, contractions ('can't' instead of 'cannot', for example) and informal constructions are out of place in these documents. Writer credibility is an important element in the success or otherwise of our essay or report, so we need to maintain an objective, rational and unbiased tone. Both essays and reports are normally written in the impersonal third person.

The report will be successful if our recommendations are implemented; that is, if our report is accepted by management and forms the basis of management decisions. This places much emphasis on our credibility. It is important, therefore, to avoid emotive language, **absolute terms** or anything that seems subjective. Reports are analytical, factual documents and our tone and style need to reflect that factual, objective perspective.

SUMMARY

This chapter has provided an overview of the distinguishing characteristics of essays and reports. Because of the centrality of the essay in academic assessments, and because many of the principles of essays apply equally to reports, more time has been spent on essays. Although reports and essays differ in terms of layout, the skills required to write a good essay are also the skills required to write a good report since both documents require analytical skills and the ability to construct a logical, sustained argument.

The first step is task analysis. In terms of the essay, this involves analysing the question and identifying the central problem or issue. In terms of the report, it involves formulating a concise aim. Both essays and reports will involve research, which can be both primary and secondary. It is important in secondary research to reference correctly the sources of any information, and the referencing style used will be determined by the demands of the faculty or organisation for which you are writing the essay or report. Since writer credibility is important in the eventual success or acceptance of any document, it is important in both essays and reports to maintain an objective, factual, unbiased tone. Emotive language and absolute terms should be avoided.

Finally, the document should be rigorously edited and proofread. Poor editing or proofreading can be as damaging to writer credibility as a subjective tone.

In academic and professional contexts, essays and reports will often be required to be presented orally, as well as in writing. Conference, seminar and tutorial papers, for example, are essays. Reports may often be presented orally to senior management. So, in the next chapter, we will deal with presenting our ideas, findings and messages orally.

KEY POINTS

- Essays and reports differ in terms of layout. They also differ in that essays require analysis of a topic or question while reports require finding solutions to problems but both require the skills of analysis and development of logical, sustained arguments.

- Formulating a clear thesis statement is integral to the development of an argument within an essay.
- Formulation of a clear statement of aim is integral to the successful solution of the problem(s) being analysed in a report.
- Both essays and reports require research and care must be taken that sources are properly documented.
- Both essays and reports have an introduction, body and conclusion. The essay finishes with the conclusion but in the report the conclusion is followed by the recommendations, which are the real focus or purpose of the report.
- Essays will normally be written in continuous prose but the various sections of the report will be divided by headings and subheadings.
- Writer credibility is important for the success of both essays and reports, so a factual, unbiased, objective tone and effective editing and proofreading are important.

REVIEW QUESTIONS

1. What are the characteristics of effective academic writing?
2. What task analysis is involved before writing an essay?
3. Essays normally require the development of a logical argument. How can you develop a logical argument in essays?
4. Why is it important to document our reference sources?
5. What task analysis is involved before writing a report?
6. What purposes are served by the transmittal document?
7. What considerations should be kept in mind when determining the organisation of the material in a report?

EXERCISES

1. Identify the task and key words in the following essay topics. What is the central issue or problem at the core of each topic?

    - External threats are often used to justify internal restrictions. Analyse the relationship between the threat of terrorism and civil liberties with particular reference to Australia.
    - There is a popular perception that young people drink, drive and have accidents. How important is alcohol as a contributory factor in fatal road accidents among young people?
    - Scientists have been talking of the effects of global warming for years but, despite international conferences and conventions, addressing the problem seems to be constantly 'put in the too hard basket'. Examine the relationship between the environment and capitalism with reference to the continuing problem of global warming.

2. Select one of your assignment topics and write an essay plan, including references and linking words/phrases. How clear does your argument seem? Is there anything that should be added or deleted? Do you have enough linking words/phrases to enable your reader to follow your logic easily?

3. Select a piece of academic writing in your discipline and analyse how the writer has constructed a logical and cohesive argument. How has the writer provided logical progression and smooth transitions between and within paragraphs? How well do the introduction and conclusion work in terms of the argument?

4. Look at your work space, either the area at work or your study at home. Assume that someone has asked you to write a report on how efficiently your space functions and what can be done to improve its efficiency. What would be the main headings and subheadings in the body of your report? What would be the best organisation of those headings and subheadings?

5. Write a short informational report on what happened on your way to work or college.

BIBLIOGRAPHY

Anderson, J. and Poole, M. 2001, *Assignment and Thesis Writing,* 4th ed., John Wiley & Sons, Milton.

Bate, D. and Sharpe, P. 1996, *Writer's Handbook for University Students,* Harcourt, Brace and Company, Sydney.

Browne, M. and Keeley, S. 2001, *Anthropology on the Internet: Evaluating Online Resources,* Prentice Hall, Englewood Cliffs.

Burdess, N. 1998, *Handbook of Student Skills,* 2nd ed., Prentice Hall, Sydney.

Burnham, S. 1994, *For Writers Only,* Ballantine Books, New York.

Clanchy, J. and Ballard, B. 1997, *Essay Writing for Students,* 3rd ed., Longman, Sydney.

Flower, L. 1989, *Problem-Solving Strategies for Writing,* 3rd ed., Harcourt, Brace and Jovanovich, Orlando, Florida.

Hay, I., Bochner, D. and Dungey, C. 1997, *Making the Grade: A Guide to Successful Communication and Study,* Oxford University Press, Melbourne.

Kogen, M. 1989, *Writing in the Business Professions,* National Council of Teachers of English and the Association for Business Communication, Urbana.

Locke, T. 1996, *English Manual: A Guide to Language and Writing,* Macmillan Education Australia, Melbourne.

Mahony, D. 2004, *Studying and Writing Effectively,* QUT Brisbane.

Morenberg, M. 1991, *Doing Grammar,* Oxford University Press, Oxford.

Palmer, R. 1992, *Write in Style: Guide to Good English,* Spon, London.

Petelin, R. and Durham, M. 1996, *The Professional Writing Guide: Writing Well and Knowing Why,* Pitman, Melbourne.

Pirie, D. 2002, *How to Write Critical Essays,* Routledge, London and New York.

Severin, W.J. and Tankard, J.W. 1992, *Communication Theories: Origins, Methods, and Uses in the Mass Media,* 3rd ed., Longman, New York.

Turabian, K.L. 1982, *A Manual for Writers of Research Papers, Theses, and Dissertations,* Heinemann, London.

Part Three

Oral Communication

Oral presentations/speeches

CHAPTER 7

Upon completing this chapter you should be able to:
- understand public speaking as a transactive process;
- recognise the different types of oral presentations and their requirements;
- demonstrate an awareness of the importance of pre-speech preparation and post-speech appraisal;
- show the capacity to analyse both task and audience to ensure an effective presentation;
- understand the ways in which oral presentations can be organised and presented; and
- realise the importance of audio-visual aids in reinforcing the oral message.

The ability to make effective oral presentations, to speak confidently in public, is an increasingly important professional skill. This chapter will, therefore, be of use not only in terms of delivering seminar papers when you are students but, more importantly, in your professional lives, especially as you begin to move up the promotion ladder.

Before we look at oral communication, making speeches or taking part in interviews, it is useful to consider the advantages and disadvantages of oral and written communication. Why do we choose to encode our message in oral form, or why do we choose to write a letter? Is it just a matter of how we happen to feel at the time, or are there reasons why one form of communication is better than another in different situations?

Advantages of written communication

Written communication:

* gives greater control over the final message. In oral communication, conversations can take different directions from those we had planned or anticipated and we can find our message being diverted or 'derailed'. We also do not have time to consider, to choose exactly the right word and so on in the flux and exchange of conversation;

* enables greater accuracy. Because we can take time to draft and redraft a document as often as we wish, or as often as the constraints of time and cost allow, we can ensure that our written communication is as precise and exact as we can make it;

* provides a cheap method of conveying information to many people with no change or distortion in the original message. Company newsletters, global emails, even newspapers and magazines reach many people with the same message simultaneously;

* provides a permanent record. It can be useful, for example, to confirm discussions in writing. This enables both parties to check the accuracy of the record and it can be referred to later if there is any dispute or uncertainty about what happened or what was decided;

* can be re-read and referred to as often as the reader requires. For these reasons written communication is better than oral communication for the transmission of complex or technical material. How much harder would it be for you to understand, say, the material in your biology or engineering text, in your literary theory text or your anthropology text if you were not able to stop, think, re-read, go back over earlier sections and so on—if, in fact, the information came to you once only and at the speed of the speaker?

* can be written at the writer's convenience and can be accessed and read at the reader's convenience.

Disadvantages of written communication

Written communication:

* is slow. It takes the sender longer to encode and it takes longer to transmit. Even email is not as instantaneous as face-to-face or telephone conversations;

* can seem cold and formal. It lacks the spontaneity and vitality of oral communication;

* can be ignored. We have no way to ensure that our letter or memo is read. We can, of course, track email messages but we can only find out whether or not our email has been opened. We cannot check if it has been read and this is even more the case with 'snail mail' or hard copy material;
* involves delayed feedback which puts greater emphasis on the need for good task and audience analysis. In conversation we can monitor the nonverbal feedback and adapt our message accordingly, perhaps by moderating our message, by providing additional detail, by asking questions to check for accuracy of decoding and so on. These feedback cues are not available in written communication so our message needs to be as exact and tailored to the task and audience as possible.

Advantages of oral communication

Oral communication:

* has a spontaneity and immediacy that can increase the persuasiveness of messages;
* allows immediate feedback, enabling the message to be adapted for more accurate transmission and enabling both sender and receiver to check for accuracy;
* is a **transactive process** which allows for meaning to be negotiated between the communicating parties;
* involves nonverbal communication—kinesics, proxemics, paralinguistics—which add to the overall message;
* is more personal than written communication.

Disadvantages of oral communication

Many of the advantages of oral communication can also be disadvantages.

* The amount and complexity of material that can be successfully assimilated by an audience is limited, so if we have much material to cover, or the material is complex or highly technical, our message may be more successful if we choose a written medium such as a report or a company newsletter.
* Presenting material orally allows for more audience bias. The appearance, mannerisms, dress or accent of a speaker make a more powerful impression than written words and therefore can influence an audience either positively or negatively.
* Spontaneity and immediacy can mean that a thoughtless or inappropriate remark can be made.
* Lack of time for consideration can mean that we find ourselves responding in ill-considered ways; giving consent or agreement that we later regret, for example.
* Nonverbal cues can undermine the verbal message.
* Variability of perception means that if oral messages are passed on they will be distorted and changed.

Oral presentations

Presenting our material in the form of an oral presentation or speech does have advantages, however. The most important advantage of presenting material orally is the transactive nature of any face-to-face communication; the fact that while we are sending our message we are also receiving audience feedback. This enables us to adapt our presentation to increase our chances of success. A speech or oral presentation enables us simultaneously to reach audiences ranging from small groups to mass audiences in a way that permits immediate feedback and provides opportunities for our listeners to ask questions, propose alternative views, provide suggestions or generally interact personally.

One of the most important and central aspects of public speaking is that every oral presentation is a transactive process. There is a tendency to think of making a speech or oral presentation as akin to shooting an arrow (the speech) at a passive target (the audience); to think of speaking in public as a one-way process. If this were so there would be nothing to be gained by presenting our material in the form of a speech. Audiences, however, are not passive targets, but are involved in giving feedback throughout any presentation. It is this transactive nature of an oral presentation that provides scope for the flexibility and spontaneity that are strengths of presenting material orally. Consciously or unconsciously, speaker and audience are involved in a continuously transactive process.

Good speakers are aware of audience reaction and monitor audience feedback *all* the time. Effective speakers are flexible and use audience reactions to guide them in their presentations. They do not consider a speech to be cast in concrete, something that cannot be changed, but use audience feedback to ensure their presentations are effective. For example, if some members of the audience look puzzled, good presenters go back over the material that the audience seemed to find difficult, perhaps using further illustrations, explaining more fully, maybe even asking questions. The good presenter notices if the audience seems to be bored or irritated, interested or restless, and adapts the presentation accordingly. One of the most important things to realise about speaking in public is the need to be aware of, and responsive to, the audience at all times. This will help to make the presentation successful and effective.

Types of speeches

Speeches range from short one- or two-minute speeches which introduce major speakers or move votes of thanks to the presentation of conference papers that may be 40 or 50 minutes in duration with a question time at the end.

Speeches of introduction and votes of thanks

These are the most common short speeches. They should be simple speeches to make and, most importantly, they should be short. However, even with these short speeches it is important to keep our purpose in the forefront of our mind.

SPEECHES OF INTRODUCTION

The speech of introduction serves three purposes.

1. At a basic level it provides time for the audience to settle down so that the main speaker can have full audience attention from the start of the speech.

2   It gets the attention of the audience and announces the speaker's topic.

3   Most importantly, it introduces the speaker, giving the speaker's experience and educational background, credentials, qualifications—in other words, why the speaker has been asked to speak on the subject.

Points to remember

* If we are making a speech of introduction it is important to obtain all the facts necessary for the introduction (including how to pronounce the speaker's name) before making the speech.

* The primary purpose of a speech of introduction is to introduce the speaker, not to preview the speech itself.

* A speech of introduction is short—one or two minutes is ample.

VOTES OF THANKS

Like the speech of introduction this is a short speech. Its purpose is quite simply to thank the speaker for taking the time and effort to speak to the group.

Points to remember

* Do not summarise the speech. The speaker should have done this in the conclusion.

* Be brief; one minute should be ample.

Extended presentations

Extended speeches range from presenting research findings to senior management to addressing the shopfloor staff on company policy; from motivational speeches to salespeople to presenting papers at conferences or seminars; from addressing assembled students/parents to after-dinner speeches; in fact, any occasion when we have to 'hold the floor' for anything from five minutes to the best part of an hour.

BEFORE THE SPEECH

Speech preparation

The success of any presentation depends to a large extent on pre-speech preparation. In fact, the most important elements in success as a presenter concern what is done before the speech, rather than what happens during the speech.

Pre-speech analysis

Pre-speech analysis can be thought of as market research. This is where we analyse our task, our audience, the occasion and the environment.

The task

In analysing our task we need to bear in mind both our general and specific purposes. The general purpose is broadly what we intend the speech to do. Do we want to inform, persuade/motivate or simply entertain? Informational presentations (lectures, conferences, seminar presentations, presentation of research findings, dissemination of information among colleagues or subordinates) aim to convey information as clearly and accurately as possible. Persuasive/motivational presentations (sales presentations, political speeches) aim to get the audience to accept certain viewpoints, or to act in certain ways. Entertaining speeches (after-dinner speeches often fall into this category) aim simply to entertain. In reality no presentation is wholly informational, or persuasive or entertaining. Presentations are usually a mixture of all three elements, but one purpose will predominate.

The specific purpose is exactly what we intend our presentation to achieve—why, in fact, we are making a presentation at all. Our general purpose may be to inform, but our specific purpose may be to demonstrate how changes to mailing procedures can halve staff time.

The specific purpose must be just that—specific. We need to refine the specific purpose down to one short, simple, straightforward sentence which can then be kept in the forefront of our minds through all the stages of our speech preparation.

The audience

The more we know about our audience, the more closely we will be able to target our speech and the greater the chance we will have of achieving our objective—an effective presentation. According to Bittner (1988) audience analysis can be broken down into demographic and psychographic characteristics. Demographic characteristics are such elements as: age, gender, socioeconomic background, level of education and religious and ethnic affiliations. The following are possible demographic questions:

* What is the composition of the audience in terms of age and sex? Are we addressing a group of senior citizens, or the graduating group from a girls-only school?
* What is the educational level of the audience?
* What is the audience level of subject knowledge?
* What is the socio-economic mix?

Psychographic characteristics are concerned with audience perceptions, opinions, values, attitudes, biases or prejudices, beliefs and feelings. For example, if we were going to talk on a proposed industrial development to a group of environmental activists we would need to take this into account in the way we structured our message.

It is important that any presentation is easily understood by the entire audience. This can sometimes be difficult. Even conferences nowadays are often multi-disciplinary, so it may not be possible to assume that all of our audience are experts in the area. Sometimes it is easy to find out about an audience. This is particularly so if we are addressing people within our own organisation or presenting a conference paper, but sometimes an audience may be mixed and difficult to analyse. Nevertheless, it is important to find out as much about the audience as possible before we begin writing the speech.

The occasion

The occasion, like the audience, should influence the speech. The primary question is, how formal or informal is the occasion? Let us put this into context. Imagine a speech of congratulation to a winning football team during the end-of-season ball and a speech of acceptance for an academic award. Would both speeches be equally informal or equally formal?

The environment

This is of more concern in terms of the actual delivery of the speech rather than the writing of it, but we will deal with it here.

* How large is the room? Will we need a microphone?
* What shape is the room? Some rooms are easier to speak in than others. For example, a long, narrow room is usually a more difficult venue than a wider, shallower room.

* What facilities are available? Most rooms contain a lectern and overhead projector as standard equipment, but what other facilities are available?
* How many power points are there and where are they positioned?
* Can the room be dimmed if we want to show slides or a video?
* Is there a central console from which we can control lights, doors and so on or will we have to move to the side of the room to switch off the lights?
* What type of screen is there? If it is a flat screen there could be sightline problems. Screens angled from the ceiling are better.
* Can the furniture be rearranged easily?

RESEARCHING THE SPEECH

When we have defined our purpose we are ready to gather the material for the speech. Material for our presentation can be primary and/or secondary. Wherever we gather our material (and we will probably use a mix of primary and secondary material) our data should be reliable, credible, factual and referenced.

A problem with many speeches is that the speaker tries to cover too much content. Listening to speeches and oral presentations requires considerable sustained concentration. We will only get our points across effectively if we limit the main points to a maximum of six in a speech lasting an hour. The bulk of any speech should consist of material supporting the main points being made. Supporting material includes:

description	explanation	comparison	contrast
examples	illustrations	anecdotes	definitions
statistics	testimony	quotations	repetition
restatement	audio-visual aids		

This list could be expanded even more but the elements noted above will give some idea of how major points in a presentation can be supported.

It is important that supporting material advances our purpose. An anecdote, for example, is only useful if it in some way underlines the point being made. If it does not support the point it will actually be a negative influence in the speech, distracting audience attention away from the point we are trying to make.

Writing the speech

Every presentation has three major parts: the introduction, the body and the conclusion. In terms of importance, the introduction and conclusion rank above the body of the speech, even though our message is contained in the body.

THE INTRODUCTION

The introduction is important because it is the first impression the audience gets of us and the speech. It establishes our rapport with the audience.

The introduction should:

* state the purpose (the exception here is the persuasive/motivational speech where the real purpose may not be apparent until the end of the speech);

* orient the audience to our topic; and
* provide an overview of the speech (how long we intend to speak, the areas we intend to cover, what audio-visuals we will be using, whether and when we will accept questions).

Points to remember

* Do not apologise. Some speakers begin with an appeal to pity. ('This is the first time I have done something like this.')
* Do not feel a speech has to begin with a joke. Using humour can be an effective way of 'breaking the ice' and relaxing both yourself and your audience; but if you are not very good at telling jokes it is better to leave the humorous opening to someone else. If you do use humour, the joke must be relevant to the topic and purpose of the presentation.

A presentation can begin with a rhetorical question, with some startling statistics, with an anecdote or with audio-visuals. In fact, speeches can begin in any way that will gain audience attention and be relevant to the topic and purpose.

THE CONCLUSION

The conclusion is important because it is the last impression the audience has of us and our presentation.

* The conclusion provides a summary of the speech. It is not the place to introduce new material but it does allow us to restate the main points of our presentation. This is particularly important in informational speeches.
* In a motivational speech the conclusion is the last chance to push the audience in the desired direction.
* The conclusion should provide closure; in other words it should tell the audience that the speech has ended. This is often the most neglected part of oral presentations. Speakers tend either to tell their audience several times that they are finishing—'Finally . . .', 'In conclusion . . .', 'To sum up . . .'—or they give audiences no indication that they have finished, other than gathering up their papers and sitting down.

Finish conclusively, unusually and/or interestingly. Try to avoid thanking the audience for listening. This has become so hackneyed that it is virtually meaningless. The devices listed as possible speech openings can also function to end a speech. Rhetorical questions, audio-visual aids and anecdotes can all provide effective closures.

Point to remember

* Finish positively. The conclusion is not the place for doubts or reservations.

THE BODY

The body of a speech is the message, the data, the facts, the research. This section should be arranged so that it is as clear and accessible as possible for the audience. How easily our audience can follow our presentation is largely determined by how well the body of the speech is organised. One point should lead smoothly and logically to the next.

Material in the body of the speech can be arranged in different ways, and the purpose and topic will to some extent determine which method is selected. We will see that most of the basic ways of organising presentations are the ones suggested for organising reports. They are: chronological order, geographical/spatial order, topical order and parallel order. We can also use the motivated sequence, or AIDA (see Chapter 5 on letters, memos and email) formula, for persuasive or motivational presentations. Let us look at these different organisational methods in relation to, for example, a presentation about a local preschool.

Chronological order

Chronological order would be suitable for a presentation tracing the history of the preschool. Our speech outline might look like this:

Before the preschool:

- community need;
- community action;
- planning for the preschool.

The early years:

- initial enrolments;
- foundation staff;
- early curriculum.

Expansion of the preschool, etc.

Geographical/spatial order

A speech dealing with a state-wide preschool organisation could be organised in terms of geographical/spatial order:

- local preschool organisations;
- area preschool associations;
- state-wide preschool associations, etc.

Topic order

Topic order lends itself to almost any type of speech. If we were talking about the importance of the preschool experience for children we could organise our speech in terms of topics and subtopics.

Topic: preschools and childhood socialisation

Subtopics:
- ownership and sharing;
- awareness of others;
- individual rights, etc.

Parallel order

Parallel order could be used to organise a presentation designed to solve a particular problem. Perhaps we intend to talk about government cuts to preschool funding. The problem is reduced funds; the solution is what can be done about it.

Problem: Reduced government funding

- expected shortfall;
- implications.

Solutions:
- raise fees;
- reduce staff;
- reduce services, etc.

Motivated sequence

The motivated sequence would be the one we would choose if our purpose was to sell the idea of the preschool experience to prospective parents who would (hopefully) enrol their children in the preschool.

The attention step could be a thought-provoking question or statement; for example, 'Did you know that, on average, children who attend preschools between the ages of three and five scholastically outperform children with no preschool experience?'

The interest step aims to generate interest. This is where we could produce statistics or illustrations to support our attention-getting question.

The desire step aims to turn interest into desire. The appeal in this section can be to logic or to the emotions (usually a mix of the two). In terms of our speech, appeals could be made to the future careers of the children or to the responsibilities of parents to give children the best start in life.

The action step is the real purpose of the presentation, what the speaker wants the listeners to do—in this case to enrol children in the preschool.

Whichever method of organisation is selected, the material needs to flow logically so that the audience can easily follow the argument. The introduction helps here because it should already have given our audience an overview of the speech, a sort of route map. However, clear, smooth transitions from point to point using linking words and phrases are still necessary to lead the audience through the logic. Using headings and subheadings on an overhead projector is one way to help the audience to follow the argument.

Audio-visual aids

Audio-visual aids are an important part of any presentation. Audio-visuals can be overhead transparencies, video clips, films, slides, flipcharts, posters, whiteboards, computer-generated images or models—just about anything that is appropriate and relevant to the speech topic and purpose.

Audio-visual aids fulfil three primary purposes:

1. They are an effective way to reinforce/illustrate the points being made. We have probably heard the adage 'a picture is worth a thousand words' and this is particularly true of audio-visual aids in oral presentations.
2. They provide interest for the audience. Being a member of an audience is not easy. Audio-visual aids provide variety and allow the message to be received through the sense of sight as well as hearing.
3. They enable the speaker to deal with nervous energy by providing something physical to do. They can help the speaker to feel less exposed by taking audience attention away from an exclusive focus on the speaker.

IMPORTANT CONSIDERATIONS

* Only use audio-visual aids that will support and reinforce the presentation. No matter how good an overhead transparency or PowerPoint slide is, if it does not help the presentation it should not be used. Nothing in a presentation is neutral. If it does not support the presentation it will detract from it. Part of the presenter's task is to assess if an audio-visual aid adds to, or detracts from, a presentation. Use only audio-visual aids that support the speech.
* All audio-visuals must be integrated into the speech.
* Audio-visuals need to be simple. An audience should be able to read and understand any audio-visual in five seconds or less.
* All audio-visuals must be legible. Avoid handwriting overhead transparencies, unless there is a particular reason for using handwriting.
* Letter height should be no less than 0.5–1 cm.
* Keep audio-visuals uncluttered. Detail should be kept to a minimum. Audio-visuals should concentrate audience attention on the main points only.
* Limit the media. No more than two media should be used in a 30–40 minute presentation. Perhaps we might use overheads and PowerPoint slides, or a video clip and overheads.
* Match your media to group size. For example, posters or charts can work well with a small group but are too small to be of real use with a larger group.
* Be careful of sightlines. This applies both to whether the projector comes between some of the audience and the screen and to your own use of the media.
* Only use audio-visuals that are of good quality.
* Overhead transparencies and, increasingly, PowerPoint slides are perhaps the most used audio-visuals in oral presentations and they are more effective if they are used well. Use of a transparency with a series of items can be enhanced by uncovering only the item to which reference is being made. We can use something as simple as a sheet of paper to do this, but some speakers use a sheet with a cutout which can be moved down the transparency. PowerPoint slides enable us to bring each item up on the screen as we refer to it.
* If pointing to any sections of an overhead transparency use a pointer (a knitting needle works well). Even better is a laser pointer that enables us to point to items on the screen without moving from the lectern.
* Avoid the temptation to talk to the screen. It is the audience that we need to address all the time.

Preparation and practice

Preparation and practice form the basis of a successful oral presentation.

Preparation

Apart from researching and writing the speech, pre-speech preparation involves:

* preparing our notes or speech outline;

* being completely familiar with the notes or outline;
* getting the mechanics right, such as checking equipment and, very importantly, knowing how to operate the equipment. For example, do we know where the on/off switch is on the overhead projector? Is there a spare overhead projector bulb and do we know how to replace the bulb if it blows during a presentation?

Practice

Practise thoroughly, but most importantly practise the speech as it will be delivered. Do not go back to the beginning of your presentation if you lose your way or forget something. You will not be able to do this when you are in front of an audience. In fact, one of the things that separates effective presenters from novices is the ability to cope with 'glitches'. We are all human. Audiences do not expect machine-like efficiency and a 'glitch' can often be turned into increased rapport with an audience by the way it is handled. For example, if you inadvertently put an overhead transparency on back to front, make a joke of it. 'Now that is just to see if you are all still awake—at least that's my story and I am sticking to it.' If possible, it is a good idea to practise the speech at least once in the actual venue to give you a feel for the space in which you will be presenting.

Gain experience

Public speaking is like any other activity—the more we do it the better we become. So take every opportunity to speak in public. It really does get easier as you go on.

Delivering the speech

There are basically three methods of delivering a speech: reading it, memorising it and extemporaneous delivery.

Reading the speech

If the exact wording of the speech is important, for example a joint communiqué from two governments, a speech can be read. However, let us go back to the point made at the start of this chapter—that an oral presentation is a transactive process. This means that most of the time speeches should definitely not be read. If we read our speech we cannot monitor our audience. In Chapter 12, 'Nonverbal communication', the point is made that eye contact is our primary means of compensating for distances when we are communicating. Making and maintaining eye contact with our audience is central to achieving rapport. However, reading a speech virtually eliminates our capacity to make and maintain eye contact. Because we are afraid of losing our place we will not take our eyes from our speech. If we are reading, our voice is going down to the lectern not out to our listeners. We might just as well print copies of the speech and save everyone's time by sending it to them in the mail instead of having them sitting listening to us.

Not only will we have no real contact with our audience, so that we will be unable to respond to audience needs, but the speech will lack spontaneity. Written and spoken language are different. Written language is grammatical, formal and polysyllabic. Spoken language is informal, colloquial and often uses incomplete sentences—but it is that very informality and lack of grammatical correctness that gives it spontaneity and naturalness.

Why are we giving an oral presentation at all? Because we want the interaction, the spontaneity that speech rather than writing affords. So avoid reading your speeches.

Memorising the speech

So what about memorising the speech? There are problem areas with memorising speeches. First, there is always the danger that we will forget part of the speech and probably 'freeze', desperately trying to remember the forgotten words. Second, a memorised speech suffers from the same lack of flexibility and spontaneity evident in the read speech. The vocabulary and sentence structures will be of the written rather than the spoken form. And, most importantly, we will be unable to adapt our presentation to meet the needs of the audience as reflected in feedback.

Extemporaneous delivery

This leaves delivering our speech **extempore**. This does not mean an impromptu, or unprepared, speech. Write the speech, then reduce it to its essence. This means reducing it not to complete sentences but to key words or phrases, perhaps adding quotations or statistics that need to be delivered accurately. Put the notes on speech cards and/or a speech outline.

SPEECH CARDS

Speech cards are usually about the size of small envelopes. It is important that we can find our place easily so use a new card for each idea. Audio-visuals can be indicated on the cards and it is helpful to indicate these in a different colour as well as the points we are going to make. Be sure to number the cards and attach them at the top left-hand corner with a split ring or ribbon or whatever is easiest to use. Whatever method is used to attach the cards, it is a good idea to check in advance that they will turn easily and lie flat on the lectern.

SPEECH OUTLINE

A speech outline is like a plan or route map of the speech. It helps to keep the speech as a whole before us. Again, it is helpful to use lots of white space so that we can instantly find what we need. Indicate audio-visuals, again preferably in a different colour. Ensure the pages are numbered. If using a speech outline it is often better not to attach the sheets together, as separate sheets are easier to turn over and they will lie flatter on the lectern, but experiment to find what works best for you.

One method to help with anxieties about forgetting what to say is to exploit audio-visuals. For example, almost all the points we are going to make in our speech can be put on overhead transparencies or PowerPoint slides.

The speech itself

* Speech dynamics—pitch, speed and volume—are the tools we use to bring the words to life for the audience. Vary pitch, volume and speed. Use pauses. You do not have to speak every second. Pauses act like rests in music, highlighting or emphasising points and providing variety.

* Speak comfortably. If you have a very quiet voice it is better to use a microphone than to strain to be heard at the back of the hall.

* Speak slowly. A rough rule of thumb is that the larger the venue the slower we should speak, within reason. Unfortunately, nerves often tend to make people speak faster so take care with the rate of delivery, and remember, it should be slower than normal speech.

- Be natural. If you have an accent do not try to change it. It is part of what makes you unique and part of what will make your presentation unique.

- Keep delivery appropriate both to the topic and audience, and that includes nonverbal elements such as clothes, posture and gestures.

- Use your delivery to reinforce the message.

Speech nerves

If it is any consolation, feeling anxious about speaking in public is not unusual. Everyone, even professional presenters and public speakers, feels nervous and apprehensive about speaking in public. Unfortunately there is no magic pill for stage fright or pre-presentation nerves. Using deep breathing, relaxation, desensitisation, meditation, visualisation or anything that helps to calm our nerves can be of assistance, but there are a few general strategies.

- Put your apprehension into perspective. How large a part of your life, even your working life, does the presentation represent—a hundredth, a thousandth? Whatever the proportion it is only a small part of your professional life. Certainly it is a high-profile part and you want to make an effective presentation but speaking in public is not your whole profession.

- Be realistic in your expectations. Presenters on television or on the radio are good speakers. They should be; it is their primary role. It is only a small part of most professional roles, so try not to judge your performance by the yardstick of professional presenters.

- Remember that the audience consists of people just like you.

- Remember, too, that the audience wants you to succeed. If you have ever sat through an amateur dramatic performance when one of the cast has forgotten the next lines you will know how embarrassing it is for the audience and how the audience wills the actor to remember the words. Your audience has come to listen to you because they want to know what you are going to say.

- The audience cannot see the butterflies in the stomach, the sweaty palms or the shaking knees. The audience will accept you as you present. You might be surprised at how confident and in control you can seem, even though you may be feeling nervous.

Seminar presentations

Much of what has been said earlier about oral presentations applies equally to seminar presentations. However, as students are increasingly expected to present seminar papers and, indeed, are often assessed on such presentations, it is appropriate to say something specifically about presenting material orally in seminars. The terms 'seminar' and 'tutorial' are often used interchangeably. However, we can think of tutorials, which are central to teaching and learning at university, as based on a free and open exchange of information, ideas and perspectives, often centred around previously distributed questions; while seminars are occasions for the presentation of one or more papers with subsequent discussion.

Let us look at seminar presentations specifically. First, the seminar paper on which the presentation is based will usually take the form of an essay, often on a set topic, which will involve the presenter in all the task and audience analysis, research and writing involved in a normal essay.

Often this seminar paper will form part of the formal assessment of a course and will be marked in much the same way as an essay is marked.

Once we have our seminar paper, however, we need to adapt it for presenting orally. We need to do more than simply read the paper. So, how can we most effectively convey the 'gist' of our paper to our audience?

* First, analyse the seminar paper. What is the thesis or main idea which the paper sets out to prove? It is vital that we get this idea across clearly to our audience.

* Second, what are the principal supporting ideas, that is, what points do we make to prove our thesis? In a normal seminar presentation (even a conference presentation) there should not be too many supporting points. Remember audiences cannot cope effectively with too much density of content. So we need to determine which points are necessary to support our main idea and ignore less important or less central points.

* Third, what evidence do we consider essential to validate the points we are putting forward?

* Fourth, what audio-visuals will best support or illustrate our points?

This is what we present to our seminar group—not our entire paper but this distilled essence of our research.

Discussion

We will not spend too much time on discussion techniques as these will be dealt with in Chapter 14, on group communication, but it is appropriate to make some mention of both discussion leading and discussion participation because discussion is so central to work at university. As mentioned earlier, tutorials are based on discussion but that does not mean simply turning up for the tutorial and having a general conversation. Discussion in tutorials needs to be based on preparation (thinking about the subject or questions for discussion and pre-reading relevant material) and must be focused on the subject or question under discussion. In terms of seminars, discussion needs to focus on the paper that has been presented and the issues that have been raised in the paper.

Seminar participation

If we are part of the audience at a seminar presentation we have certain responsibilities. These include giving appropriate feedback. Remember the transactive nature of any oral presentation? We need to look interested. Very importantly we need to pay attention and to listen actively. This means making a note of anything particularly interesting or controversial, especially anything we want to raise in the post-presentation discussion. We should think about the issues in the paper and our own responses to those issues because a very important part of seminars is the discussion that takes place after the paper has been presented. We need to be prepared to contribute our own perspective on the topic, to ask questions about content in the paper and so on. Most importantly, we should be constructive in any comments we make on the paper.

Academic scholarship relies on research which is shared through published articles and books but also through material presented at conferences. Indeed, the exchange of information, ideas and perspectives is central to conference presentations. Our seminar presentation is like a conference presentation. We are sharing the results of our research with our peers, our fellow students, with, hopefully, a fruitful exchange of ideas after the presentation.

Discussion leading

Often it will be the tutor or lecturer who will lead the post-presentation discussion but it may be the presenter of the paper who is expected to lead discussion. So, if you are to lead discussion what should you do? Often discussion flows well once it is started but simply asking if anyone has any questions can lead to a prolonged silence. So it is always a good idea to be prepared with one or two questions, perhaps ready on an overhead transparency or PowerPoint slide, to start discussion.

'Go with the flow' but keep the group focused on the topic so that the discussion remains relevant. It is important to allow discussion to flow freely. It is also important not to direct discussion along the trajectory of our own perspective. We need to be open minded. There is often more than one valid viewpoint on a topic and we need to be receptive to other perspectives. Remember, the free exchange of ideas and information is central to academic work and differing perspectives can generate interesting insights. However, it is also important that discussion does remain focused on the topic so we need to be aware of where the discussion is going at all times.

It is also important to maintain objectivity and this applies whether we are leading or participating in discussion. Academic discussion is the place for reasoned, rational debate, not for emotional outbursts, so keep discussion objective and factual.

Finally it may be useful to mention briefly the two major types of questions. These will be dealt with in more detail in Chapter 8, 'Interviews', so we will just touch on them here. The two major types of questions are open and closed. For the purposes of discussion open questions, questions which allow considerable leeway in terms of the answer, are preferable to closed questions. Closed questions, which are good for eliciting factual information, usually require short, often only one word answers, and, as the name implies, tend to close that section of discussion whereas open questions can open up the discussion.

After the speech

Every presentation should be a learning experience, enabling us to improve our performance. Post-speech appraisal can be broken down into as many detailed areas as desired but there are seven basic areas that should be reviewed: preparation, introduction, body, conclusion, audio-visuals, delivery and the speech overall.

PREPARATION

* Were you happy with your pre-speech preparation?
* Were there any areas that could be improved (perhaps your notes needed to be larger, or you needed to do more work on timing the speech)?

INTRODUCTION

* How well did the introduction work?
* Did you get the attention of the audience at the start?
* How well did you make the connection between your topic and the audience? Remember, the more closely the presentation is tailored to the audience the more effective it will be.
* Did you tell the audience all they needed to know?

BODY

* Did the body of the speech work?
* Was the material organised in the most effective way?
* Were there too many points?
* Was there enough supporting material?
* How effective was the supporting material?

CONCLUSION

* Did the conclusion provide a satisfactory summary?
* Did it succeed in convincing the audience?
* Did it provide closure?
* What final impression do you think the conclusion left with the audience?

AUDIO-VISUALS

* Were the audio-visuals effective?
* Could they be improved?
* How well were they integrated into the speech?
* How relevant were they?
* Did they add to, or detract from, the message?

DELIVERY

* How do you feel about your delivery?
* Did you establish and maintain eye contact?
* Was your delivery spontaneous and natural?
* Did you have good rapport with your audience?
* Did you avoid those irritating speech mannerisms such as 'uhm', 'you know', 'sort of'?
* Did you make use of the full range of vocal possibilities in terms of speed, volume, pitch and effective pauses?

THE SPEECH AS A WHOLE

* How do you feel about the speech as a whole?

Finally, remember that in an oral presentation there is only one chance to get the message across to the audience. Listeners cannot turn back and review something that they did not quite catch, or slow down to assimilate a difficult point. We need to put ourselves in the place of the audience. How much detail do they need? How much explanation? What needs to be defined, described or illustrated in order for the message to be received effectively?

SUMMARY

In this chapter we have looked at presenting our ideas orally in the form of a speech or oral presentation. Effective speeches exploit the transactive nature of oral communication by adapting the presentation to suit audience feedback. Whether the speech is a short speech of introduction or vote of thanks or a more extended presentation it is important to keep our purpose clearly focused in our minds. In terms of a successful presentation, what happens before the speech has as much, if not more, importance than the actual delivery. Pre-speech preparation involves analysing both task and audience, research, writing the speech, deciding on audio-visual aids and practising the speech, preferably at least once in the venue where the speech will be delivered. In delivering the speech it is important to remember that the strength of an oral presentation lies in its transactive nature. For this reason the most effective speech delivery will be extemporaneous. This enables constant monitoring of audience feedback and greater exploitation of the dynamics of spoken language. Using the full range of vocal dynamics, including pauses, is important in maintaining audience interest and getting our ideas across most effectively. Finally, every speech should be a learning exercise so each presentation should be followed by an appraisal of its strengths and weaknesses.

In the next chapter we look at oral communication taking place in a more obviously interactive communication environment—the interview.

KEY POINTS

- Presenting our material orally enables us to exploit the transactive nature of face-to-face communication.
- Pre-speech preparation has an important influence on the eventual success or otherwise of any speech.
- The most effective presentations are the ones that are tailored most specifically to both the task and the audience.
- Task and audience analysis will influence the way in which speech content is organised.
- Extemporaneous delivery provides the best method of exploiting the transactive nature of face-to-face communication and the vitality and spontaneity of spoken language.
- Each oral presentation provides opportunities to learn through post-speech appraisals.

REVIEW QUESTIONS

1. What are the advantages and disadvantages of presenting material orally?
2. What do we mean when we speak of an oral presentation as a transactive process?
3. What are the implications of thinking of a speech as a transactive process in terms of how we organise the content of any speech?
4. What factors should be taken into account in analysing the task and the audience for any oral presentation?
5. What functions do audio-visual aids serve in oral presentations?
6. What should be borne in mind in selecting audio-visual aids?

EXERCISES

1. Assume you are introducing your friend who is giving a speech to new students. List the information you would need to get from your friend in order to do that.

2. Look at a professional speaker or presenter, perhaps on television. How does the speaker make contact with the audience? How is rapport established?

3. Give a two-minute speech to your tutorial group on a topic selected at random. You will need to make one main point and provide some support for that main point.

4. Take an academic journal article and convert it into a seminar presentation, including an indication of audio-visual aids.

5. Prepare a five-minute speech about something in which you are interested or about which you feel strongly for delivery to your tutorial group. What audience factors influenced your content and approach?

6. Observe a tutorial discussion and evaluate class participation. Did every person contribute? How relevant and focused was the discussion?

BIBLIOGRAPHY

Bailey, E. P., Jr 1992, *A Practical Guide for Business Speaking,* Oxford University Press, New York.
Bittner, J. 1988, *Fundamentals of Communication,* 2nd ed., Prentice Hall, New Jersey.
Byrnes, J. H. 1994, *Speak for Yourself: An Introduction to Public Speaking,* 3rd ed., McGraw-Hill, New York.
Campbell, J. 1990, *Speak for Yourself,* BBC Books, London.
Day, E. J. 1995, *How to Perform Under Pressure: By Control of Voice and Nerves,* Daybreak Publishing, Victoria.
Dwyer, K. K. 1998, *Conquer Your Speech Fright,* Harcourt Brace, Orlando, Florida.
Gray, M. 1991, *Public Speaking,* Schwartz & Wilkinson, Melbourne.
Gregory, H. 1990, *Public Speaking for College and Career,* 2nd ed., McGraw-Hill, New York.
Hasling, J. 1993, *The Audience, The Message, The Speaker,* 5th ed., McGraw-Hill, New York.
Hatcher, C. and McCarthy, P. 1996, *Speaking Persuasively: How to Make the Most of Your Presentations,* Allen & Unwin, Sydney.
Lucas, S. E. 1995, *The Art of Public Speaking,* 5th ed., McGraw-Hill, New York.
Minnick, Wayne. 1983, *Public Speaking,* 2nd ed., Houghton Mifflin Company, Boston.

Interviews

CHAPTER 8

Upon completing this chapter you should be able to:

- demonstrate an awareness of the nature of interviews and their prominence in our lives;
- understand different types of questions and their relationship to the type and purpose of the interview;
- appreciate interview structure and the role played by the introduction or opening, the body and the conclusion of the interview; and
- demonstrate a knowledge of methods of sequencing questions for maximum effectiveness and efficiency.

You are visiting the doctor for a consultation; you have been stopped in the shopping mall to answer a market survey; you are talking to a journalist; you and your tutor are assessing your progress; you are applying for a position; your local parliamentary member is doorknocking. Communication in all these activities is conducted through an interview. In fact, interviews now form a major means of communication. Interviews can be used to solve problems and make decisions; to gather or share information; or to persuade.

The word 'interview' comes from the Latin *inter*, meaning 'between' or 'among', and the French *voir*, meaning 'to see'. This derivation provides a basic definition, because the essence of interviews is an exchange of views or information between two or more people, usually, but not always, face to face. This definition could equally apply, of course, to conversations. What distinguishes interviews from conversations is that interviews have a purpose and a structure. At least one of the participants in an interview will have a specific purpose which will influence the structure and flow of the interaction. Conversations can be random and desultory but interviews, if they are to be effective, need to be structured to achieve a particular objective.

Every interview has a purpose and an interview will only be successful if that purpose, whether it is to select the best applicant for a position or to give information on company policies, is clearly defined and kept in mind at all times. The objective of an interview is achieved through planning and preparation on the part of both the interviewer and the interviewee.

While all interviews have a purpose and a structure, not all interviews have the same structure. Minchiello *et al.* (1995) categorise interviews on a continuum from highly structured to unstructured. Highly structured interviews rely on standardised questions asked in a set order so that each interviewee is asked exactly the same questions in the same order. Market survey interviews and opinion polls fall into this category. Focused or semi-structured interviews involve a more in-depth investigation. In place of standardised questions set out in a fixed order, interviewers have a guide or schedule designed to cover a list of topics but the discussion of the topics, the wording and ordering of the questions is up to the interviewer in each situation. Unstructured interviews are at the conversational end of the continuum. Interviewer control is minimal but the interview still has an objective and the interviewer still guides discussion to meet the objectives of the interview. Research in the social sciences often involves unstructured interviews such as in-depth interviews, group interviews and oral or life-history interviews.

In professional life we can consider the continuum to move from highly structured interviews such as surveys, through less structured but still highly organised selection interviews, to the informal, unstructured discussions which can occur between peers or between managers and subordinates. The structure that is selected for any interview will depend on the purpose of the interview and the type of information we wish to elicit.

If we think of all the areas of our communicative lives where we are involved in more or less structured question-and-answer format situations which are designed to achieve some objective we can see that interviews are a pervasive communication method. It is, therefore, important to develop good interviewing skills whether we are interviewer or interviewee.

Questioning

Having said that interviews are based on a question-and-answer format, we now need to look at the types of questions that can be asked and their suitability for different purposes and types of interview. Questions can be used to gain or share information; to encourage participation; to gain insights into motives, wants or needs; to assess attitudes; and to diagnose or problem solve. Questions can be categorised as closed or open.

Closed questions

As mentioned in the previous chapter, **closed questions** are questions that require few words, often in fact only one-word answers. Opinion poll or market survey questions are usually closed.

What brand of dog food do you use?

How would you rate the government's performance: very good, good, fair, poor, very poor?

When do you expect to graduate?

These are all examples of closed questions.

ADVANTAGES OF CLOSED QUESTIONS

Closed questions limit responses. This means that they:

* are useful for getting factual data quickly;
* give a high level of control to the interviewer which can be helpful for novice interviewers;
* can be used to direct the interview into desired areas of discussion or to move discussion forward. Sometimes interviewees, particularly in selection interviews, can be over-talkative. Closed questions can stem the flow of talk and move the interview to the next point;
* can help to get a reluctant interviewee talking as they require simple, straightforward, usually easy answers;
* are useful when seeking clarification or verification of any points; and
* provide easily quantifiable information in a highly standardised form which allows for easy comparison between different interview subjects.

DISADVANTAGES OF CLOSED QUESTIONS

Some of the disadvantages of closed questions are that they:

* ignore complexities, which can result in an invalid response. This is particularly likely to occur where an interviewee is asked for a binary answer such as yes/no. 'Do you think the present government is doing a good job?' The interviewee may think the government is doing a poor job in some areas but an adequate job in others but a simple 'yes/no' does not allow for this complexity;
* can be frustrating for interviewees because of the inability of closed questions to deal with deeper, more complex levels;
* can turn an interview into an interrogation; and
* are a poor method of eliciting information about attitudes or beliefs.

Open questions

Zima (1991) defines an **open question** as one that introduces or indicates the topic for discussion, allowing wide scope in the response. 'Tell me about yourself' is perhaps the classic open question.

What do you think about the new syllabus?

How would you handle cross-cultural conflict?

Why do you think you would be suited to this position?

These are open questions which leave considerable freedom in interviewee responses.

ADVANTAGES OF OPEN QUESTIONS

Open questions are useful because they:

- establish a supportive climate and are valuable in building rapport;
- can elicit a wide variety of information;
- allow in-depth responses;
- reveal attitudes, feelings, motivations and values;
- can open up unexpected areas for discussion; and
- encourage interviewee participation.

DISADVANTAGES OF OPEN QUESTIONS

Open questions:

- take a lot of time;
- require more skill in wording than closed questions if they are to be clear and unambiguous;
- give less control to the interviewer;
- can provide too much information; and
- are less standardised than closed questions and thus make comparison between interview subjects more difficult.

Other types of questions

Most interviews will consist of a mix of closed and open questions with the proportion of closed to open questions determined by the purpose of the interview. In a selection interview, for example, most of the questions would probably be open questions: 'What is your view on worker participation in decision-making processes?', for example.

Barone and Switzer (1995) also classify questions into primary questions and probes or probing questions.

PRIMARY QUESTIONS

Primary questions introduce topics and are the first questions asked on any new topic in the interview.

Could you tell us about your experience in teaching basic skills to large groups?

How important do you consider socialisation to be for the under-fives?

These are examples of primary questions. Because the interviewer knows in advance what topic areas are to be covered in the interview, primary questions are usually prepared before the interview. It is important that primary questions deal with one idea only, are unambiguous and easily understandable by the interviewee.

PROBING QUESTIONS

Probing questions can also be called **secondary** or **follow-up questions** because they arise out of previous responses. According to Zima (1991) probing questions are useful when answers are not relevant, clear, complete or accurate. They are designed to elicit further information or detail and this can be useful if a question has not really been answered or has been only partially answered. Probing questions can also be used to:

* probe motivations;
* check accuracy;
* summarise; and
* provide opportunities for any unasked questions by either interviewer or interviewee.

Let us suppose that the person you are interviewing has made the statement that her previous position involved supervisory responsibility. You may want to probe this area further.

> What did your supervisory responsibility involve?
>
> Did any problems arise?
>
> How did you deal with them?
>
> How do you feel about continuing in a supervisory role?

The probing questions in the above sequence are all open questions which allow maximum freedom of response from the interviewee.

MIRROR QUESTIONS

A **mirror question** is a variant of the probing question. Here the interviewer paraphrases or reflects back a response to elicit more information.

> I was unhappy in my last position because there was no scope for creativity or individuality.
>
> You need scope for creativity and individuality?

LEADING QUESTIONS

Sometimes questions can be asked which make it clear what response is expected. These questions are called **leading questions**. Let us look at two questions which both require a response about a new roster.

> Don't you agree that the new roster is an improvement?
>
> What do you think about the new roster?

Which question is more unbiased? Which question is more likely to elicit the respondent's real opinion of the new roster? The first question is a leading question. The way it is worded makes it clear that the interviewer wants agreement that the new roster is an improvement. The second question has no obvious bias. There is no indication in the question itself what answer the interviewer would prefer.

If leading questions are used they should be used carefully. The interviewer should always bear in mind that leading questions may not elicit valid or accurate responses but answers geared to the interviewer's clearly indicated preferences. 'Taking sport on Saturdays won't be a problem for you, will it?' makes it clear what response is expected. Leading questions are usually part of persuasive communication, especially in sales interviews.

'Wouldn't it be preferable to buy now, rather than wait until prices have gone up?'

Mirror and leading questions may be open but are often closed.

HYPOTHETICAL QUESTIONS

Hypothetical questions are often used in selection interviews. They pose particular problems to which interviewees are asked to supply a solution.

How would you deal with a subordinate who is habitually late back from lunch?

What would you do if your manager asked you to lie for him?

Hypothetical questions can be used to gauge the interviewee's general attitude to particular situations. They are useful for probing motivations, ethics, analytical and problem-solving skills. It is important, however, that the interviewer is open to alternative responses to the hypothetical question and has not already decided on the 'right' answer. It is also important to realise that internal applicants, because of their familiarity with the organisation and its climate and systems, will probably be at an advantage in dealing with hypothetical questions.

Interview structure

Every interview will have an introduction, or opening, body and conclusion.

Introduction

Just as in an oral presentation, the introduction, or opening of an interview is important. What happens at the beginning of an interview has what Barone and Switzer (1995) call the 'primacy effect'. This means that impressions formed early in the interview have a continuing effect, impacting more powerfully than impressions formed later in the interview.

The introduction or opening of an interview should achieve several objectives. It should:

* establish rapport between interviewer and interviewee;
* establish common ground between interviewer and interviewee; and
* state the purpose of the interview.

Establishing rapport

The first step in any interview process, of course, is introductions, which should give roles as well as names. At a selection interview, for example, the interviewer may introduce himself as 'Jim Jones and I am in charge of the Payroll Section'. This enables the interviewee to 'place' Jim Jones, both in terms of his name and his role. This step also allows the interviewer to indicate the level of formality of the interview. If a lecturer introduces herself to a student as 'I am Dr Smith but please call me Carla', a more informal tone has been set than if the lecturer says 'I am Dr Smith'. The level of formality set by the interviewer will be influenced by the nature of the interview. Tone in disciplinary and selection interviews is usually formal. In sales interviews the salesperson will usually try to develop an informal tone.

An important aspect of the opening of the interview is the establishment of rapport between the parties. This can be achieved through the exchange of 'small talk'.

We are a bit out of the way here. Did you have any trouble finding us?

Comments on the weather, non-controversial news and so on can help establish rapport. Rapport can also be established by asking simple, usually closed, questions to verify data.

You are currently working for Box and Company, aren't you?

You have been with them for five years now?

The early minutes of the interview should establish common ground. This is often combined with stating the purpose of the interview. We can think of this step as orienting both interviewer and interviewee towards the objective of the interview.

As you know we are looking for someone to work in the copywriting section of our agency. What we need is someone to deal with the day-to-day administration so that the copywriters can be free to concentrate on creating award-winning advertisements.

Body

The body of the interview consists of question-and-answer exchanges designed to achieve the interview objective. This might be to find the most suitable applicant for a position, to appraise an employee's performance, to solve an employee problem in terms of a disciplinary interview, to provide counselling, to gain information for a research project, to exchange information with a colleague, to sell an idea or product and so on.

An effective interview, an interview that achieves the objective, does not just happen. It is the result of careful planning and thought. This planning starts before the interview takes place. The first and perhaps most important responsibility of the interviewer is to have a very clear idea of exactly what the interview should achieve. Having defined the objective of the interview clearly, the interviewer is in a position to decide on:

* the type, range and sequence of questions, in other words the structure of the interview;
* the level of formality appropriate to the situation; and
* the most appropriate venue for the interview.

Interviews are structured, purposeful question-and-answer exchanges so it is important that both parties to the interview prepare thoroughly. This means that both the interviewer and interviewee need to learn as much about the subject and the other parties to the interview process as possible. In the case of a selection interview, for example, the interviewer(s) will have thoroughly read the résumés of the applicants, perhaps even checking references, and will have decided on the questions to be asked and, in the case of a panel of interviewers, who will ask which questions and in what sequence.

The interviewee should have become familiar with the position and its duties and responsibilities through reading a position description, have found out as much as possible about the organisation through company publications such as annual reports, and should certainly have spoken to the contact person nominated in the job advertisement. It can also be helpful if the interviewee has tried to anticipate the types of questions that will be asked and has prepared a defence or explanation of any areas of weakness in the application, for example any areas where experience or qualifications may be less than desired.

Question sequences

It is the responsibility of the interviewer or interviewing panel to decide not only the topic areas to be covered, sometimes even the precise questions, but also the sequence of the questions. There is a variety of question sequences but we will deal only with the most common.

FUNNEL SEQUENCE

The **funnel sequence** begins with a broad or general question moving gradually to more specific or detailed questions. This sequence works well with interviewees who are knowledgeable about the topic. It also provides the opportunity for the interviewer to uncover unexpected areas that might be worth further exploration.

The following questions provide an example of a funnel sequence moving from the broad question about what the interviewee thinks about the reorganisation in general to the more specific question on how long the changes discussed would be likely to take.

1. What are your views on the office reorganisation?
2. What would you change?
3. Why do you feel that those changes would be an improvement?
4. How would you implement the changes?
5. What time frame would your changes require?

INVERTED FUNNEL SEQUENCE

The **inverted funnel sequence** is the opposite of the funnel sequence. It begins with specific and detailed questions moving gradually to broader and more general questions. The inverted funnel sequence is appropriate for counselling interviews as it can encourage reluctant interviewees to participate. It is also effective in eliciting information about the interviewee's motives and beliefs.

What specific problems have you encountered with the new equipment?

Are these problems concerned only with the new equipment or are there wider implications?

How do you see the wider implications impacting on our productivity?

TUNNEL SEQUENCE

The **tunnel sequence**, uses mainly closed questions to elicit maximum data in minimum time. This sequence is used for interviews such as loan applications or initial medical screening interviews where specific factual data is required.

What is your full name?

What is your date of birth?

What is your occupation?

Who is your employer?

QUINTAMENSIONAL DESIGN SEQUENCE

Barone and Switzer (1995) document the **quintamensional design sequence,** formulated by George Gallup in 1947. This sequence is designed to elicit information, especially about attitudes, from large numbers of people. The sequence consists of five steps:

1. the awareness step, which uncovers the interviewee's knowledge of the subject area;
2. the uninfluenced attitude step, which is designed to get the interviewee to talk about the issue in his/her own words;
3. the specific attitude step, which requires a simple yes/no response to a specific attitude in relation to the subject area;
4. the reasoning step, which asks for the interviewee's reasons for the response; and
5. the intensity of attitude step, which aims to measure the intensity of the interviewee's attitude.

A sample quintamensional design sequence follows:

What do you know about the move to ban certain dog breeds?

What do you see as the government's responsibility, if any, in relation to savage dogs?

Do you think some dog breeds should be banned?

Why do you think so?

On a scale of one to ten, how strongly do you feel about this issue?

The particular question sequence selected will depend on the type of interview, on the nature of the interviewee and on the objective of the interview.

Conclusion

The conclusion of the interview serves a number of functions. It provides a summary of the essence of the discussion. This not only reinforces the main points but provides an opportunity for any misconceptions to be dealt with. It enables both parties to ensure that their understanding of what took place is consonant. It indicates the next step. This is particularly appropriate in selection interviews where the interviewer should tell the interviewee when and by what means the interviewee can expect to know the result of the interview. It provides a sense of closure.

One area that is important in successful interviewing which we have not dealt with here, but which is covered in Chapter 12, is the nonverbal component of an interview. Our nonverbal cues can help build rapport or can demolish it. Similarly a large part of our reaction to, and final decision about, an interviewee comes from our assessment, however unconscious, of nonverbal behaviour. It is important, then, in an interview to be aware of the total communication picture, not just the words but the nonverbal cues and the communication context in general.

SUMMARY

Interviews are an important and integral part of our communicative lives. In professional and organisational life they can be used to recruit, induct, counsel, appraise or review performance or discipline. They can be used to diagnose or problem solve, to elicit information or attitudes for research purposes, to exchange information and views, to persuade or to sell a product or an idea. Interviews are conducted to achieve a particular purpose and require careful planning by both interviewer and interviewee. The interviewer is responsible for determining the structure of the interview and for formulating the questions to be asked. Most interviews will consist of a mix of open and closed questions which will be designed to achieve the interview purpose. Every interview should have an opening or introduction, a body and a conclusion.

Interviews can be used for problem solving and decision making and in the next chapter we will look at some problem-solving and decision-making strategies.

KEY POINTS

- Interviews can be thought of as conversations with a purpose and structure.
- Interviews are based on exchanges of questions and answers.
- Questions can be open or closed and most interviews will consist of a mix of both.
- Questions can also be classified as primary, probing or secondary, mirror, hypothetical or leading.
- Questions can be arranged in different sequences depending on the type and purpose of the interview and the nature of the interviewee.
- Interviews have an opening or introduction, body and conclusion.

REVIEW QUESTIONS

1. What are some of the purposes for which interviews are conducted?
2. What are the advantages and disadvantages of closed questions?
3. What are the advantages and disadvantages of open questions?
4. What function is carried out by primary questions?
5. When would you use probing questions?
6. What are the dangers of using leading questions? In what types of interviews would leading questions most likely be found?
7. What should the introduction or opening of an interview achieve?
8. What are the functions of the conclusion of an interview?

EXERCISES

1. In pairs, with each participant taking the role of interviewer and interviewee in turn, apply for a job which interests you from the 'Positions Vacant' section of your newspaper.
2. Select two television interviews, one from an 'entertainment' interview such as Michael Parkinson and one from a current affairs or investigative interview. Compare the interviewing techniques. What are the differences and why do they exist?
3. In pairs, take five minutes to find out all the factual information you need about your partner to introduce your partner to the group as a whole. Repeat the exercise trying to elicit all the attitudinal information you can. Were your questioning techniques the same in both cases, or did you use more open or more closed questions in the different situations? Why?

BIBLIOGRAPHY

Barone, J. T. and Switzer, J. Y. 1995, *Interviewing Art and Skill*, Simon & Schuster, New York.
Berman, J. A. 1997, *Competence-Based Employment Interviewing*, Quorum Books, Connecticut.
Fear, R. A. and Chiron, R. J. 1990, *The Evaluation Interview*, McGraw-Hill, New York.
Minchiello, V., Aroni, R., Timewell, E. and Alexander, L. 1995, *In-Depth Interviewing: Principles, Techniques, Analysis*, 2nd ed., Longman Australia, Melbourne.
Zima, J. P. 1991, *Interviewing: Key to Effective Management*, Macmillan Publishing Company, New York.

Part Four

Problem Solving, Decision Making and Persuasion

Decision-making strategies

CHAPTER 9

Upon completing this chapter you should be able to:
- understand the distinguishing characteristics of creative problem-solving techniques and decision-making models;
- appreciate the applicability of creative problem solving and sequential decision making to different aspects of problem solving and decision making; and
- know how to apply problem-solving and decision-making techniques to case studies.

We have a **problem** if the existing situation differs from what we want it to be (Van Gundy 1988; Brilhart and Galanes 1995). If, for example, we want everyone to have a car parking space but there are only car parking spaces for 30% of staff, we have a problem. What we do about the gap between the existing situation and the ideal, between what is and what we would like it to be, involves problem solving and decision making.

Each of us is involved in solving problems and making decisions every day. Some of our decisions involve quite trivial matters—what to have for lunch, for example, or whether to walk or drive to the shop. Some of the decisions are more important and far-reaching. Decisions on matters such as major purchases (car or house), investment decisions, career decisions (change of job, career change, education or training choices) occur less frequently but involve matters where a decision can have a major impact on our lives. So how we solve problems and make decisions has implications for both our professional and personal lives.

In this chapter we will deal with problem solving and decision making in terms of professional life, in terms of activities that are part of our working lives; however, many of the strategies are equally applicable to personal problems and decisions. We will look at the two approaches to problem solving inherent in vertical and lateral thinking and put forward a problem-solving, case study methodology.

In professional life problem solving and decision making will often be a group activity, and the strategies dealt with in this chapter are predicated on group rather than individual problem solving. Indeed, most groups in professional life exist only because of their role in solving problems and making decisions. Chapter 14, on group communication, deals with groups, group tasks and leadership styles, and with the dynamics of groups and the ways in which such dynamics can help or hinder the decision-making process. However, in this chapter we are concerned not with groups themselves but with the strategies that can be employed in solving problems and making decisions.

Logical and creative thinking

Broadly speaking, there are two ways in which problem solving and decision making can be approached in professional life: creative and logical. Edward de Bono divides thinking into two categories: lateral and vertical. **Lateral thinking** is more random, imaginative and creative while **vertical thinking** can be defined as logical and sequential (de Bono 1990). Neither type of thinking is innately superior. Both are necessary for effective decision making. Lateral and vertical thinking are complementary (de Bono 1990). Lateral thinking generates the ideas, the new approaches to problems, the creative solutions. Vertical thinking evaluates the ideas generated by lateral thinking and selects the most appropriate.

Creative problem solving

Creative problem solving is a form of applied lateral thinking which involves breaking stereotypical, logical ways of looking at a situation or problem. It means coming up with different, innovative, unusual solutions to problems. It means using imagination rather than reason.

Over the years many creative problem-solving techniques have been developed and used in organisations such as brainwriting, synectics, nominal group techniques, trigger groups and forcing techniques. Van Gundy (1988), for example, outlines some 64 ideas-generating techniques for both individuals and groups. It is, however, outside the scope of a general text such as this to go into these in detail so we will concentrate on one of the most common creative problem solving strategies and one from which many later creative problem-solving techniques have developed, and that is brainstorming. The characteristics of brainstorming—quantity of ideas; encouragement of unusual, even wild ideas; building on or adapting the ideas of others and delaying evaluation of ideas, for example—are common to almost all ideas-generation techniques.

Brainstorming

Brainstorming is one of the most common creative problem-solving strategies and uses techniques found in most creative problem-solving methodologies. The objective of brainstorming sessions is to generate as many ideas as possible in relation to a problem; preferably ideas that are different or innovative, even ideas that may seem weird, crazy or impractical. Such ideas can help members of the group to see the problem in a new light, or can act as catalysts for ideas from other participants.

Brainstorming was developed by Alex Osborne (1953). According to Napier and Gershenfeld (1999) brainstorming is designed to allow maximum freedom for individual creativity by minimising inhibiting factors such as fear of criticism or social embarrassment, status differentials and pressures to conform, while simultaneously exploiting the group forces of reinforcement, cross-stimulation and sense of belonging. The basic premise of brainstorming is that quantity will ultimately result in quality; therefore, brainstorming sessions aim to generate as many ideas as possible within a relatively short period of time, roughly 15 to 30 minutes. Brainstorming functions on the generation of freewheeling, creative ideas uncensored by prior evaluation or analysis so it works better if ideas come quickly.

Brainstorming guidelines

Although based on lateral thinking and the generation of imaginative, free-wheeling ideas, brainstorming still begins with a definition of the problem. Indeed, the problem can be set out in some detail and sent to members to allow them to think of the problem before the session.

If brainstorming sessions are to succeed in generating new and creative ideas certain guidelines need to be followed.

* There must be no evaluation of any ideas put forward and this includes comments such as 'That seems like a good idea but . . .', 'Wouldn't it cost a lot . . .' or reactions such as laughing, groaning and so on. Members of the group need to feel secure from criticism so that they can put forward ideas that may seem impractical, even weird, without fear of judgement or ridicule.

* Wild or unusual ideas should be actively encouraged. The purpose of the session is to break away from conventional ways of looking at a problem. Ideas that seem crazy can help group members to see the problem in a new way or 'spark off' new ideas.

* Hitchhiking or using the ideas of others in some way is encouraged. Ideas can be combined, modified or built on by other members of the group. Most importantly, there should be lots of ideas. In brainstorming more is definitely better.

* All ideas should be recorded so that participants can read them easily during the session.

Brainstorming leader/facilitator

Brainstorming sessions need a leader or facilitator whose responsibilities are similar to those of any group leader, in other words to regulate the flow of ideas, to ensure that all members have the opportunity to contribute and that every idea is clearly recorded. However, the primary responsibility of the leader of a brainstorming session is to ensure that the guidelines for brainstorming sessions are followed, most importantly the establishment of a welcoming, uncritical environment.

Brainstorming recorder/notetaker

A recorder or notetaker is also needed. Sometimes this can be the facilitator or it can be another member of the group. The function of the recorder is to write the ideas on a whiteboard, flipcharts, large sheets of paper or any medium that will enable all participants to read the ideas easily.

Post-meeting evaluation

It is important to remember that there is no evaluation of ideas at the brainstorming session. The brainstorming session is for ideas generation only. However, generation of ideas is only the first phase. The ultimate purpose of any creative problem-solving exercise is to make the best decision, to find the best solution, and this involves evaluation of the ideas that came from the brainstorming session. This evaluation does not occur at the original brainstorming session but takes place later at another meeting which may consist of the original brainstorming group or of a different group of people altogether.

We can think of the evaluation session as the vertical thinking aspect of the problem-solving and decision-making process, although there is still scope for creative thinking even in the evaluation session (de Bono 1990). The evaluation session is where the ideas generated in the uncritical environment of the brainstorming session are subjected to critical examination. Which ideas are feasible and capable of implementation? Which of the many ideas put forward will best solve the problem? Are there any ideas that may have future use?

Problem-solving and decision-making sequence

The very title 'problem-solving and decision-making sequence' indicates that this method of addressing problems falls within the vertical thinking category, that of working logically through a series of steps to reach a solution. John Dewey did much work on reflective thinking, which forms the basis of most problem-solving and decision-making sequences. Dewey (1933) claimed that reflective thinking involved ideas in a structured and interdependent sequence with each phase flowing logically from the previous phase and leading logically to the next phase. He considered reflective thinking to be purposeful, leading logically to a conclusion.

Dewey formulated five phases of reflective thought which were adapted in 1950 by McBurney and Hance to form the basis of the problem-solving and decision-making sequence. The five basic steps in the problem-solving and decision-making sequence are:

1. defining and analysing the problem;
2. possible solutions;
3. evaluation of possible solutions;
4. solution selection; and
5. solution implementation.

There are variations on this model. In some models defining the problem and analysing the problem are two separate steps. Some models include a step on criteria for a solution or missing information. Some models have a final step that evaluates the solution with a contingency plan if the preferred solution is not working out as expected, but analysis of the problem and selection of solution are essential.

Let us look at the steps in the problem-solving and decision-making sequence.

1. Problem definition and analysis

Sometimes this is called problem identification and analysis. Definition and analysis often merge together; however, we will separate them here to make it easier for you to understand any other problem-solving and decision-making models you may encounter.

PROBLEM DEFINITION

Problem definition or identification is necessary because problems seldom appear in a neat, orderly way. Usually problems reach us in the form of symptoms, leaving us to work our way to the problem. If you have a headache, for instance, you know you have a problem. But is the pain in your head the problem, or is it a symptom of something else, perhaps a more deep-seated problem? What has caused your headache? It may be caused by tension, a bump on the head, too much partying, or it may be an indication of a bout of 'flu, meningitis, even a brain tumour. The symptom (the headache) is obvious; the cause of the headache (the real problem) is not. To find the real problem your doctor will need to investigate and analyse, to collect data in the form of a physical history, blood tests, encephalograms and so on. This is what we need to do in the problem definition and analysis step.

If you recall the definition of a problem given early in the chapter as the gap between an undesirable present situation and an ideal desired situation, you will realise that what we term 'problems' are usually the external evidence of deeper underlying causes—the real problem in other words.

For example, let us suppose that there are problems in the mail room. There have been complaints from staff and clients. Mail, even urgent mail, sometimes takes as much as two days to be processed. Some mail is lost or damaged. Your manager asks you to look into the matter and recommend ways to solve the problem. But is the problem delayed, lost or damaged mail? No. Those things are just the evidence, the symptoms. The underlying cause, the problem, is not so obvious. However, in order to try to solve the problem, to alleviate the symptoms, we need a clear definition of the problem. This is an early stage in the process so it is important that we keep an open mind and do not limit ourselves by thinking of the problem in terms of a solution. We need to think of the problem in terms of causes rather than solutions. So in the case of the mail room situation we could ask the following questions: Are there equipment problems? What is the staffing ratio of the mail section? Is the section understaffed and, if so, why? How long has the problem existed? Did the start of the problem coincide with any changes in the section or the organisation as a whole? What is morale like in the mail section?

How do we define the problem in the mail room? We can begin by asking 'What is the problem?' If you are not sure whether what you are considering is a problem or a symptom ask 'What caused this?' If you can find a cause you are dealing with a symptom rather than a problem. It is rather like peeling an onion. You need to keep moving through the layers until you reach the core. Try to define the problem in a short, simple statement. Your problem definition can be as simple as 'what is the problem in the mail room?' 'Who', 'what', 'when' and 'why' are questions that can help in defining a problem.

PROBLEM ANALYSIS

It is sometimes difficult to make a clear demarcation between problem identification and problem analysis; however, the fundamental activity in analysing the problem is probing into deeper underlying causes. For example, if the problem in the mail room is defined in terms of poor morale we need to ask why morale is low. Is there is a systemic problem within the organisation, or is it confined to the mail section? This is also the step where we need to gather facts and data. We may, for example, observe what happens in the mail room, talk to mail room employees, survey employees (both in the mail room and within the organisation as a whole) talk to the mail room supervisor, delve into company files, perhaps even talk to people in mail sections in other organisations and so on.

2. Possible solutions

When we have defined the problem, collected data and analysed the problem, we can move on to possible solutions. This is where creative problem-solving methods such as brainstorming can be useful. If, for example, our problem identification and analysis indicated that the problem was outdated and unreliable equipment, our solution would seem to be to replace the equipment. However, there may be reasons why this is not feasible. Perhaps the company cannot afford to replace the equipment; perhaps new equipment would mean many redundancies and the company wants to avoid a large number of redundancies either because of possible union backlash or because many of the mail room staff are nearing retirement and it would be cheaper for the company to wait until they retire rather than provide redundancy payouts. There could be even more reasons why the equipment has not been replaced. So recommending replacing the equipment may not be an acceptable option, or the best solution in the circumstances. This is where adding a step on establishing criteria can be useful. Such criteria can set time and financial frameworks, for example.

3. Solution evaluation

This is where we need to ask what the likely outcome is for each possible solution. What is likely to happen if the solution is put into practice? Let us suppose, for example, that we had decided that the mail room problem was inadequate staffing levels. Possible solutions could be: do nothing (always a possible solution even if usually not a particularly effective one); increase staff; train staff; reorganise mail room systems to make them more efficient; establish a roster system throughout the organisation. What would be the likely outcome for each solution?

Doing nothing would clearly make no change at all. The mail room would still be working inefficiently, staff and clients would still be complaining. Indeed, the situation would probably deteriorate as people became more frustrated and clients became more dissatisfied and took their business elsewhere. Hiring additional staff would probably solve the problem but if the company cannot afford to hire more staff other options need to be considered. Perhaps existing staff could cope if they had training, or if the mail room systems were reorganised to increase efficiency. Perhaps there are times when some other members of staff are underutilised and could be rostered to take over some of the less skilled areas of the mail room.

There are, of course, more options, but the exercise of evaluating each solution in terms of possible advantages and disadvantages is an essential step in any problem-solving and decision-making exercise.

4. Solution selection or preferred solution

This step is self-explanatory. It involves the final selection of the solution that is regarded as most likely to solve the problem. The preferred solution may be just one of the options evaluated in the previous step, or it may be a combination of some of the options. For example, in the case of the mail room problem we may decide to adopt a mix of solutions. We may decide to reorganise the mail room systems, incorporating some training for mail room staff and institute a roster system involving other staff.

5. Solution implementation

This section is concerned with how the decision will be put into practice, with who will do what, as well as how and when it will be done. Making a decision is only part of the process. If the decision is not implemented the exercise has been a waste of time, so part of problem solving and decision making involves formulating a plan for implementing the preferred solution. In the case of the mail room problem there would need to be a plan and time line for the decision. Who would reorganise the mail room systems? Would it be the mail room supervisor, an outside consultant or someone else within the organisation? Within what time frame would the reorganisation take place? When would it be put in place? Who would organise the training for mail room staff? Would rostered staff also have any training? When would this be done? Who would organise the roster?

6. Post-solution assessment

Although this step is often omitted from problem-solving and decision-making models, it is actually an important part of the process. A decision is made and implemented, but how do we monitor whether it is working or not; whether the best decision was, in fact, made; and what do we do if the decision is not working out as we had hoped? There needs to be some mechanism for monitoring the decision, perhaps after three months and again after six months. This allows for fine tuning or adaptation if required, or for a new decision to be made if that is necessary.

Case studies

Case studies are accounts or descriptions of problem situations or events which are designed to reflect real-life situations. Sometimes they are based on actual situations. Developed at Harvard University early last century as a method of participative learning which required problem-solving and decision-making skills for their successful completion, they give experience in defining or identifying problems. They require research and data handling skills, analytical, critical and creative thinking and the ability to make appropriate judgements and decisions based on both facts and inferences. The problem-solving and decision-making elements we have just discussed form part of any case study.

Case studies can be simple or complex, long or short, and it is important to realise that there is no one right working of any case study. The important thing with case studies is the quality of analysis and how logically the study is worked from problem definition to preferred solution.

Inferences and assumptions

First, it is necessary to differentiate between inferences and assumptions. Dewey (1933) considers that an **inference** involves moving from the known to the unknown, of using what is known to deduce what is unknown. It is important, however, that inferences are based on fact and are logically consistent with what is known. **Assumptions**, on the other hand, are not based on fact and can result in a skewed working of a study.

Let me illustrate this with a case study and some assumptions that emerged as students worked through the study.

> Rowan is a student in your tutorial group. He is popular, articulate and communicates well. He studied Communication at high school, achieving quite good marks. However, he only attended two tutorials, saying that 'he doesn't need to study the subject—it's just plain commonsense', 'he already knows all that' and 'he wants to work with computers so this subject is a waste of time'. Unfortunately, Rowan failed his first assignment. He came to see you and you suggested that he attend tutorials. Rowan has been attending tutorials but his attitude is still resentful and he still does not think he needs to put in any real work. He is in danger of failing the second assignment and, probably, the subject as a whole. What can you do about Rowan?

Students who defined the problem as a personality clash between Rowan and the tutor made an assumption that had no basis in the study itself. There is nothing in the study to indicate a personality clash between Rowan and his tutor. Students who defined the problem in terms of cross-cultural barriers made another assumption that is not supported by anything in the study. A case study must be worked on the data that is given. Inferences will need to be drawn but they must be based on the available data, otherwise we end up working a completely different case study. In the case of the problem with Rowan, we are dealing with intrapersonal barriers, that is, barriers arising from Rowan's perception of himself and his abilities with regard to the subject. We are dealing with his expectations, biases and prejudices.

Let us look at a sample case study.

> Sue Smith spent many years in the Accounting Department and has recently been promoted to a supervisory position in the Customer Relations Section. The previous supervisor of the Customer Relations Section had been in the job for many years, longer than any of the employees in the section and had, in fact, developed many of the systems and procedures that were in use when Sue took over. While the section was not outstanding, it functioned efficiently and effectively. There were no problems with morale and work throughput was satisfactory. You had hoped that a new and younger supervisor might energise the section, making it even more efficient. A few months after Sue takes over, however, you have to admit that she has not improved the section. Indeed, the section is now the poorest performing section in the organisation. Morale is down, staff absentee rates are increasing and work throughput is poor. Customers are now complaining about the Customer Relations Department and questions are being asked by senior management. When you investigate you find that Sue seems unable to delegate. She tries to do everything herself on the principle that that is the only way she can be certain things will be done properly. No work is allowed to leave the section until she has checked it, with the result that staff are spending much time waiting to have their work checked by Sue. When the work is checked Sue often insists on the work being redone, sometimes as many as three

times. Sue is becoming increasingly stressed and could be headed for a breakdown. What can you do about Sue?

Case studies often require us to adopt a certain role—sometimes that of a manager within the organisation, sometimes that of an outside consultant. If we look at our study above, although it is not spelled out it is clear that we are in a managerial position with some sort of responsibility for Sue's area. This is how we know senior management is asking questions and why we have done a preliminary investigation. You can see that, although it is important in case studies to avoid making assumptions, we do have to read carefully the material that is there. We cannot expect everything to be spelled out in detail. We have to read intelligently and analytically.

In writing up our case study it is appropriate to use point form. The aim is to provide as much information as the reader needs in order to be able to follow our working, so avoid being brief to the point of ambiguity or unintelligibility, but also avoid unnecessary words. This is not an essay or a report. It is a case study and our readers need to be able to assess quickly the quality of our analysis and how logically we follow the problem-solving and decision-making steps.

Let us begin working our way through the study. We will start with **defining** or **identifying and analysing the problem**. Our problem, of course, is what to do about Sue but we need to look at the key factors in relation to Sue in the study.

* Sue is new in the job.

* She is new to the section.

* She came from long-term employment in the Accounting Department, an area where accuracy and attention to detail is important.

* She is now working in an area where people skills are more important than close attention to detail.

* She replaced a long-serving supervisor who was well known by all employees in the section and who set up most of the systems and procedures used in the section.

* She cannot delegate.

* She checks and rechecks work.

You will notice that we have not mentioned poor morale or low work throughput. These are symptoms. They are not the problem. The problem is what caused the poor morale and low work throughput. We could also add the point that Sue's manager had expected Sue to increase efficiency within the section. This has not been added here because there is an element of assumption as to whether Sue is aware of her manager's expectations. The case study does not make it clear whether she is aware of the manager's expectations or not but, especially as we are the manager, a case could be made for including this point. It is certainly likely that the manager's expectations would be known to Sue.

If we look at the key points we have elicited from the study we can see that we need to probe further. The problem is clearly Sue's management style but what has caused that management style? What are the implications for Sue of the fact that the previous supervisor had been in the job for many years, longer than any of the employees, and had set up many of the systems? It is difficult to follow someone who has become closely identified with an area over many years. This would put pressure on Sue. If Sue was aware of her manager's expectations of increased efficiency this would put further pressure on her.

What are the implications of the fact that she is new both to the supervisory role and to the area in which she is working? Is the fact that her previous area, Accounting, involved a different kind of work and skills to those involved in Customer Relations important? Why is Sue unable to delegate and why does she check and recheck work?

Is there a connection between Sue's inability to delegate, including her need to have work leaving her area perfect, and her previous work in Accounts? Is there a relationship between Sue's lack of experience in her current job and managerial expectations of her performance in her new role? Perhaps Sue is naturally a perfectionist and working in the Accounting Department suited her temperament. Did she have any training before taking up the new position? How much support and help did she receive in the early days in the supervisory position? You can see that there are many possibilities.

Let us look at *possible solutions:*

* do nothing;

* fire Sue;

* demote Sue;

* transfer Sue;

* counsel Sue;

* provide training;

* set up a mentoring system.

If we *evaluate the solutions* we can see that doing nothing will not solve the problem and, if Sue does have a breakdown, the problem will have simply worsened with costs to the organisation such as workers' compensation and so on. We could fire Sue, but she has been with the organisation for a long time and has clearly been a good employee or she would not have been promoted. It would be a pity for the organisation to lose that experience. It would have a very bad effect on Sue's morale and sense of self-worth if we demoted her. Transferring Sue may solve the problem if she is temperamentally suited to work requiring a high level of detail and accuracy as long as she is transferred to an area requiring that kind of work. However, if she is still in a supervisory area there may be a need to supply some training and support. Counselling could be an option, especially if Sue's problem is lack of confidence in her ability. This could be a reason for her insistence on absolute perfection. Training should certainly be provided, both in terms of the systems within her section and in terms of time and people management. A mentoring system could help, especially if Sue is mentored by someone at the same level who has similarly been promoted internally.

In selecting our *preferred solution* we may decide on a mix of options. If we felt the problem was Sue's temperamental suitability for highly detailed and accurate work, our preferred solution might be a mixture of transfer and training. If we felt the problem was Sue's lack of confidence in her ability we might decide on a combination of counselling, training and mentoring. There are different ways of looking at any study and consequently various ways to work through it. There are often many variations that could be equally valid.

Solution implementation would involve how our preferred solution would be put into practice. We may decide that Sue will be transferred to a vacant supervisory position in the Payroll Section and that we will liaise with the Training Officer about suitable training for Sue in supervisory and/or time management skills.

Post-solution evaluation deals with how we will monitor what happens. If our decision was to leave Sue in Customer Services with a combination of counselling, training and mentoring, we may institute review meetings with Sue at regular intervals, survey staff, increase oversight of the section and so on.

SUMMARY

In this chapter we have looked at different methods of solving problems and making decisions. Lateral thinking or creative problem solving is useful for generating solutions but vertical or logical thinking is needed to evaluate the solutions and to determine the most appropriate solution. The two methods are not antagonistic but complementary, functioning together to arrive at the optimum solution. We can see the two methods applied within the case study methodology where lateral thinking is used in conjunction with vertical thinking to analyse problems, generate possible solutions and decide on the best options.

In the next chapter we look at persuasive communication, how to recognise persuasive communication and how to use persuasive communication.

KEY POINTS

- A problem is a gap between what a situation is and what we would like it to be. Both lateral and vertical thinking are useful in solving problems and making decisions.

- Lateral thinking or creative problem solving can be thought of as the ideas-generation element in problem solving and decision making.

- Brainstorming is an example of creative problem-solving.

- Vertical or logical thinking involves thinking about a problem sequentially and logically and is used to evaluate the solutions generated by creative problem solving.

- Case studies use descriptions of realistic situations to give experience in problem solving and decision making.

- Both lateral and vertical thinking are used in working through case studies.

REVIEW QUESTIONS

1. What is lateral thinking? How is it used in creative problem-solving techniques such as brainstorming?
2. What are the defining characteristics of brainstorming?
3. What are the responsibilities of the leader or facilitator of a brainstorming session?
4. What type of thinking is involved in the post-meeting evaluations to brainstorming sessions?
5. What are the steps in the problem-solving and decision-making sequence based on Dewey's reflective thinking?
6. What is involved in problem definition and analysis?
7. What type of thinking is used in generating possible solutions?
8. What are case studies?
9. What is the difference between an inference and an assumption?

EXERCISES

1. What is a problem? Think of a problem from your experience. How did you solve it? Was your solution the best solution?

2. Form two groups. One group has 15 minutes to brainstorm possible solutions to the problem of youth, alcohol and road accidents. The remaining group then evaluates the solutions.

3. Form two groups to try to solve a problem within the class or organisation. One group uses brainstorming, the other uses the problem-solving and decision-making sequence. In plenary session compare the two decision-making strategies in terms of participation experience and outcomes.

4. Work through the following case study, either on your own or with a group of fellow students.

    Your tutorial class has been divided into groups of five to work on a case study presentation. The task involves working through the case study as a group and then presenting the working to the tutorial class as a whole. This case study presentation is worth 20% of the course mark so it is important that it is done as well as possible. You have been nominated as the leader and convenor of your group. You and two other members of the group work well. You are all prepared and turn up for every meeting. However, two of the group have never turned up for a meeting. They always have some excuse and have never done any work. You have only two weeks left before your group has to present your case study. You have spoken to your tutor but he says that it is up to the group to sort out the problem. What do you do?

BIBLIOGRAPHY

Brilhart, J. K. and Galanes, G. J. 1995, *Effective Group Discussion,* 8th ed., Wm. C. Brown Communications, Inc., Wisconsin.
de Bono, E. 1990, *Lateral Thinking,* Penguin Books, London.
Dewey, J. 1933, *How We Think: A Restatement of the Relation of Reflective Thinking to the Educative Process,* D. C. Heath and Company, Boston.
Ellis, D. G. and Fisher, B. A. 1994, *Small Group Decision Making: Communication and the Group Process,* 4th ed., McGraw-Hill, New York.
Hicks, M. J. 2004, *Problem Solving and Decision Making: Hard, Soft and Creative Approaches,* 2nd ed., Thomson, London.
McBurney, J. and Hance, K. 1950, *Discussion in Human Affairs,* Simon & Schuster, New York.
Napier, R. W. and Gershenfeld, M. K. 1999, *Groups: Theory and Experience,* 6th ed., Houghton Mifflin Company, Boston.
O'Dell, W. F. 1991, *Effective Business Decision Making and the Educated Guess,* NTC Publishing Group, Chicago.
Osborne, A. F. 1953, *applied imagination,* Scribener's, New York.
Rickards, T. 1990, *Creativity and Problem Solving at Work,* Gower Publishing Company, Vermont.
Robson, M. 1993, *Problem Solving in Groups,* 2nd ed., Gower Publishing Company, Aldershot.
Sanders, R. 1999, *The Executive Decision Making Process: Identifying Problems and Assessing Outcomes,* Quorum Books, Westport, Connecticut.
Van Gundy, A. B. 1988, *Techniques of Structured Problem Solving,* 2nd ed., Van Nostrand Reinhold Company, New York.

Persuasion

CHAPTER 10

Upon completing this chapter you should be able to:
- appreciate the pervasive nature of persuasive communication in our everyday lives;
- demonstrate an awareness of the factors involved in source credibility;
- understand emotional and rational appeals in persuasion; and
- appreciate how persuasive appeals are structured and how they operate.

In Chapter 5, on letters, memos and email, we looked at persuasive letters, in particular the AIDA formula, which involves gaining the reader's attention, stimulating the reader's interest, arousing the reader's desire for whatever we are 'selling' and finally the action step, the point towards which the letter has been leading, the actual purpose of the letter. In this chapter we will look at persuasive communication in a broader context, in terms of the persuasive communication to which we are subjected, and in which we ourselves take part on a daily basis. We will look at what persuasion is, the impact of source credibility on persuasive messages, emotional and logical appeals and some persuasive strategies.

It can be argued that there is an element of persuasion in most communicative transactions. Certainly we are subjected to persuasive communication in many forms in our daily lives. We are not, however, always passive recipients. We, in our turn, use persuasive communication all the time. The most obvious form of persuasive communication, of course, is advertising. We are exposed to advertisements every time we open a newspaper or magazine, turn on the radio or switch on the television (even the ABC has advertisements even if only for forthcoming programs). Advertising, however, is only a part of the persuasive communication with which we are surrounded.

You are running late for lectures and want to borrow your mother's car. In your attempts to get your mother to lend you the car you use persuasion. Your father wants you to work harder and achieve higher grades. He uses persuasion to try to achieve his objective of getting you to work harder. You and your friend are trying to decide what to do on Friday night. You want to go to the movies, your friend wants to go to a night club. You will both use persuasion to try to achieve your objective, having your choice adopted by the other person. These are just some of the instances of the types of persuasive transactions which occur in our daily lives. As you can see, persuasive communication is pervasive and omnipresent.

Implicit in persuasion is the idea that we are trying to get another individual to think or act in a way desired by the persuader rather than by the person being persuaded. If you suggest to your flatmate, who is already clearly getting ready to go out, that it would be a good idea if he or she went out for a while there is no attempt at persuasion. You are merely reinforcing the behaviour already explicit in the preparations your flatmate is making. However, if your flatmate is lying on the sofa watching a film on television and you want your flatmate to go out, you will need to use persuasion as the intention is clearly to stay in and watch the film, rather than go out.

There are many definitions of persuasion. Miller (1980) considers that **persuasion** is operating in situations where one individual tries to modify behaviour through messages that aim to appeal both emotionally and rationally, often with an element of coercion. Reardon (1981) defines persuasion as a conscious attempt to change another individual's behaviour in order to achieve our own goals. If we view the behaviour of another individual as inconsistent, inappropriate or ineffective, or as in some way threatening our goals, we use persuasion to try to effect the changes we desire in the other person. O'Keefe (1990) defines persuasion as an attempt, through communication, to influence another person's mental state within a context allowing some measure of freedom to the person we are trying to persuade. Perloff (1993) defines persuasion in a similar manner as an attempt to try to change beliefs, attitudes or behaviour in an individual or a group of individuals within a context which allows some element of free choice to the persuadee.

Persuasion, therefore, is a conscious activity on the part of the persuader. It is a deliberate attempt to impose ideas upon another individual. However, if the individual we are trying to persuade is in a less powerful position, we are using coercion not persuasion. If someone drives in front of you, forcing you to change driving lanes, you have not been persuaded to change driving lanes, but if your passenger asks you to make a detour which involves turning off the highway and therefore changing driving lanes, you have been persuaded by your passenger to change driving lanes. The concept of free will on the part of the person being persuaded is a central element in persuasion.

Our attempts at persuasion are made through some form of communication. The communication medium we choose may be oral (a conversation, discussion, interview); it may be written (a letter, report); it may be a mixture of writing and graphics; or it may be audio and visuals (television advertisements). Whatever communication medium we use our aim is to convey a message which will, in some way, influence our audience to think or act in a way that we desire.

Source credibility

Source credibility refers to the degree to which we believe the person originating the persuasive message. Source credibility is dependent on a number of factors. Hovland, Janis and Kelley (1953) consider that source credibility depends on expertise and trustworthiness. **Expertise** is the perceived level of knowledge or qualifications possessed by the persuader. However, as Perloff (1993) points out, expertise has differing importance in assessments of source credibility. Source expertise is most effective where the audience is uninvolved or lacks knowledge of the area. If the audience is knowledgeable the impact of expertise in persuasion falls.

Trustworthiness, according to Eagley, Wood and Chaiken (1978), is dependent on the audience's evaluation of bias on the part of the persuader. For example, in a debate on immigration laws we would expect a refugee to speak in favour of liberalisation of immigration laws. We would interpret such support for liberalisation of immigration laws as indicating a personal bias resulting from the speaker's background and would assess the message accordingly. However, if the speaker spoke against liberalisation of immigration laws, or advocated safeguards or conditions on immigration, the message would carry greater credibility because the speaker would seem to be speaking against personal bias. We evaluate message credibility according to our perception of 'what's in it for the persuader'. For example, if we attend a financial advice seminar run by a bank which advises borrowing to negatively gear investments, we are aware of bias in the advice. Bank profits depend on lending money so it is to the bank's advantage to encourage people to borrow. Let us suppose you attend another financial advice seminar. This time it is run by the local Chamber of Commerce as part of its public relations and community education role and the advice is being given as a favour by a local accountant. In this situation there is a lower perceived level of bias on the part of the speaker which gives the message greater credibility.

Berlo, Lemert and Mertz (1970) believe that source credibility is more complex, involving not only expertise and trustworthiness but also **dynamism** (being seen as bold, energetic and active) and **safety** (being perceived as kind, friendly and just). Reardon (1991) makes the point that source credibility is multi-dimensional and may alter depending on the context and the relationship between the communicators. For example, we associate professional qualifications with a high level of expertise. A pronouncement about our health from a doctor, therefore, should have a high level of source credibility. However, if we know that the doctor is currently being sued for malpractice we may not place the same reliance on what is said.

Appeals to emotion

In his work on rhetoric, the Greek philosopher Aristotle, who lived between 384 and 322 BC, divided persuasion into **ethos**, which we could equate with trustworthiness since it involved the good sense, moral character and goodwill exhibited by the persuader; **pathos**, which involved appealing to the emotions; and **logos**, which provided logical reasons for the point being made.

We have already dealt with ethos in terms of source credibility. Let us look now at pathos in terms of appeals to our emotions. In 1943 Maslow published his article, 'A theory of human motivation', putting forward the basis of what later became known as Maslow's Hierarchy of Needs (and Figure 15.3 in Chapter 15, Organisational Communication, shows this hierarchy in diagrammatic form). Maslow categorised human motivation into five divisions. At the bottom of the hierarchy are the most basic needs, the **physical needs**, which relate to the need for food and shelter. The next step of the hierarchy relates to **security needs**, such as our need for stability, order, protection, job and financial security. The **need to belong** relates to our need for acceptance within family and work groups. The **need for esteem** involves our need for self-respect, status, recognition and prestige. The highest need is the **need for self-actualisation**, which involves our need to achieve our personal potential.

If we think of advertising, for example, we can see how the needs identified by Maslow are used in order to persuade. How many advertisements do you see that use an appeal to our need for safety and security?

CAN YOU AFFORD TO TAKE THE CHANCE?

Of course you can save money by not taking out health insurance—but what happens if you or your family become ill? Can you afford $5000 or more for a simple emergency procedure and a few days in hospital? If you can't then are you really saving money by not taking out health insurance?

Advertisements for breath fresheners, toothpastes, deodorants and dandruff preparations, for example, appeal to our need to belong.

Perhaps one of the most pervasive needs targeted by advertisers is the need for esteem. All the advertisements that rely on status and a sense of elitism appeal to this need.

Grandier Champagne—simply the best!

Rational appeals

Most persuasive messages contain a combination of emotional and rational appeals. Often emotional appeal will be used to stimulate interest and generate desire but it will be supported by evidence which appeals to logic and reason. The fallacies of misuse of statistics and illegitimate appeal to authority dealt with in Chapter 11, Clear Thinking, Logic and Argumentation, provide examples of appeals to reason. In the example of health care insurance, the message may have continued by providing facts and figures relating to the likelihood of hospitalisation for a family member, statistics on average length of hospital stay and costs and so on. In the Grandier Champagne instance the advertisement could have gone on to list any medals won by the champagne and favourable comments from wine experts. Advertisements which use claims such as '9 out of 10 doctors recommend . . .', or 'most top dog breeders recommend . . .' are using appeals to reason.

In considering persuasive communication we need to think beyond the obviously persuasive messages contained in advertisements. A professional report, for example, is predominantly a factual, analytical document based on verifiable data and expert opinion, and the tone and style, the use of third person impersonal for example, reinforce the objective, unbiased nature of the document. A report, however, as well as being a factual, objective document also has a persuasive purpose. After all, we want our readers to agree with our point of view and to accept our analysis of the situation. It is important that our recommendations are accepted and implemented, so we select and organise our data to achieve that end.

A letter of application and accompanying résumé are also exercises in persuasion. It is important for the credibility of the letter and résumé that our style is objective, unemotional and factual, just as it is important in a report. The vocabulary chosen should be as unemotional as possible. However, what we put in our letter and résumé and how we organise the material will depend on our assessment of the best way to persuade our reader that we are worth interviewing.

If we think of reports, letters of application and résumés, even essays, as persuasive communication, how does the AIDA formula fit in? We can still see the AIDA formula in reports, résumés and essays but because the primary appeal is to reason, rather than emotion, the stages are less vivid or arresting. An advertisement or sales letter needs to attract attention immediately. An advertisement trying to sell managed property trusts to retirees may begin:

What would you do if term deposit interest rates fell by half tomorrow?

The attention step of your report, essay or letter of application is contained in your statement of purpose. In the report and essay this is found in the introduction. In the letter of application it is found in your opening statement that you are applying for the position of Purchasing Manager advertised in *The Daily Bugle* of 27 March. The body of your report, essay or letter of application contains the interest and desire sections. The recommendations in your report provide the action step while the conclusion, which provides the final summation and restatement of the main points in an essay, can be thought of as, if not an action step, at least a final attempt to convince your reader of the strength of your argument. The action step in a letter of application is your repetition of interest in the position, an indication of when you would be available for interview and when you could take up the appointment if your application was successful.

Persuasive strategies

Because advertising provides one of the most obviously persuasive communicative mechanisms let us look at some advertisements in terms of how the persuasive message is constructed and operates.

Which of Maslow's hierarchy of needs is targeted by the advertisement in Figure 10.1? Let us look at the advertisement analytically. What are the first things we notice? Because of the layout of the advertisement the things we are likely to notice first, the things to which the design of the advertisement initially draws our attention, are the word 'Royalty' and the illustration of a woman's hand wearing a magnificent solitaire diamond ring. The separation of the word 'Royalty' from the rest of the sentence 'visits Sydney' emphasises the status and elitism of the product(s) being advertised. This advertisement is clearly designed to appeal to our need for status, recognition and respect. Notice that even the action step of the advertisement—'By appointment 9231 3299'—reinforces the sense of elitism. This is no normal 'walk through the door' shopping expedition but one requiring an appointment.

An analysis of the text further supports the appeal to status and the elitism of the caption and illustration. Words such as 'perfect symmetry', 'irreproachable finish', 'hallmarks', 'Royal House of Asscher', 'rare and exquisite diamond', 'finest diamond craftsmen in all the world' resonate with connotations of wealth, status and royalty.

If we think of the advertisement in terms of the AIDA formula, the caption 'Royalty visits Sydney' and the illustration provide the attention step. The interest and desire section are found in the text of the advertisement. The action step, as indicated above, is the invitation to 'phone for a personal appointment'.

Let us look at the second advertisement (Figure 10.2). This advertisement appeals to our need for security, for a copier that is reliable, is easy to use and one that will not let us down. However, there is also a secondary appeal to our need for respect in the emphasis on the centrality of customers and their needs, found in sentences such as 'For over 60 years, we have focused our approach to design and technology on our customers' needs' and 'We are dedicated to creating solutions that make complex tasks easy, and routine jobs effortless'.

The emotional appeal is designed to 'humanise' the machine, the Aficio copier, and thus make it more attractive. This appeal can be found in the illustration of a friendly, tail-wagging dog over

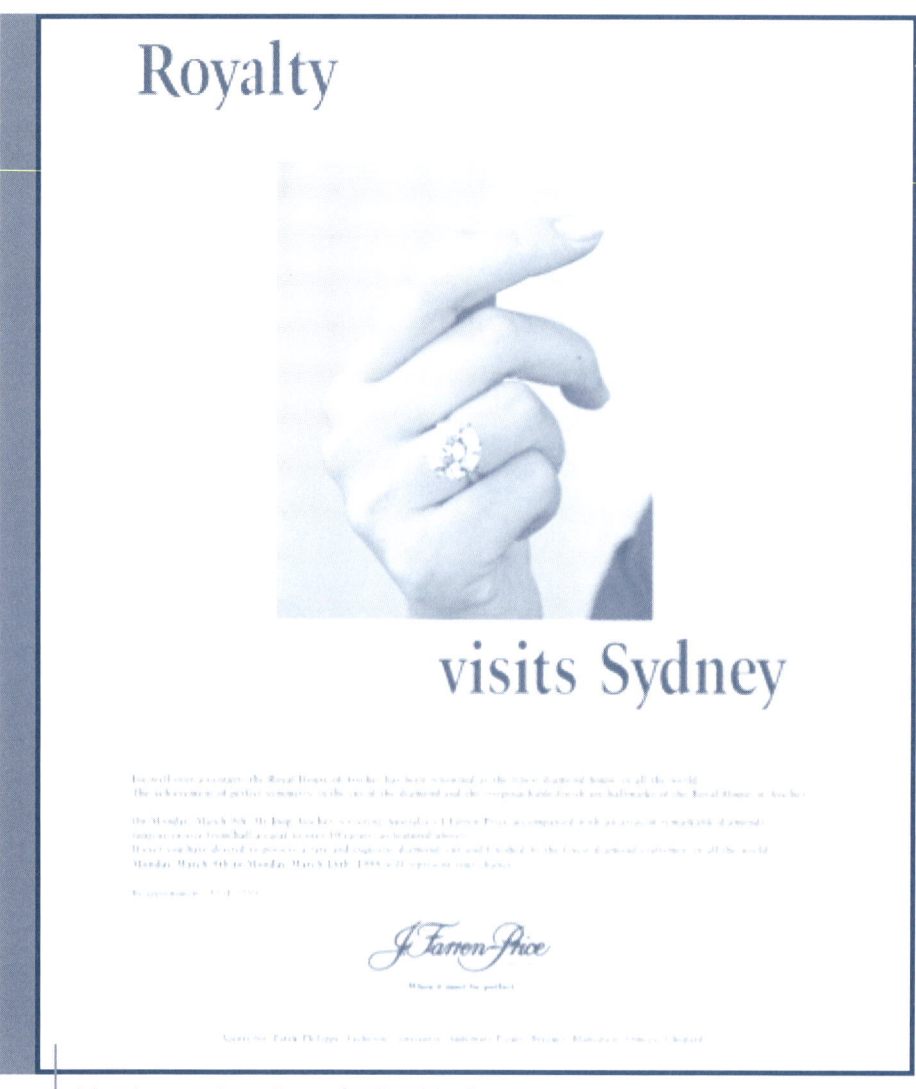

FIGURE 10.1 | Advertisement Appealing to Our Need for Status

the words 'Trustworthy. Reliable. Friendly.'. The dog has been called man's best friend and the emotional connotations attaching to the friendly, anxious-to-please graphic of the dog are linked to the Aficio copier by the repetition of the words 'Trustworthy. Reliable. Friendly.' above the illustration of the copier as well as by the claim that Aficio is 'rapidly becoming business's best friend.' The emotional appeal of this advertisement is reinforced by the slogan immediately preceding the action step, 'Simple solutions. Based on human needs.'.

Again, this advertisement can be read in terms of the AIDA formula. The graphic of the dog and the words 'Trustworthy. Reliable. Friendly.' provide the attention step. The following paragraph and the final slogan form the interest and desire steps, while the action step is the statement to contact Ricoh for more information.

While the J. Farren-Price advertisement appeals predominantly to the emotions, an analysis of the Ricoh advertisement illustrates that there is an appeal to logic as well as to the emotions.

Part Four   Problem Solving, Decision Making and Persuasion

FIGURE 10.2 Advertisement Appealing to Our Needs for Security and Respect

There is little technical information, which is in keeping with the theme of the advertisement of a machine that is friendly and easy to use, but there is information designed to provide logical support to the emotional appeal. This is found in the statements on what the Aficio can do: it can copy, fax and print from one convenient location, even if the location is a PC, and it can 'connect to your network' to give added flexibility.

We could, of course, analyse the two advertisements in more detail, looking for any fallacies and analysing the semiotic elements (which will be dealt with in Chapter 12, Nonverbal Communication) in much more detail. However, you should now have a working knowledge of how to analyse the persuasive appeals of advertisements since an analysis of most advertisements, both print and television, will show a similar adherence to the AIDA formula and a similar appeal to one or more of the needs identified in Maslow's hierarchy.

SUMMARY

Persuasive communication is part of our everyday lives. Integral to the success or otherwise of persuasive communication is our assessment of the credibility of the source of the message. Persuasive messages can be based on appeals to reason or the emotions, most usually a combination of both. Although persuasive communication can, and does, take many forms, from the highly sophisticated, professionally crafted advertisements we see in magazines and on television to the persuasive communication of everyday interpersonal exchanges, there is a high degree of commonality in the manner of persuasive appeals and the way persuasive messages are structured.

In the next chapter we will look at logic and argumentation, at the way arguments can be structured to try to persuade us to a particular viewpoint. We will also deal with fallacies and you might like to return to the two advertisements analysed in this chapter after you have the finished Chapter 11 to see if you can identify any fallacies.

KEY POINTS

- Persuasive messages are part of our lives. We both receive and send persuasive messages constantly.
- The success of any persuasive message is influenced by the credibility of the source of the message.
- Expertise, bias, trustworthiness, dynamism and safety concerns are all factors in our evaluation of source credibility.
- Persuasive communication can be based on appeals to emotion or reason, although most persuasive messages will be based on a mixture of emotional and rational appeals.
- Persuasive messages will normally follow the AIDA formula.

REVIEW QUESTIONS

1. What is persuasion? Provide examples of persuasive communication from your own experience.
2. What is involved in source credibility?
3. What are the levels in Maslow's hierarchy of needs? How does persuasive communication exploit those needs?

EXERCISES

1. Compare the source credibility of a current affairs program and a television advertisement. How do we judge source credibility and what part does source credibility play in our response to the communication?
2. Select a print or television advertisement and analyse it for emotional and rational appeals. Does one form of appeal predominate over the other? If so, why?
3. Analyse the relationship between Maslow's hierarchy of needs and an example of everyday persuasive communication. For example, what need could form the basis of an attempt to persuade you to go to the cinema rather than to a night club?
4. What is the relationship between advertisements and the AIDA formula? Analyse any print or television advertisement to support your view.

BIBLIOGRAPHY

Berlo, D. K., Lemert, J. B. and Mertz, R. I. 1970, 'Dimensions for evaluating the acceptability of message sources', *Public Opinion Quarterly,* 33, 563–76.

Dyer, G. 1988, *Advertising as Communication,* Routledge, New York.

Eagley, A. H., Wood, W. and Chaiken, S. 1978, 'Causal inferences about communicators and their effect on opinion change', *Journal of Personality and Social Psychology,* 36, 424–35.

Hovland, C. I., Janis, I. L. and Kelley, H. H. 1953, *Communication and Persuasion,* Yale University Press, New Haven.

Maslow, A. H. 1943 'A theory of human motivation', *Psychological Review,* 50, 370–96.

Miller, G. R. 1980, 'On being persuaded: Some basic distinctions', in *Persuasion: New Directions in Theory and Research,* eds M. E. Roloff and G. R. Miller, Sage Publications, California.

O'Keefe, D. J. 1990, *Persuasion: Theory and Research,* Sage Publications, California.

Perloff, R. M. 1993, *The Dynamics of Persuasion,* Lawrence Erlbaum Associates, New Jersey.

Perloff, R. M. 2003, *The Dynamics of Persuasion: Communication and Attitudes in the 21st Century,* Lawrence Erlbaum Associates, New Jersey.

Reardon, K. K. 1981, *Persuasion: Theory and Context,* Sage Publications, California.

Reardon, K. K. 1991, *Persuasion in Practice,* Sage Publications, California.

Storey, R. 1997, *The Art of Persuasive Communication,* Gower, Hampshire, England, and Brookfield, Vermont.

Williamson, J. 1987, *Decoding Advertisements: Ideology and Meaning in Advertising,* Marion Boyers Publishers Ltd, London.

Clear thinking, logic and argumentation

CHAPTER 11

Upon completing this chapter you should be able to:
- appreciate the importance of an understanding of logic and argumentation in day-to-day communication;
- determine whether or not statements constitute an argument;
- identify premises and conclusions;
- understand what is meant by deductive and inductive reasoning; and
- show an awareness of common fallacies or faults in reasoning.

Every day we are involved in making decisions, in evaluating information, in being the target of persuasion and trying to persuade in our turn. You listen to a talkback radio show on the way to university or work; do you agree with the views being put forward? Why do you agree? Perhaps what is being said happens to be what you already think, but can you provide reasons for your agreement? How rational or reasoned is your response? Perhaps you have an uneasy feeling that what is being said is not quite right but you are unable to say why.

Every time we pick up a newspaper or magazine, turn on the radio or television, we are faced with material that has been selected and presented in order to manipulate our responses or persuade us to a particular viewpoint or action. Even seemingly objective, factual programs such as news broadcasts or current affairs programs are not free of bias.

Every communicative act, whether intentionally or unintentionally, consciously or unconsciously, has elements of persuasion and manipulation. This is true not only of advertising and the mass media but of most of our communication. You and your friend discuss what to do at the weekend; you want to borrow the family car; your partner objects when you want to spend all day fishing—the exchanges that take place in these circumstances use arguments to persuade.

Because we are constantly surrounded by attempts to manipulate our responses, it could be argued that this chapter is the most important in the book. If we know when, and how, others are trying to manipulate our responses, we will be better able to make balanced, informed judgements and to resist being manipulated for the advantage of others. We will be in a position to make judgements on the basis of facts and evidence rather than merely in response to the persuasions of others. We will know whether something is logical or illogical and will be able to say why. We will know whether a cogent case has been made, or whether we are being asked to accept ideas and viewpoints with little or no evidence to support them.

What is logic and argumentation?

Studying logic provides us with the critical and analytical skills needed to evaluate the messages that reach us all the time. It also provides us with the skills to structure logical and convincing arguments ourselves—an essential requirement of most university assessments.

What do we mean when we speak of 'logic'? Holt (1987) claims that logic is directly linked to arguments. Arguments in the context of this chapter do not refer to fights or disagreements. An **argument** is a persuasive device designed to lead us to accept a certain viewpoint or opinion. Fearnside (1980) defines an argument as a linked sequence of reasoning designed to support a conclusion, an idea echoed by Holt's (1987) definition of an argument as containing ideas in a structured sequence leading to a conclusion.

Logic refers to the reasoning of the argument. It is the means by which we judge an argument, deciding whether it is good or bad, valid or invalid. In other words arguments are the way others try to persuade us or manipulate our responses, and **logic** is the means by which we judge the quality of the argument and decide whether to accept or reject the conclusion.

Arguments

Before we can assess an argument we need to be able to recognise what constitutes an argument. An argument contains a **conclusion**, the point towards which the whole argument is tending and the viewpoint or idea that we are being asked to accept, and one or more statements supporting or leading to the conclusion. The supporting statements are called **premises**. Below is an argument.

This particular form of argument is called a **syllogism** and it is a useful form to use to demonstrate premises and the conclusion.

> All artists are creative.
>
> Jane is an artist.
>
> Therefore, Jane is creative.

The conclusion is that Jane is creative. This is based on two premises. The first premise is the general statement that '[a]ll artists are creative'. This is followed by the second premise that 'Jane is an artist'. The two premises lead to the conclusion that 'Jane is creative'. Syllogisms are examples of deductive reasoning, which will be dealt with in more detail later in this chapter.

Unfortunately arguments are not always spelled out as clearly as the syllogism about Jane. Often, especially in advertisements, only the conclusion will be given. Think about the slogan 'feed the man meat'. This is the conclusion of an argument that could be expressed as:

> Meat is good for men.
>
> I want my man to be healthy.
>
> Therefore, I will feed my man meat.

Argument indicators

It is important to realise that not all series of statements are arguments. Let us look at the following statements.

> Every morning I have a shower before I have my breakfast. Then I catch the bus to work.

Do the statements about having a shower and breakfast constitute an argument? How do we decide if statements function as an argument or not? If we think back to the early definition of an argument as a sequence of ideas designed to prove a conclusion, we can see that a conclusion, a point towards which the statements are tending, is necessary for an argument to be taking place. One coarse and unsophisticated method of deciding whether an argument is taking place is to look for words which we can call **argument indicators**. Argument indicators are 'because' or, 'therefore', or any synonyms such as:

for	consequently
since	it follows that
seeing that	as a result

If such words are already present, or if we can insert them and the statements still make sense, then we have an argument. If inserting 'because' or 'therefore' makes nonsense of the statements there is no argument. So let us return to our statements about having a shower, breakfast and then catching the bus.

> Every morning I have a shower before I have my breakfast. Then I catch the bus to work.

Let us try adding the argument indicators.

> Every morning I have a shower before I have my breakfast. Therefore, I catch the bus to work.

Every morning I have a shower before I have my breakfast because I catch the bus to work.

We can see that adding, 'therefore' or 'because' really does not make sense so we can say that the statements do not constitute an argument. They are simply statements of what happens each workday morning. Let us look at the following statements.

I know the bus will be late this morning. It has been late every morning this week.

We can insert either 'because' or 'therefore' without making nonsense of the statements.

Because the bus has been late every morning this week I know it will be late this morning.

The bus has been late every morning this week so (therefore) it will be late this morning.

Here is another set of statements.

Every Thursday night I go to yoga. Then I go home.

Do these statements constitute an argument? Let us try to add 'because' or 'therefore' and see if the statements still make sense.

Because every Thursday night I go to yoga, then I go home.

Every Thursday night I go to yoga so (therefore) I then go home.

Adding 'because' or 'so' or 'therefore' does not make sense so we can say that the statements about yoga on Thursday do not represent an argument but are simply statements about what you do each Thursday night. There is no attempt to persuade anyone to a particular viewpoint.

Identifying premises and conclusions

Identifying arguments, however, is only half the task. If we think back to the definitions of arguments at the start of this chapter, we can see the importance of the conclusion. No matter where it occurs in the argument, the conclusion is the point towards which the whole argument is moving. It is what the other person is trying to convince us of, is wanting us to accept, so identification of the conclusion is critical in our evaluation of the argument as a whole. If we refer to the argument indicators we can say that 'because', 'if', 'for', 'since', 'seeing that' and so on precede premises; 'therefore' and its synonyms such as 'so', 'consequently', 'then', 'it follows that' precede conclusions.

Below is an argument. What is the conclusion?

If the weather is fine then we will go to the beach.

The conclusion is 'we will go to the beach' and it is dependent on the premise 'if the weather is fine'. If you are not sure which is the conclusion, try rewriting the argument using 'because' or, 'therefore'.

The weather is fine therefore we will go to the beach.

We will go to the beach because the weather is fine.

Notice that however we turn the argument around the conclusion remains the same. In other words, in the argument above the conclusion is always 'we will go to the beach' regardless of how we sequence the material.

Truth and validity

It is important to distinguish between **truth** and **validity**. If something is true it corresponds to the facts. If we see the rain we accept the truth of the statement that it is a rainy day. We say an argument is valid if it has consistent internal logic. In other words an argument is valid if it does not infringe the rules of logic.

Sound and unsound arguments

An argument can be valid, that is, it does not break the rules of logic, and yet be false. For example:

> All women are weak.
>
> Sue is a woman.
>
> Therefore Sue is weak.

This argument is logically consistent. If all women are weak then Sue would, logically, also be weak. However, we do not accept the argument because, although it has logical consistency, it is based on a false premise, namely that all women are weak. Although the argument is valid (logically consistent) it is false and we therefore say it is an **unsound argument**. If an argument is both valid and true it is called a **sound argument**.

Although we will return to absolute terms later when we deal with fallacies, it should be noted here that what makes the premise 'all women are weak' false is the absolute term 'all'. The problem with absolute terms is that it needs only one exception to undermine the argument.

Deductive and inductive reasoning

There are two basic ways of structuring an argument: deductive and inductive.

Deductive reasoning

Deductive reasoning uses a general or universal statement to prove a particular instance. In other words, the statements move from the general to the particular.

$$G \longrightarrow P$$

The syllogism we looked at earlier in this chapter is an example of deductive reasoning. It moves from a general statement: '[a]ll artists are creative' to prove a particular example: 'Jane is creative'.

Inductive reasoning

Inductive reasoning is sometimes called the scientific method because it uses particular examples to prove a general statement or theory. In other words it moves from the particular to the general.

$$P \longrightarrow G$$

Because any generalisation is arrived at by taking an inductive leap, that is, by assuming that what is true of a sample will be true of the whole, inductive reasoning can never have the certainty of deductive reasoning. Fearnside (1980) claims that in deductive reasoning the conclusions follow inescapably from the premises so if the premises are true the conclusion must also be true. Because of the way it operates, deductive reasoning contains an inherent certainty that is not possible for inductive reasoning. Inductive reasoning involves an inferential leap from some to all that will always create logical uncertainty because there will always be the logical possibility of an exception which will undermine the argument.

For an inductive generalisation to be convincing it must be based on a sample that is:

* sufficiently large; and

* sufficiently representative.

The Ginger Meggs comic that follows shows Cuthbert making a generalisation which is based on a sample that is both insufficiently large and insufficiently representative; in other words Cuthbert is making a false or faulty generalisation.

© Jimera Pty Ltd and Kemsley. Reproduced with permission.

Three of the most common methods of argument—generalisation, analogy and causal relationship—are examples of inductive reasoning because they all use a particular example or examples to prove a general conclusion.

If I tell you not to buy Brand X pen because I bought one recently and it was faulty, I am using inductive reasoning. I am generalising that Brand X pens are unreliable from my recent experience. However, one instance of Brand X pens not working is both an inadequate and unrepresentative sample. If I can say that Brand X pens are faulty because I have bought them on a number of occasions over the past months and 80% of those I bought did not work, my friends and family have had similar experiences with Brand X pens and I know that the government suppliers are no longer buying Brand X pens because they are unreliable, then I have a much stronger case for claiming Brand X pens do not work. However, there remains the possibility that someone down the road could have had only good experiences with Brand X pens. There is always an element of doubt with inductive reasoning.

Fallacies

A **fallacy** is a flaw or fault in the reasoning and logic. Fallacies may be conscious or unconscious. They may represent flaws in legitimate methods of argument or they may be illegitimate methods of argument. The purpose in examining fallacies is to highlight the ways in which we can sometimes be persuaded with little or no logical basis for the persuasion.

In this chapter we give names to the more common fallacies but, while it is often helpful to name things, a more important aspect of examining fallacies is to be aware of flaws in logic, to be able to judge whether arguments are valid or not.

Common fallacies

Fallacies can be categorised into many divisions. Holt (1987), for example, lists 19 fallacies; Fearnside (1980) lists 29. There can be some overlap between fallacies and it is sometimes difficult to classify fallacies neatly; however, we can be aware of the most common fallacies and these are listed below. They are arranged in two groups: those that fall within legitimate methods of argument and those that are dishonest or illegitimate methods of argument. Legitimate methods of argument become fallacies only if there is some flaw in the reasoning, some fault in the logic. Appealing to authority is something that we do all the time in academic and scholarly work. It becomes misuse of authority, or a fallacy, if there is a flaw in the logic, if the authority being appealed to is not a real or recognised authority in the area of the argument, for example.

Legitimate methods of argument:

* generalisation;
* analogy;
* causal relationship;
* classification;
* appeal to authority; and
* appeal to statistics.

Illegitimate methods of argument do not rely on reason and logic. Indeed they function to sidestep or undermine rational analysis.

Illegitimate methods of argument:

* begging the question;
* appeal to the masses;
* ad hominem (personal attack or argument against the person);
* appeal to pity;
* criticism forestaller; and
* emotive language and absolute terms.

Legitimate methods of argument

FAULTY GENERALISATION

Using generalisation is one of the most common ways in which we come to conclusions. It involves reaching a conclusion about a whole class or category on the basis of a sample. However, for a generalisation to be valid it must be based on a sufficient and representative sample.

Let us look at the following argument:

> That dentist doesn't know what he is doing. He really hurt me yesterday.

The conclusion (generalisation) is that the dentist does not know what he is doing and this is based on the premise that he hurt me yesterday. This is a faulty generalisation because it is based on a sample that is too small (just one visit) and unrepresentative (just one person and one treatment). If you had had a similar experience every time you visited that dentist and if everyone else you knew who had gone to that dentist had had a similar experience there would be some grounds for the generalisation, but one visit by one person involving only one (possibly unusually painful) treatment is neither a sufficient nor a representative sample.

FALSE (OR FAULTY) ANALOGY

Analogy depends on comparison and, like generalisation, is one of the ways we normally think about problems. Reasoning from analogy occurs when it is claimed that because such and such is true of X and because Y is like X, such and such must also be true of Y. Remember that analogy is a legitimate method of putting forward an argument, so not all analogies (or all generalisations) will be fallacies. The important element in considering analogy is whether the things being compared are really similar in terms of the conclusion. It does not matter how similar they are in other ways; for the argument to be valid the two things being compared must be similar in relation to the conclusion.

> Farmers get government help during droughts so struggling theatres should get government assistance too.

In order to judge whether the argument above works or not, we must identify the conclusion. Here the conclusion is that struggling theatres should get government help and that is based on the fact that struggling farmers get government assistance. Do you think the analogy is valid? Are the two things being compared sufficiently similar in relation to the conclusion? If they are not then the analogy fails.

FALSE CAUSE (OR FAULTY CAUSAL RELATIONSHIP)

Cause–effect relationship is another commonly used method of reaching conclusions. Like generalisation and analogy, it can be valid. However, in order for a causal relationship to be valid there must be a clear and unambiguous relationship between what is claimed to be the cause and the effect. If a tree falls on the power lines in a storm and breaks the wires I am justified in claiming that the fallen tree and broken power lines are the cause of the fact that I have no power in my home. Unfortunately the matter is often not so simple. Just because one event follows another does not necessarily mean that the first event caused the second or even that the first event alone caused the second.

> We need to keep an eye on that new waitress. Since she arrived the tips have gone down.

Here we are being asked to accept that the new waitress is taking some of the tips on the basis that since she came the tips have gone down. Is there a clear and unambiguous relationship between the new waitress and the reduction in tips? Could other factors be involved? Perhaps there have been fewer customers, or the clientele may have been less generous. The fact that fewer tips follow upon the advent of the new waitress does not prove that she is responsible.

FALSE (OR FAULTY) CLASSIFICATION (ALSO CALLED FALSE DILEMMA, BLACK AND WHITE FALLACY, OR THE EITHER/OR FALLACY)

Classification is one of the ways in which we organise our world and one of the methods we use in putting forward arguments. What happens in false classification is an oversimplification. What could be a complex situation is reduced to a binary opposition and in the process is falsified.

False classification occurs when the person putting forward the argument asserts that there are only two polarised alternatives. 'If you are not for us, you are against us' is an example of this fallacy.

> We have only two options. We can either agree to the union's demands or we can go out of business.

Are these two options really the only ones? What about discussion, negotiation, compromise and so on?

MISUSE OF AUTHORITY

Anyone who has studied or worked in an academic environment knows that supporting arguments by quoting relevant authorities is a legitimate method of validating or supporting a viewpoint. Using authorities to support an argument becomes a fallacy if the authorities quoted are not recognised authorities within the field of the argument. The important question is whether the authority quoted is:

* a recognised authority; and
* an authority in a field relevant to the argument.

To quote the Governor of the Reserve Bank to support an argument about fiscal matters would be appropriate, but to use a famous film star or model as authority for a particular brand of beauty product, soap or shampoo is a fallacy. Advertising is a rich source of the fallacy of misuse of authority: nameless dentists recommend toothbrushes or toothpaste; white coated figures extol the virtues of washing powder; famous beauties tell us about skin cream; sporting identities are seen with particular brands of drinks. However, what do we know about the nameless dentist? Does wearing a white coat make someone a recognised expert on washing powder? How does being beautiful mean that the person is an expert on skin cream? Why should being a good sportsperson mean that the person is a dietary expert?

MISUSE OF STATISTICS

Using statistics is a legitimate and often powerful way to support an argument. Statistics can provide substantiation for a claim. However, what often happens when statistics are used in an argument is that we get only part of the statistical picture. We get what could be called a censored version. Take, for example, the use of 'average'.

> This class has done well. The average mark in the examination was 70%.

What does 'average' mean here? The average mark may be 70% but that could be because a few students did very well indeed while the majority of the students may have achieved quite ordinary marks.

Illegitimate methods of argument

The fallacies that follow use illegitimate methods of argument. They rely not on logic but on emotion and try to sidestep rational, logical discussion.

BEGGING THE QUESTION (IN AN EXTENDED FORM THIS BECOMES A CIRCULAR ARGUMENT)

Begging the question is often a difficult fallacy to recognise. In essence this form of argument provides no evidence in support of the conclusion. Rather, it consists of the conclusion repeated in different words.

> Euthanasia is morally wrong. There can be no moral justification for killing another human being.

Here the conclusion is that euthanasia is morally wrong but, instead of providing evidence to support that conclusion, the conclusion is simply repeated in different words.

APPEAL TO THE MASSES (ALSO CALLED APPEAL TO POPULARITY, APPEAL TO THE CROWD OR APPEAL TO COMMONSENSE)

This method of argument functions by appealing to the likes and dislikes of the audience or by implying that everyone agrees and that to disagree is to be different from everyone else. This method of argument is the basis of advertising claims that such and such is the best selling product in Australia or overseas. Arguments using phrases such as 'everyone knows', or 'it is common knowledge' are using appeal to the masses.

AD HOMINEM (ALSO CALLED PERSONAL ATTACK OR ARGUMENT AGAINST THE PERSON)

This is a dishonest method of argument. *Ad hominem* could be called a red herring for it does not address the argument itself but seeks to distract attention from the argument to a personal attack.

> Of course he's opposed to reduced government spending. His firm does contract work for the government.

Analysis of the advantages or otherwise of reduced government spending does not take place because the argument is removed from the area of government spending to an attack on the person opposed to reduction in government spending.

APPEAL TO PITY

Appeal to pity functions in a similar manner to the *ad hominem* fallacy. It does not address the argument itself but appeals to some pathetic circumstance or situation. Situations where the family or domestic circumstances of an accused person are put forward in court (poor childhood, dependent children, aged mother and so on) are examples of this fallacy.

> How can you condemn my client to prison? What will happen to his wife and three children if he cannot work to support them?

CRITICISM FORESTALLER

This fallacy functions by using words or phrases that make it difficult to disagree with the argument. You have probably heard that unanswerable question 'when did you stop beating your wife?' Criticism forestaller operates in much the same way. A letter about hooliganism signed by 'Anzac Veteran' and using phrases such as 'every loyal Australian' is an example of criticism forestaller.

> Only those with intelligence and sensitivity are capable of appreciating the subtle complexity of Ewen Wittersand's art.

Using the phrase 'only those with intelligence and sensitivity' implies that anyone who does not like Ewen Wittersand's art is unintelligent and insensitive.

EMOTIVE LANGUAGE AND ABSOLUTE TERMS

Emotive language makes use of the connotative dimension of words. Words, as we noted earlier, have both denotative and connotative meanings. The connotative meanings are the emotions or feelings aroused by the words. Words can be chosen to be neutral or emotion laden and emotive language deliberately uses language with strong emotional overtones. The Letters to the Editor section of newspapers is usually a good place to find emotive language. Words such as 'shocked', 'do-gooders', 'bludgers' and 'alarming' are emotive terms. Emotive language however, is not always negative. Words such as 'glorious', 'worthy' and 'valued' are also emotive. Even seemingly neutral words can become emotive in certain contexts. To say that 'crossing the road without looking first could be dangerous' is fairly neutral but to say that 'to close Goulburn prison would be dangerous' is more emotive.

Absolute terms are words such as 'all', 'every', 'never' and 'none'. We live in an essentially contingent world in which absolute terms are rarely appropriate. Certainly using 'some' or 'most' rather than 'all' in an argument weakens its strength; however, when using absolute terms it requires only one exception to invalidate the argument.

Read the following letter to the editor and see if you can identify the fallacies.

> Dear Sir
>
> All intelligent people will be aghast at the proposals of the McPherson inquiry to reduce the National Orchestra and to abolish the training orchestra. But what can we expect? After all, McPherson is merely a businessman and what would a businessman know about the cultural needs of the community? For that matter what would our politicians know? I suspect that most of our politicians could not tell the difference between a musical score and a stock-market report.
>
> The cultural intelligentsia may be in a minority in Australia, but this minority must make itself heard among the rabble of Philistines at present in charge of arts funding. Many other minority groups (farmers, for example) are treated handsomely compared with the cultural elite.
>
> Australia is a wealthy country, yet we spend less than 1% of the Commonwealth budget on promoting the arts. Even Switzerland spends 9%.
>
> The civilisations of Greece and Rome declined and died after neglecting their cultural endeavours and concentrating instead on business and profit. Are we to sit back and wait for the same thing to happen here?
>
> Yours sincerely
>
> Struggling Musician's Mother

'All intelligent people' is an example of an appeal to the crowd. A case could also be made for considering it to be criticism forestaller since disagreeing would mean saying you were not intelligent.

The comments on businessmen and politicians provide examples of *ad hominem* fallacies. There is no attempt to discuss or analyse the findings of the McPherson inquiry rationally. There is simply a personal attack on McPherson in particular and politicians in general.

The cultural intelligentsia is an example of criticism forestaller.

The comparison between other minority groups and the cultural elite is an example of a false analogy.

The comparison of Australia and Switzerland could be regarded as a false analogy but it could also be regarded as misuse of statistics. Without, for example, an indication of the per capita funds available to the respective governments a comparison of Australia's 1% and Switzerland's 9% does not mean very much.

The claim about the cause of the decline of ancient Greece and Rome is an example of false cause. What is the support for the assertion that the replacement of culture with profit and loss caused the decline of ancient Greece and Rome?

'Struggling Musician's Mother' is an example of an appeal to pity.

Emotive language is found in words such as 'aghast', 'abolish', 'cultural intelligentsia', 'rabble of Philistines', 'handsomely', 'cultural elite', 'wealthy', 'neglecting', 'struggling'.

'All' is an example of an absolute term.

SUMMARY

Logic uses premises or supporting statements to prove a conclusion which we are asked to accept.

Logic and argumentation are part of the persuasive messages which we both receive and send on a daily basis. This chapter has dealt with what constitutes an argument; how arguments can be structured; and how to analyse arguments to determine whether the argument is valid or contains some logical inconsistency. We do not need to disagree or resist all attempts at persuasion but we should be aware of how arguments can be used to manipulate our responses and be able to determine whether the arguments are valid or contain fallacies.

In the next chapter we move on to considering nonverbal communication and its role in the communication process.

KEY POINTS

- Logic refers to arguments which are ideas structured in sequence to prove a certain point.
- Arguments consist of at least one premise or supporting statement and a conclusion.
- Arguments can be structured as deductive or inductive.
- Deductive reasoning uses a general example to prove a particular conclusion.
- Inductive reasoning uses particular examples to formulate a general conclusion.
- Fallacies are flaws or faults in reasoning.
- Fallacies can represent flaws in legitimate methods of argument or they can be illegitimate methods of argument.

REVIEW QUESTIONS

1. What is an argument?
2. What is the difference between truth and validity?
3. What makes an argument unsound?
4. What form of reasoning is used in syllogisms?

5. What is meant by inductive reasoning?

6. What is a fallacy?

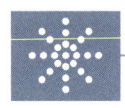

EXERCISES

1. Does the following statement constitute an argument?

    Brand X soap dried my skin so I have changed to Brand Y.

2. What is the conclusion in the following argument?

    Tom's bike must be broken. He's been walking to school all week.

3. Write a syllogism that could have as the conclusion the statement that 'my pet chases mice'.

4. Is the following argument deductive or inductive? This rose has a perfume. After all, all roses have perfume.

5. Select a letter to the editor which you think is good. Analyse it for fallacies and absolute terms. Has your perception of the persuasive appeal of the letter changed since your analysis? If so, how and why?

6. Select any advertisement and list the emotive language and absolute terms. What effect did the emotive language and absolute terms have in relation to the persuasive appeal of the advertisement?

7. Analyse the following letter, identifying fallacies and emotive language and absolute terms.

    Dear Editor

    I am writing to complain about the price of books. Every educated person knows that fewer people are reading books every year. My own children can be regarded as typical. They never open a book and I understand that on average 70% of people under twenty-five never read anything more literary than comics. A civilisation depends on the culture of its population, and that means a population that reads. Are we to sink into barbarism?

    The eminent scientist, Professor Yeovill is, quoted as saying that reading books is a central indicator of a caring society. It is, therefore, vital that we encourage reading among our population but this high cost for books is discouraging reading. Indeed, it is an active deterrent to reading. As anyone who has travelled will know, books have always been more expensive in this country than anywhere else in the world and GST has made them even more expensive. Soon we will have to save up to buy books putting impossible pressure on libraries.

    It is all very well for the Minister to talk about the Internet. His son works for an Internet company and I am sure he has a whole library full of books anyway, but for the average person the Internet provides a poor substitute for books.

    Books are still popular—just look at the Harry Potter books—but for how much longer? So I say, let's lobby for cheaper books.

    Yours sincerely

    Annabelle Lawson, teacher and mother of five.

BIBLIOGRAPHY

Allen, M. 1997, *Smart Thinking: Skills for Critical Understanding and Writing,* Oxford University Press, Melbourne.

Fearnside, W. W. 1980, *About Thinking,* Prentice Hall, New Jersey.

Gensler, H. J. 2002, *Introduction to Logic,* Routledge, London and New York.

Herrick, J. A. 1998, *Argumentation: Understanding and Shaping Arguments,* Allyn and Bacon, Boston.

Hibbins, G. M. 1990, *Stands to Reason: A Guide to Argument,* 4th ed., Macmillan, Melbourne.

Holt, R. F. 1987, *Clear Thinking: A Short Course in Everyday Logic,* Pitman Publishing Pty Ltd, South Melbourne.

Hurley, P. J. 1991, *A Concise Introduction to Logic,* 4th ed., Wadsworth Publishing Company, Belmont, California.

Kahane, H. 1995, *Logic and Philosophy: A Modern Introduction,* 7th ed., Wadsworth Publishing Company, Belmont, California.

Millgram, E. 1997, *Practical Induction,* Harvard University Press, Cambridge, Mass.

Thomas, S. N. 1986, *Practical Reasoning in Natural Language,* 3rd ed., Prentice Hall, New Jersey.

Waller, B. N. 1994, *Critical Thinking: Consider the Verdict,* 2nd ed., Prentice Hall, New Jersey.

Warwick, I. 1989, *Critical Thinking and Communication,* 3rd ed., Allyn and Bacon, Boston.

Woods, J., Irvine, A. D. and Walton, D. N. 2000, *Argument: Critical Thinking, Logic and the Fallacies,* Prentice Hall, Toronto.

Part Five

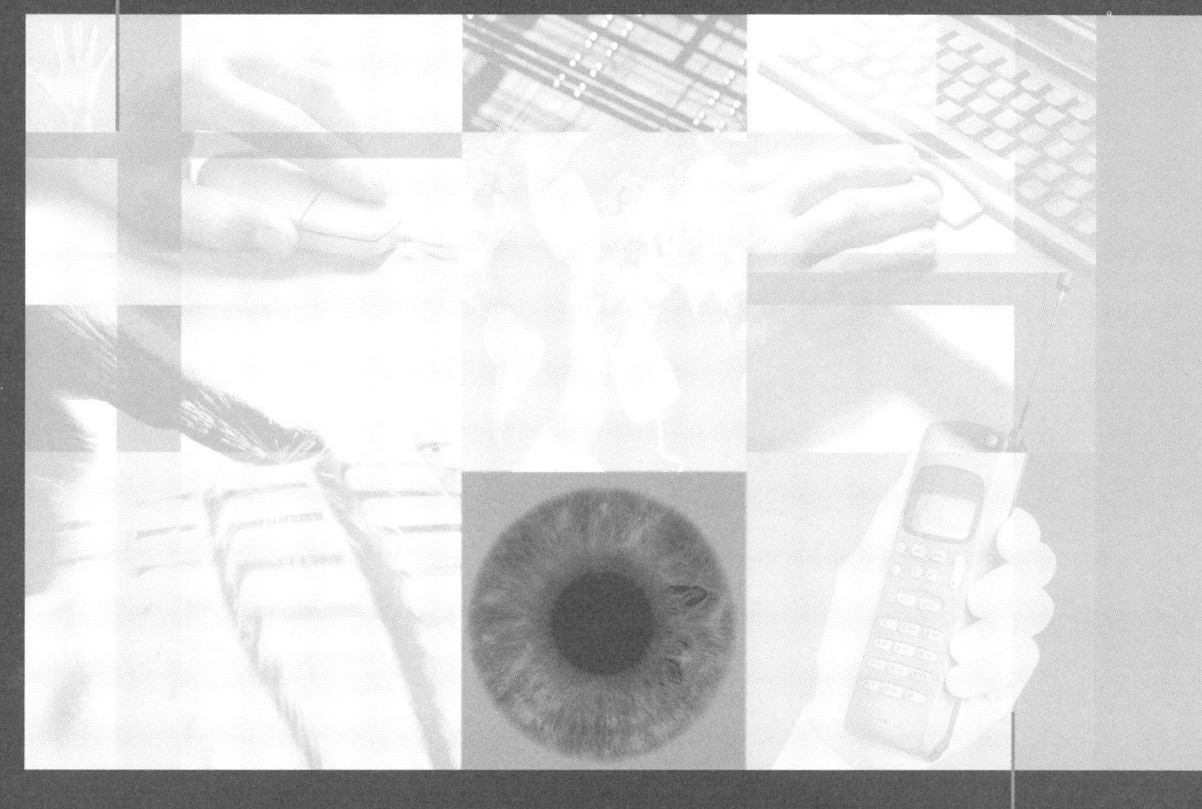

Interpersonal and Professional Communication

Nonverbal communication

CHAPTER 12

Upon completing this chapter you should be able to:
- understand what is meant by nonverbal communication;
- appreciate the importance of nonverbal communication in the communication process;
- demonstrate an awareness of the difficulties of accurate assessment of nonverbal cues;
- understand the relationship between verbal and nonverbal communication; and
- demonstrate an awareness of the six major categories of nonverbal communication and their functioning within the communication process.

Nonverbal communication includes everything about us that sends a message of some kind without words. Clothing, for example, conveys particular information and messages. Some professions have specific clothing codes—the armed forces, the police, the judiciary, chefs and so on are professionally categorised by their clothing—but each one of us sends some sort of message through the clothes we wear, our choice of hairstyle and jewellery and so on. Our surroundings also contain nonverbal cues. Have you ever wondered, for example, why fast food chains such as McDonald's and Kentucky Fried are well lit with hard, refractive surfaces, quite different from some restaurants with soft lights, soft chairs, carpets and so on? Which décor sends a message to linger, relax and stay? What message am I sending if I place a desk between myself and any visitors to my office? If I want to establish rapport would it be better to move from behind my desk?

Although nonverbal communication is commonly thought of as 'body language', we use our senses of hearing, touch and smell as well as sight in decoding nonverbal messages. So, let us look in more detail at nonverbal communication, which is defined by Malandro, Barker and Barker (1989) as the process in which nonverbal behaviours, either alone or associated with verbal behaviours, are used, within a particular situation or context, in the exchange and interpretation of messages. In its literal sense nonverbal communication means communication 'without words'. It involves all those elements of the communication process that are not embodied in words. Yet even this definition is not strictly accurate as spoken words and even written words can, and do, have nonverbal components.

Nonverbal communication is continuous and omnipresent. In Chapter 2, on communication theory, communication was described as a continuous process and the point was made that it was impossible not to communicate. Even if you sit in a corner facing the wall with your eyes closed and your arms crossed you are still communicating; indeed, you are communicating quite forcefully and you are communicating nonverbally.

In this chapter we will examine nonverbal communication in terms of its most important aspects, the interrelationship between verbal and nonverbal communication and some of the elements of nonverbal communication.

Important aspects

Nonverbal communication is continuous

Arliss (1991), writing about communication flow within conversations, argues that verbal communication is discrete, or occurs in separated segments, but nonverbal communication is continuous. In other words, while the verbal aspects of conversations are divided into separated 'turns' of speaking or listening, nonverbal communication occurs continuously. While participants either talk or listen, they communicate nonverbally whether talking or listening.

Think of any conversation you have observed. While the speaker is talking what is the listener doing? Depending on the listener's reaction to the speaker and what is being said the listener may be leaning slightly forward or leaning away, looking towards or away from the speaker, nodding, smiling, having arms crossed, frowning, shaking the head and so on. At the same time the speaker is also communicating nonverbally through gesture, posture, vocal inflection and direction of gaze. In fact we can think of any conversation as both a verbal and nonverbal dialogue.

Nonverbal communication can be both unintentional and intentional

Nonverbal behaviour can be unintentional. Leathers (1997) makes the point that, while we can control our nonverbal behaviours for a time, maintaining that conscious control is difficult. For this reason, nonverbal behaviour may 'give the lie' to what is said. Indeed, it is perhaps because we think that we have more control over words than over facial expressions and posture that we place more reliance on nonverbal cues than we do on words. Expressions of surprise and postural changes associated with an unexpected or startling occurrence and displacement activity of foot tapping or face touching to express the emotion that is being masked in facial expressions or general posture are examples of occasions when nonverbal behaviour operates without our conscious control.

How many of us still use gestures when talking on the telephone? The person we are talking to cannot see the gestures so they serve no useful purpose but we still add the nonverbal element of gestures to our telephone conversations. However, nonverbal communication can be intentional. We can regulate or control nonverbal behaviour to some extent. For example, a mother who sees her child about to do something wrong will frown and shake her head to deter the child.

Nonverbal communication conveys emotion

Words provide our main mechanism for conveying ideas or thoughts but nonverbal communication is our primary means of conveying emotion. Birdwhistell (1970) claimed that 65% of the emotional content of messages resided in nonverbal elements. Mehrabian (1972) claimed that 93% of the emotional content of any message was embodied in the nonverbal elements and only 7% in the words.

If we think of our everyday communication, dividing it into that which is concerned with the transmission of ideas and that which is concerned with emotion, we can see that, while nonverbal communication is a vital part of the communication process, its power resides in its capacity to convey emotion, not ideas. For example, if we were taking part in a debate on euthanasia it would be very difficult to put our ideas across without words, for it is in words that our argument for or against euthanasia is embodied. However, we can easily communicate tiredness or anger without words simply by nonverbal behaviour. In the photograph in Figure 12.1 it is not hard to interpret the emotion shown by Roger Federer who has just won the US Men's Tennis Open, or the emotion of the loser, Lleyton Hewitt.

Nonverbal communication provides clues not facts

Nonverbal communication can be ambiguous. While it is easy to observe nonverbal behaviour, it is not always easy to judge such behaviour accurately. For example, your flatmate comes in, plops down in a chair, arms crossed, saying nothing. Does this mean that your flatmate is angry with you, upset about something that happened before coming in or just plain tired? This is why the accuracy of our assessment of nonverbal cues increases the better we know the other person. Knowledge of the other person provides us with a **baseline**, that is, a knowledge of their normal behaviour. This helps us to know if there are any deviations from normal nonverbal behaviour.

For example, if your friend is crashing around angrily you might take little notice if your friend has a short temper and often behaves in such a way. However, if your friend is normally placid and even-tempered such an outburst would have far greater significance and you would take much more notice of it. So it is important that nonverbal behaviour should be regarded as providing clues only, not irrefutable facts.

FIGURE 12.1 Roger Federer, After Beating Lleyton Hewitt in the US Men's Tennis Open

Sydney Morning Herald 14 September 2004 'The Fourth is with him, and so is History'.
Photo: AP/Greg Bull

Nonverbal cues should be read as clusters

You will sometimes find, in books and magazines, lists of postures and gestures and their nonverbal meanings. Such lists may, for example, have withdrawal, defensiveness or defiance signalled by crossed arms, while standing with hands on hips, feet apart, signals determination. But that may not always be so. It is important to take in the whole picture. What is the facial expression? Is the person smiling, frowning, looking interested? What is the level of tension? Does the person seem relatively relaxed or tense? What is the spatial relationship between the people communicating?

Nonverbal communication occurs within a context

All communication occurs within a context but the context is particularly important in relation to nonverbal communication. A wink, for example, can have a variety of meanings depending on the context. A wink while you are making a statement can mean 'I don't really mean this' or 'this isn't really true'. A wink while someone else is speaking can mean 'here he goes again' or 'I don't really believe that, do you?'

Nonverbal communication is influenced by culture

Culture is, of course, part of the communication context so it is not surprising to find that culture influences nonverbal behaviour. Despite cultural differences, however, there are some areas of similarity or commonality. For example, according to Keating *et al.* (1981) in most cultures smiling is interpreted as evidence of happiness, while non-smiling is taken as evidence of dominance. Indeed, much research has been done, particularly by Ekman, on the universality of emotions, of the common interpretation of the emotions embodied in facial expressions across cultures, including both literate and pre-literate cultures. According to Argyle (1988) even some gestures are common across cultures. He lists pointing, shrugging, head nodding, clapping, beckoning and waving, using gestures to outline the female figure, together with the halt sign, the pat on the back, the thumbs down, head tilted with flat palm for sleep and using the flat of the hand to indicate height as being common gestures across cultures.

However, other gestures seem to be more culture dependent. According to Knapp and Hall (1992) making a ring between thumb and finger means 'OK' in the United States and northern Europe but in southern France and Belgium it means 'worthless', in Japan it means 'money', while in Greece and Turkey it is an insulting or vulgar sexual invitation. It is this culture-dependent element of nonverbal communication that can cause cross-cultural communication problems.

Nonverbal communication is gender influenced

Gender is a cultural construct so, if nonverbal communication is influenced by culture, it is inevitable that it will also be influenced by gender. In *Gender Communication* (1991), Arliss claims that women smile more than men and that their smiling has the aim of creating a pleasant communication environment while men smile in response to their own pleasant inner state. For women, smiling has a social purpose while for men it is purely a reflection of the way they feel. There are gender differences in eye contact also. Women look at their conversational partners, for example, more than men do.

Nonverbal communication is rule governed

There are no rule books for nonverbal behaviour (although it could be argued that protocol and etiquette books and articles in magazines along the lines of 'how to attract the opposite sex' are concerned with the rules of nonverbal behaviour). Nonverbal behaviour is, nonetheless, governed by rules. We learn these rules in the same way that we learn the rules of spoken language, that is, from observing nonverbal behaviours as we grow up. For example, we know that in Western cultures it is inappropriate nonverbal behaviour to look happy and cheerful at a funeral.

Interrelationships between verbal and nonverbal communication

Verbal and nonverbal communication are interrelated. Nonverbal cues can complement or add to the verbal message. They can repeat the verbal message or they can substitute for the verbal message. They can be used to accent or emphasise a point in a verbal message or they can contradict or undermine the verbal message. They can also function as a regulatory conversational mechanism.

Complementing

Nonverbal behaviour complements verbal messages when it adds to the meaning of the verbal message. A congratulatory hug accompanied with a wide smile and cheerful voice complement the message 'I am so happy for you'. They add an emotional resonance to the words.

Repeating

Nonverbal behaviour can repeat the verbal message. Telling someone that the office they want is on the next floor up and simultaneously pointing upwards is an example of nonverbal behaviour repeating the words. Watch anyone giving directions. Do they point in the direction they are talking about, circle for roundabouts, point for left- or right-hand turns? Most of us do and we are using gestures to repeat or illustrate what we are saying.

Substituting

Substitution involves the use of a nonverbal message for a verbal one. If you wave to a friend on the other side of the street, you are substituting the nonverbal communication of the wave for a verbal greeting.

Accenting

Nonverbal communication can be used to accent or emphasise a point in a verbal message. Changes in vocal tone, pitch or volume or the use of a pause can accent or emphasise particular parts of a verbal message. Gestures and facial expressions can also be used for accent. Thumping the table and frowning when saying 'stop that' emphasises the verbal content of the message.

Contradicting

There are times when our nonverbal behaviour is at variance with the verbal message. Saying 'I am not angry' while simultaneously glaring and clenching your fists sends a conflicting message. Your words deny anger but your nonverbal behaviour expresses anger. If there is a conflict between verbal and nonverbal messages we place more reliance on the nonverbal message. According to Argyle (1983) we place five times as much reliance on nonverbal messages as on words. In other words, nonverbal behaviour has more credibility than words in our assessment of any message. So, if we want our communication to be effective it is important that our verbal and nonverbal cues complement each other rather than contradict each other. In the photograph in Figure 12.2 we can see how nonverbal cues contradict the public rhetoric of a harmonious and co-operative partnership. In June 1991 there was a leadership struggle between the Prime Minister, Bob Hawke, and the Treasurer, Paul Keating. However, before a vote on the leadership could be taken, the Premiers' Conference took place in Canberra. As Prime Minister and Treasurer, Hawke and Keating were forced to sit together. The photograph in Figure 12.2 was taken at that Premiers' Conference. Notice the spatial relationship between the two men. What does the body language and use of space reveal about the way the two men, in spite of public claims of being a team, really feel about each other?

FIGURE 12.2 Hawke and Keating at the 1991 Premiers' Conference

Source: Peter Morris, The Fairfax Photo Library. Reproduced with permission.

Regulating

Nonverbal cues that control the flow of conversation are regulators. Because in conversations it is normal for listeners to look at speakers more than speakers look at listeners, increased eye contact can indicate when a speaker is finishing and the listener can take a conversational turn. Changes in vocal pitch can also regulate the conversational flow.

Types of nonverbal communication

Nonverbal communication can be divided into six categories: kinesics, proxemics, haptics, paralinguistics, chronemics, and semiotics.

Kinesics

Kinesics, sometimes called 'body language', is perhaps what most of us first think of when we think of nonverbal communication. Kinesics includes gestures, facial expressions and posture as well as eye behaviour.

GESTURES

We have already discussed some of the gestures contained in kinesics in the section dealing with the interrelationship between verbal and nonverbal communication. Gestures can be divided into different categories.

Emblems

According to Poyatos (1992) emblems are gestures with specific meanings which are used intentionally to convey a message within a particular social group, class or culture. The hitchhiker's sign, the V for victory sign, the OK sign we discussed earlier are all examples of emblems.

Illustrators

Illustrators accompany words, illustrating the verbal message in some way. Holding up three fingers when saying 'I will meet you at three o'clock' is an example of an illustrator.

Regulators

Regulators are the nonverbal behaviours that regulate conversations and include changes in eye contact, vocal pitch and inflection. Examples of how regulators function can be found in the section on eye behaviour later in this chapter.

Affect displays

Affect displays involve facial expressions, posture and level of tension. They reflect emotion and its intensity.

FACIAL EXPRESSIONS AND POSTURE

Facial expressions are the major vehicle for affect displays. Although affect displays are not always as much under conscious control as emblems and illustrators, we can manipulate affect displays. As Ekman and Friesen (1969) point out, whether our facial expressions are intentional or unintentional we are usually aware of them and conscious of any changes. The traditional 'poker face' is an example of our ability to control our facial expressions.

Posture and **level of tension** are another way in which our emotions and their intensity are revealed. Poyatos (1983) defines posture as the conscious or unconscious positioning of the body which may reveal emotional states and status differentials. Leaning forward, for example, is normally interpreted as interest, involvement or liking while a drooping posture can signal depression, sadness, tiredness and so on.

It is not only how we stand, or sit, or how we position our bodies in relation to the person with whom we are communicating that conveys information about our emotional state; it is also the level of tension or relaxation evident. In an interpersonal exchange between individuals of different status the higher status person will normally have a more relaxed posture than the lower status person. Try to be aware of your posture and level of tension or relaxation over the next few days when communicating with your friends, your parents, your lecturers or tutors. Does your posture and level of tension change depending on the status of the person with whom you are communicating?

Gender also influences posture. Males display more freedom and breadth of movement, have a more open and expansive posture, especially in relation to the arms and legs, than do females. If you saw two people sitting on a bench but you were too far away to tell whether they were male or female and one was sitting with arms stretched along the back of the bench, one leg crossed with the ankle resting on the knee, and the other person was sitting with elbows close to the sides, legs crossed at the ankle and knees together, which would you guess to be the male and which the female?

Adaptors

Adaptors are probably least under conscious control. They include such gestures as putting a hand over the mouth in dismay, fiddling with spectacles, running a hand over hair and so on. Malandro, Barker and Barker (1989) claim that adaptors are generally connected with negative feelings towards oneself or the other person.

EYE BEHAVIOUR

We have probably all heard the saying that the eyes are the mirrors of the soul and the eyes definitely play an important role in nonverbal communication. The number of sayings that involve eyes—'to catch someone's eye', 'to stare someone down', 'to give someone the eye', 'eyes only for him/her', 'making eyes at someone' and so on—indicate the importance of eye behaviour in communication. Nonverbal messages communicated by the eyes depend on the duration, direction and quality of the eye behaviour and these are culture dependent.

Argyle and Ingham, quoted in Knapp and Hall (1992) consider the average length of a gaze when interacting with another person is 2.95 seconds and if the gaze is mutual it is 1.18 seconds. If the gaze is shorter than the cultural norm we usually interpret it as meaning that the person is uninterested, shy or preoccupied. If the gaze is longer than the cultural norm we usually interpret it as meaning a higher than usual level of interest. If the gaze continues overlong we will probably interpret it as threatening. The direction of the gaze also conveys messages. Our cultural norm is that we glance alternatively at the other person's face and then away. If these directional norms are broken it can indicate an abnormally high or low interest, self-consciousness, nervousness, feeling uncomfortable or a desire to break off communication.

Eye communication serves four major functions: to seek feedback, to inform others when to talk, to signal the nature of a relationship and to compensate for increased physical distance.

To seek feedback

In conversation listeners gaze at speakers more than speakers gaze at listeners. Argyle and Ingham (1972) claim that when we are talking 41% of our time is spent in looking at the listener but when we are listening we spend 75% of our time looking at the speaker. Reversing this ratio and looking more when speaking and less when listening can convey an impression of not being interested or can be a method of establishing dominance. Again there is a gender influence in that women make eye contact more and maintain it for longer periods, both in speaking and listening, than do men.

To inform others when to speak

Eye behaviour is part of the way conversations are regulated. We tend to look at the other person when we begin and finish speaking and intermittently while speaking to monitor feedback. So if the speaker looks at the listener, especially if the look is accompanied by a vocal cue such as dropping the voice, it indicates that the speaker is handing the conversational baton over to the listener. Eye behaviour can also indicate a desire for an individual to speak, even if there is no conversation as such taking place. For example, your tutor asks a question while looking directly at one member of the group, leaving no doubt as to the person expected to provide the answer.

To signal the nature of the relationship

Eye behaviour can signal whether we regard the other person positively or negatively. If we like or are interested in the other person we will gaze at them more. If we dislike the other person our gaze will normally decrease. If we want to hide our feelings, or we feel uncomfortable, we will avoid eye contact. Status also influences eye behaviour. Individuals of greater status tend to have less direct eye contact than those of lower status. An article in *The Sydney Morning Herald* (Laurence 1997) claims that rolling eyes and grimacing in couples is evidence of a feeling of contempt and indicates a marriage that is heading for divorce.

To compensate for physical distance

We use eye contact to compensate for physical distance and to try to bridge that distance. This is particularly relevant for oral presentations where eye contact provides a means for the speaker to make a connection with even quite distant members of the audience. Conversely one of the ways we cope when too close to other people is to break off eye contact.

Proxemics

Proxemics refers to spatial relationships, or how we use space. Hall (1966), working with American subjects, divided our use of space into four zones. Each zone was divided into close and far phases. The **intimate zone** extends in the close phase from close physical contact to 0.15 metres to 0.46 metres in the far phase. The **personal zone** extends in the close phase from 0.46 metres to 0.76 metres and in the far phase from 0.76 metres to 1.22 metres. The **social zone** extends in the close phase from 1.22 metres to 2.13 metres (roughly the width of an office desk) and in the far phase from 2.13 metres to 3.66 metres. The **public zone** extends in the close phase from 3.66 metres to 7.62 metres and in the far phase from 7.62 metres.

Personal distance is the bubble of space with which we need to be surrounded in order to feel comfortable and secure. Most interpersonal interactions take place within the personal distance zone, according to Arliss (1991) at about 0.91 metres, or 3 feet. The spatial distances noted by Hall are often illustrated in texts by concentric circles but, as far as our personal distance is concerned, it is more likely to be rectangular with more space required in front of us than we require behind or beside us. This is what we regard as our personal space and we can become uncomfortable, tense, anxious or even disoriented if this space is invaded.

One way to illustrate the effect of this invasion of our personal space is to maintain a conversation while walking towards another person. As you and the other person draw closer together conversation becomes more and more difficult. When you are 'in each others' faces' it is likely that you will be unable to sustain the conversation. It will be difficult to think of what you want to say and you will probably feel tense and anxious.

Let us suppose that you are sitting on an empty park bench and someone comes and sits close to you. What do you do? The chances are that after a moment or two you will get up and move. Why? Because your personal space has been invaded. But if the bench was almost full and the only place left was next to you, would you still get up and move? Probably not, because there would be a valid reason for the other person to sit close to you. So we can, and do, cope with people invading our personal space if we feel there is a reason for us to do so.

Crowded public transport, for example, is one area where we are forced to have people very close to us indeed. However, we cope with this invasion of our personal space by what is called **barrier behaviour**, by trying to ignore the other people. We avoid eye contact and conversation. Think of waiting for a lift with other people. You may talk to one or more of the people waiting for the lift but what happens when you get into the lift? It is likely that conversation ceases and that each person in the lift looks at the floor indicator rather than at the other people in the lift.

ELEMENTS AFFECTING PROXEMICS

Proxemics is greatly influenced by culture and this can create cross-cultural communication problems. People from the Arab world, for example, tend to stand closer than people from America or Britain. In interpersonal interactions there can be constant movement as each speaker tries to reach a comfortable distance.

Context also influences our use of space. For example, we tend to stand closer together in a large space such as outside or in the street than we do in a smaller space such as an office.

Sex and age influence how close or far apart we stand. Women generally stand closer to one another than do men. Opposite sex pairs generally stand farthest apart and children generally stand closer than adults do.

We tend to stand closer to people we evaluate positively than we do to people we evaluate negatively. In other words if we like or respect someone we will be more comfortable to be closer to that person than we will be to someone we dislike or distrust.

Status also influences use of space, for we tend to allow more space to higher status individuals and figures of authority than we do to peers.

Haptics

Haptics involves tactile communication, or communication through touch. Touch is, perhaps, our most primitive and basic means of communication, beginning with the tactile communication between parents and babies. It is appropriate to discuss haptics just after proxemics because, as Leathers (1997) notes, there are correlations between how we use touch and space in communication. Both touch and space behaviour take place within norms that define what is acceptable. The sense of discomfort caused by invasion of our personal space, for example, is comparable to that which we experience if we are touched in a way that violates cultural norms. Touch, like our use of space, can also be used to define status differentials between communicators. Henley (1977) claims that relative power in a relationship is signalled by who touches and who is touched. The higher status individual is more likely to touch a subordinate than vice versa.

How we touch and what such touch means is, like much nonverbal behaviour, influenced by culture and gender. It is also influenced by age. Children touch more than adults and women touch more than men. Some cultures, Mediterranean cultures, for example, are more touch oriented than more northern European cultures such as the British.

Most importantly, touch is an important element in interpersonal communication. Touch can communicate support and sympathy, affection and aggression, commitment and control. The photograph in Figure 12.3 is of Olympic walker Nathan Deakes after he was disqualified from the Olympic 50 kilometre road race when he was coming second over two-thirds of the way to the finish. We can see how touch is communicating sympathy, comfort and support.

Touch can also gain compliance. The experiments of Kleinke (1977) show that individuals are more likely to comply with a request if the request is accompanied by a light touch on the arm.

Paralinguistics

Some people think that nonverbal communication is silent, but this is not so. **Paralinguistics** or **paralanguage** is the sound element of nonverbal communication. What happens when an audience

FIGURE 12.3 Australian Walkers Nathan Deakes After Being Disqualified from the Olympic 50 km Road Race

Sydney Morning Herald 28/29 August, 2004 Photo 'Consolation for a Bronzed Aussie' Photo: Aap/Dave Hunt

who has been kept waiting start to slow hand clap? The audience is communicating its irritation at the delay nonverbally, for no words are involved but the communication is, nevertheless, dependent on sound—the slow hand clapping. Shrieks, coughs, sighs and vocal cues such as 'hm', 'tsk' and 'ah' are all forms of paralinguistics.

However, paralinguistics does not exist only in isolation from words for the qualities of a voice, its pitch, timbre and accent, all convey information. The way words are spoken is also part of paralinguistics.

For example, let us look at a simple four word question. Notice that by altering the way we say the words we can change their meaning.

Can I help you? (Is it possible for me to help you?)

Can *I* help you? (Can I help you or would you prefer somebody else?)

Can I *help* you? (Can I help you or do you not need help?)

Can I help *you*? (Can I help you or should I help someone else?)

Chronemics

Chronemics is concerned with how we perceive, use and react to time. Like proxemics, chronemics is influenced by culture. In some cultures time is precisely expressed and strictly observed while in other cultures time may be interpreted more loosely or flexibly. There is also a status element in our observance of time. The importance of being punctual varies with the relative status of the individuals. For example, we usually ensure that we are on time for an appointment with someone important or considerably above us in status but may be late for a meeting with someone on the same or lower status level.

Semiotics

Semiotics involves communicating through signs and symbols. The presentational aspects of a piece of writing, an essay or report for example, are part of the semiotic elements of the writing. A piece of writing that looks professional immediately has more credibility than a piece of writing that has no margins, poor handwriting, dog-eared pages and a general careless and haphazard appearance.

Perhaps the most universally used signs are words; however, there are many other signs that we use in communication. Traffic lights, no smoking signs, disabled access signs and road signs are all examples of communicating through signs.

Signs can be divided into icons, indexes and symbols. The icon resembles the object it represents. A portrait photograph is an iconic sign because it resembles the person. Disabled access signs and road signs indicating a steep incline or a winding road are also examples of iconic signs.

The index involves a causal link with the object it signifies. Mohun *et al.* (1996) cite the example of an index of fire being smoke.

The symbol is arbitrary, lacking both the resemblance to the object being represented by the icon and the causal link of the index. For example, a dove is a symbol of peace, not because doves are necessarily peaceful birds but because that is the meaning that has, over time, come to be associated with the dove. Company logos, for example the logo for Telstra or BHP, are symbols.

FIGURE 12.4 | Mirroring Shown by John Howard and Woman

Source: Andrew Meares, The Fairfax Photo Library. Reproduced with permission.

Mirroring

According to La France (1979) mirroring indicates rapport between communicators and occurs when the communicators unconsciously imitate each other's posture and gestures. In Figure 12.4 you can see this mirroring of posture and gesture between a woman and John Howard. In this instance the mirroring is also influenced by the status differential between the two.

SUMMARY

In this chapter we have given a brief overview of nonverbal communication as an integral part of the communication process; as the primary means of conveying emotion. Although nonverbal cues are easy to observe they are not always easy to assess accurately. Personality, culture and the context within which the communication is taking place all influence the nonverbal behaviour. It is important to remember that nonverbal cues should be evaluated as clusters rather than isolated gestures or facial expressions. We need the whole picture, not just isolated segments, when evaluating nonverbal behaviour. Often nonverbal communication operates in conjunction with verbal communication where it can reinforce or undermine the verbal message.

In the next chapter we will move on to an analysis of how we communicate with others on an interpersonal basis.

KEY POINTS

- Nonverbal communication is concerned with the ways in which we communicate without words.
- Nonverbal communication is continuous and may be intentional or unintentional.
- Nonverbal communication conveys emotion.
- Nonverbal cues are easy to observe but not easy to assess accurately.
- Nonverbal and verbal communication interrelate.
- Nonverbal behaviour can complement, repeat, substitute for, accent or contradict words. Nonverbal behaviour is also important in regulating conversations.
- Nonverbal communication can be divided into kinesics, proxemics, haptics, paralinguistics, chronemics, and semiotics.

REVIEW QUESTIONS

1. How does the context within which nonverbal communication takes place affect our interpretation of the nonverbal communication? Provide examples from your own experience.
2. In what ways can nonverbal and verbal behaviours interrelate?
3. What nonverbal behaviours are contained within the category of kinesics?
4. How important is our personal space to us and how do we compensate if it is invaded?
5. What is involved in paralinguistics?
6. How do status differentials impact on nonverbal behaviours?

EXERCISES

1. Try to give no feedback at all when you next talk to a friend. How easy is it to give no feedback and what effect does that have on the person with whom you are talking?
2. Try to conduct a conversation when standing uncomfortably close to a friend. What effect does this closeness have on the conversation? How did you feel? How did your friend feel?
3. Take conscious note of any nonverbal communication when you are talking on the telephone. Does your nonverbal communication differ from that you use in face-to-face conversations?
4. How common is communicating with signs rather than words? Make a list of all the nonverbal signs you encounter on your way to work or college.
5. Take a television segment (an advertisement or a section of a sitcom or a soap opera) and turn off the sound. What does the nonverbal behaviour tell you about the communication that is taking place and the relationship between the people communicating?
6. Watch people in a public situation such as a coffee shop or shopping mall. How much can you judge of relationships and emotions from nonverbal cues?

BIBLIOGRAPHY

Allen, M. 1997, *Smart Thinking: Skills for Critical Understanding and Writing,* Oxford University Press, Melbourne.
Argyle, M. 1983, *The Psychology of Interpersonal Behaviour,* 4th ed., Penguin Books, Middlesex.
Argyle, M. 1988, *Bodily Communication,* 2nd ed, International Universities Press, Connecticut.
Argyle, M. and Ingham, R. 1972, 'Gaze, mutual gaze and proximity', *Semiotica,* 6, 32–59.
Arliss, L. P. 1991, *Gender Communication,* Prentice Hall, New Jersey.
Bate, D. and Sharpe, P. 1990, *Writer's Handbook for University Students,* Harcourt Brace, Sydney.
Beebe, S. A., Beebe, S. J. and Redmond, M. V. 1996, *Interpersonal Communication: Relating to Others,* Allyn and Bacon, Boston.
Birdwhistell, R.L. 1970, *Kinesics and Context,* University of Pennsylvania Press, Philadelphia.
Chen, G.O. and Starosta, W. J. 1998, *Foundations of Intercultural Communication,* Allyn and Bacon, Boston.
Dwyer, K.K. 1998, *Conquer Your Speech Fright,* Harcourt Brace, Orlando, Florida.
Ekman, P. 2003, *Emotions Revealed: Understanding Faces and Feelings,* Weidenfeld & Nicholson, London.
Ekman, P. and Friesen, W. V. 1969, 'The repertoire of nonverbal behaviour: Categories, origins, usage, and coding', *Semiotica* I, 49–67.
Hall, E. T. 1966, *The Hidden Dimension,* Doubleday, New York.
Hatcher, C. and McCarthy, P. 1996, *Speaking Persuasively: How to Make the Most of Your Presentations,* Allen & Unwin, Sydney.
Henley, N. M. 1977, *Body Politics: Power, Sex, and Nonverbal Communication,* Prentice Hall, New Jersey.
Herrick, J. A. 1998, *Argumentation: Understanding and Shaping Arguments,* Allyn and Bacon, Boston.
Heslin, R. and Patterson, M. L. 1982, *Nonverbal Behavior and Social Psychology,* Plenum Press, New York and London.
Keating, C. F., Mazur, A., Segall, M. H., Cysneiros, P. G., Divale, W. F., Kilbridge, J. E., Komin, S., Leahy, P., Thurman, B. and Wirsing, R. 1981, 'Culture and the perception of social dominance from facial expression', *Journal of Personality and Social Psychology,* 40, 615–26.
Kendon, A. 1967, 'Some functions of gaze-direction in social interaction', *Acta Psychologica,* 26, 22–63.
Kleinke, C. L. 1977, 'Compliance to requests made by gazing and touching experimenters in field settings', *Journal of Experimental Social Psychology,* 13, 218–23.
Knapp, M. L. and Hall, J. A. 1992, *Nonverbal Communication in Human Interaction,* 3rd ed., Harcourt Brace College Publishers, Florida.
La France, M. 1979, cited in Putnis, P. and Petelin, R. 1996, *Professional Communication: Principles and Applications,* Prentice Hall, Sydney.
Laurence, C. 1997, 'Rolling your eyes says a marriage is over and out', *The Sydney Morning Herald,* 18 October, p. 3.
Leathers, D. G. 1997, *Successful Nonverbal Communication: Principles and Applications,* 3rd ed., Allyn and Bacon, Boston.
Malandro, L. A., Barker, L. and Barker, D. A. 1989, *Nonverbal Communication,* 2nd ed., McGraw-Hill, New York.
Mehrabian, A. 1972, *Nonverbal Communication,* Aldine, Chicago.
Mohun, T., McGregor, H., Saunders, S. and Archer, R. 1996, *Communicating! Theory and Practice,* 4th ed., Harcourt Brace, Sydney.
Poyatos, F. 1983, *New Perspectives in Nonverbal Communication: Studies in Cultural Anthropology, Social Psychology, Linguistics, Literature and Semiotics,* Pergamon Press, Toronto.
Poyatos, F. ed. 1992, *Advances in Nonverbal Communication: Sociocultural, Clinical, Esthetic and Literary Perspectives,* John Benjamins Publishing Company, Philadelphia.
Richmond, V. P. and McCroskey, J. C. 2004, *Nonverbal Behavior in Interpersonal Relations,* 5th ed., Pearson Education, Boston.
Warwick, I. 1989, *Critical Thinking and Communication,* 3rd ed., Allyn and Baker, Boston.

Interpersonal communication

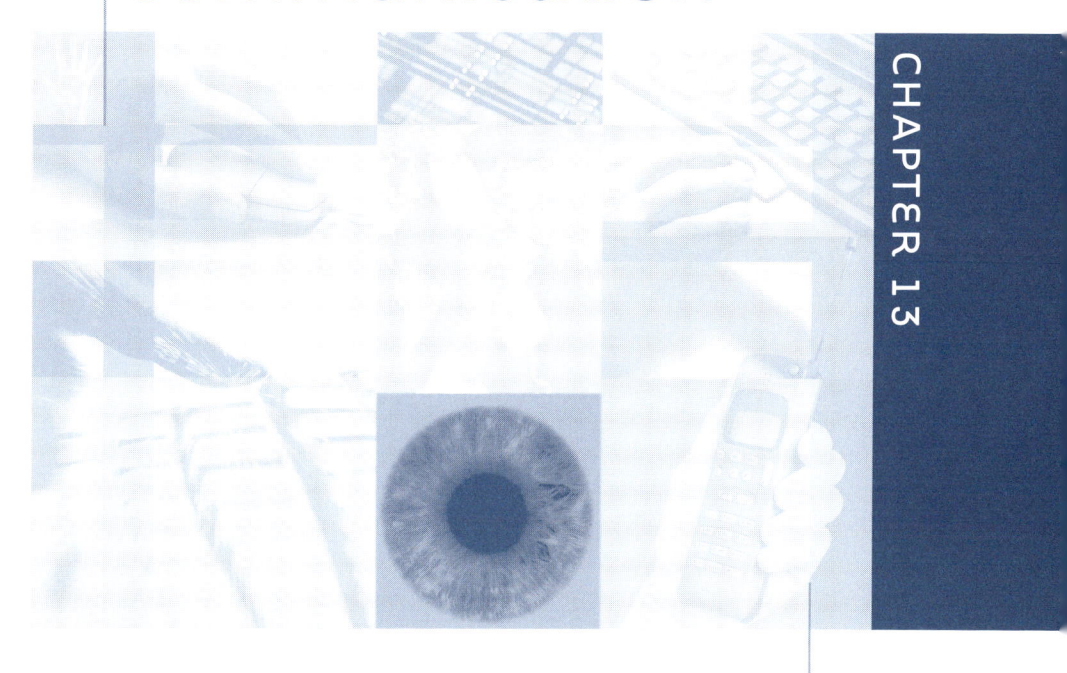

CHAPTER 13

Upon completing this chapter you should be able to:
- identify issues related to defining the term 'interpersonal communication';
- explain the nature of intrapersonal communication and its role in developing awareness of self and other and managing emotions and 'thinking habits';
- define conflict and explain its sources and forms;
- outline a range of approaches for managing conflict including assertive behaviour and the use of 'I' statements; and
- identify inappropriate tactics people sometimes use to deal with conflict.

Interpersonal communication is very often multi-contextual in nature in that it can take place within the specific context of face-to-face interaction while simultaneously occurring in a broader context, for example in an organisation (organisational communication). Once again this scenario shows that the categories we apply to the study of communication are not rigid or mutually exclusive, but often fluid and overlapping in nature. It is also important to note that interpersonal communication occupies a central position in communication, because a great deal of our communicating, for example in organisational settings (organisational communication), involves relating with others face to face, that is, interpersonally. Hence the importance of interpersonal communication skills in working or personal lives should not be underestimated.

Interpersonal communication involves the managing of relationships, whether they be close or distant, friendly or hostile or otherwise. For instance, within an organisation or workplace, people have what we call 'working' relationships with their colleagues, bosses and subordinates, and then there are those relationships outside the organisation such as those with customers, clients and suppliers. Nelson-Jones (1991) notes relationships are the major source of both human pleasure and pain. So how we deal with people (our relationships) is in essence a 'quality of life issue'. Improving the ways in which we relate to others can enhance both our personal and professional relationships and our ability to communicate effectively. It is also interesting to note how interpersonal problems at work can impinge upon our personal lives, and interpersonal problems in our personal lives can also affect our ability to perform well at work or study.

Interpersonal communication provides an appropriate juncture at which to incorporate the notion of 'satisfaction' into a definition of what goes into making communication effective. Ask yourself the question: 'Am I satisfied with the way I handle some difficult kinds of people and difficult situations that I encounter in life?' The notion of satisfaction in communication will be explored further in this chapter and will allow you to consider issues of satisfaction in ways relevant to the way you handle people and situations in your life.

Defining interpersonal communication

O'Sullivan *et al.* (1994) define interpersonal communication as being communication which is:

* between people; and

* unmediated by media (technology) such as television or print.

Interpersonal communication is typically understood as 'face-to-face' or direct 'person-to-person' communication, which is unassisted, uninterrupted and unfiltered by media technologies. While it could be argued that telephone conversations are in many ways similar to face-to-face conversations, it could also be counter-argued that telephone conversations lack the richness of information presented in interpersonal interactions by way of nonverbal features, such as facial expressions.

Choosing when to use interpersonal communication

Communication via technologies such as the telephone (including text messaging) and email can function to distance and depersonalise communication when compared with face-to-face interaction. Hence planning communication involves choosing the modes and channels that seem most appropriate to the situation. In the case of dealing with highly personal or sensitive situations, the interpersonal mode is often the most appropriate. Likewise it is often that case that there is no real substitute for face-to-face communication, that is, 'the personal touch', when it comes to maintaining strong relationships. Having said all this, communication technologies are challenging traditional boundaries as much of the communication that occurs in online chatting, emails and phone text messages involves the highly interactive and personal interactions that we tend to associate with interpersonal face-to-face communication. Hence technology-assisted communication now plays a major role in what could be referred to as 'personal communication'; however, there are still contexts in which it is unable to serve as an effective substitute for face-to-face interaction. Task analysis principles can help us to determine whether a situation would be best dealt with by using interpersonal communication or alternative modes, and of course there are many situations which require a combination of modes.

Intrapersonal communication

Intrapersonal communication is a topic that often makes its way into discussions about interpersonal communication and it takes up a substantial portion of this chapter. **Intrapersonal communication** refers to communication that takes place within the individual and consists of thoughts, including the 'internal dialogue' we have with ourselves, when thinking about and evaluating ideas and information. Intrapersonal communication involves making sense of life and situations as we encounter them, so it is integral to perception as discussed in Chapter 2 and you may wish to review that topic.

How someone thinks about and approaches day-to-day situations influences the way they behave in interpersonal communication and hence interpersonal and intrapersonal communication are intrinsically linked. Indeed it is often the case that we simultaneously communicate in both modes, for example, interpersonally when speaking to someone and intrapersonally as we think and formulate responses to what is being said to us.

Chapter 2 raised the point that our perception of the world and its events involves varying degrees of error and distortion—and that this can hinder performance in many ways and even prevent a person from reaching their true potential and result in choices and behaviour that run counter to a person's own best interests. The greater our understanding of ourselves and others, including cultural and contextual factors, the better placed we are to be able to make decisions and behave in ways that more closely serve our own best interests. Greater levels of awareness also empower because they increase our capacity for effective communication and performance. This section incorporates strategies for raising our levels of awareness of ourselves and others.

Note that while the following sections appear to place more emphasis initially on self-awareness, the strategies discussed can also help to further our understanding of other people.

Self-concept and self-awareness

Self-concept refers to our own understanding of ourselves. Interestingly, scientists agree that we are born without the notion of self (DeVito 1989). Then somewhere in the early stages of life we begin to recognise our own being as something distinct from our environment. Self-awareness starts at a basic concrete level, for example that day in life when a young child begins to recognise, 'That hand is me' (Adler *et al.* 1998, p. 108). Our understanding of ourselves develops from our experiences of interacting with 'significant' others—that is, the people who are prominent in our lives: family, friends and people we work with—and then on through to secondary influences such as mass media. The term 'self-concept' refers to one's own mental view of one's self, includes what we think we are like as a person and ideas we have about our abilities, strengths and weaknesses.

Our self-concept, or image we have of ourselves, also develops from the way we think others see us (Adler and Rodman 2000).

Self-concept, a person's own understanding and image of themself, differs from **self-awareness**, which refers to a person's level of awareness about themself. As noted in Chapter 2, some people have very accurate perceptions about themselves, in which case they are very self-aware and have an accurate and well-developed self-concept, whereas others may have a very distorted and undeveloped view of themselves, in which case they have (1) a low level of self-awareness and (2) an inaccurate self-concept (Verderber 1999). Developing an accurate self-concept and higher level of self-awareness depends largely upon a person's capacity to receive and process feedback well, even when it is subtle. A person's capacity to receive feedback is then dependent upon how open (or open-minded) they are to new ideas and alternative points of view, that is, points of view that differ from their own.

Someone with a highly developed level of self-awareness (a comprehensive and realistic self-concept) can be described as being receptive or perceptive and also as someone who 'knows their own mind'.

The Johari Window: A theoretical model for self-awareness

The **Johari Window** (named after the first names of its creators Joseph Luft and Harry Ingram) provides a model for understanding the concepts related to self-awareness (see Figure 13.1). The whole window represents all there is to know about an individual (the self), including wants, needs, desires, opinions and so on.

The *Open self (1)* represents information about an individual that is known to both that individual and to others. Someone with a large open self sector may be outgoing and willing to share information they have (including information about themselves) with others. However, if this area is small the potential for effective communication and relationship development is reduced.

	Known to self	Not known to self
Known to others	1 Open	2 Blind
Not known to others	3 Hidden	4 Unknown

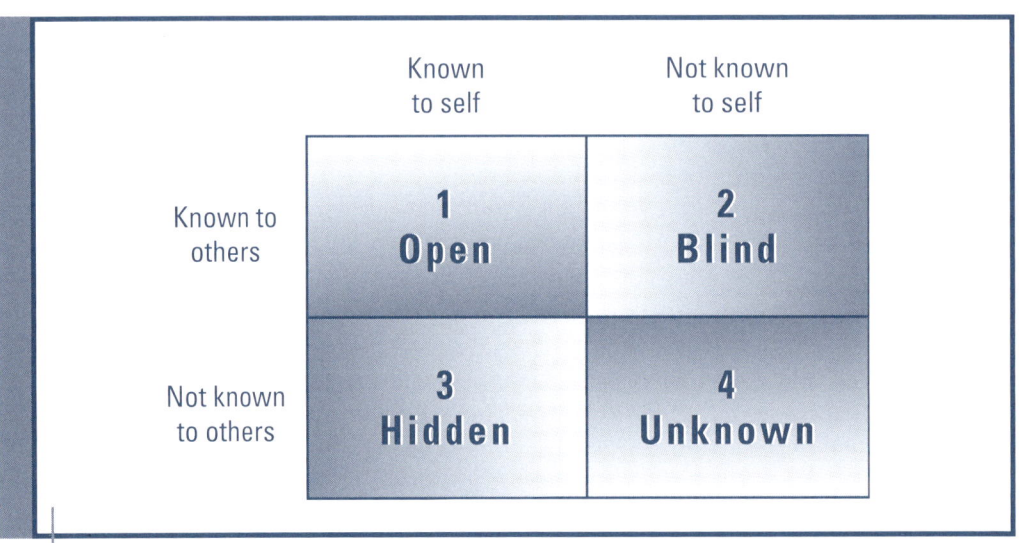

FIGURE 13.1 The Johari Window

Source: Joseph Luft, Group Processes: An Introduction to Group Dynamics, 3rd edn. Copyright © 1984 by Joseph Luft. Reprinted by permission of McGraw-Hill Companies.

The *Blind self (2)* represents information about an individual that is known to others but not to the individual. The blind area can contain information about a person's habits and character traits of which that person is unaware. For example a person who treats others in an insensitive manner may experience difficulties in developing deeper relationships with others, but may remain completely unaware (or blind) of their tendency to treat others insensitively. Again when this area is large the potential for effective communication and relationship development is reduced. People with a large blind spot tend to be closed minded and unreceptive (or unperceptive).

The *Hidden self (3)* represents information about an individual that is known to that individual only but not to others. This is the information a person keeps secret from others. Regulating this area is important to communicating effectively and self-disclosure (discussed below) provides a means of doing this.

The *Unknown self (4)* represents information about an individual that is not known to either that individual or others. This area is by far the least tangible. However, unusual or difficult circumstances may bring to light information about a person not previously known, for example you may surprise yourself and others in the way you react to an emergency situation.

Increasing self-awareness functions to decrease diagrammatically the size of the two 'not known to self' quadrants on the right, that is, the Blind self and the Unknown self in the Johari Window model.

Increasing awareness generally (e.g. of others) along with self-awareness enhances one's capacity for effective performance and interpersonal communication.

Core techniques for developing self-awareness and awareness generally include:

1. *Receptivity and monitoring feedback:* that is, being open minded and open to the feedback and responses of others and monitoring interpersonal interactions by watching how people respond to you, so that it can be given appropriate consideration (as per technique 3, below).

2. *Perception checking:* that is, testing your interpretations with others including how others may be perceiving you. For example, you can check your perceptions against those of others where appropriate (subtlety and a degree of discretion is sometimes required).

3. *Critical self-reflection:* that is, taking time out to think critically about and question aspects of your own disposition including beliefs, biases, values, likes and dislikes.

The processes of monitoring of feedback, perception checking and critical self-reflection can be done in 'real time', but can also be undertaken periodically, as a stocktake of your own views about yourself (e.g. strengths and weaknesses) and your goals (e.g. using evaluative questions about whether you should continue to pursue current goals). While the role of this kind of self-questioning is very important and very often highly beneficial, conversely becoming too self-critical, that is, hypercritical, can damage self-esteem. Taken too far it can be counter-productive and impede upon your personal and professional development.

The following section extends self-monitoring and critical self-reflection and explores in more depth the notion of addressing and managing the dynamics of self-awareness and thought processes.

Self-awareness and self-development: Insights from cognitive psychology

It is commonly accepted that genetic traits and environment, that is, experiences such as a person's upbringing, are factors that influence a person's temperament and character—and capacities and opportunities. Our parents or guardians have a great deal of influence on the way in which our *self-concept* and *perspective on life* develop in our younger and most formative years. Hence parents and guardians hold a great deal of responsibility in helping to ensure a child's psychological health and development.

Unfortunately, people can and in instances do treat others badly and this is evident in the incidents of bullying in schoolyards and workplaces that we hear about and perhaps experience. On an ethical and moral note, it is important to realise that as members of society we all carry responsibility to help to ensure that these kinds of behaviours are not tolerated and are reported and addressed in an appropriate manner.

As we mature we also become more and more responsible for developing and maintaining our own mental wellbeing—which is in addition to the responsibilities we have for our own physical wellbeing and professional development. So this then brings us back to the subject of intrapersonal communication because managing our self including self-awareness and self-esteem involves an intrapersonal process (i.e. communicating with our self). At this point we can also see that as a person we have a relationship with ourself. This being the case, it is important that we work at developing a good relationship with ourself, that is, one which is well balanced and conducive to our overall success, satisfaction and happiness.

The past three decades in particular have seen some major changes in direction in the field of psychology, a shift away from what is known as behaviourism, that is, the study of behaviour, to cognitive psychology (the latter has not been totally abandoned but is undergoing an adjustment period as a result of criticisms). A leader in the field, Martin Seligman (1996, p. 8), notes that one of the most significant findings in psychology over the past three decades has been that 'individuals can choose the way they think.' Prior to this, conventional wisdom held that people's behaviours were the result of internal drivers (genetics, for example their IQ and body/brain chemistry) and external drivers (environment, that is, events, upbringing, etc.). While the influence of these factors is not being denied, the traditional perspective had left out a third major factor of influence—a person's thought patterns (e.g. the role of optimistic or pessimistic cognitive tendencies) and even more importantly that people have the capacity to exert control over their own thought processes. Other pioneers of this new paradigm of psychology were also integrating aspects of subjective experience, notably emotion, as popularised in Goleman's (1996) book *Emotional Intelligence*.

The emotional intelligence view contends that traditional conceptions or definitions of intelligence, particularly the Intelligence Quota, or IQ, conceptualise intelligence and capacity for success in terms which are far too narrow. According to the **emotional intelligence** (EI) view, how someone copes emotionally with the challenges of life has a major influence on that person's capacity for attainment and success over the longer term. Hence how a person reacts emotionally to setbacks can influence future success or failure. For example, one individual may become so disheartened at failing a course/subject they may actually give up, whereas another individual may rebound after a short period with added determination and begin re-strategising their next attempt—by asking questions such as 'What can I learn from this experience to help ensure success next time?', 'What can I learn from the feedback?' and 'Do I need to seek out more detailed feedback for the next attempt?' People who tend to bounce back after setbacks are regarded as having emotional intelligence and as possessing a defining characteristic of EI called *resilience*. They are described in the literature as having the ability to manage their emotions in such a way that their emotions do not overpower them for extended periods after they experience setbacks or adversity. That is not to say that they do not experience painful emotions, but that they demonstrate an ability to 'get over them' in a relatively short period of time. At this juncture it is important to note (1) that how people deal with setbacks is a greater determiner of future success than the setbacks in themselves and (2) that learning to manage emotions that overwhelm the self and undermine motivation better is pivotal to future success and self-development.

It is also worth mentioning that the emotional brain has evolved over thousands upon thousands of years and serves incalculable purposes—can you even begin to imagine how different life would be without desires? In an effort to understand issues of this nature further, it is recommended that you go to the end of the chapter and undertake Exercises 1 and 2.

In the past science has sought to separate the brain (and thinking) into the rational and the emotional. However, there is a growing consensus that the emotional and the rational parts of the brain are intertwined in very complex ways, indeed they both depend upon each another to make us 'human' and guide us toward making good decisions. When you face important decisions such as 'What kind of career should I pursue?', 'What kinds of subjects should I study?' and 'Who should I date or marry?' the rational brain on its own is not very well equipped for such decisions; these decisions also have to come from the heart (i.e. emotional brain) (Seligman 1996). It is this emotional side of us that 'feels' and hence it is difficult to stay commited to decisions that do not 'feel' right. Meanwhile traditional wisdom viewed rational thinking as the saviour of humanity and emotion as an opposite and counter-productive force which should suppressed. The emotion of anxiety (or worry), for example, can and does serve a purpose; it often motivates us into action but yet we know that these kinds of emotions also have the potential to do the opposite and in some cases to the point where it paralyses us.

Advances in this area of cognitive psychology support conventional thinking on the process of perception as examined in Chapter 2, particularly that a person's ways of thinking develop into 'habits of thinking'. Research is showing that a person's thinking tendencies, especially in response to setbacks, is a major determiner of (1) future success or failure in undertakings and (2) future satisfaction or lack of satisfaction with life (Goleman 1996; Seligman 1996). For example, Seligman (1996) shows that how a person thinks about setbacks is a major determiner of how energised or defeated and helpless they become. Furthermore, research has also shown that optimistic thinking tendencies are more conducive to (1) success in undertakings, (2) higher-level performance, (3) satisfaction and (4) physical wellbeing, while pessimistic tendencies have been shown to hinder and also make a person more prone to depression (Seligman 1996).

Fortunately, our thinking habits, whether they lean toward the positive or the negative, are what we have learned, and as such they can be relearned (or unlearned and replaced). I imagine you're thinking that changing habits by definition would involve strong resolve and substantial ongoing effort, and you are right! So why try it? This brings us back to the start of the chapter—it is because the potential for improving the quality of your life is so substantial.

In addition to (1) commitment and effort, (2) some background knowledge (as covered here) and (3) the specific techniques in Chapter 16 under 'Intrapersonal barriers', there is a fourth element we need to modify existing problematic thinking habits: it is the ability to be aware of our thinking routines as they occur so that we can consciously monitor them.

This human ability to think about our thinking is what psychologists call meta-cognition (thinking about our thinking), for example when *self-monitoring* as discussed earlier. This process of operating on a higher level or 'consciousness' can be compared to (but is obviously different from) the notion of being 'health conscious'. When someone is conscious about their health they tend to pay more attention to it; where attention is being directed marks the difference between the two.

Techniques for self-monitoring are dealt with in Chapter 16 in 'Intrapersonal barriers' but in essence it involves a process of (1) self-monitoring to detect poor thinking habits when they occur and then (2) challenging them, (3) substituting more productive ways of thinking and (4) continued efforts to adopt thinking identified as more productive until these ways of thinking eventually become new habits. This involves 'real-time' self-monitoring, that is, monitoring and thinking about our own thought processes as they occur, which is in itself a skill that can be acquired through practice.

Interpersonal communication

Remember how the transactional model incorporated a *relationship dimension* into the process of communication. That is to say, when we communicate we are also involved in relationship with the person involved. Chapter 2 also noted that relationships vary from intimate relationships to 'working relationships', through to less personal kinds of relationships, such as a relationship between a customer and salesperson. From a transactional viewpoint, when communicating with people we are also relating to people and, therefore, in a relationship with other parties.

Self-disclosure: The bricks and mortar of close relationships

Self-disclosure is an important concept in interpersonal communication and the development of interpersonal relationships. **Self-disclosure** involves the imparting of personal information about oneself to another. With reference to the Johari Window (Figure 13.1) self-disclosure works to increase the left-hand 'known' areas (i.e. the open and hidden self), and as such reduces the amount of uncertainty in interpersonal communication. According to the theory the better we know someone the more accurately we can understand and communicate with them. Disclosure is something that can be both overdone or underdone. People who resist disclosing information about themselves are often described as distant, hard to talk to, difficult to get to know, shy and sometimes unfriendly. Over-disclosure overloads people with information and can be interpreted as a sign of insecurity. In addition, it is a less socially accepted behaviour, often 'puts people off' and can function as a barrier to effective communication and relationship development. The extent and rate at which we disclose information to another depends on the context of a situation including our goals and desires, whether it be to maintain a good working relationship or to develop an intimate relationship.

Self-disclosures are the bricks and mortar of relationships. The appropriate use of self-disclosure brings rewards as a means by which to deepen and strengthen relationships. However, there are no guarantees of this and there are risks involved, so it should be approached carefully. Taking time to evaluate a prospective disclosure is a worthwhile strategy. The following kinds of questions can be used to try to evaluate potential risks and problems.

REFLECTIVE SELF-EVALUATION QUESTIONS

* What could this information cost me—perhaps my job? Assess risks.
* Am I trying to enhance or deepen this relationship?
* Am I trying to hurt (or get back at) the other party?
* Am I trying to take advantage of someone? Assess motivations.

True self-disclosures are honest and this has been assumed in the discussion thus far. However, the area of interpersonal communication remains problematic. Research in psychology has shown that people have a tendency to present highly censored versions of themselves to others (see Middlebrook 1980). This notion is compatible with role theory (discussed next), in that it involves *acting* in ways that we think will promote the kind of image we want to present to others. Nevertheless, self-disclosure is critical to the development of deeper relationships and deeper relationships are typically more productive and satisfying. Honest disclosures allow us to 'be ourselves' by behaving in a more relaxed manner and enable us to turn our energies towards more fulfilling and productive pursuits.

The reciprocity principle: Self-disclosure encourages self-disclosure from others

According to the principle of reciprocity, making self-disclosure can also be an effective strategy-based technique for gaining an understanding of another person. While there is no guarantee, the principle of reciprocity means that when we disclose information about ourself it serves to encourage the other party to reciprocate with a self-disclosure of their own. A self-disclosure carries with it a subtle but often powerful expectation that it should be reciprocated. So self-disclosure can be used as a way of learning about and developing relationships with other people.

Role theory: As a tool for skill development

Goffman (1959) argues the importance of **role theory** as a means of understanding our communication with others. According to the theory, our social interactions can be seen as situations in which people perform certain roles to fulfil social expectations. Further to this, O'Sullivan et al. explain the concept of roles as:

> socially defined positions and patterns of behaviour which are characterized by specific sets of rules, norms and expectations which serve to orientate and regulate the interaction, conduct and practices of individuals in social situations.
>
> (O'Sullivan et al. 1994, p. 270)

Throughout the course of a day we fulfil a variety of roles. Some of these may include friend, student, brother or sister, mother or father, coach or player, work colleague or employer or employee. During the day people move in and out of a wide range of roles with relative ease.

As an explanatory theory of communication, role theory relies on the metaphorical construct of 'life as theatre' to communicate the idea that life is like a 'play' where roles are acted out in the 'drama' of everyday life. Its strength as a theory is its power to explain and help deepen our understanding of human action and interaction as being modelled on 'role' or patterned type behaviours.

Role theory also helps to account for the process of socialisation; that is, that we learn how to behave in accordance with the social expectations that accompany a role. For example, when starting a new job we need to learn our role in an organisation. This can include expected behaviours such as greeting customers. Schank and Abelson (1977) introduce the concept of 'scripts' which provide socially approved recipes that assist us in performing various roles. Scripts afford us great economy because they allow us to do less processing and wondering (Schank and Abelson 1977). Scripts also increase the predictability of situations and thereby reduce uncertainty. Indeed, it would be difficult to function and communicate effectively without the kind of information these scripts provide. Scripts for certain situations are much more detailed than for others. For example, formal situations such as the making of marriage vows are often highly scripted (or routine) in contrast to casual encounters which often contain greetings and discussions on topics such as the weather (which in itself reveals scripted-ness).

Uses and limitations

Role theory has been criticised by some experts as being an overly simplistic view of human interaction. Furthermore it has been argued that while it may be usefully applied to highly structured situations it neglects the complexity and spontaneity of human interaction. Trenholm (1996) maintains that we negotiate our 'performance' in life, as opposed to passively acting out roles in a predetermined manner. Hence it is important to be aware that role theory should be approached with caution as its simplicity can be limiting.

But in spite of this the concept of role theory can provide us with a useful framework for analysing and understanding roles and behavioural traits appropriate for various roles. For example, it provides a basis from which to explore questions along the lines of 'What makes Harry a good father?', 'What makes Sally a good manager?' or 'What kinds of traits help make a good police officer?' Hence role theory can help us to learn a great deal by observing and analysing the actions of others.

At this point it is recommended that you now turn to the exercises at the end of the chapter and undertake question 3.

Expanding on the concept of role theory it can be said that we present a 'public' (and censored) version of ourselves to the world. The image or version we try to project changes depending upon circumstances, the people with whom we are involved and our intentions. Thinking strategically about the image we should project and managing this image is important as it influences the way in which others will perceive us. Adler and Rodman (2000) call this **impression management** and make the point that inevitably everyone projects impressions. In other words our choices and behaviour, no matter how intentional or unintentional, will convey impressions such as casualness or formality as we cannot avoid making impressions. People behave strategically, for example in dressing for a job interview and arriving promptly in order to convey favourable impressions. Impression management need not be about 'forgery'—in the pursuit of effective communication we need to use task and audience analysis principles to assist us in managing the impressions we convey. Having said this, the gap between our presented self and our 'real' (or private) self can also be managed in an effort appropriately to reduce or reasonably contain the gap between the two. For example, on many occasions you will have heard the advice of 'just be yourself'. Indeed impression management needs to be balanced against the self because people tend to detect credibility problems when someone moves too far away from being oneself. In other words many people find it difficult to performing convincingly when they try to project an image far removed from who they really are.

Styles of relating: In interpersonal communication

In previous sections the point has been raised that our perceptions (i.e. ways of perceiving) form patterns which, by and large, become the habits we adopt and learn during our life course. These are in essence the 'coping habits' we use for dealing with the situations we experience in life. This section draws from a theoretical perspective which divides people's coping behaviours into three broad categories, or styles of relating, called assertiveness, non-assertiveness and aggression. This perspective is termed assertive behaviour theory as it promotes the idea of assertive behaviour as a highly effective style of relating to others so that we can enhance our interpersonal and relationship skills.

Assertive behaviour theory

Assertiveness training was derived from modern psychology and it became popular in the 1970s as a behaviour therapy technique and it remains popular today. It is interesting to note that the intellectual roots of assertiveness were nurtured in the activism of the 1960s in areas such as race equality, civil rights, feminism, anti-war movements and so on (Rakos 1991). Indeed, these issues and principles remain prevalent today.

DEFINING ASSERTIVE BEHAVIOUR

The first book on assertiveness training, *Your Perfect Right* (Alberti and Emmons 1970), defined assertiveness in terms of behaviours which enable an individual to:

* act in accordance with one's own best interests;
* stand up for one's self (and rights) without undue anxiety;
* express one's opinion and feelings honestly and unashamedly;
* exercise one's own rights without denying the rights of others.

(cited in Alberti and Emmons 1970)

In essence, being assertive involves having the confidence to stand up firmly for yourself, without infringing the rights of others. In spite of this the meaning of assertiveness is often misconstrued as it is frequently interpreted as being aggressive. However, according to Rakos (1991), assertiveness is theoretically conceptualised as a balanced midpoint on a continuum between non-assertive and aggressive behaviour styles. However, an understanding of non-assertive and aggressive behavioural styles is important in developing a good understanding of the assertive style.

Assertive behaviour traits include:

* being able to say 'no' without feeling guilty;
* listening to and respecting other people's points of view;
* taking responsibility for oneself (including admitting mistakes);
* acting in a self-confident manner;
* staying in control of emotions (e.g. avoiding insults);
* the right to express one's opinions and desires without undue fear (or guilt);
* the right to not be always justifying one's actions or feelings;
* the right to say 'I don't know' without loss of dignity;
* the right to change your mind;
* the right to make mistakes and be wrong without loss of dignity;
* the right to pursue and protect your own best interests.

(Adapted from Barry 1998)

Non-assertiveness

In contrast to assertiveness, non-assertive behaviour involves not standing up for one's rights. Being non-assertive means letting the needs and desires of other people take precedence over one's own. This style of relating often results in 'win–lose' outcomes, where the non-assertive person bears the loss. Non-assertiveness can often stem from learned feelings of personal inadequacy (De Vito 1989). Non-assertiveness can be broken down into the following categories:

* **situational non-assertiveness**: where an individual lacks assertiveness in certain situations;
* **generalised non-assertiveness**: which is more widespread and refers to individuals who generally lack assertiveness.

From this point one can try to identify to what degree they may be non-assertive and endeavour to change aspects of their behavioural style to develop a more assertive style. One may steadily build up a more assertive behavioural style by starting with seemingly easy situations before tackling more difficult areas. The traits of non-assertive behaviour include being overly apologetic (e.g. 'I'm sorry to disturb you but would you mind . . .?'); avoiding certain kinds of situations due to fear; and tolerating behaviour of others that infringes upon your rights.

Non-assertive behaviour traits include:

* avoidance (including not expressing your point of view for fear of upsetting others);

* complaining to others rather than dealing directly with the person concerned;

* apologising often and when unnecessary;

* non-confident body language (such as avoiding eye contact);

* not being able to say 'no' without feeling guilty.

(Adapted from Barry 1998)

Aggressiveness

Aggressive behaviour involves putting one's rights, needs and desires above those of others. This style of relating also tends to result in 'win–lose' outcomes, as the aggressor tries to force the other party into a losing situation. Understanding aggressiveness can be more complex, as it can stem from suppressed feelings of inadequacy (e.g. the flip-side of non-assertion). It tends to communicate the impression that the aggressor seems to think that they are superior. Once again, aggressiveness can be broken down into the following categories:

* **situational aggressiveness**: where an individual has aggressive tendencies in certain situations (e.g. 'road' or traffic rage, a serious and growing social problem);

* **generalised aggressiveness:** where an individual has a predominantly aggressive disposition.

People who are generally aggressive use bullying tactics to get their own way, for example being loud and/or insulting to others and in some cases using violence. Others then begin to resent the aggressor. It is a poor strategy as a behavioural style in terms of gaining and maintaining people's respect and establishing effective relationships. Aggressors often provoke aggression in others and thereby inflame situations. With this information in hand an individual can try to identify to what degree they are aggressive and endeavour to change aspects of their behavioural style to develop a more assertive style. To do this, consider what kinds of situations make you aggressive.

Aggressive behaviour traits include:

* loud and hostile tone of voice;

* insults and abusive language (including name calling);

* intolerance and impatience;

* staring and physical abuse (including pushing);

* interrupting and not listening to another's point of view.

(Adapted from Barry 1998)

Discussion

That people bring with them their learned habits (conditioned responses) is a recurring theme in communication and this extends into people's tendencies towards aggressiveness or passiveness/timidity. While most of us are capable of behaving in each of the three styles, depending on the situation, acting assertively can often be the most difficult. You can probably think of many times when you allowed someone else to dominate you simply to keep the peace and avoid the unpleasantness of conflict and hostility. In other words, some situations do not seem worth fighting over.

This raises an important question. Does adopting an assertive behavioural style mean that you have to be steadfastly assertive in every kind of situation? This question is relevant to discussions in Chapter 2, about the limitations of theory and the fact that theories need to be approached carefully and used flexibly. The theoretical idea that acting assertively in every situation is the best option is too idealistic given the complexity of 'real-life' situations. Having said this we still strongly advocate assertive behaviour theory and contend that almost everyone can benefit by developing a more assertive style in the way they relate to others.

Assertive behaviour is best approached flexibly; hence one needs to assess each situation and respond to it in a manner that seems the most appropriate under the circumstances. This, of course, is a skill in itself (situating monitoring and evaluation) and one which needs to be developed continually, as elements of aggressive and non-assertive behaviour are sometimes appropriate.

While assertiveness is theoretically straightforward and easy to comprehend, in reality it remains quite complex and difficult to put into practice in an effective and balanced way (i.e. without over- or under-reacting). In addition, our entrenched and habitualised style of relating makes change quite hard. Hence acting assertively in situations in which you typically act (and cope) non-assertively or aggressively is 'energy intensive'; for example, standing up for oneself instead of backing down non-assertively to avoid a fuss takes a great deal of emotional energy. However, these kinds of 'energy investments' can produce very worthwhile returns over the long term (e.g. the ability to better cope with difficult people and situations).

A substantial and continuing effort is required if we wish to recondition some of our behavioural traits, to try to improve our relationships, our capacity to communicate effectively and ultimately our quality of life. In contrast, dealing poorly with difficult kinds of people and situations can negatively impact on our capacity to communicate effectively and our quality of life. For instance, poorly handled problems at work can impact negatively upon our personal lives, while poorly handled problems in our personal lives can also affect a person's ability to function well at work.

The Intrapersonal Dimension to Behaving Assertively

Behaving assertively stems from thinking assertively (Nelson-Jones 1991); this cognitive component is an essential pre-condition of a truly assertive disposition, as assertive thinking underpins assertive behaviours. In other words, consistent assertive behaviour requires a strong belief in the right one has to stand up for their personal rights. In contrast, standing up for one's rights can be extremely difficult if one lacks a firm conviction that one's personal rights are of a high priority. It is also worth noting that the more difficult the situation, the more difficult behaving assertively becomes. And while life may 'sail along' quite easily for a time, it is when situations become difficult that assertive behaviour principles and techniques can benefit people the most.

Conflict

Conflict refers to disagreement between individuals who associate with one another (De Vito 1989). The level of association between individuals can vary from close and intimate, such as that between lovers and best friends, to less intimate (such as workplace relationships), down to commonplace encounters with acquaintances and shop assistants, clients and so on.

The nature of conflict

As communicators, it is important to remain aware that conflict is an inevitable part of relationships and interpersonal communication. Accordingly, Nelson-Jones (1991), as cited at the beginning of the chapter, says that relationships are the major source of human pleasure and pain.

Conflict can be both productive and destructive. Given the inevitability of conflict the success and continuance of relationships requires that we manage these conflicts sufficiently. Hence, actively dealing with conflict, as opposed to avoiding it, is often a productive strategy, which has the potential to create greater understanding and strengthen a relationship. However, conflicts, especially when handled badly with the use of poor strategies, can lead to communication breakdown and even the disintegration of a relationship.

Sources (and forms) of conflict

The definition of conflict as a disagreement between individuals raises questions about how and why individuals disagree with each other.

INTERPRETATION AND MEANING

As individuals, we perceive the world and its incoming stimuli differently for a range of reasons. Some of these were discussed in Chapter 2 under 'Variability of perception'. Consequently, conflicts often evolve out of differences in the interpretation or perceived meaning of something, such as an event or the meaning of a word. In a workplace situation, for example, the boss may direct two workers to carry out a task together in a certain way; however, the two workers may interpret these directions differently and then argue over what the boss actually meant. A specific strategy relevant to a situation like this would be to seek clarification from the boss should they be unable to resolve doubt through open discussion between themselves.

VALUES AND BELIEFS

Along with the differences in people's perceptions, people have differing and often conflicting sets of values (or standards) and beliefs, for example concerning religion, abortion or euthanasia. An appropriate strategy in these kinds of situations can be simply to agree to accept that each party is entitled to their own beliefs and values. This does not, however, rule out discussions between people on what they believe, and the merits they perceive in their respective world views. In accordance with assertiveness principles it is important to respect other people's values and beliefs as well as one's own.

COMPETING INTERESTS: RESOURCES AND DESIRES

People have needs and desires for limited amounts of available resources. Resources include property, access to equipment and access to people's time and attention. Our needs and desires for these resources can place us in a position that conflicts with the needs and desires of others. In a domestic situation, for example, arguments (productive or otherwise) can be about expenditure in areas such as entertainment, savings and pocket money for children. There are also constraints on the number of outcomes possible, for example in disagreements where one party has a desire to have something done a certain way which conflicts with the desires of another party.

A strategic approach often useful in such situations is the use of empathy; for example, trying to understand the situation from the other person's point of view, demonstrating this to them and then encouraging them to understand your position also.

BEHAVIOUR AND STATUS/POWER

Again, differences and incompatibilities between people's behavioural characteristics place them in conflicting positions. Conflict can arise due to the habits and behaviours others find annoying or hurtful. People's interests and desires function to shape the behaviours they exhibit and the behaviours they find pleasing or intolerable from others.

Relationships involve negotiation of the kinds of behaviours that will occur between individuals, and this involves negotiation of power, including the terms upon which the relationship will occur (i.e. people's respective roles and status). Hence conflicts can arise from people's desires and expectations from a relationship, in areas such as the delegation of household duties, the use of leisure time and the level of intimacy desired by each party.

While negotiations of roles and power in relationships tend to stabilise over time, the dynamic nature of interpersonal communication means that they are open to continual renegotiation. Again, establishing empathy early is a useful strategy for managing conflict situations of this kind.

A framework for managing conflict: A collaborative model

Collaboration involves working together on a problem or even just talking to the other party. The following model provides a set of steps for resolving problems particularly those involving a degree of conflict.

      Step 1: Problem analysis and identification

      Step 2: Negotiation

      Step 3: Clarification on agreement

STEP 1: PROBLEM ANALYSIS AND IDENTIFICATION

We should start by trying to determine clearly the 'real' problem and consider our own position, and the position of the other party (i.e. applying the principle of audience analysis). The importance of clearly identifying the real problem cannot be overstated. Accurate identification of problems can be difficult due to the problematic nature of **attribution**. The theory of attribution asserts that when observing the behaviour of another we attribute that behaviour to something about that person (i.e. character attribution) and also to the circumstances of the situation (situational attribution). Problems arise due to errors and biases in the attributions we make. For example, Middlebrook (1980) notes that we have a tendency to overestimate the role of personality characteristics and underestimate situational factors when making attributions. Hence we tend to view people's behaviours as largely the result of their personalities rather than their circumstances (Middlebrook 1980, p. 136).

Accordingly, careful attention is often required to identify accurately the problems underlying the surface-level symptoms of a situation. For example, if you feel that your partner is not spending much time with you lately, consider if it is (a) because they do not like you or (b) because they are heavily committed at the moment with overtime at work or examination time at university. Critical self-reflection as a strategy that involves self-analysis provides a means by which we can critically evaluate biases we may have. It can help us to guard against our tendency to come to premature judgements about people and situations.

Empathy has already been mentioned as an important communicative strategy. Not only does it help us to see things from the other's perspective, it also encourages others to see things from ours. Receptiveness to feedback is also very important if we are to understand the points being made by the other person. Generally, the more we understand ourselves and those with whom we interact, the more effective our communication is likely to be.

STEP 2: NEGOTIATION

Negotiation involves an effort by both parties to reach agreement on what the problem is and then agree on a solution designed to provide maximum benefit to both parties. Compromise is a crucial strategy in negotiating our way through conflict situations. **Compromise** involves both parties making some concessions (i.e. forgoing some desired objectives) in an effort to resolve a conflict-based problem to the mutual satisfaction of each party. The aim of this strategy is to resolve conflict by allowing both parties some of the outcomes they are seeking. Ideally it maximises the benefits and minimises the losses for both parties on a collaborative plane. This approach to conflict resolution involves taking each other's needs and desires into consideration, using empathy and aiming for what is commonly known as a 'win–win' situation—in other words, the best or most equitable outcome for both parties under the circumstances.

Negotiation requires enough willingness by each party to co-operate on resolving a given issue. Hence it is the responsibility of each party to enter into negotiation with a willingness to work together. This includes listening carefully and giving fair consideration to the points of view and position of the other party. See 'Effective listening' in Chapter 16. Negotiation is difficult, however, if one party is unwilling to commit to resolving the problem and taking part in fair negotiations. In such cases we may need to reconsider our approach to the problem. (Refer to 'Additional conflict management techniques' below.) It is also important to remember that it is unrealistic to expect all conflicts to be resolved amicably.

There are a number of other step-by-step models for solving problems collaboratively, such as the 'Dewey problem-solving model', which can at times be usefully applied in interpersonal negotiations. (Problem-solving model is outlined and discussed in Chapter 9.)

STEP 3: CLARIFICATION ON ARGEEMENT

Seeking and giving clarification provides us with another useful strategy for defining problems and negotiating solutions, as it helps both parties to 'get it straight', and understand each other. Likewise, clarifying the details of agreed outcomes at the end of negotiations and seeking final agreement on these points is important. Clarification involves restating in our own words our understanding of what the other person has said (and vice versa). For example, we could seek clarification with the following question, 'So when you say you need more time alone, you mean that . . .?' Recording negotiated outcomes in writing for later reference is often a good way of minimising future disagreement over the conditions of negotiated outcomes.

Note that applying these steps will often involve some backwarding and forwarding between the key principals. For example, problem identification and analysis may in many cases be best handled collaboratively as a negotiation process.

Additional conflict management techniques

Behaving assertively can be a useful approach for dealing with conflict. One of the important tenets of assertive behaviour is taking responsibility for your actions and wellbeing (Nelson-Jones 1991). The use of 'I' statements is an important strategy in developing assertiveness as it involves taking responsibility for our feelings and actions.

'I' statements are statements that make use of an 'I' at the beginning, and proceed with a clear enunciation of what we feel or believe at the time. Before making an 'I' statement, it is important for us to be quite certain of what it is that we actually feel or believe (e.g. clearly identify a problem), otherwise this strategy can backfire.

An 'I' statement about what we are feeling during relationship disharmony can be quite useful as a means of 'laying our cards on the table'—that is, disclosing our true feelings. This can help promote a positive 'feel' about the relationship that is based on a sense of mutual control and trust, and it also encourages (but without guarantee) the other party to disclose their true feelings.

As a communicative strategy, 'you' statements can be hazardous especially in conflict situations. A **'you' statement** focuses on the behaviour or intentions of the other person(s) involved in the conflict, such as 'You always seem to be watching TV when I want to talk' and 'You never talk about important issues'. Also note the hazards of using absolute terms such as 'always' and 'never'.

When emotions are running high, 'you' statements may feel like the most appropriate way to get a message across. However, the logic of the 'you' statement is counter-productive as it focuses the blame and responsibility for fault on the other party. 'You' statements are often interpreted by receivers as very personal and can provoke them, thereby leading to a situation which degenerates into ongoing retaliations between each party.

'I' statements, on the other hand, can be used to approach discussion about the problem in a more objective light, and can help defuse a hostile situation and establish an atmosphere conducive to honest and fair negotiation. For example, an 'I' statement may take the following form: 'I feel we have a problem and I would like to discuss it together'.

Alternative and last resort conflict management techniques

In addition to the formulation and use of sound and productive conflict management strategies, it is important for us to identify and understand the nature of some of the unproductive approaches sometimes used in dealing with conflict.

CONFRONTATION AND FORCE

An aggressive approach, for example the use of 'bullying' tactics, is sometimes used to win an argument or get one's own way. Aggressors tend to pursue a 'win–lose' outcome in which they win with little in the way of compromise on their part. However, people tend to resent aggressors and they often become quite unpopular. While aggressive behaviour may at times lead to a 'win' outcome for the aggressor, it can also provoke others into retaliation and thereby escalate hostilities to the point of communication breakdown and a 'lose–lose' outcome.

Aggressors should also be aware that aggressive retaliations are often a sign of growing resentment to the point where the retaliator feels that it is time the aggressor is made to realise that bullying tactics are no longer tolerable. Such cases can involve a 'lose' outcome for the original aggressor and a 'win' outcome for the retaliating party.

Thus it is important that we try to approach situations with a spirit of co-operation and aim for 'win–win' outcomes, rather than a competitive 'me versus them' attitude which strives for a 'winner takes all' outcome. While confrontation and force is generally considered a poor conflict management strategy, there are times when it can be considered appropriate. For instance, in some situations you can be dealing with an aggressor or with someone persistently encroaching upon your personal rights by not taking 'no' for an answer. Using a cross-domain comparison of 'war', war is viewed by many as an undesirable but nonetheless in extreme circumstances necessary and justifiable last resort. Note too that people have the lawful right to use reasonable force to protect themselves and their property. Within a workplace context managers are justified in confronting people about problems and dealing with them in a forceful manner.

Ultimately, we need to use our own judgement about communicative strategies so that we can deal with each situation on the basis of its own merits, that is, in a case specific manner.

PASSIVE NON-ASSERTION AND AVOIDANCE

Given that conflict is inevitable in communication, trying to prevent and avoid it (at all costs) is unsatisfactory. In fact, dealing with conflict helps to prevent the build-up of more intense conflict at a later stage. Nonetheless, people often adopt passive and avoidance strategies to keep the peace and prevent trouble or unpleasantness over something that does not seem worth the bother, especially when dealing with an aggressor. This strategy, of course, plays right into the hands of the aggressor and can function to establish a behavioural pattern in which the non-aggressor starts to develop a non-assertive behavioural manner. In spite of this there are circumstances where some avoidance and a passive style is the most appropriate; in severe cases not doing so may be threatening to your physical safety.

While passive and aggressive behaviour are both behavioural strategies people use for dealing and coping with interpersonal interaction, the danger is falling into the habit of over-relying on either style. Once again we have to use personal judgement in communicative situations and be aware of the pitfalls.

Inappropriate conflict management tactics

Some of these are:

* Falsely attributing blame to the other party (or any other party).
* False allegations against the other party (or any other party).
* Bullying (inappropriate use of aggression, force or intimidation).
* Lies and deceit (these are usually manipulative tactics).
* The use of flawed reasoning or false information (that is, fallacies).

Clear thinking and logic in Chapter 11 covers fallacies in arguments and is well worth revising; fallacies often provide people with powerful weaponry for winning arguments and getting their own way. An inappropriate but often used tactic involves attempts to discredit the other party using information or allegations about the other party that are not relevant to the issues in question.

Ethical issues and ramifications

The use of unfair methods is unethical and involves considerable risk. While it may on occasion result in short-term advantages for the perpetrator over the longer term, at some point others start to realise what is happening and come to the conclusion that such a person is not to be trusted. In the longer term unfair tactics destroy a person's credibility thereby limiting their capacity to communicate, persuade and, therefore, perform effectively. As such they run counter to the core theme of this book: 'strategies and techniques that we can use to help us communicate more effectively'.

SUMMARY

The categories we use to study communication often overlap; for example, some communicative situations can be considered both interpersonal and organisational. However, interpersonal communication, as a face-to-face mode of communication, occupies a central position because our performance in group and organisational settings is influenced by our ability to communicate at the interpersonal level.

This chapter has examined some of the key characteristics of interpersonal communication along with strategies for maximising effectiveness in this area. This provides us with a basis for proceeding with the following chapters on group and organisational communication.

KEY POINTS

- Interpersonal communication is often contrasted with that of intrapersonal communication, which refers to communication that takes place within the individual, such as thinking and perceiving, which then influences the way one relates to others.

- The Johari Window is a model for understanding the process of discovery of the self and others. Receptiveness and critical self-reflection are strategies that can be used to develop self-awareness. Self-disclosure can also be used as a strategy to advance self-understanding and our understanding of others.

- Role theory is useful, but limited to comparing daily interactions as the performing of roles (i.e. behaving in expected ways) in order to fulfil social expectations.

- Assertiveness is a style of relating that involves having the confidence to firmly stand up for ourselves, without infringing the rights of others. Assertiveness involves a balance between acting non-assertively and aggressively. Because behavioural styles are by and large habits, becoming more assertive is quite difficult and requires considerable ongoing effort.

- Conflict and disagreement between individuals is inevitable in communication and can be productive or destructive. Conflict can be managed using an assertive approach of firmly standing up for yourself, while also being empathetic to the views and circumstances of others. Strategies for managing conflict include determining the problem by negotiation after looking at it from both sides and then agreeing to and applying strategies deemed appropriate.

- Confrontation and force and non-assertion and avoidance are most often unproductive ways in which people deal with conflict—but can serve as last resorts in extreme circumstances.

- Lies and deceit, bullying, false allegations and falsely attributing blame are common forms of inappropriate conflict management tactics.

REVIEW QUESTIONS

1. Is interpersonal communication becoming less relevant as a result of new information and communication technologies? Support your view.

2. Define intrapersonal communication. What major processes are involved in intrapersonal communication and what is their significance?

3. How can emotional reactions and established 'thinking habits' affect the way you learn and communicate?
4. What is self-awareness and what are the benefits of developing your own self-awareness?
5. How can role theory help to build a better understanding of how to communicate more effectively in interpersonal communication?
6. What is conflict and what are some of its forms and sources?
7. What strategies can be used to manage conflict better?
8. What are common but unproductive ways in which people deal with conflict?
9. What are some of the common but inappropriate or unfair tactics people use to deal with conflict?

EXERCISES

Note: After formulating your responses it is important wherever possible to discuss them with a peer or group of peers. If you are not in a classroom setting then an appropriate electronic discussion board would be ideal.

1. This exercise is aimed at getting you to think about the role 'emotions' play in your life—and in this case feelings that you get from your interests in life.

   Identify at least three (3) of your favourite interests. You are encouraged to cast the net as widely as possible. To get you thinking, possibilities may range from watching or participating in sports to watching movies or TV soaps, listening or playing music, parties, night-clubbing and so on.

   - Why are you drawn to this activity and/or what do you like about it?
   - What underlying purpose(s) does the activity serve (e.g. TV show or sport)?

   Discuss your ideas with a group.

2. This exercise is also aimed at getting you to think about the role 'emotions' play.

   Identify the kind of career you wish to get into or alternatively identify a career that you think you might be interested in pursuing. Discuss your ideas with a group.

   - What is it that draws you to this kind of career/kind of work?
   - What kinds of aspects do you think you would like about it?

3. Discuss with a peer(s) these questions:

   - What traits and/or behaviours make someone a good teacher?
   - What traits and/or behaviours make someone an effective learner?
   - What traits and/or behaviours make an effective professional in an area of career interest to you?

4. How do you presently use the core techniques for developing self-awareness and awareness generally (*receptivity and monitoring feedback; perception checking;* and *critical self-reflection*) to help ensure that you have a high level of awareness of yourself and others?

   - Do you feel you make full use of these techniques?
   - If your answer is no, how can you begin to address your present situation better?

5. Do you feel you use many of the techniques and/or behavourial characteristics that make up assertive behaviour theory?

    If your answer is no, how can you begin to address better the ways in which you deal with difficult situations and difficult people?

6. In reference to the section titled 'A framework for managing conflict: A collaborative model' how useful do you feel a framework such as this is for managing substantial conflicts? Justify your view.

    What are some of the main causes of conflict in life? How can you address these in an effective and appropriate manner?

BIBLIOGRAPHY

Adler, R. and Rodman, G. 2000, *Understanding Human Communication,* 7th ed., Harcourt College Publishers, Florida.

Adler, R. Rosenfeld, L., Towne, N. and Proctor, R. 1998, *Interplay: The Process of Interpersonal Communication,* 7th ed., Harcourt Brace and Company, Florida.

Alberti and Emmons 1970, *Your Perfect Right,* cited in De Vito, J. A. 1989, *The Interpersonal Communication Book,* 5th ed., Harper and Row Publishers, New York.

Barry, K. 1998, *Assertive Communication,* Queensland Council of Service Inc., Kelvin Grove, Queensland.

De Vito, J. A. 1989, *The Interpersonal Communication Book,* 5th ed., Harper and Row Publishers, New York.

Goffman 1959, cited in Putnis, P. and Petlin, R. 1996, *Professional Communication: Principles and Applications,* Prentice Hall, Sydney.

Goleman, D. 1996, *Emotional Intelligence,* Bantam Books, New York.

Luft, J. 1984, *Group Processes: An Introduction to Group Dynamics,* 3rd ed., Mayfield Publishing Company, California.

Middlebrook, P. 1980, *Social Psychology and Modern Life,* 2nd ed., Alfred A. Knopf Inc., New York.

Nelson-Jones, R. 1991, *Human Relationship Skills,* 2nd ed., Holt, Rinehart and Winston, Sydney.

O'Sullivan, T., Hartley, J., Montgomery, M. and Fiske, J. 1994, *Key Concepts in Communication and Cultural Studies,* 2nd ed., Routledge, New York.

Rakos, R. 1991, *Assertive Behavior: Theory, Research and Training,* Routledge, New York.

Schank, R. and Abelson, R. 1977, *Scripts, Plans, Goals and Understanding: An Inquiry into Human Knowledge Structures,* Lawrence Erlbaum Associates Publishers, New Jersey.

Seligman, M. 1996, *Learned Optimism,* Simon & Schuster, New York.

Trenholm, S. 1996, *Interpersonal Communication,* 3rd ed., Wadsworth Publishing Co., Belmont, California.

Verderber, R. 1990, *Communicate!,* 6th ed., Wadsworth Publishing Co., Belmont, California.

Group communication

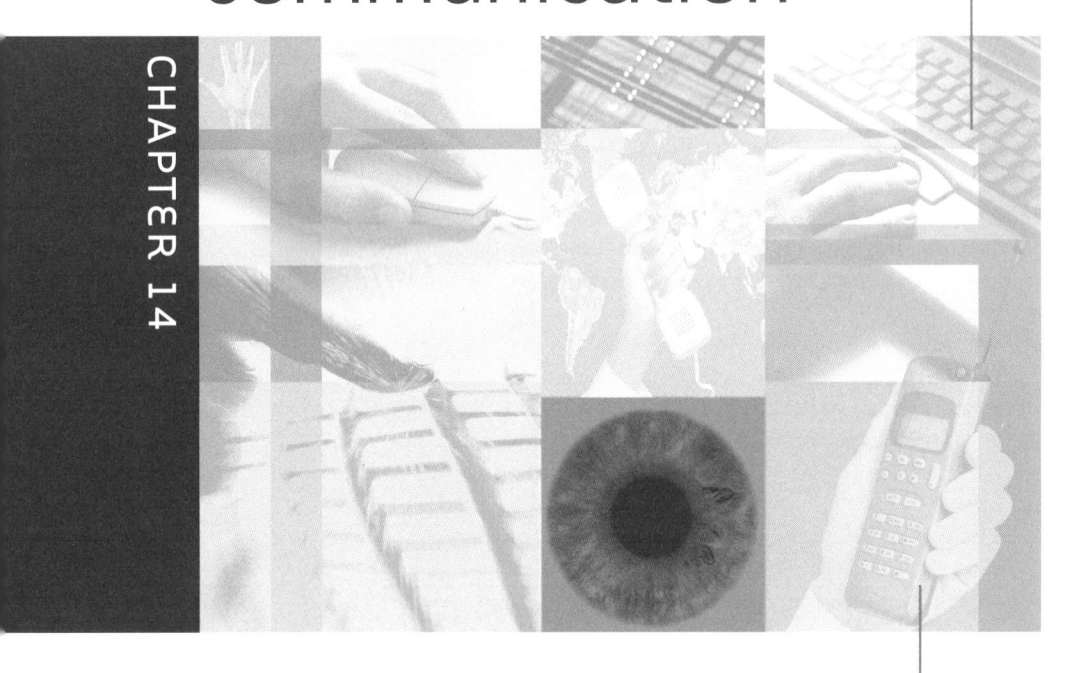

CHAPTER 14

Upon completing this chapter you should be able to:
- define the term 'group' and explain the key functions and benefits of groups;
- analyse the developmental stages of group formation and functioning;
- discuss the problems associated with 'groupthink' in relation to group decision making and strategies for overcoming such problems;
- identify strategies for managing conflicts in group communication; and
- identify issues regarding the study of leadership and evaluate a range of leadership styles.

A major issue in interpersonal communication as evidenced in the previous chapter is that of managing difficult situations and relationships with individuals. Likewise managing conflict and relationships is a major issue in group communication, but even more so because increasing the number of people involved in communicative interaction increases the level of complexity.

A group can be defined as a small collection of people who have some shared goal or interest (O'Sullivan *et al.* 1994). In addition to this, group members perceive themselves as belonging to the group and interact with other members to achieve certain aims or a common purpose (Hellreigel *et al.* 1992, p. 311).

A group of people can be contrasted with a category of people. For instance, young Australians, say those under the age of 25, are an example of a social category rather than a group of people, as are home owners or people who have the same occupation. Furthermore the passengers on a bus trip represent a category of people even if they happen to share a common purpose, that is, to arrive at the same destination at a given time. While the passengers of a bus trip may share a common purpose they do not typically interact with one another in an effort to achieve specific aims or a common purpose. In sum a group must meet the following criteria:

* The members have a shared interest or goals.
* The members perceive themselves as belonging to the group.
* The members interact with one another in an effort to achieve a shared interest (or common purpose) or specified goals.

The role of groups

Groups vary widely in terms of purpose and the degree of formality. The degree of formality of groups ranges from the informal relations between members of a group of friends or a family, through to more formally structured groups such as committees and working teams, for example marketing teams, sales teams, surgical teams and departmental teams.

In discussing *role theory* in Chapter 13, it was noted that in the course of a day we play (or function) in a variety of roles, from colleague to friend, parent to child and so on. Similarly, in the course of our daily lives we participate in a wide range of groups—family, workplace departments and committees, sports teams and so on. Given that we spend a great part of our lives communicating, interacting and working in groups it is important that we understand the functioning of groups so that we can enhance the effectiveness of our communication and performance in groups and degree of satisfaction we receive from these groups.

It is also worth bearing in mind that groups operate within and make up the organisations we are involved with. In fact groups can be viewed as the building blocks of an organisation. Workplace organisations are of particular interest to us as many people spend their working lives as employees of organisations. Hence this chapter relates closely to Chapter 15, on organisational communication.

The functioning of groups

We join groups in an effort to satisfy needs and desires. Reasons for joining groups range between achieving certain goals and our needs and desires for human interaction.

We often join groups to achieve goals that are difficult or impossible to reach as an individual, so we choose groups that have goals which are similar to, or compatible with, our needs and desires. Sports teams such as rugby or netball provide a good example of groups that enable people to share in a mutually satisfying goal.

Groups are often formed in an effort to accomplish specific tasks including the solving of problems. For example, an environmental group may come together to work towards goals of ecological preservation and to promote awareness of issues which may threaten the environment. Finally, it is also important to note that this chapter is concerned with small groups, typically between three to 16 people.

The extent to which individual members share the common goals of a group varies from individual to individual, as do points of view and individual agendas. Hence there is always some degree of tension in a group. People's motivation for being in the group and the satisfaction they derive from it will also vary. See Figure 14.1.

While the perceived rewards of being in a group outweigh the perceived costs (e.g. the degree of compromise, conflict and frustration involved), motivation among individuals to remain in the group is high. Alternatively, when the associated costs appear to outweigh the benefits, motivation for remaining in a group starts to dwindle. Hence the continuation of a group can depend on the level at which it is able to satisfy the needs and desires of its members which includes the management of inherent conflicts of interests between members. Ultimately it is up to the members of a group to negotiate the common and compatible goals and interests among themselves in an effort to achieve sufficient harmony and member commitment to the group so that it can function efficiently and effectively.

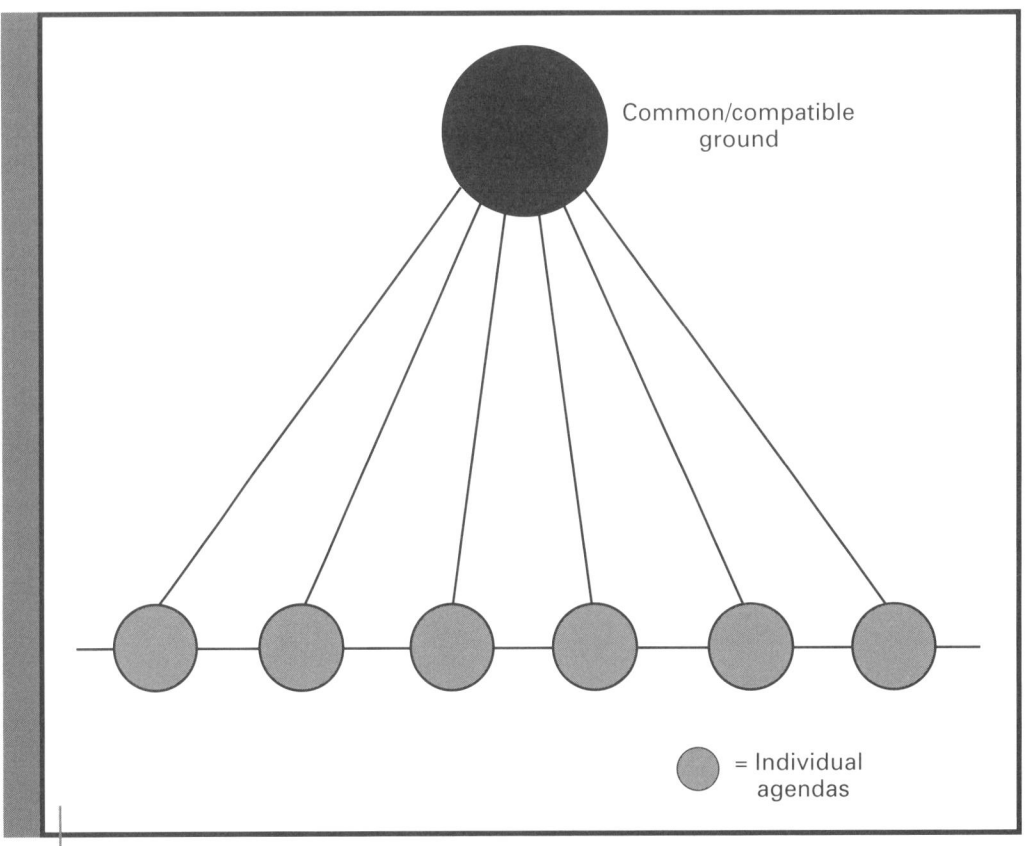

FIGURE 14.1 Building Functional Harmony

TASK- AND MAINTENANCE-BASED BEHAVIOURS

Accordingly, there are two fundamental kinds of activities that are carried out in functioning groups. First, there are **task-based behaviours** (or performance-based activities). These are actions directed towards the achievement of a group's main goals, for example the organising of events and activities for a sporting club. Second, there are **maintenance-based behaviours** (or relations-based activities) which involve the managing of conflict and morale in an effort to maintain group cohesion and functioning (Hellreigel *et al.* 1992).

Maintenance-based behaviours include giving encouragement and praise to others along with efforts to maintain a rapport with people. This can take the form of asking group members questions about their family, a sporting interest or some other topic of interest to them.

The key functions of groups

The key functions of groups can be categorised as follows:

1. To provide people with the opportunity to fulfil a need for human interaction.

2. To enable people to combine forces to pursue common goals (including needs and desires) that cannot be satisfactorily achieved by individuals on their own.

3. To pool skills and resources in an effort to achieve common or compatible goals in an effective and efficient manner.

4. To share perspectives to increase people's understanding of problems (i.e. the principle that 'two heads are better than one' and 'the more the better').

5. To increase the likelihood of significant action towards meeting goals through increased force of numbers and the added (peer) pressure on individuals to adhere to decisions made collectively and to carry out tasks assigned to them.

6. In addition, groups are often formed to deal with problems or operations. Operations refers to the functions of a group in running ongoing procedures (e.g. managing a budget, supplying a service, organising of sports fixtures).

Group dynamics

The kind of communication that is likely to occur in groups is influenced by the dynamics operating within a particular group at a given time. The nature and even the capacity of a group depends upon the abilities and character attributes of the individuals comprising the group, notwithstanding external circumstances and events impacting on the group. It is also important to acknowledge that people tend to act differently in groups than they otherwise would as individuals, for example take risks in decision making.

A group provides a means by which people can pool their knowledge and insight and as such the potential to produce outcomes beyond what an individual could achieve on their own including the ability to formulate better decisions. The concept of **synergy**, that the whole is greater than the sum of the parts, is an integral concept in the study of group dynamics. The term 'synergy' is used to refer to the idea of added energy, capability and creativity that can result from people working and interacting together.

Synergy is often understood in reference to *chemistry*—that is, the special chemistry that can result when certain people get together. The notion of synergy is central to the study of group dynamics, for example a group of people may work very well together and complement each other (i.e. bring out the best in each other). Hence we may say that a group which works together very well is one which has 'good dynamics' or positive or productive synergies.

Most of us spend a great deal of time working in and moving between various work groups or work teams and so developing an understanding of how groups operate, what they involve, is critical to a person's ability to diagnose problems and trying to resolve those problems. Understanding the dynamics of groups, including the kinds of stages that occur within groups, can also provide us with contextual information that is useful in making decisions about how to maximise our effectiveness in communication groups. Finally, group dynamics also includes the power relations operating within a group, for example the dominant members and their effect on other members.

The following section ('Life-cycle stages of groups') considers the kinds of processes and power shifts that occur within groups as they move in and out of a series of major stages common to groups. Note also that while these theorisations can be applied to informal groups this chapter is primarily concerned with formal groups, but this can also include recreational groups, sports clubs and committees.

Life-cycle stages of groups

The **developmental stages**, or 'life-cycle' stages, of groups have been explained using the terms of forming, storming, norming, performing and adjourning. The following discussion is based on these categories as outlined in Hellreigel *et al.* (1992).

1. FORMING

In the **forming** stage individuals gather together in an effort to join forces in pursuit of common goals or a common purpose. This stage often involves a 'honeymoon' period with people feeling positive because others share their goals and are optimistic about the probability of satisfactorily reaching such goals.

Communicative encounters at this stage often appear cordial and polite. This may be because of people's tendency to act cautiously when faced with uncertainty. In other words it is a time in which people are feeling each other out and in the early stages people find themselves dealing with 'an unknown quantity'. However, confusion can also develop due to uncertainties, not only about the members but with the exploration and development of the group's aims and objectives.

2. STORMING

The **storming** stage emerges when serious conflicts develop due to disagreement over policy matters—specifically the actual goals of the group and the manner in which these goals are best achieved. In addition, the growing confidence of group members along with conflicting aspirations for dominant and leadership positions also leads to hostility. Quarrels also develop over issues such as the perceived preferential treatment of some members, and the tendency for some members to dominate and get their own way. Battles over desired goals, methods of goal attainment and the power dynamics (i.e. contest for dominant and leadership positions) can become very intense. This is often referred to as the politics (i.e. derived from the word 'policy') of a situation, that is, competing and conflicting individual agendas. The formation of power-based coalitions is also a common feature in storming scenarios.

At this stage a group may disintegrate to the point of an unamicable adjournment. Sometimes a group may splinter into two different groups and it is not uncommon at this point for some members to withdraw or leave the group completely. However, groups will often overcome such turbulence and remain intact and hence move into the stage mentioned next, called norming.

3. NORMING

The **norming** stage emerges when conflict is resolved to the point where the majority of the group members agree upon the major policy direction of the group (i.e. goals, methods and leadership, as well as the power relations). At this point power relations within a group stabilise and hence the dynamics of leadership style and people's relative positions of power take root. A mood or climate of co-operation is re-established enabling the group to concentrate more energy on the business of performing.

4. PERFORMING

Performing occurs when people are working or start working towards the goals set and begin accomplishing related objectives, that is, objectives being the specific tasks which contribute to the attaining of goals.

5. ADJOURNING

The **adjourning** stage is reached by groups that were formed in an effort to achieve a specific goal (which is often a problem and may require a report) in a specified amount of time. For example, organisations often establish committee groups to investigate or resolve a problem. In some cases, however, a long-running group such as a sports team may adjourn on amicable terms, for a variety of reasons; for example, the members may feel that they have benefited sufficiently from the group and no longer have the desire to pursue the goals or purpose of the group. Of course a group can also disband or adjourn acrimoniously as a result of storming—in cases of irreconcilable differences.

DISCUSSION

As previously stated, it is important that when we work with and think about theoretical accounts on the developmental stages of groups, such as this one, we do so in a flexible manner and with a degree of sophisticated judgement. While the theoretical stages of group development are expressed in a linear form, this is not necessarily the reality. It is common for a group to proceed from stage 1, forming, to stage 4, performing, without experiencing a storming phase. On the other hand many groups move in and out of storming (stage 2) and norming (3) many times during their life-time. In this way the developmental stages of the group life cycle are non-linear but rather fluid and dynamic and hence need to be understood in this way.

Indeed, a performing group may move into a storming phase due to dissatisfaction with the power relations of the group. Stormy battles over power, status and desired direction of a group often result in renegotiation of the dynamics of a group in which certain members emerge with less or more influential roles. Cabinet reshuffles provide a particularly insightful example of this—where one group member may challenge a leader for reasons which may be related to dissatisfaction with the existing leader. In the case of a successful challenge, significant changes to group dynamics and distribution of power may result, while the status quo may continue should a challenge be unsuccessful.

It is interesting to compare how these kinds of processes also appear to occur in other types of groupings—even friends and families weather stormy periods.

Some groups may remain relatively stable for long periods while others may engage in periods of frequent and protracted turbulence. But once again, being able to identify which stage a group is in can assist us in formulating communicative strategies to maximise our effectiveness in serving our own and common group interests by taking the group climate and politics into account.

Information flow in groups

Research has shown that satisfaction of group members is greater when information flows are decentralised, that is, in groups where all members are free to communicate and share information freely with all other members (Middlebrook 1980). This is in contrast to having important information and knowledge concentrated in a hierarchical structure in which information is vetted and selectively filtered down to many of the group members. Figure 14.2 contrasts centralised and decentralised communication flow systems. Climate is a concept used to explain these aspects of group dynamics; an open communication climate is one which promotes the sharing of ideas, information and importantly opinions.

HIERARCHICAL CLOSED (Centralised)   **CIRCULAR OPEN** (Decentralised)

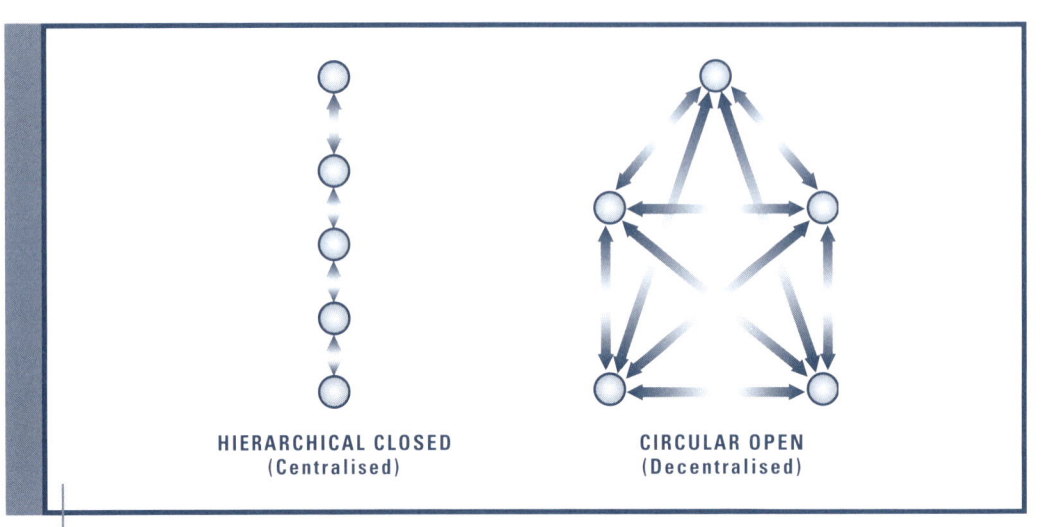

FIGURE 14.2 Communication Flows

Source: Based on Rasberry and Lemoine (1986).

Benefits of group decision making

There are significant advantages associated with the making of decisions within groups. Many of these are evident in the earlier sections 'The functioning of groups' and the 'The key functions of groups'. As previously noted, groups are often formed to deal with problems, such as a committee or a taskforce set up to investigate police corruption, and operations, such as a committee formed to help manage some aspect of the day-to-day functioning of an organisation, for example a finance or resources committee.

The advantages associated with using groups to deal with and make decisions concerning the investigation of problems or to deal with the operations of an organisation or larger group include:

* Groups are often formed on the basis of what is perceived as the best available expertise, that is, the best people available for the job.

* The dynamic interactions made possible by groups allow for the development of a deeper understanding of a situation or problem through the sharing of ideas and perspectives, as opposed to the restrictions of one individual viewpoint.

* Again, the interactional nature of groups facilitates the development of a better range of possible solutions or actions and the evaluation of options in an effort to try to determine the best possible course of action.

It is apparent from the preceding points that the 'two heads are better than one' principle is a crucial feature of groups and is important in both gaining an understanding of a situation and generating and evaluating solutions. You will be aware that in group dynamics, this pooling of skills, perspectives and knowledge to achieve outcomes beyond individual capability is typically referred to as *synergy*. Groups are often formed for the purpose of making decisions in relation to set problems or tasks. Specific problem-solving techniques that can be used in groups are examined in Chapter 9.

Cohesion in groups

Cohesion in a group refers to the strength of each member's commitment to the group and their desire to remain in it. Cohesion in groups is influenced by the degree of compatibility that exists between the goals of the group and the goals of its individual members (Hellreigel *et al.* 1992). The word 'compatibility' is significant as cohesive groups do not necessarily require all group members to have the same goals.

Cohesion can be likened to a kind of 'glue' that binds the members of a group together. Hence highly cohesive groups have a strong structure because their members are highly committed to the group and co-operate to preserve it.

Cohesion can have a positive influence on the effectiveness of groups and it does seem logical that a higher level of commitment by group members is often conducive to higher levels of performance. One of the main functions of a coach of a sports team is to promote cohesion within the group in an effort to maximise the chances of goal attainment, in this case winning against the competitors. Cohesion can enable group members to focus their energy and attention towards performance as it can dramatically reduce the time and energy being devoted to dealing with group conflict.

But despite all of this, conflict can contribute immensely to group performance and decision making, while certain levels and kinds of cohesion can impact upon group performance very badly. Unhealthy high cohesion, that is, *dysfunctional cohesion* among group members, can produce an insular climate in which many of the benefits that accrue, for example synergies of shared insight and creativity and innovation, can quickly disappear.

Pitfalls in group decision making

NEGATIVE COHESION AND CONFORMITY IN GROUPS

In the interests of exploring problems fully and evaluating solutions thoroughly, members of cohesive groups may encourage the expression of conflicting points of view (i.e. those that may not conform to the expectations and views of the wider group). However, research on groups has shown that the pressure to conform is much more intense in highly cohesive groups (Middlebrook 1980). Furthermore, research has consistently shown that many of us are prepared to compromise and even disregard our own judgement in order to conform to group expectations (Macionis 1989).

High levels of cohesiveness and conformity in groups can interfere with the group's ability to make decisions effectively, giving rise to a phenomenon called 'groupthink'.

PROBLEMS ASSOCIATED WITH GROUPTHINK

Groupthink, a term coined by Irving Janis, refers to a propensity in highly cohesive groups to make poor decisions because of a group culture that discourages alternative points of view, as they are seen as a threat to group cohesion and the status quo (e.g. existing power distribution).

Characteristics associated with groupthink include:

* *Illusions of invulnerability among members.* This creates excessive optimism and confidence in the ability of the group and increases the likelihood of risky and poorly thought out decisions. Furthermore the anonymity of members means that no one person has to take the blame or responsibility for a poor or risky decision.

* *Over-confidence* in the group—a perception that it is not vulnerable to making poor decisions. Hence an initially proposed option (often made hastily) often becomes a favoured course of action without time given to due consideration of less obvious pitfalls and contingency plans or other options.

* *Unquestioned beliefs* in the group's moral sense of what is right and just. This can lead to ignoring the moral and ethical consequences of decisions.

* *Stereotyped views about rivals* and potential competitors. Decisions made solely on this basis can blind the group and thereby lead to poor decisions.

* *'Peer' pressure* exerted on those who tender views and options that conflict with the group's beliefs in its ability, reasoning, viewpoints or status quo.

* *Censorship of information.* This can occur through 'mind guards' who shelter the group members from outside information that may conflict with the apparent validity of the group's decisions, direction, practices, prevailing views and credibility of the group's leadership.

(Based on Janis 1982)

The following provides further insight into the dynamics of groupthink and its potential to produce serious adverse outcomes.

> Janis labelled the closed decision-making process 'groupthink'. When individuals become insulated from outside information, they are likely to perceive external inputs as a threat rather than as important information. The group develops a likeness of thinking, or purpose, which blinds them to additional information. The examples Janis used to support his theory are not limited to friendships. In fact, they are more linked to the closed nature of the network to outside information during the decision-making process. Janis counselled the establishment of weak ties to prevent the group from being closed. As a careful analysis of the 1986 *Challenger* spacecraft disaster demonstrates, the pressure to launch the spacecraft apparently allowed individuals to reject outside information and proceed with a deeply flawed decision (Gouran, Hirokawa & Martz 1986). The result was a tragic loss of lives and a decrease in the credibility of NASA. One author labelled the process 'freeze-think', because the commitment to launch was so great that the decision makers failed to examine crucial evidence (Kruglanski 1986). Studies of the *Challenger* disaster indicate that the information was available to justify aborting the flight, but it was ignored, discredited, downplayed, or reframed to appear less ominous.
>
> *(Cited in Harris 1993, pp. 174–5)*

More recently, conclusions reached from investigations into communication in the lead-up to the 2003 *Columbia* space shuttle disaster are strikingly close to that of the *Challenger* described above. So much so that it is hard not to come to the conclusion that history had repeated itself and that virtually nothing had been learned from the 1986 experience. Once again there were many pieces of evidence showing communication breakdowns due to repeated 'passing over' of warnings of imminent disaster as a result of a culture of complacency among management across numerous work teams. Hence it is argued that the disaster should have been prevented had proper attention and consideration been given to the information available including warnings by a number of staff.

Historically, many post-disaster analyses have pointed towards groupthink as a leading cause of past disasters including the World War II bombing of Pear Harbour. More detailed discussion of group dynamics and organisational culture in relation to the *Columbia* incident can be retrieved online from the archive video of an American news and current affairs program, 'The News Hour', at <http://www.pbs.org/newshour/bb/science/columbia/>. Then select Ray Suarez who discusses the *Columbia* Accident Investigation Board's findings with a former NASA program manager and historian. Then click here to watch this segment in streaming video.

There are a range of strategies and techniques available to help establish and maintain healthy group dynamics and to guard against negative cohesion, that is, groupthink. *Vigilant interaction theory* (cited in Daniels *et al.* 1997) posits that ensuring effective decision making is dependent upon an awareness of, and attentiveness to, factors that can lead to flaws in decision-making and problem-solving processes and practices. The list below provides measures to help prevent and counter groupthink.

Countering groupthink

Here are some preventative strategies.

* *Encourage constructive criticism and critical evaluation input from all members (i.e. an open communicative climate).* Each member should be encouraged to evaluate ideas critically and air objections and doubts. For example, encourage the constructing of worst case scenarios that may result from decisions and explore alternatives and plan contingencies.

* *Issues to be dealt with should be presented impartially* at the start without stated preferences or expectations (particularly from leaders).

* *Encourage open-minded thinking*—alternative thinking and creativity (i.e. brainstorming)—into decision-making and problem-solving processes.

* *Adopt a structured process to problem solving and decision making,* for example Dewey's critical sequence model in Chapter 9 under 'Problem-solving and decision-making sequence'.

* *Hold 'second-chance' meetings* on important issues wherever possible—allowing time for further reflection in a 'cooling-off' period.

* *Seek additional consultation* outside the group from experts and/or trusted colleagues in cases when the decisions or problems being dealt with are of a critical nature.

(Based on Janis 1982)

Conflict in groups

Disagreement, or conflict (storming), is virtually inevitable in communication; however, it can also have positive consequences. For example, we have just seen that expressing criticism, putting forward opposing views to provoke 'healthy' debate can help prevent groupthink and, therefore, maximise the effectiveness of group decision making. However, conflict can also be counter-productive and if poorly managed can severely reduce group productivity and lead to high-level dysfunction.

Factors that can contribute to group conflict

As mentioned earlier, conflict arises out of incompatibility, conflicting interests and perceived conflicting interests between individuals' goals and desires. Goals can differ for many reasons, starting with the fact that as individuals we have our own unique world views and ways of interpreting the world. Differences in people's motivation and status can also contribute to conflict, for example the differences between the goals of leaders, bosses and employees. Sometimes individuals find themselves in a situation where their membership of a group is compulsory and they possibly resent the group and its purpose. Conflict can also develop if individuals resent the style of leadership (leadership is discussed below) or the kinds of communicative strategies people are using to persuade and direct others, for example unfair strategies such as intimidation and the use of bullying tactics.

Conflict management strategies

Communicating in groups involves varying degrees of interpersonal communication (including one-on-one interactions); hence it is important to remain mindful that the issues and strategies such as assertive communication, as discussed in Chapter 13, are also relevant here. With this in mind the following list provides a range of additional strategies that can be used to manage conflict in groups. Of course, the strategies we choose and they way in which we apply them depends on the particular circumstances of a situation. Remember, poor strategy selection and application can serve to exacerbate conflict and the unproductive tendencies of a group.

1. *Authoritative commands* Where a person in authority uses that authority to direct the members of a group, for example in cases where there is a deadline looming for a decision or a conflict has been going on too long and is deemed counter-productive or detrimental to the group.

2. *Conflict avoidance* For example, directing a group away from quibbling over a minor time-wasting issue towards something more constructive.

3. *De-emphasising conflict* Similar to that of 'avoidance'; one can try to downplay an issue of contention.

4. *Goal setting* To try to reach agreement on a productive set of goals for members to work towards.

5. *Focusing on the problem* To try to deal with the issue directly by determining the best course of action for solving it.

6. *Compromise (or negotiation)* Where conflicting parties seek genuinely to negotiate a 'win–win' outcome by making the concessions necessary for such an outcome.

(Adapted from Arnold et al. 1991)

Leadership

Leadership is another important element in group dynamics and can be crucial to the effective functioning of task-oriented groups. However, despite extensive research on the area there has been little agreement on what makes a good leader or on any general theory of leadership. This may indicate that leadership is an extremely complex dynamic and one that demands a great deal more research in an effort to understand it better. This section provides a brief introduction to some of the aspects and issues associated with the study of leadership.

Defining leadership

The inherent complexity of leadership demands a broad working definition. Hence it has been defined as a process whereby one person influences other people (Hellreigel *et al.* 1992). Despite the difficulties involved in identifying what kinds of characteristics make a good leader, effective communication skills appear to be one universal imperative. In accordance with the definition, if leaders are to influence others they must be effective communicators.

Theories of leadership

TRAIT-BASED THEORIES

Some people hold that leaders are born to lead. Early theorists attempted to explain leadership in terms of *the great-man theory* of leadership, commonly citing examples such as Adolf Hitler and Winston Churchill. The view that leaders are endowed with superior qualities (such as high IQ) that distinguish them from others gave rise to trait-oriented theories of leadership (Bass 1981). However, trait theories have been discounted because effective leaders do not appear to possess common sets of traits.

SITUATIONAL AND SOCIAL-CONTEXT-BASED THEORIES

Situational theorists focus on the relationship between the traits of an individual and the needs of a particular situation. The key assumption of this theory is that leadership can be understood only by taking into account the interactional dynamics between an individual and the situation. According to this theory, effective leadership is dependent on a good match between the needs of a particular situation and the traits or strengths of the individuals available and most suitable. This theory is more specific and built upon that of the context theory perspective. However, these theories have also been met with limited acceptance.

DISCUSSION

As stated initially, a great deal of work remains to be done in the area of leadership research and theory development. Bass (1981) feels that leadership theory to date often works to obscure understanding rather than advance it. However, a successful leader is often someone who emerges in a particular situation as best suited to both the management of people and the tasks required at a given time. It is also widely accepted that leadership skills for specific situations can be taught and so people can be trained for this role, hence the prevalence of management traineeship positions in organisations. Despite their limitations leadership theories do provide some perspective on how leadership can be studied and thought about.

Primary leadership styles

The study of leadership requires more than an understanding of the theoretical perspectives of traits and situations as discussed above. The functioning of any group will be influenced by the style of leadership being used. Here we consider four basic leadership styles: authoritarian, paternalistic, democratic or participative, and *laissez-faire*.

AUTHORITARIAN LEADERSHIP

An **authoritarian leadership** style is where the leader of a group makes the decisions for the group and commands compliance from their subordinates. Authoritarian leaders are often successful in coercing people into compliance owing to the authority bestowed on their position and their ability to dominate others.

The authoritarian leadership style works to negate many of the benefits associated with groups and group decision making because these kinds of leaders by and large oppose the perspectives and criticisms of other members of the group. Research has consistently shown that people are more satisfied in groups where their opinions are appreciated and, furthermore, people do not like being bullied. Authoritarian leaders are generally resented by group members and they fail to harness effectively the talents of group members. However, the authoritarian style can be seen as appropriate for certain situations, for example crisis situations where immediate decisions are necessary and group discipline must remain high (Macionis 1989). The leadership style used in certain sections of the military provides a good example of formalised authoritarian leadership in action.

PATERNALISTIC/SUPERVISORY LEADERSHIP

Paternalistic leadership is directive in much the same way as authoritarian leadership, but far less malicious. This type of leader often takes it upon themselves to make the decisions but may listen to feedback (Gibson and Hodgetts 1991). The paternalistic style sometimes appears evident, but to varying degrees, in the style of the leadership exercised by supervisors and managers.

Paternalistic leaders tend to be very much like a parent; they try to sell subordinates on their ideas using stock phrases such as, 'If you do it this way it will be good for your career' and 'Trust me, I would not lie or tell you to do something that is not in your best interests' (based on Gibson and Hodgetts 1991).

While stopping short of autocratic control, supervisory leaders often introduce problems and issues for discussion with a lengthy description, making clear in the process how they want to treat the problem. They tend to set the agenda for how the problem is to be tackled, and do not see themselves as 'one among equals' within the group. As a result the synergetic benefits that can accrue with the multiple view of individuals are typically greatly diminished.

DEMOCRATIC/PARTICIPATIVE LEADERSHIP

Democratic leadership involves encouraging group members to determine their own goals and methods for goal attainment and problem solving. This is a much more inclusive leadership style in which the members of a group become active stakeholders (i.e. are more likely to have a sense of ownership). This helps to motivate members and harness more effectively the talents of group members. Once again, research shows that members of participative groups enjoy greater satisfaction than those of the more directive kind.

Democratic leadership is difficult and typically requires more maturity (and sometimes education). Decision making in democratic groups can, at times, be quite difficult and time consuming and does have certain limitations, for instance in urgent or crisis situations. To be effective this style of leader must be able to coordinate both the task and the group maintenance functions.

While it can slow down the decision-making process, group performance and achievement have the potential to be higher under this style of leadership than the preceding styles. It empowers people to give their best and capitalises on the potential for synergies that become possible with a diversity of people and the views and expertise they bring as individuals. The democratic model (in a more sophisticated form) provides the basis upon which countries like Australia are governed. Modern democratic principles incorporate inclusivity, equality and freedom of speech—allowing opposing views and choice. Often referred to as an adversial model, competition between the ruling party and the opposition party is something which is highly valued. Because competition between parties over ideas helps lead them towards the best policy ideas and decisions. A group working under this leadership style is also less prone to the serious problems that can result from groupthink.

LAISSEZ-FAIRE LEADERSHIP

Laissez-faire leadership is where leaders resist exerting their influence on the group. Some theorists go so far as to say that *laissez-faire* leaders are derelict in their duties in that they actively avoid their responsibilities (Bass 1981). This style of leadership is usually ineffective unless the members of a group are self-directed and quite motivated.

It is interesting to note that the term *laissez-faire* is sometimes used to refer to a philosophy of a 'hands-off' approach as being best. For instance, the philosophy of *laissez-faire* capitalism operates under the assumption that an unregulated marketplace is the best determiner of an efficient market system and as such opposes government regulation, which is seen as interference. This theory model underpins free-market economics and is also known as economic rationalism, and *laissez-faire* leadership can be the result of deliberate choice rather than simply laziness. This style of leadership may be conducive to high-level creativity and jobs in which a great deal of individual autonomy is required. However, when this is not the case a group may become permissive and derelict in the carrying out of its duties.

DISCUSSION

It is interesting that each of these fundamental leadership styles is based on a different political ideology, indicating where the root ideas have come from. Having a Western-type cultural background, one may be inclined to see 'democratic' as good and 'authoritarian' as bad; however, this is not necessarily the case. For example, in the military a major aim of the 'lines of authority' in peace time is to prepare for a state of war.

These categories also need to be approached flexibly because, apart from extreme cases, most leaders will have their own style. However, we can view a leader's particular style as being based on a combination of one of the styles above along with tendencies towards a particular style. For example, a person who appears to work hard at being democratic may nonetheless exhibit paternalistic tendencies.

Again it is worth remembering that leadership theory is still quite tentative with little in the way of clear lines of consensus coming out of the literature and so it continues to elude clear explanation. Nonetheless, leaders can play a significant role in shaping the dynamics of a group. Yet it has also been argued that Western cultures tend to attribute too much to the role of leaders in the success or failure of a group (Baker *et al.* 2002).

Not too surprisingly good leaders often appear to be dynamic—that is, they are flexible and responsive to the problems and purpose at hand and the needs of the members within a group and hence they tend not to over-rely on any particular style but use a range of well-balanced blends.

Factors that can be conducive to effective leadership

While assembling a list of factors common to effective leadership is problematic and hence needs to be approached with caution, a synthesis of the literature reveals the following:

* *Flexibility:* the ability to respond according to people and situations as they change.

* *Ability to relate:* to be able to communicate and relate to group members effectively.

* *Sufficient support:* perceived trust and credibility by group members.

* *Perceived suitability:* perceived level of competency and ability to carry out this particular role in comparison to alternative members—including the ability to deal with situations and problems as required.

* *Ability to lead:* to envision direction, change or reform and then to influence others to pursue goals related to such change.

This last characteristic can be used to define the major difference between a manager who works at ensuring procedures are followed in order to maintain the status quo of an operation and a leader who goes beyond this to lead, that is, envision direction and influence others accordingly.

SUMMARY

Because we spend a great deal of our lives communicating and working in groups it is important that we develop an understanding of group dynamics so we can enhance our performance in group situations. This chapter has examined key features of group communication including the functions of groups, communication flows, managing costs and benefits associated with groups and group leadership. Given that groups often occur as smaller units within the organisations that pervade society, we are now well placed to proceed with the next chapter, on organisational communication.

KEY POINTS

- A group is a small collection of people who have some shared interest or goal and perceive themselves as members of a group. Groups are formed in order to achieve goals which are difficult or impossible for individuals to achieve alone. Groups are often formed to accomplish specific tasks or solve problems, for example environmental groups.

- People's motivation for remaining in a group is likely to remain relatively high if they feel the benefits received are worth the personal costs (e.g. compromise and conflict).

- Task-based behaviours are those directed towards achieving group goals, while maintenance-based behaviours involve the managing of conflict, morale and cohesion. Satisfaction tends to be higher in groups where communication is less restricted and members are able to share information freely.

- Group dynamics refers to the kinds of processes that occur in groups including the stages of forming, norming, storming, performing and adjourning.

- The advantages associated with groups include utilisation of available expertise and the developing of deeper understandings through the sharing of ideas.

- Cohesion refers to the strength of each member's commitment to a group, which can be a positive influence but also give rise to negative effects such as those associated with groupthink.

- Conflict management strategies that can be used in groups include authoritative commands, conflict avoidance, de-emphasising conflict, goal setting, focusing on the problem and compromise/negotiation.
- While leadership is very important in groups there is little agreement on what makes a good leader, and the theories of leadership include trait theory, social context theory and situational context theory. The four basic styles of leadership are authoritarian, paternalistic, democratic/participative and *laissez-faire*.

REVIEW QUESTIONS

1. What are the key advantages and functions of groups?
2. Explain the dynamics associated with the stages of group development.
3. What are the benefits and problems associated with group decision making?
4. What are the symptoms of groupthink?
5. What kinds of strategies can be used to counter groupthink?
6. What strategies can be used to manage conflict in groups?

EXERCISES

Note: After formulating your responses it is important wherever possible to discuss them with a peer or group of peers. If you are not in a classroom setting then an appropriate electronic discussion board would be ideal.

1. Identify a group in which you have been (or are) a member that you felt was a particularly effective group.
    - List and analyse, in relation to chapter content, factors you believe made the group so effective.
    - In terms of the factors that make a group effective what conclusions can you draw?

2. Identify a group in which you have been (or are) a member that you felt was a particularly ineffective or dysfunctional group.
    - List and analyse, in relation to chapter content, factors you believe made the group so dysfunctional.
    - In terms of the factors that make a group dysfunctional what conclusions can you draw?
    - What measure(s) can be taken to prevent dysfunction and/or maintain an effective group?

3. Identify and analyse the traits of someone who seems to be an effective leader.
    - List and analyse, in relation to chapter content, factors you believe make this leader effective.
    - How important is leadership as a factor contributing toward effective group functioning?
    - As a leader, what kinds leadership styles (e.g. democratic) would describe your style?

4. In what way should conflict be dealt with, and what should you avoid?
    - Identify and analyse the benefits of conflict.
    - How can group conflict be managed to capitalise on potential benefits?

5. How common a problem is groupthink?
   If you were in charge of communication at the NASA space agency, what measures would you take to help ensure that the alleged oversights and failure to pay serious attention to advice among technical staff of an imminent disaster does not happen a third time?

BIBLIOGRAPHY

Arnold, J., Gleeson, F. and Peterson, C. 1991, *Moving into Management,* Swinburne Press, Hawthorne.
Baker, E., Barrett, M. and Roberts, L. 2002, *Working Communication,* John Wiley and Sons, Milton, Queensland.
Bass, B. 1981, *Stogdill's Handbook of Leadership: A Survey of Theory and Research,* The Free Press, New York.
Daniels, T. D., Spiker, B. K. and Papa, M. J. 1997, *Perspectives on Organisational Communication,* 4th ed., McGraw-Hill, Boston.
Gibson, J. and Hodgetts, R. 1991, *Organizational Communication: A Management Perspective,* 2nd ed., HarperCollins Publishers, New York.
Harris, T. 1993, *Applied Organizational Communication: Perspectives, Principles and Pragmatics,* Lawrence Erlbaum Associates Publishers, New Jersey.
Hellreigel, D., Slocum, J. and Woodman, R. 1992, *Organizational Behavior,* 6th ed., West Publishing Company, St Paul.
Janis, I. 1982, *Groupthink: Psychological Studies of Policy Decisions and Fiascoess,* revised ed., Houghton Mifflin, Boston.
Kahn, R. 1996, 'Opportunities, aspirations, and goodness of fit', in *Age and Structural Lag,* eds M. Riley, R. Kahn and A. Foner, Wiley and Sons, New York.
Littlejohn, 1992, *Theories of Human Communication,* 4th ed., Wadsworth Publishing Co., California.
Macionis, J. 1989, *Sociology,* Prentice Hall, New Jersey.
Middlebrook, P. 1980, *Social Psychology and Modern Life,* 2nd ed., Alfred A. Knopf, New York.
O'Sullivan, T., Hartley, J., Montgomery, M. and Fiske, J. 1994, *Key Concepts in Communication and Cultural Studies,* 2nd ed., Routledge, New York.
Rasberry, R. W. and Lemoine, L. F. 1986, *Effective Managerial Communication,* PWS Kent Publishing Co., Boston.

Organisational communication

Upon completing this chapter you should be able to:

- understand scientific management and human resource development (HRD) as two major schools of thought in organisational communication
- explain the merits and pitfalls associated with (tall) hierarchical and devolved (flattened) organisational structures;
- identify measures to help ensure an effective communication in organisations;
- identify factors that shape organisational culture including those which can lead to dysfunctional organisational culture; and
- identify measures to establish and maintain a functional organisational culture.

Our society today is one based on organisations. Organisations pervade most aspects of our lives in one way or another. Amatai Etzioni expresses this sentiment in the following way:

> Our society is an organizational society. We are born into organizations, educated in organizations, and most of us spend much of our lives working for organizations. We spend much of our leisure time playing and praying in organizations. Most of us will die in an organization, and when the time comes for burial, the largest organization of all—the state—must grant official permission.
>
> *(Etzioni 1964, p. 1)*

The evolution of organisations has been traced back to when human beings started to move away from nomadic hunter–gatherer societies to more permanently settled agrarian societies, and then more recently industrialisation, the latter being the major driving force in the shaping of today's modern organisation. An **organisation** can be described as a large association of people run on (relatively) impersonal lines, set up to achieve specific objectives (Giddens 1989). Communication, or more specifically *organisational communication,* is the lifeblood of organisations, as it is communication that enables people to work in coordinated ways that make the attainment of organisational goals and objectives possible. Formal organisations, including 'for profit', 'non-profit' and 'government based', provide the communication structures required for achieving the goals they set, by way of chains of command and policies and procedures. In order to advance our understanding of contemporary organisations we will now take a look at some of the key historical developments which have shaped contemporary thought and perspectives on organisational communication.

The scientific management approach

In the early 1900s modern economies were largely based on manufacturing industries and theorists pursued a mechanical approach to organisational communication and sought tightly run command and control procedures as the most effective way to maximise productivity. In 1911 Taylor introduced **scientific management** as a way of scientifically determining the most efficient way of accomplishing tasks and then training workers to use the prescribed methods for carrying out work tasks (Daniels *et al.* 1997). While scientific management produced major gains in productivity it also lowered the demand for labour which at the time led to job losses. However, it can also be argued that over the longer term the efficiencies gained improved the economy, generating new work and ultimately the standards of living we have today. Nonetheless, the scientific management approach viewed communication as a linear process, that is, as a one-way flow of information from managers-as-senders to workers-as-receivers, thus establishing a firm division of labour between managers and workers.

Bureaucratic principles

Another feature of modern organisations is that they are based on bureaucratic principles. **Bureaucracy** has been referred to as 'rule by officials' and is based on the regulating of tasks by officially sanctioned rules and procedures. Many see it as the most efficient form of organisation devised by human beings and the only way to cope with large-scale systems (Giddens 1989). A major feature of bureaucracy itself is its hierarchical structuring of authority. The bureaucratic structure of a large organisation looks like a pyramid with a 'chain of command' which distributes

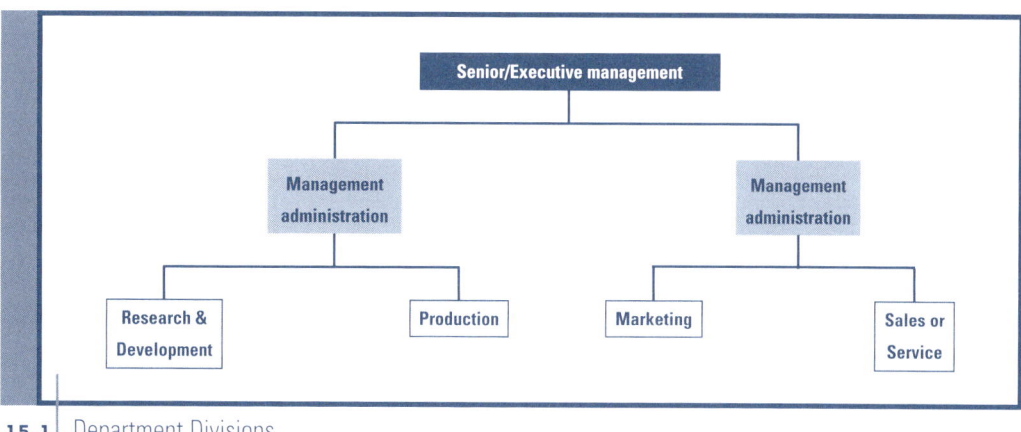

FIGURE 15.1 Department Divisions

authority from the most authoritative or executive management level through to middle-level management and then to supervisors and workers. Large bureaucratic organisations are also structured around many specialised divisions or groupings, for example research and development, marketing and sales departments (refer to Figure 15.1).

This kind of structuring, combined with set rules and procedures, provides a means by which organisations can coordinate the activities of staff members in a manner designed to achieve organisational goals. Different departments serve different purposes and of these each will have policies and procedures specific to its particular function. However, the departments within an organisation are also interdependent (ultimately depend on one another) and therefore need to be coordinated via the higher levels of management and administration.

While bureaucratic structuring in organisations has been praised for the benefits it brings through efficiency, it has also been heavily criticised on the basis that it is often perceived to be impersonal and inefficient in terms of the rigidity of the rules and procedures used. These kinds of procedures can at times seem time intensive and inflexible and are referred to pejoratively as 'red tape'.

While organisations have traditionally been based on bureaucratic, that is, hierarchical structuring, many organisations today are moving away from this centralised model of power, opting instead to 'devolve' power to lower levels. This process is often described as the **flattening out** of organisational structures. Devolving power in this way also affects the way information flows in an organisation and the dynamics of communication within it, a point examined later in the chapter. Figure 15.2 diagrammatically contrasts flat and tall organisational structuring.

The human resource development approach

Post-World War II, the **human resource development (HRD)** approach emerged out of an earlier human relations movement which started as a reaction to scientific management and sought to challenge its validity. It sought to emphasise the relationship between the worker and the organisation and opposed the traditional view of the worker as merely a 'cog' in a machine. Furthermore revolutionary new studies helped to invalidate core scientific management assumptions about how to maximise productivity thereby giving support to HRD's emphasis on humanising the organisational workplace (Daniels *et al.* 1997).

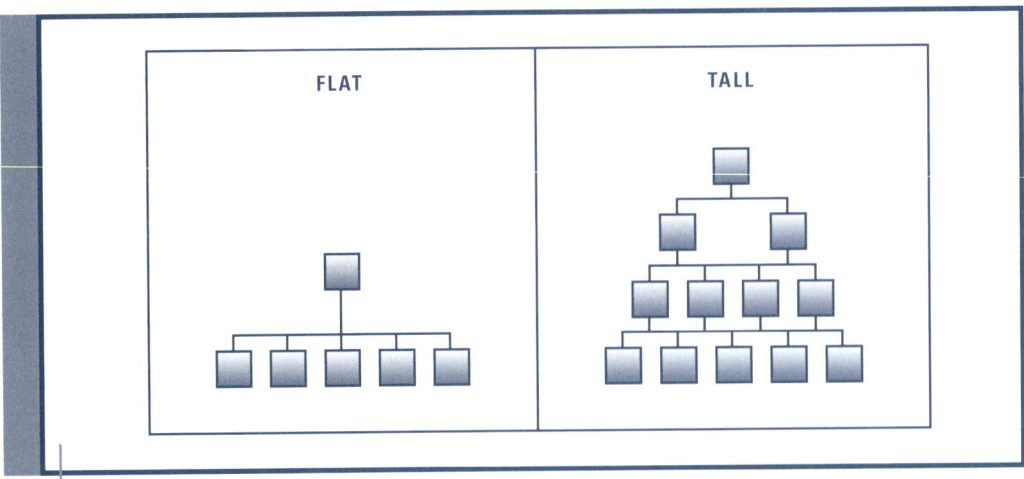

FIGURE 15.2 | Flat and Tall Organisational Structures

The HRD approach leans towards the view that empowering workers is an effective way to motivate them toward higher levels of productivity and is therefore in the best interests of the organisation. This view is based on a key assumption that workers typically desire opportunities for meaningful work and taking on responsibility; this is also known as McGregor's *Theory Y*. The scientific approach was based on the assumption that workers are adverse to work, that is, lazy (also known as McGregor's *Theory X*), and therefore financial reward and strict supervision provide the best means by which to motivate people toward productivity (McGregor 1960, cited in Daniels *et al.* 1997). Organisational thinking today is influenced by aspects of both of these approaches and in more recent decades a new combination of the two which also integrates some Asian approaches, a hybrid known as McGregor's *Theory Z* (McGregor 1960, cited in Daniels *et al.* 1997).

According to the HRD school of thought, organisations should seek to motivate their workers by working towards the meeting of their higher-order needs as put forward by Maslow (1954) (cited in Daniels *et al.* 1997) in his hiearchy of needs (refer to Figure 15.3).

The post-industrial organisation: The information age and knowledge age

Continuing industrialisation has seen a shift away from the amount of people involved in primary sector work (farming and generation of raw materials) and secondary sector work (manufacturing) as developments in mechanisation and computerised automation have led to decreases in the demand for this kind of labour. The post Industrial Age we now find ourselves in is commonly referred to as the **Information Age** and more recently the **Knowledge Age**.

This new economy has led to the emergence of many new fields of work along with increased demand for more tertiary sector workers. Some of these include recreation, hospitality and tourism, public relations, social workers, financial planning, information system services and many forms of consultancy work, and there are many more. These trends are predicted to continue for the foreseeable future and hence there is now an increased emphasis on higher education and training to produce the **knowledge workers** needed for the new economy. Post-industrial trends have also seen a reduction in managerial positions—in particular in middle management.

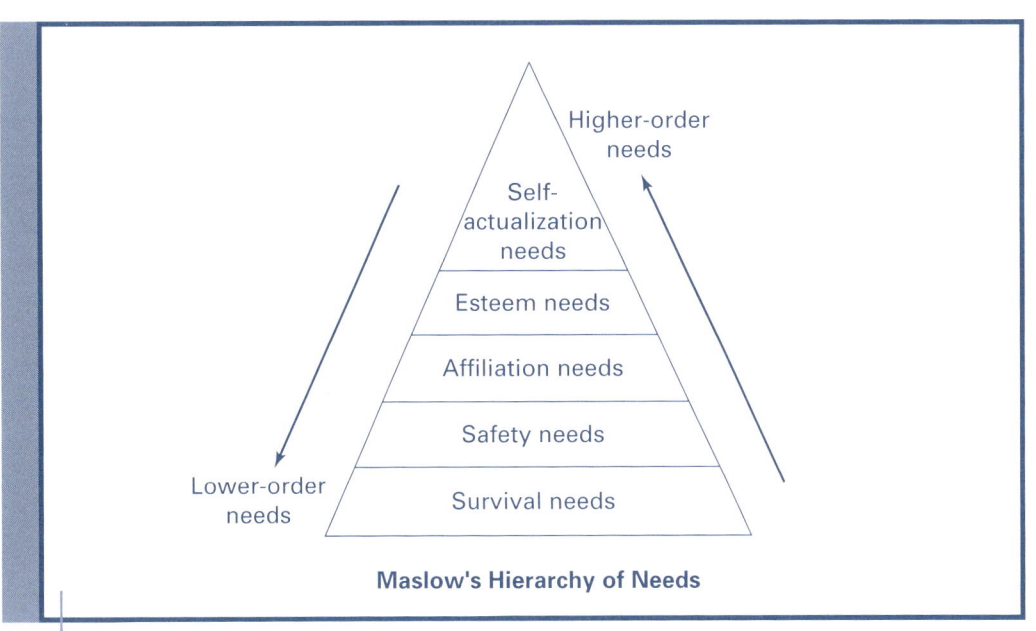

FIGURE 15.3 Maslow's Hierarchy of Needs

Maslow, A. H., Frager R. D., Faldman, J (ed.) (1997) Motivation and Personality, 3rd edition. Reprinted by permission of Pearson Education.

Figure 15.4 provides a graphic representation of the change in demand for labour towards knowledge workers and away from unskilled and middle level management workers.

It is also important to note that the nature of post-industrial work is changing at a rapid pace and this places demands upon workers to be flexible and multiskilled, and also to have strong generic communication skills including 'people skills' (interpersonal skills), 'independent self-management skills' and 'research and critical thinking skills' (Lawrence 2001).

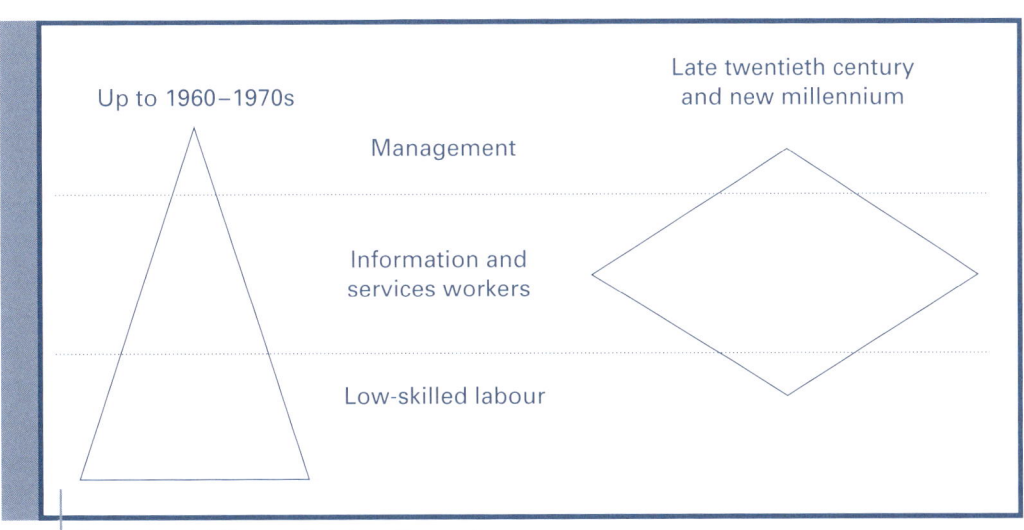

FIGURE 15.4 Post-Industrial Changes in Labour Demand

Thus far the chapter has sought to provide a brief outline of some of the major developments in thinking and practice that have influenced how organisational communication is thought about and managed in today's environment. In sum we can conclude that organisational communication today has moved more towards the HRD model and away from the scientific model; however, to varying degrees ideas from the scientific model still inform ideas and practices in organisations today.

The communicative climate

The communicative climate of an organisation refers to the degree to which the organisation allows and encourages the free flow of information, ideas and opinions between those involved in the organisation, including communication between employees and management. Establishing and maintaining effective communication flows in organisations can be very challenging due to the complex relationships and divisions between organisational substructures. Communication in organisations can also be thought of as something that flows in a number of main directions and these are discussed below.

The flow of communication in organisations

The traditional structure of centralised hierarchical information networks is still common in many organisations whereby information travels vertically; that is, either **downward communication**, such as orders from management which travel down a chain of command to workers, or **upward communication** from workers up through various levels of management.

DOWNWARD COMMUNICATION

The traditional downward flow of communication is viewed by many as the most powerful form of communication as management holds the power to direct subordinates to perform tasks in ways designed to maximise effective attainment of goals which are also determined by management (Daniels *et al.* 1997). Over-reliance by management on the use of downward information flows, especially when delivered in an authoritative tone, often results in lower levels of employee morale.

Communicating in this manner tends to make employees suspicious of management and works to create an antagonistic and contemptuous 'us versus them' dynamic. This kind of 'closed' communication climate does not normally foster a spirit of co-operation between workers and management and can impact negatively on the efficiency and effectiveness of a work environment. It also raises humanistic issues concerning quality of life and wellbeing for workers, to whom employers have moral and legal 'duty of care' responsibilities.

Nonetheless downward communication is necessary in organisations and it can provide an important means by which to:

* give directions and instructions;
* provide feedback on work performance;
* convey and explain organisational visions, goals and values as well as policies and procedures; and
* keep workers informed on important developments.

UPWARD COMMUNICATION

The second type of vertical communication—upward communication—refers to information sent from lower to higher levels within an organisation, for example from a worker to a manager. Upward communication can provide a primary means by which to keep those in positions of authority informed about workplace operations. Upward communication can be used to provide:

* information pertaining to productivity and progress in workplace operations;
* information and updates on issues and problems as the emerge (before they become larger problems);
* formal written reports on problems or progress (e.g. sales reports); and
* ideas and suggestions for efficiency improvements (e.g. suggestion boxes).

Many of the more traditional organisations still retain a strong focus on downward rather than upward communication flow (Rasberry and Lemoine 1986). Organisations with a strong focus on authoritative hierarchies often discourage upward communication, which results in a closed communication climate. Furthermore lower-level workers can become more inclined to distort and filter information they send upward in an effort to pacify bosses and managers (Gibson and Hodgetts 1991) and this kind of miscommunication is not in the interests of the organisation or its members, including workers.

IMPROVING VERTICAL COMMUNICATION

There are a number of strategic and policy approaches that can be used to improve vertical communication and hence the communicative climate in organisations. Common approaches to enhancing vertical communication include:

* The setting of clear organisational objectives, including position descriptions, which should be delivered to employees in a clear and direct but also receiver-oriented manner (i.e. in terms that employees can relate to and in a way that takes employees' perspective into account).
* Keeping employees informed about developments in the organisation and how these relate to workers.
* The use of regular and direct contact with workers—this technique is often referred to as 'management by walking around' or 'hands-on management'.
* Actively encouraged upward communication; these methods may include regular meetings (e.g. the use of meetings where employees raise issues and concerns to management), the use of suggestion boxes and employee satisfaction surveys.
* Managing change in a consultative manner, that is, in consultation with workers at lower levels.
* Flattening out hierarchical structures (as discussed below).

(Based on Rasberry and Lemoine 1986)

DEMOCRATISING AND FLATTENING OUT ORGANISATIONAL STRUCTURES

In response to some of the negative impacts of hierarchical structures and their tendency towards a concentration of authoritative downward information flows, many organisations have adopted policies of decentralising communication networks and authority by 'flattening out' their organisational structures.

The strategy of decentralisation has been advocated as a means for reducing the concentration of authority in high-level positions in an effort to reduce distance between management and workers (Bass 1981). Also referred to as democratising of the workplace (or *industrial democracy*) flattening out is an inclusive as opposed to exclusive strategic approach to employee relations and has been used as a way of empowering workers with a view ultimately to increasing efficiency. This HRD strategy is used by many organisations and is based on McGregor's Theory Y (discussed earlier) that posits that people are motivated to work given the opportunity and appropriate support.

Accordingly many organisations have adopted a system based on more autonomous **self-managed work teams**. These kinds of teams are often responsible for: (1) setting their own work goals; (2) coordinating their own work schedules and allocation of duties; and (3) evaluating their own productivity. The aim of this approach is to provide a more co-operative organisational culture and one which more fully utilises the skills of workers. In this way it also tries to overcome the view that employees' interests are in conflict with organisational interests (i.e. 'us versus them' mentality), preferring instead to work on establishing common interests between the organisation and its employees. Ideally, the HRD approach places an emphasis on upward and horizontal communication and on the developing organisational goals which are of mutual benefit to management and workers.

HORIZONTAL COMMUNICATION

Horizontal communication refers to communication that travels in a more open or decentralised manner than does vertical communication. Horizontal communication is often considered the most common kind of communication flow in any organisation because individuals at the same level talk to each other constantly about work-related events, personal matters and, quite importantly, their evaluations about the organisation and its managers (Daniels *et al.* 1997). Furthermore horizontal communication provides an important and primary means by which working teams and their members can:

* convey information on developments;
* coordinate and collaborate on activities to meet organisational goals; and
* collaborate to resolve workplace problems (drawing on expertise from other work teams).

THE GRAPEVINE (INFORMAL COMMUNICATION)

While horizontal communication takes place at an official level via telephone messages, email, letters, memoranda and so on, a great deal of communication in organisations, such as employees' opinions about management, occurs via informal conversations. The informal communication network which inevitably exists in organisations is often referred to as the grapevine and sometimes referred to as the 'rumour mill'. Many managers perceive it as harmful to the organisation and would prefer it was destroyed. However, research has shown that the grapevine is a natural part of an organisation's communication system and not inherently bad (Rasberry and Lemoine 1986). On the contrary, the non-work-related communication that takes place in workplaces can facilitate the development of harmonious working relationships between staff. It helps to engender a spirit of co-operation between staff which can be conducive to effective workplace practices.

Human beings are social by nature and a healthy working relationship with other colleagues is something which people have to build. Chapter 13 shows that self-disclosure (sharing of personal information) provides the bricks and mortar of most functional relationships.

However, dysfunctional grapevine communication can foster antagonistic relationships between staff and also undermine the authority of those in supervisory and managerial positions in cases when work teams perceive managers and other work teams with great suspicion. For example, if a manager is widely perceived as tyrant, then workers may join forces to subvert and undermine that person's authority.

Causes of poor horizontal communication

Poor morale brought about by the poor management of communication by superiors, (e.g. the distant and dictatorial use of downward communication, withholding of information and workplace bullying unchecked), tends to feed the unhealthy 'rumour mill' of grapevine communication. This can be detrimental to an organisation's communication climate. Dysfunctional climates are very often based on a spirit of unproductive rivalry and competition over resources and status as opposed to a climate of co-operation, mutual respect and concern for the greater good of the organisation.

In addition to departmental rivalry, too high levels of isolation between departments and sections in an organisation can lead to what is often referred to a miscommunication, that is, the conveying of incorrect information. Indeed this may be, in part, a result of the negative side of too much bureaucratic structuring, with deep divisions between sections and departments, as it can leave them too isolated from one another. In these cases people can easily start to lose sight of the 'bigger picture', that is, that the sections of an organisation exist to serve the goals of the whole organisation and that to do so they need to be able to work with one another in co-operative and well-coordinated ways. Ultimately each section of an organisation depends upon the other sections. Figure 15.5 tries to demonstrate in a satirical way the consequences of horizontal communication gone wrong.

Improving horizontal communication

The methods available for improving horizontal communication are largely the same in approach as those used to enhance vertical communication and create an open and constructive communicative climate and subsequently one conducive to productivity.

* Promoting an open and co-operative communication (climate) between all sections and departments of the organisation.
* Promoting a culture of mutual respect and trust between all sections of the organisation.
* Promoting understanding of the organization and its goals as a whole (e.g. mission statements and objectives) and the need to work co-operatively with other sections.
* Setting procedures for formal cross-checking (i.e. double checking) procedures to help ensure information and details exchanged between departments are kept accurate.
* Keeping employees informed with accurate information in a clear and direct and receiver-oriented manner. Accurate information should be disseminated as quickly as possible as a way of dealing with harmful 'grapevine' rumours.

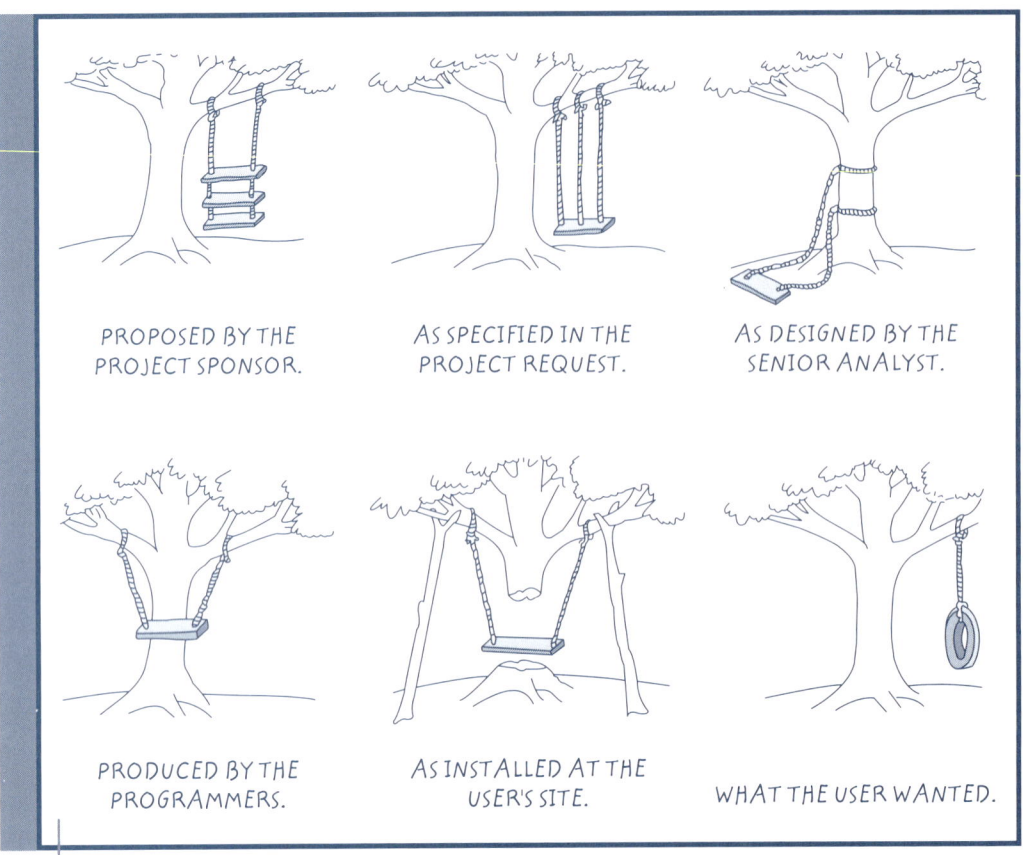

FIGURE 15.5 | An Example of what Happens when there is a Lack of Horizontal Communication

Source: From Harris, T. E. 1993, Applied Organizational Communication: Perspectives, Principles and Pragmatics, Lawrence Erlbaum Associated Inc., New Jersey.

* Maintaining regular and direct contact with workers across all sections and actively encouraging feedback from employees regarding management and procedures.
* Flattening out of unnecessary hierarchies of authority, as well as promoting occasional social gatherings and team-building initiatives, for example retreats and workshops.

Recording procedures to ensure effective horizontal and vertical communication

The appropriate retention and management of organisational activity is necessary so that an organisation can function in effective and accountable ways. Often referred to as an 'audit trail' or a 'paper trail', the recording, storage and management of organisational communication and activity is imperative as information vital to efficient management and decision making and for meeting obligations for transparency and accountability.

This is typically achieved through workplace practices such as:

* sending requests and inquiries in writing via memoranda or email;
* recording of minutes for meetings;
* keeping records of important discussions; and
* recording complaints on standardised reporting forms and so on.

Note also the writing of formal documents including letters and emails outlined in Chapters 5 and 3, and reports covered in Chapter 6.

In some, albeit distant way, the scenario outlined in Figure 15.5 is reminiscent of the space shuttle disasters discussed in Chapter 14, in so far as it prompts the questions, 'How can people get it so wrong?' 'How is it that people can end up so far off track?' While some reasons for horizontal miscommunication were outlined above, to gain an even better understanding of this we need to consider more closely the nature of the context in which these kinds of things happen. We need to consider the organisational operating environment from within the organisation itself, in other words, the **organisational culture**. At this point it is important to note and remember that **group dynamics** (a major subject in the previous chapter) and organisational culture (a major subject in this chapter) are two concepts which are very closely interlinked, indeed they overlap to the point where it can become difficult to distinguish between the two—in many ways the concepts of dynamics and culture are alternative approaches to examining the same phenomenon. Having said this, organisational culture can be used to study the organisation on a larger scale than that of a group.

Organisational culture

The concept of organisational culture has become increasingly important in the field of organisational communication and behaviour. The concept of culture is so integral to communication that it has been addressed in various parts of this book, and at this point it is recommended that you review a small section in Chapter 2 titled 'Cultural World View (commonsense knowledge)'.

Culture can be understood as something which is 'socially constructed', that is, a 'social reality' produced through the process of negotiation growing out of people's interactions with one another. This 'negotiation' process accords with that of negotiation as explained in the *transaction theory model* of communication in Chapter 2. It is also important to note that some people have more influence than others, for example management may have a greater say in the creating of organisational realities such as work routines and procedures which are often officially documented in manuals. In contrast, workers may also have the power to deviate from officially set procedures and hence there can be differences between what management stipulate and how workers actually go about their day-to-day work. Hence we can expect to see many cultures or subcultures within an organisation including management culture, departmental cultures and work team cultures.

Officially sanctioned information about management culture can be found in strategic plan documentation often available online, and it takes the form of 'officially articulated cultural information' such as that found in mission statements, organisational goals and organisational values. Ideally, management seek to promote and instil these elements into the culture of people's working lives in an effort to produce the kind of common organisation-wide culture they desire.

Executive management teams often develop organisational philosophies along the lines of 'a culture of excellence', 'a commitment to high quality' or 'commitment to excellent client service'. Woolworths supermarkets in Australia have an organisational philosophy of Woolworths as 'The fresh food people' and promote supporting values that 'being fresh food people is much more that just a job—it's an obsession'. This philosophy has been heavily promoted within the organisation (to its staff) and to its customers.

Function and dysfunction in organisational culture

Cultures within an organisation also incorporate customs, rituals and folk stories or myths shared in a cultural grouping or work team. Myths are normally very important in constructing culture, because they are the stories people within a grouping produce to explain and make sense of their lives within the cultural setting. These myths function to project and sustain ideologies (the dominant values of a group), for example the use of hero and villain stories, to delineate that which is considered good practice (valued) and that which is considered bad practice (discouraged and not tolerated). These cultural factors can function in ways which are positive but they can also lead to dysfunction.

Organisational cultures are vulnerable to a myriad of problems including various forms of corruption, bullying and harassment. Without wanting to focus too much attention on any one kind of organisation, you will be aware that issues of organisational corruption, for example corporate fraud, police force corruption and workplace bullying (e.g. brutality in the armed forces and construction industries) are regularly reported by the media. In addition to this, discrimination and harassment in workplaces often take place in subtle ways that can be difficult to prove.

Organisational cultures can become dysfunctional for a variety of reasons including the emergence of groupthink (discussed in Chapter 14) and other reasons also related to the closing down of a communicative climate and cultural environment. Corruption can flourish in closed cultures where there is little or no disclosure on organisational practices, which can include the lack of procedures designed to ensure accountability. Likewise intimidation and bullying can flourish in a closed climate where cultural norms forbid people from speaking out.

Allegations of corporate corruption appears to be a perennial issue that receives a fair amount of media coverage. The online news piece referred to in the URL below provides some insight and detail into corrupt corporate accounting practices and factors influencing motivation. The practice discussed in this video link is referred to as 'Stuffing the channels' and can be retrieved from an online archive of the American news and current affairs program 'The News Hour' at <http://www.pbs.org/newshour/>. Then search 'stuffing the channels' for <http://www.pbs.org/newshour/bb/business/jan-june02/street_4-2.html>. Then click here to watch this segment in streaming video.

The devolving of power to self-managed work teams can also lead to team cultures which are more stressful and inhumane for workers than they may otherwise be. To illustrate, groups that have the power to set their own productivity can be tempted to start setting much higher targets than those expected by management—in many cases this has led to workers having to work long hours of unpaid overtime due to peer pressure called *concertive control*, to meet unrealistically high productivity goals that they as a group have set (Daniels *et al.* 1997).

Working toward functional organisational culture

There are measures we can adopt to help guard against cultural dysfunction. Many of these are rooted in a core philosophy of establishing and maintaining 'openness' in organisational cultures.

Systems theory, or more specifically **open systems theory**, provides a useful model from which to conceptualise and build a functional and effective organisational culture.

Systems theory views organisations as *adaptive organisms* rather than *machines*. Systems theory is particularly concerned with the relationship dynamics between parts of the system as they are related to the whole. Ideally, the organisation (and its subsystems) has permeable boundaries so that information and feedback flow freely into the organisations from its environment, in which case it is classed as an 'open system'. Feedback provides the organisation with information that allows it to monitor and evaluate changes in the environment including political, legislative, economic and social factors and then strategically adapt to these.

Degrees of openness and closedness can vary, and organisations that have highly 'evolved' levels of openness have been described as 'learning organisations', that is, organisational systems that are able to learn very effectively (Senge 1998). These open/learning characteristics can enable organisations to become more dynamic and innovative and hence leading edge. In addition this attribute of 'openness' helps to fend off the dysfunctions of bullying and intimidation, corruption and preventable errors and oversights which can result in disaster, as alleged in the case of the two space shuttle disasters discussed in Chapter 14.

The basis of a healthy organisational culture is 'openness' as opposed to states of insular 'closedness' (being cut off). The open system view provides the foundations for transparency and accountability, that is, having organisational practices and processes that are open to scrutiny. In principle, the open systems approach views the organisation as a part of the wider environment, and does so to the extent that the organisation sees itself as carrying with it a host of responsibilities regarding the wider environment. Not only is the organisation working to ensure its practices are ecologically sustainable, but it is also working towards ensuring accountability to the wider community and as such its practices should be open to scrutiny. These principles and values have great merit as they are aimed at doing what is morally virtuous and in the best long-term interests of an organisation, its members and the wider community. However, these values are also arguably quite idealistic and not all organisations and their members uphold them. Indeed major instances of poor corporate governance over past years have given legislators additional motivation to do more to help ensure fair, safe and accountable practices by organisations.

Measures to help ensure accountable and just organisational practices include:

* Procedures designed to ensure high standards of transparency and accountability including financial accountability (formal auditing, reporting and disclosure procedures) (including keeping the records as outlined earlier on).

* Procedures designed to encourage and ensure the reporting of unjust and corrupt practices including sturdy procedures to protect and support those who report such practices.

* Quality control systems (e.g. cross-checking to ensure the integrity of information and activity).

* Setting and promoting healthy organisational philosophies and values.

* Processes for reporting bullying, sexual and other kinds of harassment (with sufficient support and protection of privacy and sensitive information, for example).

* Processes and procedures to help ensure equality and equitable treatment (i.e. to guard against discriminatory practices) and promotion of principles of 'reward based on merit' (i.e. as opposed to discriminatory reasons).

* Well-designed safety policies and procedures which also need to be rigorously adhered to.

SUMMARY

This chapter has explored current organisational theory and practice along with strategies that can be used to achieve effective communication in organisational contexts. This chapter concludes Part V, 'Interpersonal and professional communication'. In the final chapter we will consider the process of communication at a general level and examine common barriers to effective communication and strategies and techniques for minimising their effects.

KEY POINTS

- Organisations consist of large groupings of people organised for the purpose of achieving specific objectives and tend to be bureaucratic in nature (i.e. have highly regulated procedures). While bureaucratic structuring can provide benefits in terms of efficiency, factors like high rigidity can also lead to inefficiencies.

- Organisations have been traditionally based on rigid and hierarchical structures. However, many organisations are now flattening out their structures in an effort to foster more effective communication and increase efficiency. Hence organisations are now relying more on horizontal communication and less on vertical (especially downward) communication. This, along with the decentralisation of authority, reduces the distance between management and workers, leading towards a more inclusive work environment and as such a greater emphasis is now being placed on self-regulating work groups and teams.

- Other approaches to improving the communication climate include setting clear organisational objectives, keeping employees informed about developments in the organisation, keeping records, regular contact with staff and the active encouragement of upward communication.

- Poor communication management techniques like the dictatorial use of downward communication and withholding of information from staff can lead to an unhealthy climate whereby potentially damaging information (e.g. damaging to staff morale) is produced/rumoured through the informal 'grapevine'.

- The culture(s) within an organisation is made up of the behavioural norms that develop within it. Organisational cultures can be functional or dysfunctional, but are vulnerable to a myriad of problems including various forms of corruption and bullying and harassment.

- There are measures organisations and their members can adopt to help guard against cultural dysfunction and many of these are rooted in a core philosophy of establishing and maintaining 'openness' in organisational cultures. Can be achieved by adopting procedures to ensure high standards of transparency and accountability including financial reporting and auditing.

REVIEW QUESTIONS

1. What are the features of scientific management and bureaucratic structuring?
2. What benefits arise from a scientific management approach and bureaucratic structuring?
3. What are the features of the human resource development (HRD) approach to organisational communication?
4. What benefits arise from the human resource development (HRD) approach to organisational communication?
5. What are the benefits and potential pitfalls associated with devolving power (industrial democratisation) in organisations?

6. Describe the ways (or directions) in which communication flows in organisations and their potential impacts on the communicative climate and work performance.

7. What measures can be used to help ensure an effective flow of communication in organisations?

8. Identify factors that shape organisational culture including those which can lead to dysfunctional organisational culture.

9. What kinds of measures can be used to establish and maintain a functional organisational culture?

EXERCISES

Note: After formulating your responses it is important wherever possible to discuss them with a peer or group of peers. If you are not in a classroom setting then an appropriate electronic discussion board would be ideal.

1. How appropriate is scientific management and bureaucratic structuring today?
    - What kinds of organisations do you think may be better suited to these (if any)?
    - What kinds of organisations are not suited to these kinds of approaches?

    Justify your views.

2. To what extent do you agree or disagree with McGregor's opposing theories?
    - Theory X: workers are lazy by nature and not naturally inclined to work.
    - Theory Y: workers are naturally motivated towards meaningful work.

    Justify your views.

3. How useful do you think Maslow's hierarchy of needs (Figure 15.3 on page 239) is in informing and applying the human resource development (HRD) approach? Justify your views.

4. What do you think are the root causes of dysfunction in organisational culture?
    - Do you think corruption is prevalent in organisations today?
    - What can you and others do to try to prevent corruption in organisations?
    - Do you think bullying and harassment are prevalent in organisations today?
    - To what degrees (high or low intensity) do you feel bullying and harassment occur?
    - What can you and others do to try to prevent bullying and harassment in organisations?

BIBLIOGRAPHY

Bass, B. 1981, *Stogdill's Handbook of Leadership: A Survey of Theory and Research,* The Free Press, New York.

Daniels, T. D., Spiker, B. K. and Papa, M. J. 1997, *Perspectives on Organisational Communication,* 4th ed., McGraw-Hill, Boston.

Etzioni, A. 1964, *Modern Organizations,* Prentice Hall, New Jersey.

Gibson, J. and Hodgetts, R. 1991, *Organisational Communication: A Managerial Perspective,* 2nd ed., HarperCollins, New York.

Giddens, A. 1989, *Sociology,* Polity Press, Cambridge.

Harris, T. E. 1993, *Applied Organizational Communication: Perspectives, Principles and Pragmatics,* Lawrence Erlbaum Associates Publishers, New Jersey.

Lawrence, J. 2001, 'Academics and first year students: Collaborating to access success in an unfamiliar culture, widening participation and lifelong learning', *The Journal of the Institute of Access Studies and the European Access Network,* 3, 4–14.

Macionis, J. 1989, *Sociology,* Prentice Hall, New Jersey.

Manning, G. and Curtis, K. 1988, *Communication: The Miracle of Dialogue,* South-Western, Cincinnati.

Maslow, A. H. 1954, *Motivation and Personality,* Harper & Row, New York.

Maslow, A. H., Frager, R.D. and Faldman, J.(ed.), 1997, *Motivation and Personality,* 3rd ed., Harper & Row, New York.

Rasberry, R. W. and Lemoine, L. F. 1986, *Effective Managerial Communication,* PWS Kent Publishing Co., Boston.

Senge, P. 1998, *Executive Development and Organizational Learning for Global Business,* International Business Press, New York.

Part Six

Communication Problems and Solutions

Barriers

CHAPTER 16

Upon completing this chapter you should be able to:

- understand the notion of 'barriers' and the major kinds of barriers to communication;
- apply a range of strategies to help minimise barriers including combating counterproductive thinking and counterproductive emotional reactions;
- incorporate and apply a strategic planning model to manage barriers and become a more receptive and responsive communicator; and
- more deeply appreciate planning communication as a process of striving for the best balance of strategies and techniques for each task or situation.

This chapter marks a turning point in the text as we return to consider communication at a more general level, as in Chapter 2 when developing general theory-models of communication. This is because barriers in communication are general in nature, in that they occur at virtually all points of the communication process, whether it be at the nonverbal, organisational, written, oral levels, or otherwise. This barriers approach to communication can quite rightly be considered a theoretical perspective of its own. The barriers view of communication is one which views and approaches communication as an 'obstacle course' in which effective communication is achieved by a process of overcoming a series of obstacles. It can also be thought of as a 'trouble shooting' approach to communication. But perhaps it is best to develop a positive (rather than 'problem-based') point of view and associate barriers with a positive or an enjoyable pursuit like that of a 'game' or 'sport'. Indeed, obstacle courses are often used as a kind of sporting pursuit.

Given that barriers are ever present, we can communicate strategically by anticipating potential barriers and planning communicative action around them. The strategies and techniques covered so far provide the means by which to manage communication barriers. Hence it is recommended that you also revise parts of the textbook related to each barrier as you progress barrier by barrier through this chapter. The purpose of this final chapter is to supplement and somewhat synthesise the content presented in the preceding chapters.

What are barriers in communication?

The term **barrier** refers to anything that interferes with or stands in the way of effective communication. The concept of barriers is based on that of 'noise', which was introduced in Chapter 2, hence barriers and noise can be thought of as one and the same. However, we use the notion of barriers as a way of regrouping the kinds of 'interference' that can occur in communication, so that we can examine them with a strategic emphasis.

Communication is most effective when the barriers present in communicative situations are minimal or are managed in a way that diminishes their effect. Being able to identify and understand barriers is imperative for those interested in enhancing their ability to communicate effectively. It is also very important to remember that barriers are ever-present in communication, and while we can implement strategies to minimise barriers we can never eliminate them totally. In other words the notion that communication can be perfect, pure and free from barriers is a practical as well as theoretical nonsense.

Physical barriers (or external barriers)

Physical barriers are the equivalent of 'physical noise', as introduced in Chapter 2. The physical barriers are any physical (i.e. environmental) factors that interfere with the sending and receiving of messages. Examples are:

* Lack of access to resources or functioning equipment such as a malfunctioning computer.
* Sound—noise interference (e.g. loud noises from a construction site).
* Visual—visual distractions or poor lighting.
* Comfort factors (e.g. temperature, lack of space).

Physical barriers are so conceptually straightforward that their importance is often overlooked (as a result of a perceptual barrier/intrapersonal barrier) and hence they are often poorly managed. Despite this if you are to present a talk then it is often the case that you are responsible for managing the physical aspects of the situation, such as the clear projection of your voice and arranging amplifications if necessary. On the other hand, as a receiver/audience member you carry responsibility for managing distractions and coping with other sources of physical interference, for instance by making sure to turn off your mobile phone.

Information and computer technologies

Today, information and computer technologies (ICT's) provide us with unprecedented levels of convenience including quick access to information online such as official reports and now many reputable academic and scientific journals are also becoming available online. However, it is easy to lose sight of the fact that these technologies, especially personal computers, are not one hundred per cent reliable as they can and do 'crash' and lose information from time to time. Accordingly, backing up, that is, regularly making copies of work produced on media separate to your computer file, for example on disks and so on, is a wise practice in order to protect yourself from the physical barrier of computer system breakdown. Loss of information due to computer breakdown is a major threat to electronically produced work and one which is by and large preventable.

It also worth noting that with assignment work the onus is on the student to be able to reproduce a copy should it go missing.

Intrapersonal barriers

Intrapersonal barriers are the barriers that lie within the 'self,' in other words within people's own minds. Intrapersonal communication involves the processes of perception and thinking. As a recurring issue in the study of communication we are now well aware of how a person's ways of thinking and perceiving develop into mental models which are in essence thinking habits. In the following sections we use the terms 'ways of thinking', 'ways of perceiving', 'ways of seeing', 'thought patterns' and 'thinking habits' interchangeably. These terms are also being used as shorthand to refer to a complex 'Rubik' made up of a person's beliefs, attitudes, expectations, values and disposition or personality. Thinking habits are our learned cognitive ways of reacting to and interpreting stimuli and thinking about that which we encounter. These established mental models are what we have learned from experience and as such they function in two profound ways:

1. they empower us by providing us with the ability to be able perceive and think,
2. but the 'baggage' or biases that come with these mental models distort and hinder this very ability (to perceive and think), thereby having a disempowering effect upon us.

Hence it can be concluded that the lessons we learn from life experiences are not always realistic or helpful. 'Common tendencies that distort perception' as outlined in Chapter 2 are summarised below. These distortive tendencies are:

* to view the world in ways that suit established, conditioned ways of thinking such as overlooking or refiguring information that contradicts these;
* to believe that most people think and feel the same way as we do and to be critical of those whose views and preferences differ;
* to judge ourselves more generously and others more harshly (and when convenient the reverse);

* to exaggerate perceptions of those we like and those we do not (the halo effect);
* to view things in overly simplistic ways rather than developing more detailed and comprehensive understandings (the basis of rigid thinking and stereotypical views).

People can become so accustomed to their established ways of thinking that they become prone to what is in essence an addiction to them, even when these ways of thinking work to their own detriment and in many cases even work to make a person outrightly unhappy. For example, some people have learned to receive some form of comfort from an entrenched bleak or pessimistic outlook.

Relying heavily on ways of thinking that are obstructive and/or harmful is highly problematic because the more entrenched they become the less likely they are to change. It is interesting to note how the processes of perceiving and thinking also involve **self-talk** (intrapersonal self-dialogue), in which people talk themselves in or out of seeing things in the manner they prefer. Mackay uses the metaphor of 'prison bars' to describe the distortive effects of our own personal **world view**:

> Because we look at the world through the bars of the cage, the bars impose their own pattern on what we see: our values and beliefs affect the way we perceive and interpret what's out there. From inside the cage, the cage itself is part of what we see.
>
> (Mackay 1994, p. 62)

This gives rise to popular clichés, referred to as 'folk theory' in Chapter 2, such as 'people see what they want to see and hear what they want to hear', and we are all prone to this. So what can we do about it?

Our thinking habits are in sum the ways we have learned to cope in life (and of course we learn a lot by observing others and from the media); however, we do not have an all-wise guardian angel helping us to learn the right kinds of coping lessons, and hence we are susceptible to learning poor coping/**thinking habits**. But we do have the benefits of extensive research from behavioural science, cognitive psychology and communication studies—all of which inform the content of textbooks such as this one. In fact there are large bodies of literature from which we can learn and benefit.

We now know that research shows that established thinking patterns are resistant to change, but not completely, and that they can be changed or relearned. Science has also been able to demonstrate that as individuals we carry the capacity to gain a high degree of control over our thinking processes and as such we can choose to relearn or instil new habits in the place of existing ones (Seligman 1996).

Of course embarking upon such change is a major undertaking. There are four fundamentals required to change established thought patterns. They are:

1. sufficient desire or motivation for change;
2. heightened self-awareness—the ability to engage consciously and deliberately in monitoring and thinking about our own thought patterns in order to identify potential problem areas;
3. the determination and endurance required to challenge existing unproductive patterns in order to establish new ones; and
4. knowledge and understanding of the common pitfalls in thinking and perceiving to which we are susceptible (covered in this textbook, for example 'Common tendencies that distort perception').

In an effort to reduce these distortive barriers we need to acknowledge that they exist within us and make a committed effort to identify and manage them. However, confronting ourselves in this way is not always easy, but nonetheless it is in all of our best interests to do so. In order to develop a better understanding of a complex world, we must also be prepared to give open consideration to views and perspectives which conflict with our already existing knowledge and understanding.

Here are some strategies and techniques for minimising distortive intrapersonal effects.

* Acknowledge and commit to the idea that a need exists for managing perceptual biases within established ways of thinking.

* Receptivity and open mindedness—try to be as receptive and open-minded as possible without compromising your personal integrity (i.e. losing all faith in your own judgement and always giving in to others).

* Critical self-reflection—periodically taking time out to think critically about, and question, aspects of your own perceptual inclinations, including likes and dislikes, possible stereotypes and prejudices, values and aspirations, present understandings and established thinking patterns.

Common counter-productive thinking patterns and processes

PESSIMISTIC OUTLOOK: NEGATIVE AND SELF-DEFEATING THOUGHT PATTERNS

Self-doubting is a way of thinking that can seriously hamper one's ability to learn, develop and grow. Self-doubting and other forms of negative thinking can cause us to behave in ways that help to produce **self-fulfilling prophecies**—once a negative thought becomes a reality it then reinforces that way of thinking as being correct. These kinds of restrictive thinking habits and attitudes can be identified in 'self-defeating' thoughts that typically involve cue words and phrases like:

> I can't . . .
>
> I'll never be good . . .
>
> I'm not very good at expressing myself in writing.

Resulting self-fulfilling prophecies:

> Therefore, 'I'll never be any good at writing. . .
>
> If I keep on trying, I'll probably fail.
>
> Therefore, I may as well quit now.
>
> I'm just not cut out for writing and/or the profession I'm studying for.

A pessimistic outlook including doubting one's ability to develop skills, such as good writing skills, puts one at a huge psychological disadvantage. A lack of confidence not only impedes performance, it typically leads to avoidance behaviours which prevent the development of these kinds of skills. While we do not dispute that people have differing levels of ability in given areas and at given points in time, extensive research shows that the vast majority of people have the potential to acquire and substantially advance their existing abilities in most areas (Seligman 1996).

However, developing and acquiring specific skills is put into jeopardy when people undermine their own opportunities to do so.

OBSESSIVE AND INTENSIVE ANXIETY (WORRY)

Chapter 13 acknowledged that anxiety (commonly referred to as worry and stress) has the potential to motivate us into action, but the reality is that worrying in itself does not usually solve problems. Really intense anxiety is highly problematic as it often leads to fixation, that is, where one becomes so preoccupied with thoughts and feelings of worry that they dominate the mind to the point where they make it difficult to think about anything else. With this kind of fixated pattern a person can be described as 'being caught in a loop' because breaking this cycle of recycling of worrying thoughts can be difficult. This not uncommon pitfall tends to paralyse people as it makes taking any action to address related issues virtually impossible, which is in addition to the mental suffering it inflicts and perpetuates. If a person finds that they do a great deal of this then chances are it has become an unproductive and harmful thinking habit. Seligman (1996) explains that people's thinking habits are characterised by what he calls an 'explanatory style'; for example, one may have an optimistic or pessimistic explanatory style. A person's explanatory style can be determined by the kind of self-talk they tend to use—these are personal theories or explanations one gives one self. For example:

Negative Worrying Loop

'I can't write this essay.'	→	'I'm going to fail it.'
'I can't afford to fail it.'	→	'But I am going to fail it.'
'But I can't afford to fail it.'	→	'My life is going to be a disaster.'
which leads back into the loop	→	'All because . . . I can't write an essay.'

Seligman (1996) also calls this 'learned helplessness' and this kind of thinking can result in wild and even potentially dangerous thinking in which self-talk escalates into what Albert Ellis (a somewhat colourful but also highly regarded cognitive therapist) calls 'catastrophizing'. This is self-talk which leads one to conclude that there is no hope and that disaster is looming and inevitable. Most of us may be susceptible to catastrophizing a little. However, this explanatory style renders people more susceptible to depression, in which case even small obstacles seem to appear like insurmountable barriers (Seligman 1996, p. 57). If we stand back and try to look at this scenario from a rational point of view, it becomes clear that this kind of thinking is not only highly self-defeating, it is not realistic. Unrealistic thinking is the root cause of many intrapersonal barriers, for example in the unrealistically high expectations examined below.

UNREALISTICALLY HIGH EXPECTATIONS

Unrealistically high expectations are also obstructive, and often include absolute terms such as 'must', 'cannot' and 'have to'. For example:

I must not make a mistake; if I do then I'm a failure.

I have to get at least an 'A' grade, anything less is a fail as far as I am concerned.

I must be able to acquire good writing skills by the end of next week.

The danger with unrealistic expectations is precisely that they move people too far away from reality and hence make it highly unlikely that these expectations will be met; for example, 'that you must not make mistake' leads to painful and potentially destructive emotional outcomes such as bitter disappointment, feelings of helplessness and anger. Setting unrealistic expectations sets people up for failure. The harsh emotional reactions that follow can lead to the loss of hope, a negative thinking loop and subsequent giving up on any future attempts. Unrealistic expectations are an intrapersonal pitfall or vulnerability that sets people up for failure. It can be argued that expectations based on quick returns are in part culturally conditioned, that is, that we live in a culture that promotes unrealistic notions, for example a 'quick fix society', as commonly projected in media advertising. Another commonly used term is that of 'instant gratification'—the idea that people expect this more and more.

This kind of thinking can also extend into searching for 'shortcuts' and in this context shortcuts refers to the use of 'inappropriate or unfair means' such as cheating or plagiarism. While it is possible to understand the motivations behind such strategies, the consequences are many including very poor odds of not getting caught, especially if it becomes a habit, and that in the process a person cheats themselves out of their own development. It is ironic but worth keeping in mind that 'the easy way out', often an unrealistic expectation in itself, often turns out to be 'the longest and hardest way of all' in the long run.

TENDENCIES TO BE OVERWHELMED BY SETBACKS (ADVERSITY)

The word 'failure' carries a lot of negative connotation and is better framed and viewed as a temporary state, for example 'I did not manage to succeed this time'. Setbacks and hardship are also a normal part of life, but losing sight of this fact is another unrealistic expectation and pitfall that can swamp our thoughts and emotions and thereby interfere with our ability to manage problems in an effective manner. Chapter 13 provided insights in the section dealing with cognitive psychology and emotional intelligence (EI) and the following major section, 'Productive beliefs and thought patterns,' provides information on how to manage intrapersonal barriers including how we think about the setbacks we experience.

MENTAL BLOCKS

Mental blocks are another normal part of life; everyone gets 'bogged down' on tasks or assignments from time to time but it is how we react to these 'realities' that is most important. However, it is yet another pitfall that can overwhelm emotions by producing enough frustration and anxiety to obstruct our ability to concentrate, think clearly and therefore manage this situation, and it can also lead into a negative worrying loop. Mental blocks can include a feeling of getting lost or not knowing how to start or what to do next. At their worst they can trigger panic causing mental turmoil and anguish and take a very high emotional toll. Like other intrapersonal barriers they can unnecessarily hamper us in achieving goals and also cause a great deal of mental anguish.

'SCAPEGOAT' ATTRIBUTIONS

We must be very careful when attributing cause and blame. Inappropriately turning blame away from ourselves and directing it toward others can be unproductive. Examples could include the following:

* It's because my father didn't encourage me that I find writing at university too difficult and not very interesting.

* Lecturers don't know much—so there's nothing worthwhile I can learn from them. Therefore it is a waste of my time even trying.

Getting into the habit of 'blaming others' for negative outcomes and feelings is yet another distortion of reality and, therefore, fails to help us focus and act in a productive manner. It stands in sharp contrast to the self-doubting style of thinking and it is interesting to note that people with the 'blame others' style of thinking are less likely to become clinically depressed than those with a 'self-doubting' habit. Nonetheless it is a pessimistic disposition and people who tend more towards optimistic outlook often achieve more, perform better and enjoy better mental and physical health (Goleman 1996; Seligman 1996; Zukav and Francis 2001).

Productive beliefs and thought patterns

FLEXIBLE OPTIMISM

Extensive research shows that people who lean toward a positive and optimistic outlook are more likely to accomplish more, exhibit higher levels of performance in their pursuits and maintain better mental and physical health than those with pessimistic mental tendencies and habits (Goleman 1996; Seligman 1996; Zukav and Francis 2001). However, it must be acknowledged that degrees of measured pessimism play a vital role in productive thinking and prudent decision making. Seligman (1996) calls for 'flexible optimism' in what we refer to as **flexible optimism** based on the notion of 'balance' as conducive to health and productivity. In contrast, unbalanced *over-optimism* leads into unrealistic expectations and thinking that can go on to generate a host of undesirable outcomes as discussed in the preceding section.

REALISTIC VIEWS: EXPECT 'HARDSHIP' AND 'SETBACKS' OVER THE LONG TERM

Unrealistic expectations about the hardships of life can confound and overwhelm us to the point whereby it becomes very difficult to retain focus and progress in a productive direction. The cliché 'Life wasn't meant to be easy' is a truism, and expectations that fail to balance or temper an over-optimistic outlook leave us vulnerable to undue mental anguish and impair our ability to perform. While it is widely accepted that life incurs many hardships, we can easily forget this and find ourselves reacting badly, for example angrily, when we experience setbacks, and this can then lead to thoughts and feelings that undermine motivation. By maintaining a realistic view of setbacks as being normal we can refrain from poor reactions and the sooner our mental alarm bells send a warning about reactions which are unhealthy and counter-productive the better. Strategies and techniques for developing productive thinking styles along with alarm systems are discussed further below.

Understanding the nature of a large and long-term undertaking can also help us to stay focused and maintain motivation over extended periods. **Human capital theory** (Becker 1993) has been used to conceptualise self-investment—that is, our self-investment in our education and training as a means for increasing future returns (higher earnings) for the sale of our labour. Study can best be thought of as a long-term 'investment' from which we can gain sustained returns in the future. In principle, capital investment in business infrastructure can work in this way; for example, millions of dollars may be spent over a number of years and the expected return on such investment may be quite a number of years into the future. This is a major reason why studying is so demanding, as it entails very large amounts of personal effort, over a long time, and with much of the gratification such as financial and lifestyle returns delayed for years.

Another common pitfall is the expectation that the world is fair and just. While we all carry responsibility for working toward these most important ideals, the expectation that the world is always fair, that everyone or nearly everyone is honest and has good intentions and treats people fairly is an unrealistic expectation and one that can hurt us greatly. This does not mean that we should simply accept unfair practices where they occur, but that we need to realise we are not always able to control situations—as a realistic expectation.

THE STRATEGY OF PERSISTENCE FOR SELF-DEVELOPMENT AND ACHIEVING GOALS

In addition to believing in ourselves, believing that practice and persistence pays off is another critical strategy for maximising our chances of success in any undertaking. Conversely, the alternative—of giving up—dramatically decreases the likelihood of success in our endeavours. That persistence helps increase the likelihood of attainment is logical, realistic and a hallmark quality of both flexible optimism and emotional intelligence. It is common for people new to tertiary learning to experience difficulties in acquiring skills in academic writing. Ideally this should not surprise or dissuade those new to the tertiary environment. It is not uncommon for some students to approach lecturers for advice when experiencing difficulties with writing.

> I understand the material, and I can even explain it to others—but I just can't seem to put it down on paper.

We do a great deal more talking than writing in our daily lives, and that is why it is not too surprising that people find writing more difficult. Further frustration can develop because people expect to be able to develop advanced writing skills very quickly. On the contrary, writing skills, like other skills, are acquired and develop over time through practice, that is, 'doing' and persistence. The same principles apply in other endeavours, for example becoming proficient with a musical instrument that requires effort and practice over time.

PROACTIVE STRATEGY: SOURCING INFORMATION AND SEEKING ADVICE AND SUPPORT

Seeking advice and support as appropriate soon after you feel you have exhausted your own resources is a hallmark of success for many students and professional achievers. Time management is also very important for students with tight deadlines. Assignments need to be attempted well ahead of time so that problems can be discovered and sufficiently addressed. Seeking support is a valuable survival skill. In contrast by failing to seek clarification or assistance you may be leaving things to chance; indeed it is often the case that students easily assume that they have met the requirements of a task (so it is a major pitfall). On this note Lawrence (2002) points out that:

> The ability to seek help and information. . . is a crucial socio-cultural competency that needs to be consistently demonstrated by students in and across a variety of university cultures and sub-cultures. Students need to be able to canvass a wide range of resources and be able to determine which one will best meet a specific need for specific discipline areas. They need to be able to access for themselves, locating, utilising and assessing for example, information gleaned from handbooks, booklets and web sites, as well as discipline specific assistance such as peer assisted learning programs, consultation with tutors and lecturers, library and computer support services, and study skills sessions. They also need to know how to. . . access learning enhancement support and [develop] personalised coping mechanisms to help them negotiate the bureaucratic infrastructures in a variety of departments and faculties. There is also the help and support available from a plethora of counsellors: careers, peer and clinical counsellors.
>
> *(Available at* <http://ultibase.rmit.edu.au/Articles/march03/lawrence1.htm>)

THE CONCEPT OF LIFELONG LEARNING AND DEVELOPMENT

The concept of lifelong learning has particular relevance to communication. Indeed life is a journey of learning and development. Take written expression for example; expressing oneself in writing is a skill and it is a skill that most of us will continue to develop through out the rest of our lives. The philosophies of self-development and strategic communication both emphasise the need to work continually at developing and improving skills and also the fact that our life experiences provide us with opportunities to do this. Hence learning extends beyond formal learning as 'we are all students of life', and if we are not trying to learn as much as we can from our day-to-day experiences we are limiting our capacity to learn.

Managing motivation

Thinking realistically, we need to acknowledge that we will experience motivational lows during any large endeavour. So once again, it is better to accept and expect this as a natural and inevitable part of life. How we cope and manage ourselves through these periods is most important. Approaches to managing motivation, especially in reference to study-related goals, include the following.

1. STRATEGIC PLANNING: COMMIT TO GOALS, REALISTIC TIMETABLING AND PACING

In an effort to maximise our chances of successfully accomplishing any significant undertaking, we should first give ourselves the best possible chance by making a serious commitment to a primary goal. Before doing this we should try to determine our level of motivation, by assessing our level of desire and our reasons for wanting to achieve a given goal. Given that we all experience motivational lows, mental blocks and a host of other obstacles periodically, we can draw strength from our motivation and commitment to primary 'bigger picture' goals to help us remain persistent. Of course to achieve long-term goals and visions we also need to set and commit to realistic short-term goals and realistic time frames. Timetabling is an invaluable tool, especially for studying, as is setting day-to-day goals such as a list of what we aim to achieve in a two-hour study block. It is also important to schedule breaks, a day of rest per week and reward ourselves in an effort to maintain positive and committed.

2. POSITIVE ATTITUDE AND ACTIVE ENGAGEMENT

The importance of developing an attitude and outlook conducive to effective performance should never be underestimated, and feelings of apprehension or negativity toward certain subjects or tasks is not conducive to good performance. In contrast we tend to enjoy the things we are good at doing. Despite the challenges and hardships, study should also provide us with experiences of satisfaction and enjoyment. Hence it is in our best interest to invoke an optimistic outlook and look for ways in which to 'make' a task interesting to ourselves. This is an astute strategy that can minimise mental anguish while also increasing the likelihood of good performance in a task.

Making a determined effort to engage actively with information, material and situations we encounter also helps to create and maintain interest. This non-passive approach also facilitates deeper understanding and memory retention. Active engagement involves habitually asking ourselves probing questions, such as:

Why does this theory work in this way?

In which kinds of situations does this theory seem to hold true?

How does this theory relate to the general topic?

How does the theory relate to my life—could it enhance my friendships, or increase my chances of employment in a job in an interview?

And, quite importantly:

> How can this help me to produce a good assignment or examination paper?

In essence, active engagement strengthens retention and understanding because it involves trying actively to incorporate new information into our existing knowledge base. Active engagement also requires the use of active listening, which is discussed below under the heading 'Effective listening' in the interpersonal barriers section.

3. RECEPTIVITY: CAPITALISE ON FEEDBACK

Feedback provides us with the primary means by which we can enhance our communicative performance. For example, being perceptive to written feedback on assignments helps us progressively to produce work of a higher and higher quality. Hence the importance of actively reading and thinking over written feedback on returned assignments cannot be overemphasised. In addition, our perceptiveness to the feedback we receive from friends and colleagues in our daily interactions helps deepen our understandings in the most appropriate and beneficial manner. For example, if you are thinking of asking the boss for a pay rise and when you arrive you can see she is preoccupied or in a bad mood then this feedback tells you that it is not the most appropriate time to ask for the raise. Barriers to perceptive ability restrict our ability to adapt and improve and as a result we would be more inclined to keep stumbling across the same kinds of mistakes and pitfalls. Feedback approached with a positive or optimistic outlook can be viewed as opportunities to learn and to do this we need to fend off our tendencies to view feedback as purely negative and an attack on our character. Viewing feedback as a valuable opportunity to learn is a more positive and productive strategy.

4. MANAGING MENTAL BLOCKS

As discussed earlier, mental blocks include things such as feelings of being lost or at a loss, that is, not knowing how to start or what to do next, or feeling lost with what may seem to be an unsolvable problem or task. In dealing with this we can first acknowledge that mental blocks are a natural part of life and that we should expect them. There are many strategies we can use, such as taking a break (sometimes answers to problems can come to us while taking a break for coffee or a walk), seeking advice or support (a survival strategy mentioned earlier) or exploring options that we think will work for us. (e.g. see the fifth approach below). But remember it is important that we proactively manage and contain the pitfalls of negative thinking and self-doubt as they can produce undue anxiety and impair motivation.

5. PERSONALISED STRATEGIES AND TECHNIQUES: LEARNING ABOUT HOW WE LEARN BEST

Effective communication, especially for large tasks and where study is involved, requires that we customise a range of strategies that are suited to us and enable us to progress effectively. Different people find different approaches useful. Some of us find making lists useful, for example creating a list of tasks we wish to complete in a particular study session. Success in communication and learning typically involves developing strategies that 'work for us' in tackling goals. Students embarking on tertiary study typically find that they learn a great deal about 'how they learn' particularly in the first year. The technical definition for this is *meta-learning* (learning about learning).

In sitting for final examinations for instance, we may find it useful to psychologically prepare ourselves in some way; for example, to go in with an attitude of determination, to show the examiner our capabilities, as opposed to defensive demeanour ('I hope I'm good enough to pass'). This psychological strategy appears to be common among successful sports people; boxers, for example, typically approach a match with great determination to win.

6. EMOTIONAL INTELLIGENCE: MANAGING EMOTIONS AND THOUGHT PATTERNS

To develop successfully and realise our potential we not only need to build on our strengths but also work on our weaknesses, particularly thought patterns and emotions that can impair our ability to manage future challenges and hardships we will encounter. As human beings we can become vulnerable to our own emotional reactions, which have the potential to hijack our ability to think rationally and send us into a state of paralysis (Goleman 1996). However, there are skills we can choose to acquire and master to manage our way through our lives and endeavours better. We now know that how we react to problems and setbacks is much more important than the setbacks themselves and that our reactions have an immense influence over well-being and likelihood of future success (Goleman 1996; Seligman 1996).

As explained in Chapter 13, changing poor ways of thinking and reacting requires heightened levels of self-awareness so that we can consciously monitor our thinking and feelings (emotional reactions) for potential problems so that we can intercept them. Self-monitoring in itself is a skill and a habit we need to work at developing; it can be likened to making sure we 'have our radar on' so that 'mental alarm bells' ring when potentially poor self-management reactions start to occur. We may also need to take time out to 'cool off' and recompose, and we can then start to challenge the validity of the thoughts and/or feelings and try to instil better balanced and more optimistic alternatives.

Flexible optimism requires nurturing an *explanatory style,* that is, thinking patterns and self-talk that function to guard against and protect us from slipping into extended and excessive states of worry. But once again we need to be consciously on guard to intercept negative thinking and feelings as they occur. The following example gives you an idea of how someone may use self-talk techniques:

'I'm not a failure, and I need to realise that worrying and thinking like this is not realistic, it is unproductive and making me feel worse.'

'Instead—I'll choose to learn from this experience. I'll get the feedback I need and make sure I'm really well prepared to pass that exam next time.'

In addition to developing and maintaining our self-confidence [a belief in our own abilities to succeed cannot be overemphasised.] De Vito (1989) recommends the use of *self-affirmation*; that is, to take time to think about our positive qualities and strengths as opposed to destructive preoccupations with weaknesses or 'perceived' weaknesses. This involves the use of positive yet realistic self-talk.

The following steps provide guidelines for self-management of negative thought patterns. These steps are based, in part, on rational emotive therapy originally developed by Albert Ellis (1974) as a cognitive self-therapy methodology.

Step-by-step guide for cognitive self-intervention

1. *Self-monitoring* to detect poor thinking habits and views when they occur.
2. Challenging these by comparing them with more productive interpretations and ways of thinking.
3. Replacing them with more productive interpretations and ways of understanding.
4. Continued effort to use a newly identified (productive) 'view' until it becomes established as a new thinking habit or view.

Managing our emotions

These steps can also be used in tandem to monitor our emotions, that is, our feelings. We can develop skills to help ensure that negative emotions do not persist for extended periods. This ability to 'bounce back' after upsets has been referred to as *resilience* and it is a hallmark quality of *emotional intelligence*. In addition to detecting emotions that can potentially cause prolonged and undue distress (as per step 1 above), deliberately redirecting our attention away from a troubling matter for a period—to cool off—helps us to refresh and come back to the matter with a more productive perspective. This skill or ability is common among people who exhibit the capacity to 'bounce back' after setbacks and hardship (Goleman 1996; Seligman 1996).

Daniel Goleman (1996) identifies the following as some of the key characteristics of emotional intelligence EI:

* *emotional awareness:* the ability to notice our feelings and as they occur;

* *resilience:* the ability to soothe ourselves, to move out of, or bounce back from, states of distress by being able to 'take time out', to stop, 'cool off' and recompose;

* *self-control:* the ability to delay gratification and persist with goals despite setbacks and upsets; for example, commitment to, and persistence in, pursuing longer-terms goals;

* *empathy:* a fundamental social skill, being able to understand people by being better attuned to their feelings.

While the emotional part of our brain is of indispensable value, our initial emotional responses are often 'sloppy'. So the ability to take time out to separate ourselves for a period and delay action provides us with the means to be able to think things through more carefully. Legislators are aware of this hence it is law in many States that there be a 'cooling off period' when signing agreements for major purchases including motor vehicles and real estate. When we delay action, for example 'sleep on it', we often see that our feelings settle in a way that serves us better, that is, before we have done or said things that we will live to regret. It is hard to overstate the importance of this skill!

Concluding comments

Thus far we have examined physical and now intrapersonal barriers and the 'obstacle course' view that barriers theory provides has proved to be a very useful way to think about and identify the many factors that need to be taken into account to help ensure effective communication and performance generally. It has enabled us to realise that there are many obstacles out there and that the paths we need to navigate are often very slippery indeed. We need to work at being positive and vigilant as we can all too easily succumb to the many tempting pitfalls that surround us.

Interpersonal barriers

The study of **interpersonal barriers** seeks to focus on factors that impede communication between people. The kinds of interpersonal barriers that can impede communication vary greatly, many stemming from the intrapersonal differences between individuals. Clashes between people often occur because of misunderstandings and incompatibilities in people's viewpoints, values and beliefs and competition over limited resources, that is, conflicting interests.

A critical first step in managing conflicts and problems between people is to gain a good understanding of the people with whom we wish to communicate (audience analysis), including an appreciation of the issues relevant to the *life world* of others.

Assess potential intrapersonal barriers of other party

So far intrapersonal barriers have been discussed in terms of the personal barriers that can impede our ability to communicate as effectively as possible. Of course, the second major aspect of intrapersonal barriers involves the perceptual biases and attitudes of those with whom we wish to communicate.

The kinds of barriers we encounter when endeavouring to communicate with others vary greatly. The preceding chapters of this text contain a range of techniques and strategies for minimising such barriers, and these are more easily identifiable once you have identified the kinds of barriers involved in a particular situation.

Identifying barriers (potential and otherwise) requires analysing not only the problem or task at hand but analysing your intended audience/receiver through audience analysis. The principal tenet of audience analysis is that the more we know about those with whom we are dealing, the better equipped we are to do so effectively.

Structure messages to target receiver/other party

The next stage of audience analysis then involves using seemingly the most appropriate strategies for tailoring messages so that they appeal to the receivers in the way we intend. Core methods of appeal include:

* persuasive appeals (e.g. appeal to people's interests);
* logical/rational appeals (e.g. use of scientific research and logical argument);
* education and awareness promotion initiatives (based on logical/rational appeals).

These kinds of strategies can be used to help manage intrapersonal impediments like fear, opposition or disinterest in new information or ideas, for example fear of computers or technology. In the media you will have seen many promotional education-based campaigns on issues such as road safety, which are aimed at educating and encouraging people to adhere to safe driving practices.

It is also important to use careful ethical judgement in developing strategies for our dealings with others. The detection of unfair and unethical tactics works to undermine a communicator's credibility and the likelihood of productive communication outcomes.

Effective listening

Listening involves more than mere hearing, and its importance cannot be overstated. In spite of this it remains a very underdeveloped skill for many people. Like any other skill it is acquired and developed through practice and effort over time. Effective listening requires considerable effort as it often requires more concentration than speaking. Barriers to effective listening arise for a variety of reasons but many stem from poor listening habits.

Barriers to effective listening include:

* Concentrating on something else or what you are going to say next while the other party is speaking.

* Assuming that the topic/story is boring or that you already know all there is to know on the topic.
* Disinterest or personal dislike/lack of respect for the other party (regardless of whether they are making a worthwhile point or not).
* Dominating a conversation, negating another's opportunity to express ideas.
* Tiredness, physical noise or mannerisms you find distracting (e.g. another's nervousness).
* Lack of understanding of the topic.
* Lack of cultural and/or technical understanding.

Key strategies for enhancing effective listening skills include:

* Make a committed effort to listen despite distractions including physical noise or any negative feelings about the other person and their mannerisms.
* Make an effort to be open minded by concentrating and considering carefully what is being said (and resisting premature judgements).
* Do not dominate conversations and resist an excessive preoccupation with other ideas (such as what you want to say next).
* Ask questions and give encouragement (nods, smiles, eye contact, etc.).
* Use empathy—understanding the person helps you to understand the message better.

Empathy

Empathy means developing an understanding and appreciation of another person's circumstances and point of view. It is a genuine attempt to 'stand in the other person's shoes' to see what the world looks like from their perspective. Empathy is significantly different from sympathy and sympathy does not necessarily follow empathy. Empathy helps us to understand better the people we are relating to; but it does not require us either to agree with them or feel pity for them.

Empathy is an integral part of the audience analysis approach and hence one of the most fundamental principles of strategic communication. People who lack empathy are self-centred because they are unable to or fail to appreciate adequately other people's circumstances and other people's ideas and points of view. A lack of ability to empathise isolates us from the lives of others and our very 'social world' and as such impedes our interpersonal skills, often referred to as people skills.

It is now recommended that you reread the 'Conflict' and 'Assertive behaviour theory' sections in Chapter 13 to refamiliarise yourself with strategies and techniques for dealing with difficult people and situations.

Many interpersonal barriers to communication occur in workplaces. Given that most people have little choice over who they work with, it is important to try to establish and maintain a productive and congenial working relationship. Increasingly, we need to work as a part of a group or function in and manage teams. Hence it is also recommended that you reread the sections 'Pitfalls in group decision making' and 'Conflict in groups' in Chapter 14 'Group Communication'.

Intercultural barriers

Australia, like many other countries, has a history of a large amount of immigration, and has become what is commonly called a multicultural society. More recent developments in information and communication technologies (ICTs) and increased affordability of international travel have also produced an environment which facilitates increased intercultural interactions. Many people today travel internationally to work in other countries or to study and obtain educational qualifications. Yet many also work for, or study with, overseas organisations without leaving their country of origin.

The march of globalisation is continuing to change our business and social environments into international ones. As a consequence, the need to communicate and work with a diverse range of people who have cultural backgrounds different from our own is becoming increasingly important. The need for competencies in communicating interculturally is growing as our economies continue to become integrated into a global system which is highly competitive. Organisations are beginning to realise that the synergies and depth of intercultural perspectives that cultural diversity can generate in the workplace have the potential to provide them with a great deal of competitive advantage.

What is culture?

Culture, in essence, is a society's shared and systematic ways of living. It consists of the norms and conventions (such as language) which enable us to interact socially and make sense of the world. It refers to all socially conditioned ways of behaving that are not strictly biological, so it affects nearly every aspect of life. To demonstrate, eating is considered biological, while the kinds of foods we eat, the ways in which we prepare and eat them are all cultural (the ways of eating common to a given culture).

Culture has been defined as 'the collective programming of mind which distinguishes the members of one human group from another' (Hofstede 2001, p. 4). Culture is the result of socialisation, that is, we learn culture from our interactions within a culture. A culture is characterised by its language system; its knowledge and belief systems such as religions and sciences, including what is regarded as commonsense; and the myths or accepted explanations and values that underpin these systems. At this point it is recommended that you reread a brief section in Chapter 2 under the heading 'Cultural world view'.

The concept of culture is complex and broad as it also covers the concept of *subculture*. Subculture refers to groups of people within a culture, that exhibit variations and/or specific cultural characteristics. Subculture in itself is also a broad concept and is used to refer to wide-ranging groupings of people, for example surf culture, football culture, team or workplace culture, youth culture, music culture and so on. Subcultural variations commonly include technical and informal language and knowledge, norms and behaviours (e.g. clothing) and values. At this point it is recommended that you review the section in Chapter 15 under the heading 'Organisational culture'. The remainder of this section focuses on a societal level of culture, pertaining to whole societies rather than subcultures.

Core barriers to intercultural communication

1. ETHNOCENTRISM (LACK OF CULTURAL SENSITIVITY)

Ethnocentrism refers to the practice of viewing and making judgements about other cultures and cultural practices based on one's own culture. It is based on a flawed assumption that one's own culture provides the most appropriate benchmark of what is correct and appropriate, that is, it involves assuming the practices of another culture are 'incorrect' on the basis that our own culture is the 'correct' one (Marshall 1994). While ethnocentricity in the extreme can lead to racism, its manifestations are often unintentional and unconscious. Hence a person with ethnocentric views is not necessarily nasty or racist. Ethnocentrism involves attitudes and understandings which are insensitive to other cultures and as such undermines the foundations upon which intercultural communication and understanding can take place.

2. LACK OF APPROPRIATE CULTURAL KNOWLEDGE

The lack of accurate information about a particular culture is the other core barrier to effective intercultural communication and this is especially difficult in cases where people cannot speak one another's languages. Depending on the circumstances, the use of an interpreter or a multilingual friend may be required. There is no substitute to 'doing our homework', in other words using audience analysis methods to research and develop the cultural knowledge required for the task(s) at hand.

Addressing core intercultural barriers

1. DEVELOP A SENSE OF CULTURAL SENSITIVITY (RELATIVITY)

It is difficult to truly comprehend the subjective and constructed nature of our own culture; that is, the extent to which our cultural practices and norms are simply one set of ways of doing things, and that there are many other cultures that have very different but equally valid ways of doing things. We all have a natural tendency towards viewing our own culture as normal (this applies to all cultures and, therefore, technically speaking is a *cultural universal*), especially if we have had limited experience with another culture. However, those who have some depth of experience in another culture will normally have a deep understanding and appreciation that cultures differ, in other words they have *cultural sensitivity*.

The first step toward effective intercultural communication is to develop a sense of cultural sensitivity. This involves curtailing our ethnocentric tendency to see our own practices, so familiar to us, as being 'correct' and 'normal', so that we can appreciate and respect different cultural practices.

You would also be aware that tolerance and acceptance of cultural difference are core underlying principles of social justice in Western democratic multicultural societies. We also need to bear in mind that differences in cultural values, belief systems and ways of living between quite a number of cultures appears so great that it leads to strong feelings of hatred which at its worst leads to atrocities, war, acts of terror and international instability. Like relationships between people, relationships between nations, even those with strong diplomatic ties, can and do experience difficulties over conflicting national interests—real or perceived—and conflicting points of view. Like all significant relationships international relationships have to be taken seriously and treated carefully.

2. ACQUIRE CULTURAL UNDERSTANDING APPROPRIATE TO THE SITUATION ('CULTURAL AUDIENCE ANALYSIS')

We should try to gain knowledge of another's culture in an effort to become more informed about the person or persons with whom we wish to communicate. This will help in conveying and interpreting information in ways that both parties can understand and thereby reduce misinterpretation. Understanding can be further developed during intercultural interaction by asking questions. Also remember that inaccurate myths and stereotypes about another culture can be misguiding.

Culture is comprised of behavioural norms (customs and values) so norms that constitute respectful manners and etiquette vary according to culture. Once again there is no substitute for 'doing our homework'. Usually, it important to show a host culture that we have made an effort to gain cultural knowledge on matters such as manners; however, we can go too far as a host culture will not expect us to try to master their culture, and attempts to do so may appear silly and even offensive.

Individualist and collectivist cultures: A comparison

Individualist cultures place an emphasis on individual achievement and self-reliance while collectivist cultures place an emphasis on collective wellbeing (the wellbeing of a group) and social harmony. People are expected to be more conformist as loyalty to the group is regarded paramount (Hofstede 2001). Collectivist cultures tend to reach decisions through careful consensus as group harmony is considered very important and hence there is a tendency to avoid conflict and speaking out against issues. In comparison in individualistic cultures people are permitted to speak out, challenge ideas being put forward by other group members and so conflict is much more readily accepted (Hofstede 2001). Given the emphasis placed on harmony and conformity, collectivist cultures tend to communicate less directly and much more politely, in contrast to individualistic cultures where communication tends to be more direct or 'to the point'. An example of this kind of indirectness comes from a library sign in South Korea which reads 'There is much laughter and fun in our trees and park outside'. A cultural translation in many English-speaking countries would be 'Silence in the library.' This shows how cultural norms relating to manners can require a substantial shift in the way we think about, and approach communication, as there can be large differences in people's cultural sensibilities.

There seems to be merits in all aspects of difference between collectivist and individualistic approaches. On the one hand people from collectivist backgrounds can be really well suited to teamwork and averting group conflict, while the tolerance of group conflict in individualistic cultures promotes competition between ideas which can also help to produce effective outcomes. Hence intercultural communication provides all parties with great opportunities to learn from one another.

Finally, *seeking clarification regularly* is an effective way to manage and reduce misunderstandings; it helps to ensure that both parties are understanding each other and do not offend each other. This is a strategy similar to that used in conflict resolutions whereby respective parties check carefully that everyone has a clear understanding of agreements made—in an effort to negate the continuation of conflict or generation of any new conflict.

The cultural construction of gender

The gender roles and expectations within a society are also culturally constructed. The cultural construction of gender is changing in Australian society and in many other societies. Our use of language is also changing to accommodate and reflect new relations between women and men. The use of gender-biased language is being tolerated less in our society; for example, a gender-specific position description is rarely tolerated in job advertisements, that is, the gender-biased word 'foreman' has been replaced with the term 'supervisor'.

Gender-biased language will frequently produce a barrier because a receiver may become preoccupied with what seems an insult rather than what may have been the intended message. It is important to note here that gender-biased language is not accepted in professional or academic discourse. Hence it is not tolerated in tertiary level assignments. Using 'barriers' as theoretical categorisations has helped us to focus closely on factors that can hinder effective communication. But once again these categorisations are highly complex as they are closely interrelated and the boundaries between them are not always clear. For instance, we have just seen how gender roles are culturally constructed. Indeed the next major category of barriers, semantic barriers (semantics is the study of the meaning), is very much influenced by culture.

Education and awareness promotion strategies

Education—the promotion of public/people's awareness of the inappropriateness and unfairness of prejudiced attitudes and other unjust and inequitable practices—has been traditionally used, and with a considerable degree of success, as a means of addressing social barriers at this level, for example the inequitable and discriminatory forms of sexism, racism, ageism and discrimination on the basis of disabilities. In addition to this, governments have legislated to make discrimination on these characteristics illegal in most cases. At an organisational level companies and organisations can, and in many cases do, also provide educational awareness initiatives and adopt appropriate policies.

Awareness promotion strategies often require a sustained effort over time, often many decades, for example changing behaviours and attitudes so that we as a society, women and men, can effectively remove cultural barriers that, for instance, marginalise women for fields of employment including executive management, engineering and automotive industries. Ongoing education and awareness promotion are important strategies as it is also widely known and accepted that anti-discrimination legislation on its own has very little impact.

Semantic barriers

The term 'semantics' refers to the study of meaning, as generated from language. Semantic barriers (also discussed in Chapter 2 as 'semantic noise') refer to problems in meaning when communicating with words. **Semantic barriers** arise in cases when the receivers and senders of messages have a different understanding of the word or words used in a message. Semantic barriers also arise when a sender uses words that are unfamiliar to the receiver, for example technical jargon.

The colloquial use of language can also cause meaning problems in intercultural communication. Overseas visitors whose first language is not English may have studied English at school; however, there is a difference between 'textbook' English and the way it is used by many Australians. For example, the Australian phrase 'How are you?' may seem to be a question about one's wellbeing, when in fact it is used as a standard acknowledgement or greeting (with a meaning similar to 'hello'). Hence the literal meaning of the phrase is quite different from its meaning in the Australian colloquial context. It is interesting to note that the standard response to greetings such as 'How are you?' and 'How are you going?' is 'Good' or 'Well, thank you' even if one is feeling quite unwell.

Semantic barriers can occur at the denotative level (the literal or dictionary meaning of a word) and also at the connotative level (the emotional tone being conveyed). For example, if we were to talk about a 'cheap' shirt compared with an 'inexpensive' shirt, at the denotative level the words 'cheap' and 'inexpensive' have the same meaning. However, at the connotative level 'cheap' can imply that the shirt is of inferior quality, whereas 'inexpensive' does not.

Key strategies for reducing semantic barriers

The principal approach to minimising semantic barriers is to choose words carefully so that they are appropriate for the receiver and so that they can understand the messages in the way intended.

Key strategies include the following:

* Choose words that the receiver(s) is likely to understand and strive to explain as clearly as possible. Take care with the use of colloquial terms, especially in intercultural situations.

* Consider the denotative and especially connotative meanings of words in an effort to avoid misunderstandings; some words may offend by what they imply or they may seem condescending.

* Use jargon (specialist terms) carefully. For example, in presenting an informative talk about universities to primary school children, we would avoid using university jargon the way one might when conversing with a lecturer.

* When communication requires the use of jargon, then explain these terms clearly using examples wherever possible.

* Use questions to test whether messages are being interpreted the way you intended. (Do not assume understanding, especially at the intercultural level.)

* As a receiver of messages in communicative exchanges we should ask questions for clarification when unsure about our own interpretation of what has been said (or read).

* Avoid culture specific clichés. For example, it is often the case that they do not make literal 'textbook English' sense; for example, 'She's apples' is a cliché meaning 'Things are OK' but it could be literally interpreted as a reference to a female whose name is 'Apples'.

Additional barrier management approaches

Strategic planning

This textbook is primarily concerned with the development of strategies that can be used to enhance the effectiveness of communicative performance. Strategically planning communication, especially for significant tasks, provides us with the means by which to enhance the effectiveness of our communication.

Accordingly, we reintroduce at this point a modified version of the generic strategic task management model to include responsiveness (discussed below). This task, incorporating audience, analysis model involves working out what we want, or what needs to be achieved, with due consideration to the needs and desires of the audience or receiver. Using this model as a guide we begin to choose and apply strategies and techniques to help achieve our aims and objectives in an effective and efficient manner.

Strategic planning model

Task Analysis

* Analyse the task, question or problem to determine the aim and objectives.
* Divide into manageable subtasks and formulate a plan/schedule.
* Select strategies and contingencies and incorporate into the plan.
* Begin with initial subtasks (e.g. research literature).

Audience Analysis

* Analyse the audience/receiver: needs and expectations, desires and so on.
* Select strategies and techniques as appropriate to target and cater for them effectively and incorporate these into the plan (e.g. format, layout and style of language to be used).

The Responsive Execution of (Sub)Tasks

* Execute subtasks step by step.
* Monitor and assess chosen strategies and techniques: e.g. 'Will my argument be convincing and clear for receiver/target audience?'
* Responsive flexibility: monitor and adjust strategies and techniques according to the situation as it develops, so you can change tactics and keep pace with changes if need be.
* Periodically monitor and manage your own intrapersonal and motivational performance and state for intrapersonal barriers.

Post-Task Evaluation

* Re-evaluate strategies after task completion.
* Use feedback to evaluate performance and identify lessons learned (for future reference)

Responsiveness

Responsiveness means responding and behaving in a manner which is likely to be the most appropriate and effective under the given (and changing) circumstances (Richmond and McCroskey 1985). It is important to remain mindful of the fact that things do not usually go exactly as planned. Planning is nonetheless important as it provides the direction and strategies to help maximise successful outcomes.

Contingencies are also an important planning strategy—often referred to as a 'plan B'. In many cases it is important to incorporate strategies for coping with problems that may arise. Sometimes we need to adopt contingencies that have not been planned. For example, if we were presenting a talk and it became obvious in the early stages that the audience was having difficulty understanding the topic (their faces were puzzled), then it may be necessary to re-strategise. At this point we may give more detailed explanations than we had planned originally and perhaps leave out some of the more complex ideas. Being responsive and flexible, 'thinking on our feet', is an important skill for effective communicators. Responsiveness is a skill that can be developed by continually striving to do our best in situations as they develop.

Research: Communication barriers analysis

When conducting research into communication barriers the first step requires an analysis of situations to identify and then explain any barriers to communication. Once a communication barrier is identified and more fully understood we are in a better position to start looking at ways to overcome or minimise the problems associated with that barrier.

FORMING WORKING GROUPS AND COMMITTEES

It is quite common for organisations to set up special working groups or teams for the purpose of investigating problems and exploring new initiatives. The most common kinds of working groups include task- or problem-dedicated committees and taskforces. Chapter 14, on group communication, examines the dynamics of working in groups. At this point we highly recommend that you review Chapter 14, particularly the section headed 'Benefits of group decision making'.

Building redundancy into communication

The term 'redundancy' in the study of communication refers to repetition in messages. It is a valuable communicative strategy and one that is used every day when repeating information or rephrasing a certain point. Redundancy can be used to try to overcome a physical barrier, such as loud machinery, when repeating a message more loudly and also accompanying it with nonverbal gestures. Redundancy can take many forms and can be planned into communication. For example, redundancy is typically built into the structure of a presentational talk by providing:

* an introduction for the main points;
* the main body in which the main points are presented in more detail; and
* a conclusion in which the main points are reiterated.

This provides the audience with more opportunities to comprehend and remember the messages being conveyed. It is interesting to note that people typically build redundancy into structuring essays in much the same way, that is, with an introduction, a main body and a conclusion.

Redundancy can also take the form of follow-up communication, for example confirming a spoken agreement in writing or sending a memorandum or email as a reminder after a telephone conversation.

Finally, while structuring redundancy into communication is an important strategy, it can be inappropriately applied or overdone and much repetition can even occur unintentionally. Too much repetition is a barrier to communication because it puts people off, causing them to 'tune out'. We sometimes take offence at others when they over-apply repetition, and often interpret it as patronising, an insult to our intelligence and an indication that the other party is trying to 'control' us.

The meta-theoretical principle of communication as balance

The point just covered, that redundancy can be either underdone or overdone, once again demonstrates that the key to effective communication involves achieving the best possible balance (or mix) of strategies and the most appropriate application of those strategies. This is a meta-theoretical point (meta-theory was discussed in Chapter 2) because it involves consideration about theory ('meta' means about) and its application. Maximising the benefits of communication theory and principles requires the building up of our 'balancing' skills through application/practice and the development of deeper understanding through engagement with, and reflection upon, that knowledge.

In conclusion, the study of communication is about striving for the best possible mix of strategies from the knowledge available to us, in order to manage a given task or reach a certain goal under the given circumstances. Indeed the developing of our skills to apply knowledge well in responsive and innovative ways will be a large determiner of future success: personally, academically and professionally. A strategic planning approach including the use of a robust model helps guide us toward an effective balance of strategies and techniques for achieving successful outcomes.

SUMMARY

This final chapter supplements and rounds off the textbook with a general discussion of the common kinds of barriers to communication and approaches to minimising their impact. The ability to identify, understand and manage barriers is imperative for those interested in enhancing their ability to communicate effectively.

The barriers theory approach is very useful in helping to ensure that we communicate effectively. The barriers approach allows us to anticipate likely and potential problems and pitfalls of a situation so that we can strategically plan to overcome or minimise obstacles that can interfere with and reduce our chances of communicating effectively. Commonsense dictates that the more important a situation (e.g. what is at stake) the more important it is to take the time and plan thoroughly.

KEY POINTS

- A barrier is anything that interferes with or stands in the way of effective communication and as such is the conceptual equivalent of noise.

- Physical barriers are those impediments that are due to physical or environmental factors and constraints.

- Intrapersonal barriers are those characteristics that impede an individual's ability to communicate and develop as effectively as possible. Differences between people's intrapersonal (or psychological) make-up, such as their interests, values and so on, also give rise to what are called interpersonal communication barriers.

- Intercultural barriers arise from differences in perspectives and practices between people due to differing cultural backgrounds. Cultural barriers often give rise to semantic barriers, that is, problems associated with the meaning of words between two parties. Gender barriers are also in part the result of cultural conditioning.

- The kinds of barriers we encounter when endeavouring to communicate with others vary greatly. Strategies for minimising barriers are more easily identifiable once the kinds of barriers involved are identified.

- Incorporating audience analysis into the planning of communication is the primary means by which barriers can be identified and appropriate communicative strategies developed. Communicative strategies can be used to tailor messages in an effort to try to appeal to receivers in the way we intend.

- Strategic planning (including planning around potential barriers) provides a useful means by which to help ensure that we communicate effectively.

- Planning for effective communication involves a process of striving for the best balance (or mix) of strategies and techniques to suit a particular situation.

REVIEW QUESTIONS

1. What kinds of physical barriers do you believe are the most commonly overlooked?
2. What kinds of intrapersonal barriers do you believe affect a person's ability to learn and become more effective communicators?
3. What strategies do you feel would be most helpful for managing counter-productive thinking and counter-productive emotions?
4. Why is empathy so important in communication and what problems can arise if one lacks empathy?
5. Drawing on your own experience, what kinds of interpersonal barriers occur most often? What are the best ways to manage these?
6. Why are the concepts of ethnocentricism and cultural sensitivity important in intercultural communication?
7. What strategies can be used to minimise semantic barriers?
8. Why is incorporating a responsive approach to communicative tasks important?

EXERCISES

Note: After formulating your responses it is important wherever possible to discuss them with a peer or group of peers. If you are not in a classroom setting then an appropriate electronic discussion board would be ideal.

1. Identify what you believe to be the common physical barriers that impede upon your day-to-day life. Put forward some new measures you could use to manage these better.

2. What are the main barriers to an effective oral presentation? Put forward measures you could use to overcome these.

3. The literature on perception indicates that we are susceptible to a range of factors that distort our perception and understanding.

    - To what extent do you agree or disagree with this view? Justify your views.
    - Put forward some new measures you could use to help counter distortive influence.

4. Today there is substantial scientific support for the claim that 'flexible optimism' is conducive to achieving goals, higher levels of performance and one's general wellbeing.

    To what extend do you agree or disagree with this claim? Justify your views.

5. What do you believe are the key survival skills for success at university and in a career? Justify your views.

6. What elements are important in helping to ensure effective intercultural communication?

BIBLIOGRAPHY

Adler, R. B. and Towne, N. 1993, *Looking Out/Looking In,* 7th ed., Harcourt Brace Javanovich, Florida.

Becker, G. 1993, *Human Capital,* University of Chicago Press, Chicago.

De Vito, J. A. 1989, *The Interpersonal Communication Book,* 5th ed., Harper and Row Publishers, New York.

Ellis, A. 1974, *Humanistic Psychotherapy,* McGraw-Hill, New York.

Goleman, D. 1996, *Emotional Intelligence,* Bantam Books, New York.

Hofstede, G. 2001, *Culture's Consequences: Comparing Values, Behaviours, Institutions, and Organisations Across Nations,* Sage Publications, Newbury Park.

Lawrence J. 2002, "The deficit-discourse shift: University teachers and their role in helping first year students persevere and succeed in the new university culture', presented to *The 6th Pacific Rim First Year in Higher Education Conference* held at the University of Canterbury, Christchurch, New Zealand, 8–10 July 2002. Also available from <http://ultibase.rmit.edu.au/Articles/march03/lawrence1.htm>.

Mackay, H. 1994, Why Don't People Listen? Solving the Communication Problem, Pan Macmillan, Sydney.

Marshall, G. 1994, *Oxford Concise Dictionary of Sociology,* Oxford University Press, Oxford.

O'Sullivan, T., Hartley, J., Montgomery, M. and Fiske, J. 1994, *Key Concepts in Communication and Cultural Studies,* 2nd ed., Routledge, New York.

Richmond, V. and McCroskey, J. 1985, *Communication: Apprehension, Avoidance and Effectiveness,* Gorsuch Scarisbrick, Scottsdale.

Seligman, M. 1996, *Learned Optimism,* Simon & Schuster, New York.

Zukav, G. and Francis, L. 2001, *The Heart of the Soul: Emotional Awareness,* Simon & Schuster, London.

Glossary

absolute terms: words or phrases that allow for no exceptions, such as 'never', 'every', 'all', 'none'.

abstract words: words which either refer to abstract concepts such as 'love', 'happiness', 'responsibility' or are vague, general, lacking in specificity.

acronyms: initials used to represent words such as UNESCO.

active voice: in active voice the subject does the action.

adjourning (in groups): the stage in group dynamics where a group ceases operation and disbands.

aggressiveness: a hostile behavioural style that involves putting one's rights, needs and desires above those of others.

analogy: involves comparison.

analytical reports: sometimes called 'formal' reports because of the formal elements that need to be included. These are usually documents which aim to solve problems and suggest solutions.

argument: a structured sequence of ideas designed to lead to, or support, a conclusion.

argument indicator: words such as 'because', 'therefore', which indicate that an argument is taking place.

assertiveness: a style of relating which involves having the confidence to stand up for yourself firmly, without infringing the rights of others.

assumption: involves moving from the known to the unknown but is not based on facts.

attitude: a predisposition to responding to stimuli in a particular way. (Taylor, Rosegrant, Meyer & Samples 1983).

attribution: the process of attributing reasons/causes in relations to outcomes and situations. Attribution is problematic as errors arise due to the biases that influence our attributions.

audience: the person(s) to whom communication is sent; our listener, reader, etc.

audience analysis: involves researching the needs and desires of those with whom we wish to communicate in an effort to help tailor communication to them effectively.

authoritarian leadership: a style of leadership whereby the leader of a group makes the decisions for the group and commands compliance.

barrier behaviour: methods to compensate when circumstances force us to allow people within our personal space.

barrier (communication barrier): anything that interferes with or stands in the way of effective communication (see 'noise').

baseline: knowledge of an individual's normal behaviour which can be used to judge how usual or unusual an individual's behaviour is in a given situation.

brainstorming: a creative problem-solving technique that relies on quantity of ideas produced quickly and without evaluation.

bureaucracy: the use of and adherence to specific procedures for the regulation of tasks (common in organisations).

case study: accounts or descriptions of problem situations or events designed to reflect real-life situations as a method of participative learning involving problem-solving and decision-making skills.

cause–effect relationship: requires a clear causal link to be successful, that is, the effect must be a direct result of the cause.

channel: the means or medium used to convey a message (e.g. telephone, print).

chronemics: how we perceive, use and react to time.

closed questions: require few words, sometimes only one-word answers.

code: the system through which a message is conveyed (e.g. English language is a code).

cohesion: in reference to groups refers to the strength of each member's commitment to the group and desire to remain in it.

communication climate: the communicative atmosphere in an organisation (i.e. the extent to which there is an atmosphere which encourages a free flow of ideas).

compromise: a conflict resolution strategy whereby all parties make mutual concessions in an effort to reach an outcome satisfactory to all parties.

computer-mediated communications (CMC): any use of computers to initiate communications, store the communication contents, deliver to one or more participants and to process the communications. Chat programs, discussion groups, electronic mail and voice mail are some common examples of CMC.

computer networks: the physical connection between two or more computers that allows computers to exchange electronic data or 'talk to each other'.

concepts: the mental names and categories we assign to phenomena (theoretical concepts are sometimes referred as variables).

conclusion: the point towards which an argument is tending; the viewpoint or idea that the argument is designed to prove or support.

concrete words: words which either refer to concrete, physical phenomena or which are sufficiently detailed and specific to present a clear and precise idea.

conflict: disagreement between individuals (stated and unstated) which emerges from incompatibilities between people's views and desires.

connotative meaning: the meaning given to a word by each individual, that is, the individual interpretation of a word.

context: the situation or setting within which communication takes place including the particular circumstances involved.

contingency theory perspective (of leadership): holds that leadership is contingent upon the demands of a situation in terms of the relations between leader and group members and leader and task.

critical self-reflection: taking time out to think critically about and question aspects of one's own thinking, perception and disposition including beliefs, biases, values, likes and dislikes. This can be used to help detect and critically challenge unproductive ideas, perceptions and thinking in an effort to replace them with more productive ones.

decoding: involves a receiver interpreting encoded messages (e.g. the code of spoken English) by a sender.

deductive reasoning: reasoning which uses a general statement to prove a particular conclusion.

democratic leadership: a style of leadership whereby the leader involves and encourages group members to determine group goals and methods of attainment.

demographic factors: characteristics about a receiver or audience that are relatively accessible such as gender, age group, occupation and so on.

denotative meaning: the dictionary definition or the commonly accepted meaning of a word.

developmental stages: of groups, refers to the phases groups experience (specifically, forming, storming, norming, performing and adjourning).

disclosure: involves the imparting of information about one's self to another (also known as self-disclosure).

discourse: the systematic ways in which people (or groups) within a society produce and communicate information which then becomes the areas of knowledge in a society.

discussion groups: newsgroups within an organisation with access restricted to members of the organisation. They may be available for all members of the organisation or limited to a defined group.

distribution list: a list of email addresses of users who have a defined focus of interest. Postings, some after moderation, are forwarded to all the addresses on the list.

downward communication: information and instruction from those with more authority to those with less authority in an organisation.

dynamism: being seen as bold, energetic and active.

electronic bulletin board: electronic version of a traditional noticeboard. Authorised persons can post electronic messages for all to read. These messages may result in a user contacting the person who posted the notice directly, but rarely results in a group discussion.

electronic communication: any person to person(s) interaction that occurs via or with the support of a computer network and the appropriate communication software.

electronic mail (email): a text-based messaging system similar to a memorandum or a letter that is delivered electronically from one computer to another via a computer network.

electronic mail attachment: a file that is attached to an email and delivered with it. Any type of file may be attached, for example a wordprocessing file, a spreadsheet file or a clip art file.

electronic media: any computer hardware or software that supports rapid communication between two or more persons situated at different localities: across the desk, down the hall, down the street or around the world.

emotional appeal: an appeal to our feelings or emotional needs such as our need to belong.

emotional intelligence: an emerging body of literature addressing the role of emotions in performance including strategies and techniques to assist in managing emotions more intelligently.

emotive language: words with emotional overtones; emotion-laden words.

empathy: imaginatively putting ourselves in the other's position.

encoding: involves the formulating of ideas by a sender into a form that can be understood by a receiver (e.g. the code of spoken English).

enhanced email: electronic mail software packages that have extra functions such as filters which allow users to set up folders in which to filter incoming email. The filters check the incoming mail and deliver the mail to a particular folder according to a user-defined set of rules.

essay: a sustained piece of writing which tests the ability to analyse, research, write effectively and develop a sustained, logical argument.

ethnocentrism: a tendency to view one's own culture as being 'normal' (and hence superior) in comparison to other cultures and, therefore, judging other cultures on that basis.

expertise: perceived level of knowledge or qualifications of the persuader.
extempore: delivering speech material using only brief notes.
facial expressions: smiles, frowns, pouts and so on which convey emotion and which can be intentional or unintentional.
fallacy: a flaw or fault in the logic in an argument.
false classification: putting forward only two polarised alternatives.
feedback: a receiver's response to a message.
field of experience: the past experiences of an individual which ultimately influence the way one perceives the world.
flattening out: the reducing of levels of command and management in organisations.
flexible optimism: maintaining an optimistic as opposed to pessimistic view and disposition, but one which is also tempered with realistic expectations. It is regarded as a productive as opposed to unproductive (self-defeating) way of thinking.
folk theories: informal explanations like myths and stereotypes and as such are accepted by people to varying degrees.
formal reports: see 'analytical reports'.
forming (in groups): the stage in group dynamics where individuals gather together in an effort to join forces in pursuit of common goals.
funnel sequence: questioning sequence moving from broad or general questions to more specific or detailed questions.
generalisation: involves reaching a conclusion about a whole class or category on the basis of a sample.
generalised aggressiveness: a predominantly aggressive disposition.
generalised non-assertiveness: a predominantly non-assertive disposition.
grapevine: the informal network by which information flows in an organisation.
group: a small collection of people with a shared interest and who perceive themselves as members of a group.
group dynamics: the kinds of processes that occur in groups including the stages of forming, norming, storming, performing and adjourning, conflicts and so on.
groupthink: refers to an agreement-at-any-cost mentality that results in ineffectual decision making.
haptics: tactile communication; communication through touch.
hierarchical structuring: in organisational communication refers to organisational structures characterised by a rigidly authoritative and relatively long 'chain of command' (i.e. levels of management).

historical dimension/context: our historical place in time, (i.e. the early twenty-first century including the kinds of technology and knowledge that now exist).
human capital theory: a term used to conceptualise self-investment—for example, self-investment into one's education and training as a means for increasing future returns (i.e. higher earnings) for the sale of one's labour.
human resource development (HRD): a view (gaining wide acceptance) of organisational behaviour that operates under the assumption that people in general are naturally motivated to work if they can find satisfaction in their work (Daniels & Spiher 1994). It favours reducing supervisory roles, fostering a more participative approach to managing the workplace as a means of increasing worker motivation and ultimately productivity.
hypothetical questions: posing particular problems to be solved to gauge general attitudes, motivations, ethics and analytical and problem-solving skills.
'I' statements: statements that make use of an 'I' at the beginning as a means of trying to take responsibility for one's thoughts and feelings.
idealised cognitive models (ICMs): the mental models or mental structures people use to organise and interpret information. Also known as preconceptions they develop out of past experiences and work to simply information. In principle ICMs function in a similar way to stereotypes.
ideology: the kinds of values (or value systems) which underpin a discourse (e.g. the discourse of environmentalism values the protection of the environment).
impression management: deliberately acting in particular ways in order to project a desired image of one's self, for example dressing well for an interview to make a good impression.
inductive reasoning: reasoning that uses particular examples to prove a general conclusion.
inference: made by moving logically from the known to the unknown on the basis of facts.
informal report: a report, usually not long, that is not set out according to the formal requirements of longer, formal reports; informal reports are often set out in the form of a memo or letter.
informational reports: sometimes called 'informal' reports. These are usually short documents, sometimes merely a form to be filled out, which aim simply to provide information.
interactive process model: an advance on the linear model incorporating feedback, unintentional communication, people's fields of experience and noise beyond physical impediments.

intercultural barriers: arise from differences in perspectives and practices among people due to differing cultural backgrounds.
Internet: a worldwide collection of open computer networks. It enables the transfer of data, text, voice and/or video between any two computers connected to this network.
interpersonal barriers: factors that impede communication between people due to differences and incompatibilities in people's perspectives and personalities.
interpersonal communication: normally refers to face-to-face communication that takes place between individuals (e.g. two or three).
intimate zone: the distance that allows for close physical contact.
intrapersonal barriers: those characteristics that impede an individual's ability to communicate effectively, and also impede one's capacity for personal development and learning.
intrapersonal communication: communication within the individual (e.g. thinking and perceiving).
inverted funnel sequence: questioning sequence moving from specific questions to broader and more general questions.
jargon: a technical language; a type of professional shorthand.
Johari Window: a model that is useful for understanding the process of discovery of the self and others.
key words: words that define the areas we are to investigate.
kinesics: sometimes called 'body language'; involves gestures, facial expressions and posture.
laissez-faire leadership: a 'hands-off' style of leadership where the leader resists exerting their influence on the group.
lateral thinking: ideas-generating thinking; random, imaginative and creative.
leadership: commonly defined in terms of a process whereby one person influences others towards achieving a goal(s).
leading questions: questions which make it clear what response is expected or desired.
level of tension: the degree to which a person is relaxed or tense.
linear (or transmission) process model: commonly known as the most rudimentary of communication models, emphasises the notion of communication as a sender sending messages to a receiver.
linguistic relativity: a theoretical perspective that holds that different kinds of languages (i.e. systems for conceptualising) give rise to different views of the world.
logic: the means we use to judge the validity or invalidity of arguments.

maintenance-based behaviours: directed towards maintaining the group and involve the managing of conflict and morale.
Maslow's hierarchy of needs: a system of categorising human motivation.
message: the meanings conveyed in communicative exchanges via the code (see 'code').
meta-conceptual: pursuits concerning questions about the nature of conceptualisation and its implications.
meta-theoretical: pursuits concerning questions about the nature of theory construction and the implications of this.
mirroring: involves an unconscious similarity of posture and gesture between communicators and indicates a level of rapport between the individuals.
mirror questions: variants of probing questions involving paraphrasing or reflecting back responses to elicit more information.
models: diagrammatic representations of a theoretical nature (often simplified representations of a theory).
monitoring feedback: deliberately paying a good deal of attention to feedback. Also see 'receptivity'.
myth: the common beliefs (or belief systems) that reside in a discourse (e.g. the idea that Australia is an egalitarian society where people get 'a fair go').
need for esteem: the fourth step in Maslow's hierarchy; our need for self-respect, status, recognition, prestige.
need for self-actualisation: the highest need in Maslow's hierarchy; our need to achieve our personal potential.
need to belong: the third step in Maslow's hierarchy; our need for acceptance.
negotiation: involves a collaborative effort between two or more parties to reach a mutually beneficial outcome to a problem.
newsgroup: an electronic noticeboard with a specific focus. Any user of the Internet may read or post a message to a newsgroup.
noise: all the kinds of interference that can impact upon a message (as it was originally intended). (See 'barrier', 'physical noise', 'psychological noise' and 'semantic noise'.)
non-assertiveness: a submissive behavioural style that involves not standing up for one's rights.
nonverbal communication: communication without words.
norming (in groups): the stage in group dynamics involving the resolving of conflict. Generally, the resolving of conflict can lead to two outcomes: (1) the continuation of previous order (i.e. where the same people continue to hold the same influence), or (2) the

emergence of a new order (where the distribution of power and status among members has changed).

open questions: allow wide scope in the response.

open systems theory/system theory: views organisations in biological as opposed to mechanical terms. Open systems are desirable as they refer to organisations that have practices that are open and accountable.

organisation: a large grouping of people organised for the purpose of achieving specific objectives.

organisation/interpretation (in perception): the way in which people organise/process information and interpret phenomena (according to the kind of perspective they have developed).

organisational communication: the communication processes occuring within and about organisations.

organisational culture: ways of understanding and behaving common to individuals in an organisation (and can include its subcultures). Organisational cultures can become dysfunctional, for example widespread corruption in an organisation is often discussed in terms of organisational culture.

paradigm: a term commonly used today to refer to a particular orthodoxy (or orthodox view's beliefs and thinking). Also see 'world view (cultural)'.

paralinguistics, paralanguage: the sound element of nonverbal communication including indeterminate sounds and vocal inflection.

passive voice: in passive voice the subject receives the action which gives prominence to the object rather than the subject.

paternalistic leadership: a style of leadership whereby the leader is authoritative and directive but is still open to feedback.

peer reviewed/refereed: many scholarly/academic journals are peer reviewed or refereed. This means that articles that appear in these journals have been assessed by one or more experts in the area before they are accepted for publication.

perception: involves a process of selecting and organising/interpreting stimuli being observed.

perception checking: testing one's interpretations against those of others. For example, seeking clarification to see whether your perception of a situation is similar to those of others.

performing (in groups): the stage in group dynamics where a group is functioning—that is, performing tasks.

personal distance: the area of uninvaded space we need around us to feel comfortable and secure.

personal zone: from 0.46 to 1.22 metres.

persuasion: the attempt of one individual to influence the behaviour or beliefs of another individual.

physical barriers: (1) those impediments that are due to physical or environmental factors and constraints; (2) any physical source of interference in communication (see 'physical noise').

physical needs: the most basic need in Maslow's hierarchy—our need for food and shelter.

physical noise: any physical/environmental interference in communication (e.g. from loud machinery to poor lighting).

plagiarism: the theft of intellectual property or using someone else's ideas without acknowledgement.

posture: conscious or unconscious positioning of the body which can reveal emotion and indicate the nature of the relationship.

premise: statement designed to support or lead to a conclusion.

primary questions: introduce topics.

primary sources: there are variations from discipline to discipline but primary sources are normally unpublished material; our own research which may take the form of surveys, questionnaires, observation, interviews or experimentation.

probing, secondary, follow-up questions: arise out of and are designed to follow up previous responses.

problem: when what is differs from what we would like it to be.

proxemics: concerned with how we use space; with spatial relationships.

psychographic factors: the psychological characteristics of a receiver or audience such as personal biases, assumptions.

psychological noise: the influences of individual factors including psychological make-up, mood and emotion.

public zone: from 3.66 metres to at least 7.62 metres.

quintamensional design sequence: sequence designed to elicit information, especially about attitudes from large numbers of people.

rational appeal: a persuasive appeal based on logic and reason.

receiver: a person involved in receiving messages from another (see 'audience').

receptiveness/receptivity: the degree to which one is open and able to detect and intelligently process feedback. And also the degree one is open to giving consideration to ideas that conflict with one's established views.

redundancy (in communication): repetition in messages.

referencing: acknowledging the source of the quotation or idea being used.

reports: part of professional written communication providing one of the primary means of problem analysis and management advice within organisations.

responsiveness (in communication): means responding to and behaving effectively under given and changing circumstances.

role theory: a view that compares daily interactions with the performing of roles in order to fulfil social expectations.

scientific management: a traditional view of organisational behaviour that operates under the assumption that workers are not intrinsically (i.e. naturally) motivated to work (Daniels & Spiher 1994). Hence it favours hierarchical structures with high concentrations of supervisory power as a means of maximising productivity.

secondary sources: usually published material such as books, journals, newspapers, government publications, electronic sources such as discussions lists and so on; research done by others.

security needs: the second step in Maslow's hierarchy; our need for stability, order, protection, job and financial security.

selection (in perception): involves selecting what kinds of information we focus our attention upon.

self-awareness: a person's level of awareness about themselves. Some people have very accurate perceptions about themselves, that is, 'self-concept', in which case they are very self-aware.

self-concept: one's own understanding of oneself including one's abilities, strengths and weaknesses. People who are self-aware have a more accurate self-concept. See 'self-awareness'.

self-disclosure: the imparting of information about one's self (usually of a personal nature) to another.

self-fulfilling prophecy: how certain belief a person has tends to influence the behaviour of that person in a way that increases the likelihood of an outcome that supports, or appears to support, that belief (Adler, Rosenfeld, Towne & Proctor 1998).

self-talk: a feature of intrapersonal communication, it refers to one's own internal dialogue, for example the things you tell yourself when thinking and interpreting situations.

semantic barriers: problems in understanding the meaning of certain words when communicating.

semantic noise: distortion due to differences in people's understanding of the meanings generated via the signals being used (e.g. jargon words can create confusion).

semiotics: often referred to as the science of signs, it is concerned with the levels at which signs generate meaning (including the levels of discourse, ideology and myth).

sender: a person involved in sending/communicating messages to another.

Short Message Service (SMS): a service that allows alphanumeric messages to be sent from mobile phones, fax machines and/or a computer connected to the Internet. The message has either a maximum of 160 or 244 characters depending on the bit mode available.

situational aggressiveness: the tendency to be aggressive in certain situations.

situational context: specific contextual aspects such as the kind of event (e.g. lunch).

situational non-assertiveness: the tendency to be non-assertive in certain situations.

situational theory perspective (of leadership): holds that leaders emerge from a combination of the traits of the individual and the needs of a particular situation.

Social constructivism: a body of theory (or theoretical position) that views the human world as one which is socially constructed. In principle, but in very simple terms demonstrated by the following: we create social order (eg. laws and norms) by negotiation through our social interactions (eg. laws are made by elected parliamentary representatives who are influenced by public debate).

social context theory perspective (of leadership): holds that the emergence of effective leaders is a result of the social context and historical circumstances of a given time.

social zone: area within which most professional interactions take place.

sociocultural dimension/context: our cultural setting and positioning (e.g. a rural Australian, a Japanese tourist, someone involved in surfing culture).

sound argument: an argument which is both valid and true.

source credibility: the degree to which we believe the source or sender of a message.

storming (in groups): the stage in group dynamics where serious conflicts develop.

strategic communication: taking a strategic approach to communication, that is, consciously and deliberately taking a planned approach to communication in order to achieve a specific goal which includes your needs and desires.

style: the result of the vocabulary, sentence and paragraph structure chosen by the writer.

syllogism: form of argument which uses a general or universal statement to prove a particular example.

synergy: the idea that added energy, capability and creativity can result from people working and interacting together ('chemistry' is sometimes used to describe this phenomenon).

task analysis: determining what needs to be achieved, dividing this into more manageable subtasks and the most appropriate kinds of strategies to be used.

task-based behaviours: those directed towards achieving group goals.

task words: words that tell us what we should be doing; how we should treat the areas to be considered.

temporal dimension/context: the immediate time frame (e.g. time of day, after work, lunch time and so on).

theory: an explanation which is considered to be formal or scientific.

thesis: a theory we hope to prove; our viewpoint or stance in relation to a topic.

thesis statement: the clear, precise expression of our thesis or viewpoint on the topic.

thinking habits: largely self-explanatory, it is an informal term that refers to tendencies in one's thinking (e.g. optimist, pessimist or realist). See 'idealised cognitive models'.

tone: the feeling created by the style of the writing.

topic sentence: the sentence which embodies the central idea of a paragraph.

trait theory perspective (of leadership): holds that leaders are endowed with superior qualities that distinguish them from their followers and as such have considerable capacity to influence others.

transactional process model: this more advanced model views communication as an ongoing process involving relationships between participants who occupy individual but overlapping fields of experience, who are involved in the simultaneous sending and receiving of messages. These messages are then also subject to various forms of noise.

transactive process: process in which both source and audience are involved in simultaneously sending and receiving.

trustworthiness: dependent on audience evaluation of bias on the part of the message sender.

truth: something is true if it corresponds to the facts.

tunnel sequence: a sequence of usually closed questions designed to elicit factual information quickly.

upward communication: information from those with less authority to those with more authority in an organisation.

unsound argument: an argument which is valid, is logically consistent, but is false, being based on a false premise.

validity: an argument is valid if it has consistent internal logic.

variability of perception: the differences between the ways in which individuals perceive information and experience the world.

vertical thinking: can also be called 'logical' thinking; logical, sequential thought.

vigilant interaction theory: the idea that vigilance in respect of factors that can contribute to poor group decision making is an effective way to guard against poor decision making.

Web services: functions that are placed on a company's website that facilitate contact with the company via the website.

world view (personal): a person's unique view and understanding of the world including cognitive tendencies (e.g. optimist, pessimist or realist).

world view (cultural): commonsense knowledge and taken for granted knowledge of a cultural group—which produces particular understandings of the world (e.g. Western individualism or Eastern collectivism).

'you' statements: (1) in the context of interpersonal communication and relationship skills, statements that make use of a 'you' at the beginning and often involve the focusing and attribution of blame on the other party; (2) in the context of persuasive communication, can refer to statements which focus attention on the receiver/audience (e.g. 'you will gain these kinds of benefits if ...).

Index

A
absolute terms
abstraction level, vocabulary, 62–3
abstract of report, 98
academic life
   communication areas, 4
academic writing, effective
   essay structure, 91–6
   referencing, 91
   research, 89–91
   text evaluation, 90–1
   thesis development, 89
   topic/question, analysis, 87–9
accenting, nonverbal communication, 186
active and passive voice
   writing, effective, 64–5
active engagement, 262–3
adaptors, 189
ad hominem, 173
advanced communication theory, 25–6
adversity, 259
advice, seeking, 261
affect displays, 188
aggressiveness, 208
agreement clarification
   conflict management, 212
alternative and last resort conflict management techniques, 213–14
analogy, 171
analytical reports, 96
anxiety, 258
appeal to masses argument, 173
appeal to pity, 173
appendices and glossary of terms, reports, 102
appropriate writing, 60
argument, 165–7
   argument indicators, 166–7
   deductive and inductive reasoning, 168–9, *169*
   illegitimate methods, 172–5
   legitimate methods, 170–2
   premises and conclusions, identification, 167
   sound and unsound, 168
   truth and validity, 168
argument development, 95
assertive behaviour
   defining, 207
   intrapersonal dimension, 209
assertive behaviour theory, 206–7
assertiveness training, 206
assignments
   audience analysis, benefit, 32
assumptions, 150
asynchronous mode, 44
attachments, email, 50
attitude, 29
attribution, 211
audience, speech preparation, 116
audience analysis
   communication tailoring, 32
   writing skills, 59
audio-visual aids, 120–1
authoritarian leadership style, 230
authority, misuse, 172

B
backing up computer information, 255
barrier behaviour, 191
barriers
   adversity, 259
   anxiety, 258
   counter-productive thinking patterns and processes, 257–60
   expectations, unrealistically high, 258–9
   generally, 254
   information and computer technologies, 255
   intercultural barriers, 267–71
   intrapersonal, 255–7
   management approaches
      building redundancy into communication, 274
      responsiveness, 272
      strategic planning model, 272
      work groups and committees, 273
   mental blocks, 259
   physical, 254–5
   'scapegoat' attributions, 259–60
   worry, 258
behaviour and status, conflict, 211
bibliography, reports, 102
black and white fallacy, 172
brainstorming, 145
   guidelines, 145
   leader/facilitator, 145–6
   post-meeting evaluation, 146
   recorder/notetaker, 146
bureaucracy, 236
bureaucratic principles, 236–7, *237*
business letters, *75*

C
case studies, problem situations, 149–53
cause–effect relationship, 171
centrality of communication, 4
chronemics, nonverbal communication, 193
circular argument, 173
closed questions, 132
close relationships, 204–5
code and channel, 17
cognitive psychology, 201–3
cognitive self-intervention guide, 264
cohesion, 225
collaborative model of conflict management, 211–12
commonsense knowledge, 31–2
communication, 'structured,' 24
communication cues, email, 51
communication tailoring
   audience analysis, 32
communication theory
   communication definitions, 9–10
communication theory, nature
   functions and features of theories, 10–11
   structure: formal and folk theories, 13
   theory application, 15
   theory as an explanation, 10
communicative climate, organisations, 240
competing interests, conflict, 210–11
complementing, nonverbal communication, 186
compound sentences, 63–4
comprehension, 9
compromise, 212
computer-mediated communications (CMC), 45–6
   discussion groups, 53–4
   electronic bulletin board (EBB), 54
   newsgroups, 53
   Short Message Service (SMS), 52
   web services, 52
conceptualisation, costs associated, 11–13
conclusion, arguments, 165
conflict
   behaviour and status, 211
   competing interests: resources and desires, 210–11
   groups
      contributing factors, 228
      management strategies, 228
   interpretation and meaning, 210
   management framework, collaborative model, 211–12
   nature, 210
   sources and forms, 210–11
   values and beliefs, 210
conflict management
   additional techniques, 213
   alternative and last resort techniques, 213–14
   ethical issues, 214–15
   inappropriate tactics, 214
   passive non-assertion and avoidance, 214

conformity in groups, 225–7
Construction of Theoretical
    Knowledge, 12
context, 23–4
contradicting, nonverbal
    communication, 187, *187*
countering groupthink, 227
counter-productive thinking
    patterns and processes,
    257–60
creating email, 46–9, *47–8*
creative problem solving, 144–6
criticism forestaller, 173–4
cultural audience analysis, 269–70
cultural knowledge, lack of
    appropriate, 269
cultural sensitivity, development, 269
cultural world view, 31–2
culture, defined, 268
culture influence, nonverbal
    communication, 185

D
deductive and inductive reasoning
    arguments, 168–9, *169*
definitions of communication, 9–10
democratic leadership style, 230–1
demographic factors
    perception, influence, 30
direct method, letter structure, 76–7
discourse, 25
discussion, 125, 209, 223, 229
    leadership styles, 231
    leading, 126
discussion groups
    computer-mediated
        communications, 53–4
distribution lists, email, 50–1
downward communication
    flow, 240
dynamism, 157

E
editing, 104–5
education and awareness promotion
    strategies, 271
effective listening, 266–7
either/or fallacy, 172
electronic bulletin board (EBB)
    computer-mediated
        communications, 54
electronic communication
    generally, *44*, 44–5
electronic mail, 46–51
email
    attachments, 50
    communication cues, 51
    creating, 46–9, *47–8*
    distribution lists, 50–1
    incoming, organising, 49
    information dissemination, 50
    information overload, 51
    receipts, 49
    reply times, 49
    storage and search, 50
    tone and style, 82–3
emblems, nonverbal communication,
    188
emotion, nonverbal communication,
    183, *184*
emotional appeals, persuasion,
    157–8
emotional intelligence, 264, 265
emotions, managing, 265
emotive language, 174–5
empathy, 267
environment, speech preparation,
    116–17
essays
    academic life, 4
    academic writing, effective, 86
    tone and style, 105
essay structure, 91–6
    body, 94–6
    conclusion, 96
    introduction, 92–4
ethical communication, 6, 22
ethical issues, conflict management,
    214–15
ethnocentrism, 268–9
expectations, unrealistically high,
    258–9
expression, 9
extempore, 123
extended presentations, 115–17
    audio-visual aids, 120–1
extended writing *see* essays; reports
external barriers, 254–5
eye behaviour, 189–90

F
facial expressions, 188–94
fallacies, 169–70
false analogy, 171
false classification, 172
false dilemma, 172
familiarity, vocabulary, 61
faulty causal relationship, 171
faulty classification, 172
faulty generalisation, 170–1
feedback, 19
    eye behaviour, 189
fields of experience, 19
flat and tall organisational structures,
    237, *237*
flexible optimism, 260
focus, maintenance, 94
folk theories, 13
follow-up questions, 134
functioning of concepts, 11–13
functioning of groups, 219, 219–20
funnel sequence of questions, 137

G
gender, 88
    cultural construction, 270
    influence, nonverbal
        communication, 185
generalised aggressiveness, 208
generalised non-assertiveness, 207–8
generic approach to task analysis,
    34–5
gesture, nonverbal communication,
    182
gestures, 188–94
goal achievement
    persistence strategy, 261
grapevine communication, 242–3
graphics, reports, 104
group communication *see also* groups
    functioning of groups, *219*, 219–20
    generally, 219
    role of groups, 219
    task-based behaviours, 221
group decision making
    benefits, 224
    pitfalls, 225–7
group dynamics, 245
groups
    cohesion, 225
    conflict, 227–8
    discussion, 223
    group dynamics, 221–2
    groupthink, 226–7
    information flow, 224, *224*
    key functions, 221
    life-cycle stages, 222–3
groupthink, 226–7

H
haptics, nonverbal communication,
    191–2, *192*
historical context, 23
horizontal communication, 242
    improving, 243–4
    poor, causes, 243
    recording procedures, 244–5, *245*
human capital theory, 260
human resource development, 237
hypothetical questions, 135

I
idealised cognitive models (ICMs), 28
ideology, 26
illustrators, nonverbal
    communication, 188
incoming email, organising, 49
indexes, 193
    function, 90
indirect method
    letter structure, 77–8
    memos, 81–2, *82*
individualist/collectivist cultures,
    comparison, 270
inductive reasoning, 168–9, *169*
inference, 150
informal communication
    (grapevine), 242–3
informal reports, 102–4, *103*
information
    finding, 55–6
    storing, 56

Information Age, 238
informational reports, 96
information and computer technologies, 255
information censorship, groupthink, 226
information dissemination, email, 50
information flow, groups, 224, 224
information overload, email, 51
information sourcing, 261
interactive process model
    theories of communication, 18–20, 19
intercultural barriers, 267–71
intercultural communication, core barriers
    addressing
        cultural audience analysis, 269–70
        cultural sensitivity, development, 269
        cultural knowledge, lack of appropriate, 269
        ethnocentrism, 268–9
Internet, 44, 44–5
    knowledge acquisition and management, 54–5
interpersonal barriers, 265–7
interpersonal communication
    assertive behaviour theory, 206–7
    defining, 198
    generally, 198
    Johari Window, 200, 200–1
    role theory, skill development tool, 205–6
    self-concept and self-awareness, 199–200
    self-disclosure, 204–5
    use, choosing, 198–9
interpersonal skills, 5–6
interpretation and meaning, conflict, 210
interpretation in perception
    organisation, 28–30, 29
interviews
    generally, 131
    questioning, 131–5
    structure, 135–8
intimate zone, 190
intrapersonal barriers, 255–7
introductory speeches, 114–16
inverted funnel sequence of questions, 137
'I' statements, 213

J
jargon and acronyms, 63
job advertisements, 5
Johari Window, 200, 200–1

K
key words, 88
kinesics, 188

knowledge acquisition and management, 54–5
Knowledge Age, 238
knowledge workers, 238

L
labour demands, 238–40, 239
laissez-faire leadership style, 231
lateral thinking, 144
leadership
    conducive factors, 232
    defining, 229
leadership styles
    authoritarian, 230
    democratic/participative, 230–1
    laissez-faire, 231
    paternalistic/supervisory, 230
leadership theories
    discussion, 229
    situational and social-context-based, 229
    trait-based, 229
leading questions, 134–5
letters
    essential elements, 72–3
    optional elements, 73–4
    purpose and structure, 76–9
    types, 74–5
level of tension, 188
life-cycle stages of groups, 222–3
    adjourning, 223
    forming, 222
    norming, 223
    performing, 223
    storming, 222
lifelong learning and development, concept, 261–2
linear process model
    theories of communication, 16, 16–18, 18, 24
local area network (LAN), 46
logical and creative thinking, 144
logic and argumentation, 165
logos, 157

M
mainstream institutionalised domains of knowledge
    discourse types, 25
maintenance-based behaviours, 221
McGregor's *Theory X*, 238
McGregor's *Theory Y*, 238
McGregor's *Theory Z*, 238
memos
    elements, 80–1, 81
    indirect method, 81–2, 82
mental block, 259
    managing, 263
message structure, 266
meta-theoretical inquiry, 10
meta-theoretical principle of communication as balance, 274
mirroring, 194
mirror questions, 134

miscommunication, 4
motivation, managing, 262–4
    emotional intelligence, 264
    mental blocks, managing, 263
    personalised strategies, 263–4
    positive attitude, 262–3
    receptivity, 263
    strategic planning, 262
myth, 26

N
nature of conflict, 210
negative, self-defeating thought patterns, 257–8
negative cohesion, groups, 225–7
negotiation
    conflict management, 212
neutral/good news letters, 74
newsgroups
    computer-mediated communications, 53
noise, 17
    psychological noise, 20
    semantic noise, 20
non-assertiveness, 207–8
nonverbal communication, 182
    ambiguity, 183–4
    chronemics, 193
    clues read as clusters, 185
    context, 185
    continuous, 182
    culture influence, 185
    emotion, 183, 184
    eye behaviour, 189–90
    facial expressions, 188–94
    gender influence, 185
    gestures, 188–94
    haptics, 191–2
    intentional and unintentional, 183
    kinesics, 188
    mirroring, 194
    paralinguistics, 192–3
    posture, 188–9
    rule governed, 186
    semiotics, 193
    types, 188–94
    verbal communication, interrelationships, 186–8

O
obsessive and intensive anxiety, 258
occasion, speech preparation, 116
open questions, 132–3
optimum balance, theory application, 15
oral communication
    advantages/disadvantages, 113
    seminar presentations, 124–5
oral presentations, 114
    practice, 122
    preparation, 121–2
organisation
    interpretation in perception, 28–30, 29

organisational communication
  bureaucratic principles, 236–7, *237*
  communication flow
    downward, 240
    upward, 241
  communicative climate, 240
  generally, 236
  horizontal communication
    improving, 243–4
  human resource development approach, 237–8
  informal communication (grapevine), 242–3
  scientific management approach, 236
  vertical, improving, 241
organisational culture, 245–7
  functional, working toward, 246–7
  function and dysfunction, 246
  transaction theory model, *21*, 21–3, 245
organisational structures
  democratising and flattening out, 241–2
over-confidence, 226
own perceptions, impacts on ourselves, 33–4

P
paradigm, 32
paragraph structure
  writing, effective, 65–6
paralinguistics, nonverbal communication, 192–3
passive non-assertion and avoidance, 214
paternalistic leadership style, 230
pathos, 157
'peer' pressure, 226
perception, 26–7
  influence factors
    demographic factors, 30
    psychographic factors, 31
    organisation/interpretation, 28–30, *29*
  tendencies that distort, 29–30
perceptions, differences in people's, 30
personal attack argument, 173
personal distance, 190
personalised strategies
  motivation, managing, 263–4
personal world view, 28
personal zone, 190
persuasion, 156–7
  appeals to emotion, 157–8
  rational appeals, 158–9
  source credibility, 157
  strategies, 159–61, *161*, *162*
persuasive letters, 75, 78–9
physical barriers, 254–5
physical noise
  physical barriers, 254–5

positive attitude
  motivation, managing, 262–3
post-industrial organisation, 238–40
post-speech appraisal, 126–8
posture, nonverbal communication, 182, 188–9
power and status, 88
primary questions, 133
probing questions, 134
problem analysis, 148
problem analysis and identification
  conflict management, 211–12
problem definition, 147
problem-solving and decision making sequence, 146–7
process models, comments, 24
productive beliefs and thought patterns, 260–2
professional life
  'people-oriented,' communication demands, 4–5
proofreading, 104–5
psychographic factors
  perception, influence, 31
psychological noise, 20

Q
quintamensional design sequence of questions, 137–8

R
rapport, establishing in interviews, 135–6
rational appeals, persuasion, 158–9
realistic views, 260
receipts, email, 49
receptivity
  motivation, managing, 263
reciprocity principle, 205
referencing, 91
reflective self-evaluation questions, 204
reflective thought, phases, 146
refusal
  letters, 75
  memos, 81–2, *82*
regulating, nonverbal communication, 187–8
regulators, 188
repeating, nonverbal communication, 186
reply time, email, 49
reports
  abstract, 98
  appendices and glossary of terms, 102
  bibliography, 102
  body, 100–1
  conclusion, 102
  formal, format, 96–102, *97*, *98*, *99*
  graphics, 104
  informal, 102–4, *103*

  introduction, 100
  organisation, 104
  recommendations, 102
  summary, 98, *99*
  tone and style, 105
  types, 96
research, 89–91
  source material, selection, 90
Rigid Versus Fluid Thinking on Categorisation, *14*
role theory, 219
role theory, skill development tool, 205–6
  uses and limitations, 205–6

S
salutation
  email, 48
  letters, 73
'scapegoat' attributions, 259–60
scientific management, 236
scientific management approach, organisational communication, 236
secondary questions, 134
selection, 27–8
self-awareness
  cognitive psychology, 201–3
  Johari Window, theoretical model, *200*, 200–1
self-concept, 199
self-development
  cognitive psychology, 201–3
  persistence strategy, 261
self-disclosure
  close relationships, 204–5
  reciprocity principle, 205
self-fulfilling prophecy, 27, 257
self-managed work teams, 242
self-talk, 256
semantic barriers, 271
  reducing, key strategies, 271–2
semantic noise, 20
seminar participation, 125–6
seminar presentations, 124–5
semiotics, 24, 25, 26, 193
sentence structure
  writing, effective, 63–4
Short Message Service (SMS), 45, 52
situational, social-context-based leadership theory, 229
situational aggressiveness, 208
situational context, 23
situational non-assertiveness, 207
social constructivism, 26, 31
social zone, 190
sociocultural context, 23
solution evaluation, 148
solution implementation, 149
source credibility, persuasion, 157
source material, selection, 90
speech cards, 123
speech dynamics, 123

speeches
  audience, 116
  delivery
    extemporaneous, 123
    memorising, 123
    reading, 122–3
    speaking, 123–4
  environment, 116–17
  extended presentations, 115–17
  occasion, 116
  post-speech appraisal, 126–8
  preparation, 115
  researching, 117
  types, 114–15
  votes of thanks, 115
  writing, 117–20
speech nerves, 124
speech outline, 123
speech preparation, 115
spelling, grammar and punctuation
  effective writing, 60
  proofreading, 104–5
  report writing, 104–5
statistics, misuse, 172
storage and search, email, 50
strategic approach to communication
  task analysis, *34*, 34–6
strategic planning, motivation, 262
structuralism, 24
structuralist perspective, 24
structured communication, 24–5
summary, reports, 98, *99*
synchronous mode, 44
synergy, 221

T
table of contents, reports, 98, *99*, *101*
task analysis
  communication, strategic
    approach, 34–6
  generic approach, 34–5
  writing skills, 59–60
task-based behaviours, 221
  maintenance-based behaviours, 221
task management, generic model, 35–6
temporal context, 23
text evaluation, 90–1
theories of communication
  interactive process model, 18–20, *19*
  linear process model, *16*, 16–18, *18*
  transactional process model, *21*, 21–4
theory and practice, gap, *12*, 13–14, *14*
thesis development, 89
thesis statement, 92
thinking habits, 256
title page, reports, 98, *98*
topic/question, analysis
  academic writing, effective, 87–9
touch, nonverbal communication, 191–2, *192*
traditional/electronic functionality, comparison, *46*
trait-based leadership theory, 229
transaction and negotiation, 22
transaction theory model, *21*, 21–3, 245
transmittal document, *97*, 97–8
trustworthiness, 157
truth and validity, arguments, 168
tunnel sequence of questions, 137

U
unity and transitions, 66–7
unquestioned beliefs, 226
upward communication flow, 241

V
values and beliefs, conflict, 210
verbal/nonverbal communication
  interrelationships, 186–8
vertical communication, organisations, 241
vertical thinking, 144
vocabulary
  abstraction level, 62–3
  familiarity, 61
  freshness and vitality, 62
  jargon and acronyms, 63
  simplicity, 62
votes of thanks, 115

W
web services, 52–3
workers
  post-industrial work demands, 239
world view, 31, 256
worry, 258
writing, effective
  active and passive voice, 64–5
  audience analysis, 59–60
  criteria
    accessible, 60–1
    appropriate, 60
    correct, 60
  logical sequence, 67
  paragraph structure, 65–6
  sentence structure, 63–4
  style and tone, 67–8
  task analysis, 59
  unity and transitions, 66–7
  vocabulary, 61–3
written communication
  advantages/disadvantages, 112–13

Y
'you' statements, 213